More Advanced Praise for *Fast-Track Business Growth*

"Once again, Andrew Sherman proves that he's got his finger on the pulse of entrepreneurship. It's all about growth, and if anyone knows the hard-and-fast key strategies of business expansion, it's this veteran observer of business trends. *Fast Track Business Growth* provides a vital blueprint that will aid entrepreneurs and managers alike in their efforts to stay focused."

DON J. DEBOLT
president, International Franchise Association

"In today's business environment, growth is essential to a company's survival and success. *Fast Track Business Growth* should be required reading for anyone charged with making growth a reality."

STEPHEN K. KRULL
vice president and general counsel, operations, Owens Corning World Headquarters

"Andrew Sherman's work is always thorough, and this is no exception. If you're trying to grow your company, *Fast Track Business Growth* is a must. It's a complete reference to the ins and outs of raising capital and managing growth."

RIPLEY HOTCH
editor in chief, SUCCESS Magazine

"If I were limited to five experts with which to build a dream team to help me grow my company, Andrew Sherman would be on that list. With this book, EVERY business owner can put Andrew on their dream team."

JIM BLASINGAME
host of The Small Business Advocate, a nationally syndicated radio and Internet talk show and author of Small Business Is Like a Bunch of Bananas

"Sherman will help you understand the day-to-day needs and operating challenges of a fast-growth company. Keep this book close to you. It is a winner!"

BRIEN BIONDI
CEO, Young Entrepreneurs' Organization

FAST-TRACK
BUSINESS GROWTH

FAST-TRACK
BUSINESS GROWTH

SMART
STRATEGIES
TO GROW
WITHOUT
GETTING
DERAILED

ANDREW J. SHERMAN

KIPLINGER BOOKS
Washington, DC

Published by
The Kiplinger Washington Editors, Inc.
1729 H Street, N.W.
Washington, DC 20006

Library of Congress Cataloging-in-Publication Data

Sherman, Andrew J.
   Fast track business growth : smart strategies to grow without getting derailed / Andrew
J. Sherman.
      p. cm.
   ISBN 0-938721-88-7 (cloth)
      1. Small business--United States--Management. 2. Strategic planning--United States.
   I. Title.

HF62.7 .S5265 2001
658.02'2--dc21   2001038526

This publication is intended to provide guidance in regard to the subject matter covered.
It is sold with the understanding that the author and publisher are not herein engaged
in rendering legal, accounting, tax or other professional services. If such services are
required, professional assistance should be sought.

First edition. Printed in the United States of America.
9 8 7 6 5 4 3 2 1

Kiplinger publishes books and videos on a wide variety of personal-finance and business-
management subjects. Check our Web site (www.kiplinger.com) for a complete list of titles,
additional information and excerpts. Or write:
   Cindy Greene
   Kiplinger Books & Tapes
   1729 H Street, N.W.
   Washington, DC 20006
   email: cgreene@kiplinger.com
To order, call 800-280-7165; for information about volume discounts, call 202-887-6431.

Dedication

For my sisters Joy and Stacey.
A family that grows together stays together.

In loving memory of Bernie Hunter.

Acknowledgments

AFTER TWENTY YEARS OF TEACHING, WRITING AND working with clients of all sizes and from all industries on the legal and strategic aspects of business growth, it would take me several hundred pages to acknowledge everyone who has helped me along this exciting path. But since I promised my wife and children that this was my last book for a while, I want to make sure that there is nobody that I forget to mention.

First, I want to thank my partners and all of the excellent lawyers and staff worldwide at McDermott, Will & Emery for their support, particularly Tim Waters for his mentoring and guidance in Washington, DC and Larry Gerber for his leadership globally. I want to especially thank my partners Al Schaeffer, Debra Harrison and Andy Friedman for their loyalty and for putting up with me on a daily basis and associate Ben Krein for his research and assistance on several chapters. For the tenth book in a row, thanks to corporate and franchising paralegal Michele Woodfolk for her loyalty, dedication, organizational skills and word processing assistance.

At Kiplinger's, I owe a large debt of gratitude to David Harrison for his support and advocacy for our three books and countless related projects that we have had the pleasure of work on together and Gloria Suzia, a freelance editor for her editing of this manuscript. Thanks, too, to Heather Waugh for her excellent cover and interior design, to Allison Leopold for a fine copy-editing job, and to Kiplinger Books editorial assistant Cindy Greene for her organizational skills used to keep the project moving along. None of this would be possible without the vision and resources of Knight Kiplinger, who is at the helm of one of the world's finest business and financial publishing companies.

Finally, my wife, Judy, and children, Matthew and Jennifer, again deserve a lot of recognition for their patience, chapter after chapter taking time away from them. I am very proud of their accomplishments and they seem to be growing up as fast as many of my rapid-growth clients.

Table of Contents

Introduction

BIGGER AND BIGGER, FASTER AND FASTER. THIS ISN'T just the mantra of the folks who design SUVs and sports cars. These days, it seems, the imperative of ever-increasing size and velocity is everywhere, from sports stadiums and 20-ounce steaks to high-speed Internet and drive-through grocery stores.

Sure, there is an undercurrent of thoughtful dissent out there—people preaching and practicing that "less is more," pulling back from the rat race to slow down, smell the roses, and simplify their lives.

But you won't find many entrepreneurs in the "small is beautiful" movement. Successful entrepreneurs are, by nature, type-A people, thriving on the speed and stress inherent in starting and developing a new business. Their goal is growth—the faster the better.

Andrew J. Sherman, an accomplished lawyer and business consultant based in Washington, D.C., calls this phenomenon "fast-track growth," and now he has written a marvelous book that shows every executive how to do it right. In its breadth, insight and clarity, *Fast-Track Business Growth* is a like an entire MBA program between the two covers of one book. In chapter after chapter of compelling advice and examples, Sherman rolls out multiple blueprints for business growth without undue risk.

Sherman starts with the assumption (broadly embraced today, especially by financial markets) that a strong rate of growth is good—indeed, necessary—for most companies. In his opening chapter, he lays out the leading factors impelling fast-track business growth today, including compulsive creativity and innovation ("The Edison Syndrome"), fear of being overtaken by one's competitors, and restlessness and ego on the part of executives who are bored by mere stewardship. To these factors he could add the high—often unreasonably high—expectations of venture capitalists and public shareholders.

This assumption that fast growth is desirable, interestingly, has not always been universally held, even by business owners themselves.

In every era, but especially in the aftermath of business crises such as the Great Depression, some entrepreneurs chose a path of slow, steady growth. They didn't want to rely too much on outside funding and didn't want to take excessive risk. Businesses grew by what we call "internal growth"—conceiving and developing every new product or service in house; financing expansion with the retained earnings of current operations; borrowing sparingly; and keeping the business a private, closely held firm, with no outside shareholders looking over their shoulder and second-guessing their every move. If a new idea was "not invented here," they didn't want to hear about it.

These business owners were content to grow their revenue and earnings at a rate healthily, but not dramatically, above some modest benchmark . . . the average growth in demand for their kind of product, or maybe the average growth rate of their local economy or the national economy. They didn't intend to sell their business in the near future, either to a private buyer or to public shareholders, so they didn't need to dazzle anyone with a rapid rate of growth which, they suspected, would be unsustainable for a longer period. They were content with generating enough sales growth—and productivity gains—to fund steadily rising compensation for themselves and their employees, without eroding profit margins.

Many highly profitable, admired businesses still run on principles such as these, but this is certainly not the prevailing model today. While most new businesses still start out closely held, the typical modern entrepreneur dreams of going public or selling to a larger company early in the life of the enterprise.

And if he or she is one of that restless breed of "serial entrepreneurs," the next goal is to go right out and do it all over again—founding, growing and selling one business after another. Achieving this dream requires rapid growth, and fast-track growth just can't be achieved today by the old business model of internally financed expansion.

That's why Andrew Sherman's new book devotes so much time to business-growth strategies that were never a part of management manuals a generation ago. He shows how Web operations can be a sensible vehicle for growth—not the drain on profitability seen at most companies. You'll learn, too, how to grow by acquiring other product lines or entire companies, rather than reinventing the wheel. Sherman will show you how to structure joint ventures and strategic alliances without losing control of your own operations. The ins and outs of licensing your technologies, brands and products to other firms get close attention, too.

There is also a strong international component in Sherman's business-growth strategy. Any business that is not content with the modest economic growth of the world's largest and richest economy—the United States—must look at ways to sells its goods and services to the 95% of the world that lives off our shores.

Finally, Sherman explores the dark side of fast-track growth—the pitfalls of overly rapid, careless growth and how to avoid them, as well as antitrust issues that can arise if you are too successful in achieving market dominance.

Rapid growth isn't every executive's goal, but if it's yours, you can't find a better trail guide and mentor than Andrew Sherman. We at the Kiplinger organization have been advising business owners and managers since 1920, and we are proud to publish this superbly practical guide to the fast lane of commerce. Our best wishes to you for success with your fast-track business growth.

Knight Kiplinger

Knight A. Kiplinger
Editor in Chief, *The Kiplinger Letter* and *kiplingerforecasts.com*
Washington, D.C.
October 2001

Preface

I HAVE SPENT THE BETTER PART OF MY PROFESSIONAL LIFE helping companies of all sizes and in many different industries develop strategies to grow their businesses, and I've observed that companies of all types and sizes want their companies to grow in one way or another—whether it's in terms of growth of revenues, profits, number of employees or customers, market share, or number of locations (or these days, the amount of new traffic to their Web site). Not everyone has aspirations to build the next Roman Empire, but all entrepreneurs want to see progress from year to year, even if it's just in the amount of money that they can take home to their families.

From a legal perspective, the more things change, the more they seem to stay the same. Owners of fast-track growing businesses continue to worry about some of the same issues that plagued such businesses at the turn of the last century, such as OSHA health and safety standards, minimum wage standards, personal injury and workmen's compensation claims, and product-liability litigation. These issues may never be entirely resolved, but as our economy shifts, new legal, financial and organizational issues have begun to emerge involving protection of intellectual property, doing business in the global village, transacting business via the Internet and the renewed focus on satisfying the customer. These economic and organizational shifts are creating new legal challenges. Global competition and rapid technological advancements are creating new business-management models, such as geographically dispensed work forces; flattened organizational structures; and strategic partnering among customers, vendors, suppliers, and even competitors. And companies of all sizes are developing work teams that communicate and collaborate electronically instead of around a conference table or by the water cooler. The virtual workplace where there is significantly less human interaction brings new challenges in the areas of protection of privacy, confidentiality and copyright laws.

- **Given these rapidly moving changes in our marketplace,** the challenge is—*how* and *when* to grow? And this question leads to other key questions that can be difficult to answer.
- **What strategies should be used** to facilitate growth?
- **How do you know whether these strategies are appropriate** for your business?
- **Are there problems with your business structure** that need resolving before you can implement the growth strategy selected?
- **How can you build** on your strengths and compensate for your weaknesses?
- **How might the growth strategy selected** present new risks or make you vulnerable? To whom?
- **Is this the right time to grow?** That is, have you put a proper foundation for growth in place?
- **Is capital available to fuel growth?** Are market conditions ripe for growth opportunities?

The challenges and problems associated with building a company beyond the start-up phase have certainly taken a toll on the many entrepreneurs who began new businesses over the past few years. There are a wide variety of changes that are caused by growth, all of which present different management, legal and financial challenges. Growth means that new employees will be hired who will be looking to top management for leadership. Growth means the company's management will become increasingly decentralized, which may create greater levels of internal politics, protectionism and dissension over the goals and projects the company should pursue. Growth means that market share will expand, calling for new strategies for dealing with larger competitors. Growth also means that additional capital will be required, creating new responsibilities to shareholders, investors and institutional lenders. Thus growth brings with it a variety of changes in the company's structure, needs and objectives.

The plans and strategies developed by management to cope with the changes caused by rapid growth cannot be made in a vacuum. Legal implications, costs, benefits and risks of each proposed decision, transaction, plan or strategy must be understood. An understanding of the legal issues raised by the inevitable changes that are caused by business growth is a necessary prerequisite to effectively managing the organization and ensuring the company's long-term success and continued profitability.

Business growth is truly a two-edged sword. When it's controlled and well-managed, it has the potential of providing tremendous rewards to the managers and shareholders of the company. When growth is poorly planned and uncontrolled, it often leads to financial distress and failure.

Rapid growth for many companies is the only way to survive in highly competitive industries. These companies are faced with a choice of either acting quickly to capture additional market share or sitting on the sidelines and watching others play the game. But do these competitive conditions justify unplanned and unbridled growth, where sound management, legal and accounting principles are disregarded? Certainly not. What these conditions do mean is that the need of the organization to grow must be tempered by the need to understand that meaningful, long-term, profitable growth is the by-product of effective management and planning. A strategy that focuses on sensible and logical growth dictates that a balance is created between the need for organizational flexibility to quickly seize upon market opportunities, adapt to changes in the marketplace and develop creative solutions for problems that arise versus the need for a controlled and well-managed expansion plan. Failure to create this balance will result in a vulnerability to attack by competitors, creditors, hostile employees and creative takeover specialists.

A commitment to properly growing the company will invariably trigger the need for management to undertake greater risks. These risks must be managed from a legal perspective, as must the changes that the organization will experience as a result of the growth. Accelerated growth will mean that these risks and changes will occur with greater frequency and with more serious implications. The requirements and restrictions imposed by the law that affect most business objectives and transactions will typically retard the rate at which a company can grow. The delays caused by legal drafting and negotiation of documents, filings with regulators and meeting statutory requirements, however, are inevitable setbacks and costs of doing business. Since the law is not likely to go away any time soon, prudent owners and managers of growing companies should take the time to learn the fundamental legal issues that govern their plans and strategies.

An emerging-growth business is likely to experience a wide variety of changes in its structure, its products and services, its markets and its capital requirements. Each change will raise a host of legal issues that must be considered prior to the implementation of the particular strategy that has been selected to achieve the company's growth objectives. Naturally, the specific legal requirements of a growing company will depend on:

- **the market segments and industry sectors** in which the business operates;
- **the exact stage of the company's development;**
- **the current and projected capital needs** of the business; and
- **the types of barriers that the company must overcome** to achieve its objectives.

I wrote *Fast-Track Business Growth* to help you decide which growth strategy is appropriate for your business and understand the key challenges and issues you may face once you select one or more growth strategies. It is also designed to help your company stay on a growth track, even when the economy is slowing down. The book generally follows the decisional path shown in the box on the next page to help you determine what types of growth are best for your company and what challenges you may encounter in implementing the strategy selected.

Chapter 1 discusses the foundation that needs to be in place for growth to be effective and feasible. Chapters 2 to 4 describe growth objectives that are commonly selected by fast-track growing companies and the development of a business-growth plan. Chapters 5 through 10 look at the internal and

---

┌───┐
| **Decisional Path Toward Selecting a Growth Strategy** |
| |
| **Understanding the dynamics**   ■ Mergers and acquisitions |
| **and challenges of business growth** ■ Licensing |
| How and why do businesses grow?   ■ E-commerce |
| ■ Joint ventures |
| **Building a foundation for growth** ■ Global business |
| Is your business ready to grow?   ■ Strategic alliances |
| What needs to be in place? |
| **Growth strategies audit** |
| **Determining growth objectives** Self-assessment and decisional |
| Do you want to achieve growth in   matrix for help in selecting a given |
| terms of sales, profits, employees, strategy. |
| customer base or geography? |
| **Selecting a growth strategy** |
| **Understanding growth strategies** Which growth strategy or strategies |
| An overview of the ways that fast- are most appropriate for meeting |
| track companies typically grow: these objectives? |
| ■ Internal strategies |
| ■ External strategies   **Implementing a growth strategy** |
| ■ Capital formation   How to develop a business-growth |
| ■ Franchising   plan. |
└───┘

external human-resources challenges in building a rapidly-growing business. Chapters 11 through 14 look at how to raise the capital needed to implement growth plans and strategies. In Chapters 15 through 17, I look at some commonly selected internal or organic-leveraging strategies, such as acquisitions, e-commerce and international expansion. In Chapters 18 through 21, external-growth strategies such as franchising, licensing and joint ventures are discussed. In Chapters 22 through 24, business-growth problems, such as litigation, financial stress and antitrust challenges, are examined. Finally, the Appendix offers a resource directory that highlights some of the organizations and resources that may be helpful as your company follows its growth path. As we move along the decisional path, I'll discuss the following issues:

■ **What factors influence** a company's selection of a particular growth strategy?

■ **What are the advantages and disadvantages** of each growth strategy?

- **How can intellectual property and other intangible assets** be leveraged when access to capital is limited or too costly?
- **What technological developments and current business trends** influence the selection of a particular growth strategy?
- **How does a company avoid "growth for growth's sake?"** How does an entrepreneur regulate the pace and rate of growth?
- **Is the proposed growth strategy profitable?** How will it add to the bottom line or otherwise enhance your business? What about other parties affected by your strategy? Is this path viable for them as well? *Avoid growth to feed ego.*
- **If the growth strategy requires the establishment** of *interdependent relationships,* such as *franchising* and *licensing,* are you considering: Who will control what issues? Who needs the other the most? What does each party bring to the table? What are the financial implications for each party?

Over the years, I have found that there are very few things that are more professionally gratifying than helping an entrepreneur or fast-track growth company find new ways to grow. I hope that *Fast-Track Business Growth* becomes a resource and a tool to help your company leverage its strengths and achieve its full potential and that you enjoy the journey as you follow the business-growth plan.

ANDREW J. SHERMAN
Bethesda, Maryland
October 2001

FAST-TRACK
BUSINESS GROWTH

Building a Platform
and Developing a
Growth Strategy

Building a Foundation for Business Growth

I N THE WORLD OF BUSINESS, THERE ARE VERY FEW challenges that are as exciting and as complicated as the task of growing a company. As we begin our journey examining the legal, financial and strategic issues that arise when growing a business, it is critical to first establish an understanding of the foundation that must be in place to allow a company to begin its growth path. The elements of this foundation include the company's brands, its relationships with its customers, its commitment to its products and services and the management of its distribution channels.

Factors Driving Business Growth

What factors drive a company to fast-track business growth? What motivates an entrepreneurial growth company to get bigger, faster, diversify, enter new markets, and develop new products? The reasons for business growth are many and varied. They are as likely to include the leadership attitudes and the personalities of the business owners as they are to include external market pressures. Here's a sampling of the most common factors.

THE EDISON SYNDROME. Some companies develop a culture of creativity and innovation that drives them toward new product development and technological breakthroughs. The pride of inventiveness is combined with skillful management to provide the fuel for growth. Cisco Systems would be an example of a modern success story that is driven by innovation—both internally and via acquisition of developing companies and technologies.

FEAR. Some companies are driven by fear of competition, the fear of missing an opportunity or the fear of not being the market leader. Andy Grove, the founder of Intel, stated that "only the paranoid survive"—and certainly the fear of failure or the insecurity of the company's leadership can, if harnessed properly, be a strong motivator for growth. A healthy level of anxiety will keep the company sharp and competitive but must not be an excuse for deadlocking the decision-making process or leading to "analysis paralysis."

BOREDOM. One entrepreneur I met recently told me that he and his team decided to triple the size of their building-supplies conglomerate through recapitalization, the establishment of new offices and the acquisition of existing businesses primarily because they got bored with the business as it was. When a business is running smoothly, the entrepreneurial challenge can be significantly diminished. In such circumstances, many companies remain stagnant (and often begin to deteriorate slowly) because ownership and management become "fat, dumb and happy" with the EBIT (Earnings Before Interest and Taxes) and cash flow. Unless the leadership of the company chooses to develop new challenges, they go from being agile like a gazelle to being sluggish like an elephant. The failure of the business to continue to evolve may also eventually lead to the loss of key employees, key customers and other important strategic relationships. Never, ever take business growth for granted. Getting bored relatively easily and always striving for new challenges can be strong characteristics for a growth company.

PUBLISH OR PERISH. Some industries, particularly those that are technology-driven, mimic the old publish-or-perish culture in the world of university academic tenure. Businesses in such industries must continue to be productive and innovative, or the markets and their customers will punish and abandon them. The misjudgment of a market or the mistiming of a new product winds up being very costly. In 2000, Lucent Technologies Inc. lost 70% of its market capitalization as a result of such a misstep by not keeping pace with industry innovations and product offerings.

FIRST-MOVER ADVANTAGE. Many emerging industries are driven by who has the first-mover advantage—that is, which company can get its product or service out the fastest and begin building brand equity with its targeted group of customers. This market dynamic becomes a market and business-growth motivator because strategies need to be put in place to be first to market, first to build brand, and so forth. The theory here is that the company that grabs the most market share the fastest wins the bat-

The theory here is that the company that grabs the most market share the fastest wins the battle and the war. Said another way, the view never gets any better for the second dog pulling the sled.

tle *and* the war. Said another way, the view never gets any better for the second dog pulling the sled. Although this approach has long been a strong business-growth motivator, it came under attack in 2000 when a "Best Beats First" mentality crept into the marketplace. The first to market in the dot.com arena didn't guarantee that the company would be around 12 months later. For example, discount online retailer ValueAmerica.com is now bankrupt but Walmart.com is just hitting its stride. Amazon.com has survived as a first mover, but with a significant reduction in its market value. And first-mover Netscape, whose innovative *Navigator* software introduced the world to Web surfing, ultimately lost the browser wars to rival Microsoft's *Explorer*. In pursuing a first-mover-advantage strategy for business growth, it is important to ensure that this strategy will withstand the best-beats-first challenge.

EGO. The stereotypical public image of an entrepreneur at the helm of a growth company is that he or she has an ego the size of the state of New Jersey. It is often true that entrepreneurs have very large egos, and their self-confidence and pride can become the motivators for continued business growth. But a successful company cannot be built on the basis of ego alone. If the founder views the company as basically a monument to himself, then it will surely fail at some point. Similarly, if selfish greed is at the heart of the company's compensation and own-

If the founder views the company as basically a monument to himself, then it will surely fail at some point.

ership structure, the company will often fail or lose momentum. Smart entrepreneurs such as Sam Walton or Bill Gates took great pride in helping thousands of employees and shareholders build wealth, knowing that their rewards would be even greater if they could have everyone around them prosper. To paraphrase Rabbi Hillel, a famous Talmudic scholar, wrote, "If I am not for myself, then what shall be for me? But if I am only for myself, then who am I?" The entrepreneur or management team that is focused on the enrichment of its employees, the satisfaction of its customers and a steady increase in its shareholder value will build wealth by helping others along the way.

THE "CHIP ON MY SHOULDER" PHENOMENON. Many entrepreneurs who are at the helm of rapid-growth companies have some external motivating factors that drive them to succeed day in and day out. They may have been the kids who never got picked in schoolyard basketball, the product of a broken home or raised under difficult economic or social conditions. This "I've got something to prove" syndrome becomes part of the corporate culture, and employees who share similar backgrounds are attracted to this culture in which "geeks can rule" or where "David beats Goliath."

Momentum Is the Key Factor

In all of the key motivators for business growth, momentum is a critical component. The "Big Mo," as entrepreneurs and venture capitalists often refer to momentum, is critical to continued success. The leadership of an organization must ensure that the resources and the systems are in place to provide for forward progress toward stated objectives. Every day, week, month, quarter and year, the management must establish benchmarks and milestones and measure its progress against these goals. A loss of momentum for an extended period can be detrimental, and will also stand in the way of the company's ability to raise additional rounds of capital or get access to other resources needed for continued business growth. The measuring of performance against established benchmarks, together with a leadership focused on maintaining high employee motivation and strong customer relationships, will ensure continued momentum. The need to avoid complacency should be balanced against the need to maintain your culture and core values. The challenge is: How can we continue to grow without sacrificing *who* we are *now* and what makes us special?

Building a Foundation for Growth

To grow your business successfully, your company should have a strong foundation on which the growth strategy will be built, launched and monitored. As you build a platform for growth, make sure that the following relevant components are in place:

A clearly defined mission statement, vision and core values . These must be adopted by management and embraced by your employees. If your mission statement sits on a plaque behind your desk, and it's not embedded in the corporate culture, that means your company is not yet in a position to grow effectively. To achieve corporate goals, your employees must be com-

---

Ensuring Business Growth

Identifying and
understanding your + Leadership + Momentum = Continuous
growth motivation   business growth

7

mitted to sharing and living by your vision and core values.

A proven prototype that will serve as a basis or model for the growth strategy you have selected. The business prototype must have been tested, refined and operated successfully and should be consistently profitable. The success of the business model should not be too dependent on the physical presence or specific expertise of the founders of the system.

A strong and leadership-oriented management team made up of internal officers and directors (as well as outside advisers) who are committed to growth. The team must understand both your industry and the legal and business aspects of the strategy selected as a method of expansion, and must be committed to creating or fostering a corporate culture that encourages and rewards teamwork and innovation.

Sufficient capitalization to implement and sustain the growth strategy.

A distinctive and protected trade identity that includes federal and state registered trademarks, as well as a uniform trade appearance, signage, slogans, trade dress and overall image. This creates a competitive advantage.

Three Key Aspects of Business Growth

HUMAN RESOURCES	CAPITAL	INTANGIBLES
Co-founders, team,	Current capital, strategic and distribution channel relationships	Intellectual future needs, property financial and capital structure

Key Question: How do we leverage these assets to facilitate growth? The better managed fast-track growth companies learn how to leverage their three critical sets of assets—their people, their capital resources and their intangibles. As will be discussed later in this book, the company's ability to create core businesses and incremental revenue streams from these assets are key to healthy growth.

Proven methods of operation and proprietary processes that can be reduced to a comprehensive operations manual that cannot be easily duplicated by competitors. The processes must maintain their value to any market-channel partners over an extended period of time, and be enforced through clearly drafted and objective quality-control standards.

Comprehensive training programs for employees and any market-channel partners. The programs should integrate the latest education and training technologies and take place both at your headquarters and on-site at the channel partner's proposed location. The latter should be done at the outset of the relationship and on an ongoing basis.

A commitment to, and genuine understanding of, your customers, so that you will be positioned for growth, your company must take the time to understand the short-term as well as long-term needs and wants of its customers, and its organization and products must be modified to meet these needs and wants.

A demonstrated market demand for the products and services that will be offered through the channels created by the growth strategy selected. Your company's products and services should meet certain minimum quality standards, not be subject to rapid shifts in consumer preferences (as is the case with fads), and be proprietary in nature. Market research and analysis should be sensitive to trends in the economy and your industry, the plans of direct and indirect competitors, and shifts in consumer preferences.

A genuine understanding of the competition (both direct and indirect) that your company will face in the adoption and implementation of the given growth strategy. Your company should have a strategic and systematic way of gathering and analyzing this market intelligence, rather than on a random or ad hoc basis.

Research and development capabilities for the ongoing introduction of new products and services that can be distributed to consumers through the channels that have been built in connection with the growth strategy.

A proven system for attracting, training, motivating and retaining key employees at all levels.

A strong set of external advisers and outside members on your board of directors.

A capital and ownership structure that makes sense given your growth objectives, and that is compatible with other similarly situated competitors in your industry.

A passion and devotion to creating, protecting and leveraging your company's intellectual property and related intangible assets.

A commitment to using all available technologies, including developing an e-commerce strategy, to enhance the adoption of your particular growth strategy.

A little bit of luck.

Common Traits and Best Practices of Successful Rapid-Growth Companies

Successful rapid-growth companies possess many of the following characteristics. The more of these characteristics your company acquires, the greater your chances will be for its success.

BEYOND SEED CAPITAL. The company has already received early rounds of capital and has shifted its focus from "How do we get start-up capital" to "We've been seeded, but now how do we grow?"

PROVEN TEAM. Each of the company's teams has demonstrated an ability to work together and proved an ability to execute important decisions. Their peers and employees view them as leaders. They are committed to reinvesting resources back into the company.

SCALABLE BUSINESS MODEL. The founders of the company developed a business model and infrastructure that fits with *current* customer demand patterns, but that can *evolve* as the market embraces the company's products and services and *future* demand patterns increase. The company's leaders must monitor and enhance demand and ensure that infrastructure and capacity are in place to handle the demand that has been generated.

> **Rapid-growth companies often aim for "ten times" as the goal because they understand that by the time the product or service hits the marketplace, it will be only three times better.**

RECOGNIZABLE INNOVATION. Many of rapid-growth companies today are truly innovative pioneers. They are focused on the creation of products and services that are ten times faster, cheaper or more convenient for the user than the products the competition creates. Rapid-growth companies often aim for "ten times" as the goal because they understand that by the time the product or service hits the marketplace, it will be only three times better. Your rapid-growth company must demonstrate that its products or services are several times better and more valuable for targeted customers or it will be virtually impossible to get consumers to switch over.

INTELLECTUAL VISION AND AN ABILITY TO EVOLVE. The company's founders have created a vision and a culture devoted to the intellectual challenge of developing a great idea into a great product or service that customers will want. The founders have anticipated change, stayed ahead of the curve and ensured that the company's plans were flexible enough to change directions when circumstances dictated. A continuing commitment to the development of new initiatives is critical.

LOYAL CUSTOMER BASE. Real customers who have paid real dollars (and are happy they did so) for the company's products and services help to demonstrate that the company's solutions work and that somebody wants what it offers. These customers are initially attracted to the differentiation of the products or services; the company's ability to deliver on its promises builds brand loyalty.

SUSTAINED COMPETITIVE ANALYSIS AND ADVANTAGE. The fast-growth company has a strong sense of its current position in the marketplace and has demonstrated some sustainable competitive advantage—either by being first to the marketplace, building brand loyalty, developing a portfolio of intellectual property that creates barriers to entry, or by finding a niche to exploit and then building a product or service around that opening in the market.

CULTURE OF TEAMWORK. The leaders of successful emerging companies create a genuine culture of teamwork that avoids internal politics and backstabbing. These leaders teach their employees to compete externally, not internally. It is difficult enough to compete with the outside world without employees worrying about excessive internal competitive pressures.

HEALTHY FINANCIAL PERFORMANCE. The company has developed a stream of durable revenues and profits that are built on a foundation of defensible accounting and revenue-recognition practices.

A HEALTHY ATTITUDE TOWARD FUTURE RISK. Rapid-growth companies know how to put risk into proper perspective. They understand that entrepreneurial companies need to be prepared to fail to succeed. They view some degree of failure as inevitable; when it happens their culture of resiliency helps them quickly rebound without getting too discouraged. These companies know how to learn from their mistakes. The healthy attitude toward risk is a part of their culture that drives ongoing innovation.

COMMITMENT TO GENUINE EMPOWERMENT. The leadership of the company is committed to empowering team members at all levels with the resources and the decisional authority to do their jobs effectively, without excessive red-tape or decisional hurdles. Management authority becomes more horizontal and far less vertical in nature. The leaders of the company continuously set goals and benchmarks, communicate these goals to employees at all levels and regularly measure the company's performance against these benchmarks. The company develops compensation and reward systems around the accomplishment of (and the ability to exceed) these benchmarks.

ONGOING MONITORING OF COMPETITIVE TRENDS. Successful rapid-growth companies are never caught with their hands in their pockets. They devote capital and resources to develop market-information systems and to gathering and analyzing market intelligence. They carefully monitor key market trends, indicators and the moves made by their competitors but also avoid an overfocus on competitors at the expense of being attentive to the needs of current customers.

THE ART OF SPIN CONTROL. Rapid-growth companies learn quickly how to manage the rumor mill. Along the growth path, these companies are especially vulnerable to attack by jealous competitors, disgruntled employees and Wall Street analysts. The smarter companies stay ahead of this information and control the flow of data effectively. When bad news does hit, they deal with the problem in a direct and straightforward manner that will often prevent employees and customers from abandoning them.

Getting Ready for Growth

Before you can get your company ready for more growth, you need to know its strengths and weaknesses. Being alert to what's working well serves to concentrate your efforts where you have the best chance of success. And by looking for strengths, you'll also spot the weaknesses. Your answers to the following questions will give you an idea of where your company is strong and where it could improve, as well as which type of growth strategy would be best for your company.

COSTS AND REVENUES. Examine these for every part of your business. Are revenues rising or falling? How about profit margins? Which divisions or departments stand out? Why? Does your company have a strong positive cash flow?

PERSONNEL. Do certain employees show exceptional skills or produce outstanding results? Where in the company is the strongest management, organization and planning? Do you have the talent on staff to handle anticipated growth, or would you have to hire new personnel?

OPERATIONS. Are these areas that seem to be trouble-free, functioning with little supervision but always delivering results? How do the managers in those areas achieve such consistent results? If operations are not running at peak effectiveness, what improvements need to be made?

PHILOSOPHY OR MISSION. Do you have a written statement describing your company's philosophy or mission? Does it define the essence of your business exactly so that you know which kinds of activities fit your company's goals and which do not? Are you diluting your resources by engaging in any activities outside your mission? Have you developed a set of core values, and have your employees embraced them? After you've sized up your internal operations, take a long and careful look at your market, your competitors and the current economic climate. This external examination should reveal whether you are in a position to take advantage of current business trends and cycles.

YOUR MARKET. Is your market share—your company's percentage of estimated total business available—increasing or decreasing? Is your marketing strategy based on careful research or on instinct and hunches? Is your customer or client base growing or shrinking?

YOUR COMPETITION. Do you know exactly who your competitors are, and where they pose the largest threat? Which part of your business is most vulnerable to competition and which is

---

Will Your Business Make It?

Honest answers to the following questions will indicate whether you're using the kinds of management practices that will give your business the best chance of success. The more "yes" answers, the better.

_____ Do you have a written plan that sets out the goals you want to achieve in the next five years? Has it been revised recently?

_____ Can you prove that you've made progress toward the goals with hard numbers?

_____ Can you generate a cash flow without having to suffer through too many dry spells?

_____ Does your accountant prepare and thoroughly explain reports other than tax returns, such as monthly profit-and-loss statements and balance sheets?

_____ Have you consulted experts recently about financial or marketing strategy?

_____ Have you talked about your business with your bank's loan officer even though a loan wasn't the object at the time?

_____ Do you know your break-even point and whether you are on target for reaching it?

_____ Do you know how much it actually costs to make each sale?

_____ Do you know exactly how much inventory you have on hand?

_____ Do you belong to a trade association for your industry?

_____ Do you read the same publications that your competitors and customers read?

_____ Do you talk regularly about business-related topics with other business owners?

_____ Do you get regular feedback from your customers and base changes on their suggestions?

_____ Do you consistently study your competitors' ads and read their sales literature?

_____ Do you have training sessions for and regular motivational meetings with your employees?

---

least vulnerable? Are some parts of your market becoming crowded with competitors?

ECONOMIC CLIMATE. Are changes in economic conditions—interest rates, inflation, housing starts, and industry earnings—likely to affect your company? Do you make efforts to anticipate changes in the marketplace, or are you often surprised by developments that affect your company?

Finally, remember that long-term growth is not about sexy trends or management fads. To enjoy sustained business growth over longer periods of time, your company and its leadership must maintain an intense focus on creating and building value for your company's shareholders, your employees and your customers. To accomplish this, your company must have its ears close to the ground—always listening and responding to the needs of your customers and the challenges of your employees—which will in turn build long-term shareholder value. The key is to balance a long-term focus with the need to move quickly enough to respond and adjust to short-term opportunities to expand your core business and to short-term problems that threaten your long-term viability.

Defining Your Growth Objectives

I N CHAPTER 1, WE LOOKED AT WHY COMPANIES GROW, in this chapter we will look at the importance of clearly defining the company's objectives prior to the implementation of a business growth plan or strategy. Effective growth management involves:

- **understanding why** the company wants or needs to grow;
- **clearly defining the objectives** that growth will achieve or problems that growth will solve;
- **management's understanding** of the challenges and risks that rapid growth will pose to the company, especially if the growth process is not well managed;
- **understanding the various phases of growth** the company will experience as it evolves towards maturity; and
- **implementing a growth-management process** that is responsive to and reflective of your company's current stage of growth.

As discussed in Chapter 1, when ego, impatience or boredom serve as a primary driver for growth, the consequences can be severe. At the heart of your company's growth objectives should always be the desire to meet your customer's need or solve your customer's problem. This customercentric focus on defining business-growth objectives will help you ensure that the analysis has been done to demonstrate whether the market demand is in place to support your plans for growth.

The Strategic Audit

A *customercentric* focus on business growth requires that you conduct market research before you execute your growth strategy in order to prove that a promising niche really exists. Concurrent with this market research, you should conduct a *strategic audit* to make sure that you have the proper infrastructure in place to support your proposed growth plan. The strategic audit will assess the strength of your current management and advisory team; define the key sections of your business-growth strategic plan, which needs to be drafted; examine your current systems, distribution channels and financial resources that are available to determine whether your plans for growth can be supported; and look at industry trends and macroeconomic factors that will either support and expedite your growth plans or serve as a barrier to its implementation. The strategic audit is also important as a benchmark for comparing your company's performance to date and its plans for growth against direct or indirect competitors.

The strategic audit may reveal that your initial set of growth objectives were misdirected, overly conservative, too aggressive or just plain inconsistent with market trends. It will serve as a reality test and an opportunity to refine objectives before you expend resources to implement the wrong set of objectives. The audit will help you identify holes or weaknesses in your organizational chart, processes or controls that are antiquated or need to be streamlined and where available technology can make your company more productive or efficient. Following the strategic audit, you can adjust your business-growth strategic plan and put in place any missing resources.

Categories of Growth

The strategic audit should also help your company define which specific categories or aspects of your business you've targeted for growth. For example, your business plan might revolve around a desire to grow profits while holding the number of employees steady, or it may be that you want to achieve growth by increasing the number of distribution channels while holding the number of new products and services steady, or vice-versa. The process of choosing which aspects of the business are slated for growth and what strategy will be most effective for meeting these objectives is a critical part of the overall growth planning process.

There are many categories of business operations that could be targeted for growth, as demonstrated by the box below.

Growth Strategies to Solve a Problem

Growth strategies are often developed to solve a specific problem or to help jump over a hurdle in the business-growth evolution. The need to stay competitive, to foster creativity and innovation, to encourage career advancement among top management, to build your brand, to respond to the challenge of overseas expansion, to strengthen the balance sheet, and to better leverage your portfolio of intellectual property may all

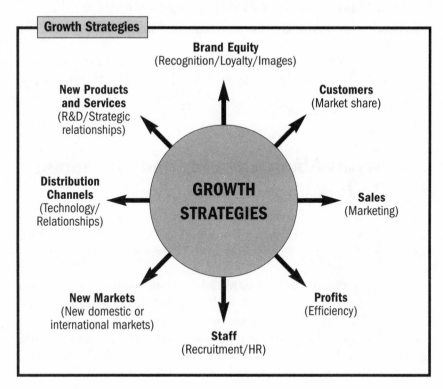

Sample Growth Problems and Solutions

Problem: A growing office- supply manufacturer is losing the loyalty of its sales representatives who desire to have their own businesses, while at the same time the manufacturer is seeking stronger control over its distribution network.
Solution: Convert the sales representative to franchisees.

Problem: A small but growing developer of software has created a state-of-the-art system for engineering support, but lacks the capital and the marketing expertise to bring the product to market.
Solution: Develop a strategic alliance with a cash-rich Fortune 500 software company that is weak in new-product development.

Problem: A venture-capital company is left with only the technology of a failed portfolio company and no means for providing a return to its investors.
Solution: Enter into a licensing agreement with a competitor of the failed company that will provide ongoing royalty fees that could eventually recoup the original investment if technology is properly developed.

---

be problems your company is facing. The right growth strategy will solve any of these problems, if it is properly formulated and implemented as illustrated in the box above.

Myths About Defining and Developing Business-Growth Objectives

Before you undertake a rapid-growth strategy for your company, you must be able to recognize the myths about business growth. Here are some of the more common ones.

YOU MUST BE FIRST TO MARKET TO WIN THE GAME. This is often wrong, wrong, wrong. Fred Smith did not invent mail delivery, Ray Kroc did not invent the hamburger and Bill Gates did not invent software. The entrepreneurial focus on "First to Market" or "First-Mover Advantage" is slowly being replaced with a "Best Beats First" business mantra. In other

---

Characteristics of Leading Growth Companies

- Brand recognized by customers and respected by competitors
- Strong channel relationships and market partners
- Business and revenue model is durable and stable but also adaptable to rapid-moving market conditions and quick to react when changes or shifts in trends are identified
- Sophisticated technology deployment and adaptation strategy that balances the need to stay

current against the temptation to grossly overspend
- Management style is innovative, flexible and responsive
- Focused on building and strengthening customer interactions from a quality and quantity perspective
- Clear and annual goals for increasing market share
- Culture that encourages creativity but also tolerates failure (as long as lessons are truly learned)

---

words, being best often means improving on what's already out there, not necessarily pioneering or discovering the product or service. The follower often prevails over the innovator in the battle for market share, just as Boeing did over DeHavilland in the fight for jet-airliner sales, as Texas Instruments did over Bowmar in the fight for pocket-calculator sales and as Coca-Cola did over R.C. Cola in the battle for diet-cola sales. The follower usually must have improved on the original pioneer's product, either in technological features, price, availability, service or user-friendliness. The follower must differentiate itself in some significant way, not just offer a me-too product or service.

GROWTH IS THE RESULT OF A CONSCIOUS CHOICE. Some companies grow even if they don't want or intend to do so. The market dynamics causing this may be a fast-moving, "grow or die" environment, as was the case with Internet commerce in 1999 and 2000, where there was no choice but to grow and usually no time to plan for it properly. In these types of markets, growth is a matter of survival. This go-go dynamic lead to inflated valuations—and inflated egos. Many of the companies that experienced growth in this type of environment have died or are near death. Others have needed to completely re-tool their business models around more sensible growth plans and more durable revenue streams. In other situations, the founders of a company may intend for the business to stay small, but the market demand for their products or services is so strong that market forces drag them into a rapid-growth plan. In this situation, the management team is ill prepared for growth because they were not expecting it—and growth as a result of surprise or accident can be deadly to the future of the enterprise. The ultimate irony is that many of these entrepreneurs had been trying to keep their companies small by design in order to keep better control over their role, their company and their lives, but the accidental or unavoidable pull of the markets into hypergrowth mode dictated otherwise.

GROWTH IS FUN. Growing your business can be fun, but that's not always the case. Often the founders or managers of the business do not get much of a feel in advance for what it really takes to achieve rapid growth and what is like to actually experience it. Growing a business can take a heavy emotional toll on the business owners and managers, and can wreak havoc on their personal lives. For many entrepreneurs, the pressures of growing a business have led to broken marriages; weight gain due to lack of time to exercise or eat properly; personality and management-style changes as the stress begins to mount or the ego begins to swell; drug and alcohol abuse; a limited social life (as the company becomes a jealous mistress); limited time to enjoy the wealth they have built; and mounting personal debt. Along with this, owners must face the new moral and ethical pressures of having hundreds of employees and their families depending on them for their livelihoods. Many entrepreneurs are ill-equipped for these new pressures and demands and wind up becoming very frustrated or disappointed with the whole process.

IF YOU REALLY WANT TO GROW, THEN FOLLOW THE PATH OF YOUR LARGER COMPETITORS. When it comes to certain types of industry practices, a decision to emulate your largest competitors is a good strategy. But to achieve fast-track business growth, following

Some Management Tips To Sustain Business Growth

Think in many directions. Business growth is not always linear and you need to see and manage the many linkages in the networks you build. Understand the interdependency of the relationships you manage.

Get everyone at all levels involved in the growth-planning process. Seek the input of employees at all levels in your organization as well as the advice of outside professionals, vendors and customers.

Think big, act small. Big dreamers and broad visions match well with the need to be nimble, pay attention to detail and adapt quickly to changes in demand, trends, or market conditions.

Focus on progress in bite-sized increments. Growth will often be fast-paced, but that does not mean it will always be in giant leaps forward. Appreciate and reward the incremental progress that moves the company toward its growth objectives.

Avoid being penny-wise and pound-foolish. Successful growth companies are not afraid to spend money and devote resources to information technology, research and design, which bring new products and services to the markets faster. They are also not afraid to invest in training to make sure they have a human-resources infrastructure capable of sustaining business growth.

Creativity is the engine of growth. Companies that successfully sustain growth are not afraid to experiment, not afraid to fail, reward innovations by employees and strategic partners, and understand that risk and the possibility of failure are part of the growth game. Growth companies may make more mistakes than others, but they also learn from those mistakes more quickly and use this knowledge to identify new opportunities.

Understand that the management of business growth is hard work. Very few worthwhile endeavors are accomplished easily, and this is certainly true of rapid business growth. Be prepared for bucket-loads of stress, financial pressures and extended periods of loneliness, but stay focused on the prize, which can be quite significant if your growth objectives are achieved.

Have fun. If you are not enjoying the ride, leave the business-growth amusement park.

the path of another is not a good idea. No two companies follow the exact path to growth, and a small company is not a little big company. Many features of the small company such as management structures, strategies, operations, distribution channels, market partners, and access to resources, may differ from those of the big company. Different factors will spur a period of rapid growth for different companies at different times in different markets, even though sometimes overall market conditions may be driving companies on an industrywide basis into a particular growth spurt or slowdown. In some cases, entrepreneurs start their companies fresh out of management positions at their larger competitors and then are too quick to adopt the styles and practices of their former employer in an effort emulate their path of growth. If only it were that easy! This is especially true in management buy-out (MBO) situations, where the team may have trouble making the transition out of the big-company mentality. Things will be different than they were at the big company. The early-stage company will have less access to capital and resources than their already larger competitor, and systems and decision-making must be adjusted down to scale.

Avoiding Some of the Classic Business-Growth Problems

Growth spurts can hit a company at any time, especially in a fast-moving economy and fast-paced business environment. The impetus for growth could be development of new technology, demise of a competitor (or even a competitor's area of weakness short of a total demise), hiring of new personnel, infusion of fresh capital, newly discovered opportunities or marketing breakthroughs or a favorable shift in economic conditions. These developments can happen over an extended period or virtually overnight. When they happen quickly, some of the more commonly experienced problems include cash-flow shortages, mismanagement, inadequate customer-service responsiveness, overhead costs spiraling out of

---

Understanding the Inhibitors to Growth

Some companies really want to grow but often have internal or external barriers that get in the way of adopting and implementing creative and aggressive growth plans. The first step in removing the growth "handcuffs" is to identify whether the problem is external or internal and then determine its cause. Examples of typical inhibitors are listed below.

External Growth Inhibitors
- Economic conditions
- Competitive threats
- Broken distribution channels
- Poor selection of market partners

Internal Growth Inhibitors
- Traditional/cultural challenges
- Internal politics/red tape
- Resource scarcity
- Education and training deficiencies

---

control, communications logjams, high employee turnover, inexperienced senior management and a slip in quality control.

If not properly managed, these problems can take your company quickly off its growth path and lead to a violent crash. The key to managing the growth process is for your management team to anticipate the risks of a given growth strategy or of market conditions that provide the impetus for growth, and prepare for overcoming them.

Steps that can help keep your company on course include: getting high quality advice from consultants and professional advisers; recruiting senior executives to help the founders manage the growth; and heavy doses of training for the employees to help them understand the implications of business growth. Other steps to help your growing company stay on course as it works toward its growth objectives include: developing strong financial controls and accounting/reporting systems (to manage and monitor the costs of growth, for example); building internal working teams that have clear focus and accountability for meeting goals; keeping a strong focus on the evolving needs of your current and future customers; creating a culture that views risks as opportunities; raising additional capital; and maintaining the discipline to stay focused on the end game, rather than getting frustrated or celebrating prematurely with lavish spending and perks.

Internal Versus External Growth Strategies

I N FORMULATING ONE OR MORE GROWTH STRATEGIES FOR your company, your management team needs to determine whether the focus will be on internal strategies, external strategies or a combination of the two. Internal growth strategies tend to rely on actions such as hiring more employees, growing the customer base, opening new company-owned locations or developing new products through internal research and development. External growth strategies tend to focus on meeting growth objectives by establishing relationships with third parties, such as strategic-alliance partners, licensees, franchisees and co-branding allies.

Internal Business Growth

Although the use of external-growth strategies is becoming more common, not all growth is accomplished through the establishment of external strategic relationships. Some types of business-growth strategies, such as raising capital to build additional locations, hire more sales staff or develop additional products, are more internally focused, or "organic," growth strategies. Another type of organic growth is through merger-and-acquisition, where the growing company chooses to buy a third party in lieu of establishing a strategic rela-

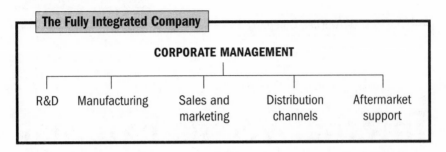

The Fully Integrated Company

CORPORATE MANAGEMENT

R&D | Manufacturing | Sales and marketing | Distribution channels | Aftermarket support

tionship with it, although the acquiror may use a strategic relationship as a due-diligence precursor to an actual acquisition.

External Business Growth

As recently as ten or 20 years ago, most large and even midsize companies were fully integrated. In other words, all major business functions and operations took place under one roof, under one management structure and under common management, as seen in the box at the top of this page.

But in today's networked economy, even the largest of companies—and most certainly the small to midsize ones—rely on a series of strategic relationships to get things done (as outlined in the box at the top of the next page). And the expansion in the number and scope of these relationships often serve at the heart of a company's growth strategy

The new organizational structure puts a greater emphasis on leveraging the company's intellectual and intangible assets, such as its brands, systems and relationships, in order to reduce its overhead and increase shareholder value. It also raises key legal and strategic issues regarding the degree of interdependency of these relationships (for example, who needs the other the most?), the allocation of control in these relationships (how will decisions be reached and who governs in the event of a disagreement?), the resources that will be committed to these relationships (what does each party bring to the table?) and the unwinding of these relationships (what happens when a change needs to be made?).

The range of choices of external growth strategies and the

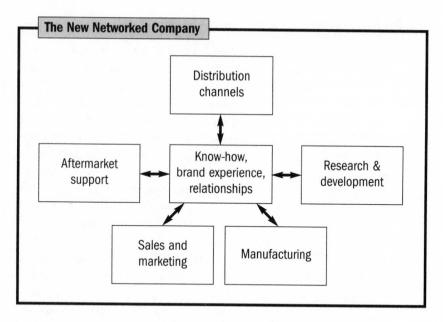

The New Networked Company

Distribution channels

Aftermarket support

Know-how, brand experience, relationships

Research & development

Sales and marketing

Manufacturing

structure of the relationships is vast and can include franchising, licensing, joint ventures, strategic alliances, outsourcing, spin-offs, research and distribution cooperatives, federations, associations, and networks—all of which are discussed in greater detail later in this book.

The new business model creates a "hollow" or even "virtual" corporation that redefines the linear functions that are present in the fully integrated company, as a comparison of the organizational structures on these pages illustrate. In the old model, illustrated on the previous page, each function is taken step-by-step by one company with its own resources. In the new model, illustrated above, the functions are more dynamic—the company relies on outsourcing and relationships to get things done.

Today, companies in growth mode are more likely to focus on leveraging their core assets and their core competencies, and to use strategic relationships to take care of other business functions. The skilled CEO (and his or her team) essentially becomes a manager of networks and strategic relationships. Henry Ford's vision of owning and controlling every step in the production cycle has been replaced with strategic alliances and outsourcing, where everything from research and design engineering to manufacturing, sales and distribution, maintenance and repair is accomplished through relationships with third-party strategic allies. For example, Sara Lee, the Chicago-based baked-goods manufacturer recently announced that many of its manufacturing and marketing functions would now be outsourced or licensed to third parties—allowing the company to stay focused on the building of its brands and new-product development. The performance of all companies in such an alliance becomes inextricably linked in a complex web, where the market value of companies A and B is tied to company C because of their strategic interdependence on each other, and where company C's value is in turn dependent on the performance of companies D, E and F, its primary distribution channels to its targeted customers.

> **For rapidly growing smaller companies, the emphasis on relationship management and building valuable networks helps to level the playing field in competing against larger companies.**

External Relationships and the Growing Company

For rapidly growing smaller companies, this new emphasis on relationship management and building valuable networks helps to level the playing field in competing against larger companies. The ability to leverage your knowledge, establish key strategic relationships (and maintain them as happy marriages), be flexible in establishing new relationships as necessary and bring products and services to the market faster (using these strategic relationships) gives small and medium companies an edge over the larger companies that you compete against. This contrast in agility is the source of the term "gazelle" to describe such a small company, because the gazelle is able to survive by being nimble, fast and smart, thereby compensating for the size and strength that the larger companies (the elephants) may possess.

The ability to leverage knowledge and establish key strategic relationships also creates opportunities for smaller companies, because now they can find their niche within the networked economy and fill that niche better than anybody else.

Internal Versus External Growth Strategies

Internal and external growth strategies are closely examined in chapters 15 through 17, which focus on organic strategies, and chapters 19 through 21, which focus on strategies that are primarily driven by the establishment of independent strategic relationships.

INTERNAL	EXTERNAL
Resources	**Resources**
■ Board of Directors	■ Outside advisers
■ Leadership team	■ Strategic partners
■ Middle-level management	■ Outsourcing
Capital	**Capital**
■ Current resources without dilution of ownership	■ Infusions of equity
	■ Debt financing
	■ Hybrids
Strategies	**Strategies**
■ Organic growth of customers, Markets, revenues, and profits	■ Formal expansion of channel relationships through franchising, licensing, etc.
■ Informal expansion of channel relationships	■ Formal joint ventures
■ Mergers and acquisitions	■ Strategic alliances
■ Expansion of current distribution models via e-commerce or international markets	■ Federations, cooperatives and networks

For example, Milcom Technologies, in Orlando, Florida, has built its entire business by partnering with large defense contractors. Its founder, Peter Atwal, has convinced companies like Lockheed, Raytheon and ITT to allow Milcom to partner with them to find commercial opportunities and niches for technologies that have been developed for defense-industry applications.

Smaller and more nimble growth companies can use a rapidly developing, more-common best practice such as outsourcing as a strategy for growth. Such companies can reduce costs and the need for capital by outsourcing key functions to third parties who can typically perform the task faster and cheaper. Once the key task or function has been outsourced, the fast-track growth company can better focus on its remaining core activities that are pivotal to its business. But overreliance on outsourcing or failing to carefully monitor the performance of the outsourced solution provider can lead to multiple problems. For example, turning over the reins of your customer-service support functions to an outsourced call center may result in significant savings, but look at the damage that can be done to one of your most important assets—customer relationships—if the call center is not professionally managed

Fast-track growth companies can also use this practice to create a source of capital by *being* the solution provider to other companies. Outsourcing has been a valuable means of growth for many companies. For example, in 1993, Flextronics was a midsize manufacturer with sales of a few hundred million dollars. When many high-tech companies either abandoned or chose to outsource their manufacturing functions, Flextronics filled the void by making itself available as a manufacturing partner. As a result, Flextronics has expanded to 70,000 employees working in 150 factories in 27 countries, with estimated annual sales in 2001 of more than $20 billion. In early 2001, Ericsson turned over its factories and manufacturing operations entirely to Flextronics, a relationship that could be worth as much as $5 billion a year to the growing company. Several other companies, such as Solectron, Celestica and SCI Systems have also experienced dramatic growth over the past several years by offering a full range of research, development and manufacturing services.

In today's networked economy, an early-stage semiconductor company could stay totally focused on design, and in turn outsource its manufacturing, sales, distribution and aftermarket services, allowing it to focus on creativity and brand-building as its top priorities.

Planning for Business Growth

EFFECTIVE BUSINESS AND STRATEGIC PLANNING IS critical to your company's long-term success and its ability to raise capital and sustain growth. Bankers, accountants, consultants and academics have written volumes about business-growth plans. Yet, it seems the more information there is, the more confused businesspeople become. Ultimately, there is no single formula. A business-growth plan should tell a story, make an argument and conservatively predict the future. All companies have different stories to tell, different arguments to make and different futures to predict; thus their strategies for growth—and yours—will also differ.

Business-growth planning is the process of setting goals and explaining objectives, then mapping out a plan to achieve these goals and objectives. A well-written plan maps out the best growth path and strategy as well as the rationale for the selection of the strategy over others. In essence, a business-growth plan is the articulation and explanation of why your chosen strategy makes sense, what resources you will need to implement the strategy, who will make up the team that will have the vision and leadership to execute the strategy, and what path you will follow to achieve your growth objectives. It will also answer the following questions about your company:

- **Who are you?**
- **What do you do?**

- **What is your business model?** How do you make money? Who is your customer? What problem do you solve? How do you solve it better, faster or cheaper than your competitors?
- **How do your customers pay you?**
- **How loyal are they?**
- **How should you grow?**
- **Why is the strategy you've chosen better** than others that may be available?
- **What do you need to implement** the growth strategy selected?
- **How crowded is the market?** Who are your current customers as well as likely future customers?
- **What vehicles (and at what costs)** will you use to sell the customer your product or service? Why are they the best vehicles?
- **What market research have you done** to be sure that anyone wants to buy this product or service at this price—or at all?
- **Does your company modify the way business is being done** in your industry (as a change agent) or is this more of a fad or a trend?

Not even the most savvy investor or the most veteran entrepreneur can predict with certainty which strategies for growth will work and which won't, but the better the analysis, the better the chances that most of the goals set forth in the business-growth plan will be achieved.

A well-written business-growth plan doesn't oversell the good, undersell the bad or ignore the ugly! It is essentially a plan to manage the risks and challenges involved in implementing a new growth strategy. Business-growth plans should acknowledge that growth and success are moving targets by anticipating as many future events or circumstances as possible that will affect the company's objectives.

Preparing the Business-Growth Plan

Emerging companies as well as established ones use business-growth plans. For example, a company operating for several years will need to draft a plan to raise the necessary capital to reach the next stage in its development. In any instance, the business-growth plan should be prepared with the assistance of a financial consultant, an investment banker, and the internal management team, and should be thoroughly vetted by attorneys and accountants. Here's an outline of a sample fast-track business-growth plan.

I. EXECUTIVE SUMMARY
   a. Brief history of your company
   b. Overview of your products and services
   c. Background of your management team (summary)
   d. Mission statement (Why are you in this business?)
   e. Summary of your company's financial performance to date (where applicable)
   f. Key features of your market

II. THE COMPANY: AN OVERVIEW
   a. Organizational and management structure
   b. Operational and management policies
   c. Description of products and services (both current and anticipated)
   d. Overview of trends in the industry and marketplace in which you compete (or plan to compete)
   e. Key strengths and weaknesses of your company

III. GROWTH-STRATEGY ANALYSIS
   a. How and why did you adopt this growth strategy?
   b. What hurdles and risks might you encounter in the implementation of this strategy?
   c. What resources will you need to implement this strategy?

IV. MARKET ANALYSIS
   a. Extended description of the markets in which you compete (size, trends, growth, etc.)
   b. Analysis of key competitors and likely future competitors (and how your business model and growth strategy will change or evolve to face the new competitors)
   c. Description and analysis of key customers and clients (current and anticipated)
   d. Market research supporting current and anticipated product lines

e. Analysis of barriers to entry and your sustainable competitive advantage

V. MARKETING AND ADVERTISING STRATEGY

a. Strategies for reaching current and anticipated customers
b. Pricing policies and strategies
c. Advertising and public-relations plans and strategies
d. Discussion of potential market partners and strategic alliances

VI. FINANCIAL PLAN AND STRATEGIES

a. Summary of financial performance for past three to five years
b. Current financial condition (include recent income statements and balance sheets as attachments)
c. Projected financial condition (forecasts for three to five years)
d. Extended discussion of anticipated allocation of proceeds and parallel budgets

VII. SUGGESTED EXHIBITS AND ATTACHMENTS

a. Résumés of key members of your management team
b. Organizational chart
c. Timetables for completion of goals and objectives
d. Copies of key documents and contracts
e. Copies of recent media coverage
f. Pictures of key products or advertising materials for services offered
g. List of customer and professional references

Common Myths Regarding Business-Growth Plans

As you draft your business-growth plan, beware of some of the more common misperceptions about business-growth plans, and avoid some of the common mistakes entrepreneurs make in preparing them.

MYTH: Business-growth plans are only for start-up companies.
REALITY: Companies at all stages of development need to prepare or revise business-growth plans, either for the planning and financing of a specific project or for general expansion financing, mergers or acquisitions, or the overall improvement of the company's financial and managerial performance.

MYTH: Your plan should be as detailed and slick as possible, because the more money that you spend preparing the plan, the better the chance that your project will be financed.
REALITY: Sophisticated investors will not have the time to review hundreds of pages of text, and they will commit funds based on the quality and clarity of your document, not its thickness. Your plan must be concise, well-written and should focus on the lender's or investor's principal areas of concern. It should not include overly technical descriptions of your company's processes or operations. Although business-growth plans ought to be presented professionally, a very expensive binder or presentation will often demonstrate inefficient resource management.

MYTH: Your business-growth plan should emphasize ideas and concepts, not people.
REALITY: Many entrepreneurs fear that if the success of a company depends too heavily on any specific person, an investor will shy away. Although this is partially true, experienced venture capitalists will tell you that they would prefer to invest in a company that has great people and only a good concept, rather than in a company that has a great concept and a weak management team. Ultimately, lenders and investors will commit funds based on the strength of your management team.

MYTH: Only the founding entrepreneur should prepare your business-growth plan.
REALITY: Most entrepreneurs are highly skilled in a particular profession or area of management, but may not necessarily possess the ability to prepare a business-growth plan. Ideally, your plan should be developed by a team of managers within your company and then reviewed by qualified experts, such as

accountants, attorneys and your board of directors. Conversely, your business-growth plan should never be prepared solely by outside advisers. A venture capitalist will be quick to recognize a "cooked" plan or one that reflects the views and efforts of professional advisers instead of those of the people who are responsible for running the company on a day-to-day basis.

MYTH: Business-growth plans should be distributed as widely as possible.
REALITY: Your plan will inevitably contain proprietary and confidential company information. Therefore, keep distribution closely controlled and maintain careful records as to who has been provided with copies of the plan. The cover sheet should contain a conspicuously positioned management disclaimer reminding the reader that these are only the plans of the company, the success of which cannot be assured, as well as a notice of proprietary information. If your business-growth plan is intended as a financing proposal, carefully consider all applicable federal and state securities rules. However, do not use your plan in lieu of a formal private-placement memorandum. Finally, certain institutional investors will consider investments only in certain kinds of companies or industries. Research these criteria before sending your plan to save the time and resources of all concerned parties.

MYTH: Your business-growth plan should follow a specified format, regardless of the industry in which your company operates.
REALITY: While it may be true that all companies face certain common challenges in the areas of marketing, management, administration and finance, companies at different stages of growth face different problems. And companies operating in different industries will require different sets of topics that must be included in their business-growth plans. For example, plans for a start-up manufacturing company may be more concerned with financing of the plant, equipment, patents, inventory, and production schedules, whereas an already established service-oriented company may be more focused on personnel, marketing costs and the protection of trade secrets and goodwill.

MYTH: In preparing your business-growth plan, optimism should prevail over realism.

REALITY: Although your plan should demonstrate your enthusiasm and that of other founders of the company, as well as generate excitement in the reader, it should be credible and accurate. Investors will want to know all of your company's strengths and its weaknesses. In fact, if you include a realistic discussion of your company's problems, along with a reasonable plan for dealing with those challenges, your plan will have a much more positive impact on the prospective investor. As a rule, investors would rather invest in someone who has learned from previous business failures than in a person who has never managed a company. Finally, substantiate in the plan, with accompanying footnotes, any budgets, sales projections, company valuations, or related forecasts, for both legal and business reasons. Unrealistic or unsubstantiated financial projections and budgets will reveal inexperience or lack of attention to detail to an interested investor, or even lead to litigation by disgruntled investors if there are wide disparities between what was represented in the plan and what really exists.

> **As a rule, investors would rather invest in someone who has learned from previous business failures than in a person who has never managed a company.**

MYTH: A well-written business-growth plan should contain an executive summary written before the full text of the document is prepared.

REALITY: Institutional investors are exposed to hundreds of business-growth plans every month. As a result, they will initially devote only a few minutes to the review of each business-growth plan, often making the decision to either consider or discard the plan based on the executive summary. The executive summary (generally one to three pages in length) should contain all of the information that will be critical in the investment decision, such as: the nature of your company and its founders, the amount of money sought, the allocation of the proceeds, a summary of key financial projections, and an overview of marketing considerations. Therefore, it is much more effective to prepare the main body of the plan, then draft the executive summary in order to ensure that it will truly be a preview of the details of the plan.

MYTH: You write a business-growth plan only when your company needs to raise capital.
REALITY: Although most business-growth plans are written in connection with the search for capital, a well-written plan will serve a variety of valuable purposes. It serves as a management tool and a road map for growth; a realistic self-appraisal of your company's progress to date, as well as its projected goals and objectives; and a foundation for the development of a more detailed strategic and growth-management plan.

The Importance of Strategic Planning for Business Growth

In your company's early stages, your emphasis will be on the initial business-growth plan. Among your key concerns will be how to launch the plan to attract customers and how to identify the necessary resources you'll need to sustain the strategy selected. But once your emerging-growth company reaches its initial set of core objectives, your focus shifts away from mere business-growth planning to strategic planning.

Strategic planning should be ongoing and should take the form of periodic meetings among your emerging company's leadership, periodic strategic-planning retreats, and an annually updated written strategic plan.

Objectives for a Strategic-Planning Meeting
Focus your strategic-planning meetings and retreats on a specific theme. Topics that should be addressed in strategic planning efforts include:
- **the quality and sophistication of the technology and communications systems** used to support your customers and for internal communication;
- **the quality and sophistication** of your training and support systems;
- **the development of operating systems,** practices and procedures

based upon internal company "best practices" as well as over-all industry "best practices";

- **the exploration** of new domestic and international markets;
- **the organization of supplier councils,** co-branding alliances, brand-extension licensing and other key strategic relationships;
- **the development of strategies** for alternative sites and related new-market penetration strategies; and
- **the value and recognition** of your emerging company's brand from a customer-awareness perspective;
- **the development of advanced branding** and intellectual-property protection strategies;
- **the improved recruitment** of women and minorities;
- **rebuilding trust** and value with customers;
- **litigation prevention** and compliance;
- **leadership** and productivity issues;
- **financial management** and performance issues.

The Strategic-Planning Meeting Agenda

Any of the preceding topics are appropriate for one meeting or for discussion on a continuing basis. The strategic-planning meeting could be lead by an outside facilitator, such as an indus-try expert, or by your company's senior-management team. Here's a model agenda for a general strategic-planning retreat:

EVALUATING OUR STRATEGIC ASSETS AND RELATIONSHIPS
1. Overview
- Goals and objectives of the meeting
- Key trends in domestic and international business growth
2. Assessing the strengths of our customer relations
- State of the Union
- Common critical success factors
3. Evaluating our team
- Code of values—reality and practice
- Motivating and rewarding employees
- What are the common characteristics of our most successful employees?
- What can we do to attract more people like this in the recruit-ment and selection process?

- Protecting the knowledge worker
- Providing genuine leadership

4. Our strategic partners

- What do we expect from our vendors and professional advisers?
- What can we do to enhance the efficiency and productivity of these relationships?
- Building the national accounts program
- Do all of our strategic relationships provide mutual reward?

5. Our targeted customers

- What are the common characteristics of our targeted customers?
- Identifying and dealing with the competition
- Customer perceptions of quality and value
- Building the relationship with the customer
- Customer satisfaction surveys
- Exploring two-tier marketing strategies
- Our competitive landscape
- Analysis of our direct and indirect competitors
- Potential future competitors and competitive threats
- Analysis of current alliances, pilot projects and co-branding relationships within our industry

ASSET-BUILDING STRATEGIES

1. Building and leveraging brand awareness

- Building overall brand awareness
- Brand-leveraging strategies
- Building an arsenal of intangible assets

2. Co-branding and strategic alliances

- Identifying goals and objectives
- Targeting and selecting partners
- Structuring the deal

3. Shared goals and values

- Enhancing intracompany communications
- Building trust and respect

4. Role and value of technology

- How technology is changing the way we work and consume products and services
- The impact of technology on recruiting, training and sup-

porting employees

- The impact of technology on how the emerging-growth company will market its products and services to targeted customers

5. Development of branded products and services to strengthen our revenue base

- Business training and assistance resources for customers
- Product review (i.e., review of specific company products or product lines, such as home cleaning and refinishing products)
- Co-branded products and services (e.g., securities sales, financial planning, home improvement and remodeling, etc.)
- Affinity-group purchasing programs

The result of an effective strategic-planning meeting is to develop a list of specific action items. Some items may be implemented right away; others may take some time.

In sum, the strategic-planning process is a commitment to strive for the continuous improvement of your business-growth objectives. The process is designed to ensure that your company delivers maximum value, day in and day out, to your growing company's executive team, employees, shareholders, vendors and suppliers and, of course, your customers. The strategic-planning process doesn't fear asking questions such as: Where are we? Where do we want to be? What do we need to do to get there? What is currently standing in the way of our achieving these objectives? Strategic planning is about making sure that your company takes the time to develop a mission statement and define a collective vision and then develop a series of plans to achieve these goals. Your executives must stay focused on these objectives and provide leadership to your growing company's management team in order to achieve those objectives and demonstrate to your customers how the company's goals will be achieved. The focus must be on brand equity, customer value and loyalty and shareholder profitability. The guidelines and protocols for internal communications must encourage honesty and openness, without fear of retaliation or politics.

The Six Habits of Highly Successful Emerging-Growth Companies

To develop and maintain a highly successful organization, the leadership of an emerging-growth company must examine its procedures, relationships, and culture. The following six habits of the highly successful growth company can be achieved by careful examination of the questions that follow.

An Ability to Adapt to Challenges and Changes in the Marketplace

- How do we react to inevitable and constant changes in the environment?
- How well do we plan in advance, anticipate change and face the reality of what's really happening in the trenches?
- Do we really listen to our customers?

A Genuine Commitment to the Success of Every Employee

- A chain is only as strong as its weakest link. Have we mended weak links in our organizational chain?
- How is this commitment demonstrated?
- Is this how our employees truly perceive our commitment?

A Culture Committed to Overcoming Complacency

- Are we committed to research and development?
- What steps are in place to constantly improve and expand our systems and capabilities?

A Team Ready to Break Old Paradigms

- Are we committed to thinking outside the box?

Planning for Business Growth

Once the general business- and strategic-planning processes have been completed, a foundation exists upon which you can build a specific business-growth plan. The plan looks at specific growth opportunities and analyzes the alternatives for implementation. For example, if your company develops a new product or technology, fundamental corporate-venturing principles would dictate the following structural analysis:

- **Should you fold this new project** into an existing business division or operating unit? Why? Which one offers the best fit?
- **If not, should you structure this new project** as a newly created

- What recent examples do we have where creative thinking solved a problem or created a new opportunity?
- Are we using computer and communications technologies such as e-mail, intranet interactive computer training and private satellite networks to help us support and communicate with our market partners?

A Total Devotion to Excellent Customer Service

- What systems do we have in place to ensure excellence in our interactions with targeted home and business customers?
- Do we have a procedure for gathering feedback and reacting to problems in the field?
- When is the last time we spoke directly with our customers?

- What are we doing to educate our targeted customers on quality and product/service differentiation issues?
- How can we set the standards for quality by achieving "Good Housekeeping Seal of Approval" type status with our customers How can we enhance the customer's buying experience to promote and enhance this image?
- Do we treat our employees and market partners as customers?

A Commitment to Taking the Time to Truly Understand and Analyze the Economics of the Core Business (by all key players in the organization, Not just the CFO!)

- Do our current pricing and sales models make sense?
- What steps can we take to improve our profitability?

subsidiary? If yes, what are the corporate and tax implications? What approvals may be necessary to transfer assets and resources into this new subsidiary?

- **If you'll be creating a new subsidiary,** will the parent company wholly own it? Will it be partially owned by the employees? Or will you spin it off as a standalone entity with separate management and capitalization? Will you invite third-party investors or strategic partners to invest in the subsidiary? Which ones? How will you structure the deal? Or should the subsidiary be co-owned as an operating joint-venture corporation with one or more joint-venture partners? Which partner makes the most senses for this new venture?

These are just some of the questions that may need to be answered. Essentially, you must first analyze each new corporate opportunity from a structural point of view before you can develop other elements of the business-growth plan. And for highly innovative rapid-growth companies, this means that dozens of new corporate opportunities must go through this rigid analysis each year.

You must first analyze each new corporate opportunity from a structural point of view before you can develop other elements of the business-growth plan.

Your impetus for developing a business-growth plan may be that innovation within your company has created new products or opportunities, but that is not always the case. As shown in the box on page 47, other reasons for growth may include market-driven factors (for example, the market is growing rapidly and you must grow with it or perish); increasing customer demand for your specific products or services; or the problems or even failure of a given competitor, which create a void that your company can fill. These types of growth drivers do not typically require an internal analysis to determine which projects are worth pursuing, but they nevertheless dictate the need for a business-growth plan, the key components of which are discussed below.

Key Components of the Business-Growth Plan

A well-prepared business-growth plan builds on the basic business and strategic plan discussed earlier in this chapter but also specifically focuses on:

Developing a budget. You must analyze the resources that will be required to implement the selected strategy. Your analysis must be conservative, realistic and well-documented. The type of strategy your company decides to adopt—whether it's an organic, internal-growth strategy, an external-growth strategy (which relies prominently on resources to be deployed by others), or some hybrid of the two will often drive the budget.

Distribution channels. You must explain how the product or ser-

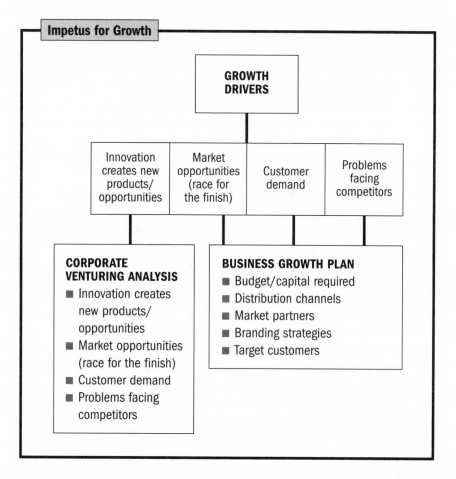

Impetus for Growth

GROWTH DRIVERS

| Innovation creates new products/ opportunities | Market opportunities (race for the finish) | Customer demand | Problems facing competitors |

CORPORATE VENTURING ANALYSIS
- Innovation creates new products/ opportunities
- Market opportunities (race for the finish)
- Customer demand
- Problems facing competitors

BUSINESS GROWTH PLAN
- Budget/capital required
- Distribution channels
- Market partners
- Branding strategies
- Target customers

vice will reach the marketplace and the targeted consumer. Most rapid-growth companies will have a multichannel strategy to ensure maximum market penetration and to increase the chances of success. For example, Ariba (ARBA, Nasdaq), a developer of e-commerce software products and services, employs a direct sales force of more than 700 full-time sales professionals around the world, but the company does not rely exclusively on that sales force to meet its growth objectives. Ariba uses strategic partnerships in the areas of logistics, hardware platforms, software platforms, electronic commerce and systems integrators to enhance its marketing, sales and distribution capabilities. Ariba relies on these strategic relationships to implement, support and recommend its products during the evaluation stage of a target customer's purchasing-decision process.

Market partners. A key component of the business-growth plan will be to identify the appropriate strategic market partners and get to them before your competitors do, particularly if you expect to enjoy an exclusive or partially exclusive relationship.

> **Your business-growth plan must also analyze your company's current branding and marketing practices to see how they fit into the new growth strategy.**

Again using the Ariba example: Their hardware partners include Cisco Systems, Hewlett-Packard and Sun Microsystems, which helps ensure the reliability, scalability and performance of the Ariba solution on these platforms. Their electronic-commerce partners include American Express, Sterling Commerce and Visa International, and they have marketing relationships with IBM and other software providers, including J.D. Edwards, i2 Technologies, Siebel Systems, and BEA Systems. These partners either resell or co-sell Ariba's products to their respective customers. Ariba also has strategic relationships with Softbank in Japan and Telefonica in Europe and Latin America. Ariba has also developed system-integrator relationships with various parties to implement its products and to assist them with sales-lead generation. They have certified and trained consultants in these organizations for the implementation and operation of Ariba's products.

Branding strategies. Your business-growth plan must also analyze your company's current branding and marketing practices to see how they fit into the new growth strategy. What new advertising or sales campaigns will you need to develop? Would co-branding with other strategic partners be a way to expedite or enhance the pace of the growth? Do you need to do any repositioning of the brand (or the development of new brands or sub-brands) to offer this new suite of services or family of products? For example, say your base of customers associates your company's brand with a baseline level of quality at a very competitive price. Would a new-product introduction that features much higher quality at an increased price require a brand

Variables Likely to Affect the Implementation of Your Plan

No matter how well you plan, things can and will change. Your business-growth plan includes hundreds of variables, which means that thousands of unexpected events could affect your company's actual performance. Among the factors that could affect your company's actual growth results are the following:

- **increased or reduced demand** for your products and services;
- **actions taken by your competitors,** such as new-product introductions and enhancements;
- **your ability to scale your network and operations** to support large numbers of customers, suppliers and transactions;
- **your ability to develop, introduce and market new products** and enhancements to your existing products on a timely basis;
- **changes in your competitors' pricing policies** and business model;
- **integration of your recent acquisitions** and any future acquisitions;

- **ability to expand your sales and marketing operations,** including hiring additional sales personnel;
- **size and timing of sales of your products and services,** including the recognition of a significant portion of your sales at the end of the quarter;
- **success in maintaining and enhancing existing relationships** and developing new relationships with strategic partners, including systems integrators and other implementation partners;
- **compensation policies** for sales personnel based on achieving annual quotas;
- **ability to control costs;**
- **technological changes** in your markets;
- **deferrals of customer orders** in anticipation of product enhancements or new products;
- **customer budget cycles** and changes in these budget cycles; and
- **general economic factors,** including an economic slow-down or recession.

overhaul or even a new brand, especially if the existing line of products or services will remain intact?

Customer relationships. Your business-growth plan should address whether the growth strategy you've selected relies on the company's ability to sell more products and services to existing customers or is more dependent on establishing new customer relationships. If it is the former, what strategies will you put in place to get existing customers to spend more? If it is the latter, have you identified these new customers? From whom are these targeted new customers currently getting their products or services? Will they shift their loyalty from their current provider and give you their business? Why?

The Importance of Sensitivity Analysis in Building a Business-Growth Plan

As previously discussed, a well-drafted business-growth plan becomes the roadmap for implementing your company's growth strategies by outlining the steps that need to be taken, when, how and by whom. It focuses on key components such as resources, branding, market partners and distribution channels. But it must also deal with the inevitable contingencies and be reflective of changing business models. For example, if the success of your plan relies on your company's products being faster, cheaper, more reliable and capable of solving more complicated problems than those offered by your competitors, then how does the strategy change when your competitor introduces a product better, faster and cheaper than yours? Or what if the customer is slow to adopt or even recognize the benefits of your new product or service? These are the types of problems that sensitivity analysis in the business-growth plan seeks to address.

Sensitivity analysis is a tool for looking at a wide range of variables and assumptions in the business-growth plan to determine the impact on the company and the viability of the plan if and when these planning assumptions change—and they inevitably will. Sensitivity analysis might raise the following kinds of questions:

- **Will our business-growth plan still be viable** if 20% of the target customers that we assume will adopt this new product don't? What if 30% or 40% do not?
- **What impact will it have on our plan** if two of the key potential competitors we have identified become actual competitors?
- **What impact will it have on our business-growth plan** if we can't attract new employees or strategic partners that we have

identified as critical to implementation?

■ **What if we can't raise the equity capital we need** to implement the strategy? What if we have to give up more ownership and control than we had anticipated to raise the capital?

■ **If we planned to borrow money** to implement the strategy, what impact would higher interest rates have on the economics of the strategy? If our customers will need to borrow to buy our products and services, what impact will higher rates have on these buying decisions?

■ **What if the market rejects the pricing structure** that underlies the introduction of the new product or service? What if deeper discounts need to be offered to compel customers to make the switch to our product or service? What impact will this have on our margins?

The bottom line is that overly optimistic or poorly researched assumptions in your business-growth plan can and will come back to haunt you. And even if you are conservative in your assumptions and conduct adequate research, there are still many variables that can and will change (see the box on the next page). Sensitivity analysis seeks to anticipate these changes so that you are not caught by surprise.

Some Final Thoughts on Effective Business-Growth Planning

You can see that effective business-growth planning is not an easy process. The chapters that follow will give your company some of the tools and strategies that you will need to remain viable and competitive. In working with hundreds of companies of all sizes and in many different industries over the years to develop business-growth strategies, I have gathered the following tips, thoughts and observations that should govern your planning process:

■ **Have the right mix** of talent to develop and maintain your plan. The wrong planning team will yield the wrong planning decisions, leading the company down a path of disaster.

- **Think long-term but act short-term.** Be ready to modify the plan based on changes in market conditions but without taking your eye off the long-term goals.
- **Understand your company's strategic velocity and capacity.** In other words, how quickly can new strategies be implemented? How quickly can you align everyone's interests to make things happen, and do you have the right team in place to execute the vision?
- **Effective business-growth planning is an ongoing process, not a stand-alone task.** Spending thousands of hours developing a thick five-year plan that collects dust in an oversized three-ring binder while praying that market conditions will fall into place as expected is not a rapid path toward building share-holder value.
- **Don't buy in to the mantra** that planning is a thing of the past. There are some who believe that market conditions are too dynamic and uncertain to make long-term business-growth strategic planning possible. This is simply not true! In fact, fast-moving business conditions make the need for strategic planning more critical than ever, provided that the plan is monitored and modified as conditions may warrant.

  As your focus turns from strategy toward execution, this commitment to careful monitoring to keep a close watch on changing market conditions, the emergence of new and disruptive technologies or shifts in consumer-demand patterns becomes a critical step in the planning process. Poor execution will kill even the best-prepared business-growth plans.
- **Invest in systems that will gather competitive intelligence.** Information rules. If you don't have good data on the trends affecting your competitors and customers, you are dead in the water. The competitive intelligence you gather should become a key component of your plan and a trigger point for changes to the plan or strategy selected.
- **Protect your key assets.** You can develop business-growth plans until you are blue in the face. But if the success of your strategy depends on your ability to keep and leverage your key intangible assets, such as intellectual property (see Chapter 18) and employees (see Chapter 8), then you must first work to protect those assets.

■ **Learn to recognize the market forces that affect your business.** A well-drafted business-growth plan understands and anticipates how all of the market forces and players fit together, taking into account social, environmental, political and economic influences and figuring out how these factors come together to affect your growth plans. And because these market conditions are never static and the relationships that connect them are always changing, you need to constantly review each of these components and how they fit together. Be prepared for strains in the relationships with your existing market partners as you experiment with new distribution channels—but do not let these tensions stand in the way of an overhaul if necessary.

■ **Build an organization that has a deeply rooted commitment to growth.** The commitment must begin with the leader or founder of the company, whose mission and passion become contagious. Then, everyone in the company will focus his or her efforts on meeting business-growth objectives. To achieve this, your company's leadership must clearly communicate and reinforce the company's growth plans, objectives and strategies; reward those who contribute to the achievement of these goals; and monitor the company's progress, changing its course as necessary. If the course does need to change, these shifts in direction must be regularly shared with your company's employees, together with an explanation of the need for the change. Employees at all levels will resent a change in direction if they don't know or understand the reasons for it, especially if the change affects their roles within the company.

■ **Don't be afraid to measure and monitor performance.** It is critical to develop an objective set of metrics for each key area of the business-growth plan that can be continuously monitored and periodically measured against your key goals. The metrics may include sales, profitability, the number of new customer relationships added, the growth-market partners, the number of new employees, customer satisfaction, the level of employee turnover, inventory cycles, the number of new offices or sites opened, warranty returns, or even the number of new rounds of capital raised at favorable valuation rates.

Regardless of the specific metrics selected, the growing company must build systems to track and measure these performance indicators and have the expertise in place to understand, analyze and properly react to this data once it has been reported.

■ **Develop high quality products and services.** As veteran entrepreneurs and professional advisers will always tell you, a business-growth plan will be completely ineffective if the "dogs will not eat the dog food." Ultimately, all business-growth plans must revolve around a set of high-quality products and services that customers want and need.

The Human Side
of Business Growth

Partnership Dynamics and Their Impact on Business Growth

A S YOUR BUSINESS GROWS, YOU MAY DETERMINE that it would best be served by the talents and resources that one or more partners can contribute. Or perhaps in establishing your business, you looked to others and have had partners from the start. This is a natural choice, the impetus for which may be one or more of the following reasons:

- **friendship and having a "sounding board"** for discussing ideas and strategies;
- **pairing technical expertise with capital** or other resources in which one co-founder may be deficient;
- **sharing and mitigation of risk;** and
- **bonding among family members** or friends to start new ventures together.

But as John D. Rockefeller once said, "A friendship founded on business is better than a business founded on friendship." Rockefeller knew many decades ago what many technology company founders have only recently learned—that building a business can be a cruel and difficult process that eats at the core of a friendship when things are not going as planned.

Business partners owe it to each other as well as to their employees, customers, investors and even their families to develop a genuine understanding of what brought them together in the first place, what strengths each brings to the venture, what goals and expectations hold them together and what will happen to the business if their relationship goes awry.

Although friendship, love or bloodlines may be what brought you and your partners together, it is foolish to assume that emotions or genetics alone will hold the business partnership together. Just like a good marriage, business partners must learn to communicate, compromise and evolve together as challenges arise. They must be able to agree on all of the key strategic issues, even if they disagree on minor issues that may not be as critical to the long-term success of the business.

Establishing a Relationship Charter

Many industrial psychologists and business mediators strongly suggest that business partners develop a relationship charter as a starting point for clarifying their objectives and expectations. The relationship charter is a broad statement of key principles and is a precursor to the more detailed shareholders agreement. The logic is that if the partners can't agree on a basic constitution of core values and rules, they should reconsider being in business together. The development of the relationship charter should be based on an open and honest dialogue regarding concerns that each partner may have about the other's commitment, personality, ability to fund the company, track record and experience or liability for future problems. Each partner should do a little homework on the other's prior business experiences and relationships, by talking to former or current co-workers or business partners, friends, family, spouses or significant others. Requiring each partner to provide a personal financial statement is also a good way to avoid unpleasant surprises in the future. The relationship charter may include topics such as:

- common goals (short, medium and long-term);
- resources to be contributed to the business;
- capitalization of the company;
- loyalty and commitment to the business;

■ expectations;

■ values;

■ principles of equity and fairness;

■ hiring and firing of personnel;

■ communication and governance;

■ procedures for resolving disagreements; and

■ rules for admitting additional partners.

Planning Issues for Business Partners

When a company is started or run by multiple founders or owners, it's not uncommon to have written agreements or understandings in place to restrict the ability of any given owner to pass his or her shares (and thereby ownership and control rights) on to a spouse or children. There is usually a mechanism, such as the buy-sell agreement, for providing the surviving spouse or estate with either a lump-sum payment or installment payments in exchange for the shares owned by the departing partner.

As co-owner of a business, make sure that you have considered the following issues with your partners:

■ **Do you have a plan or agreement** in place that determines (or controls) the ownership of the shares upon one partner's death? How will things be different in case of disability? Retirement?

■ **How will these issues be dealt with in case of dispute**—such as a breach of a non-compete clause, embezzlement, or failure to perform key responsibilities—that leads to a partner's departure from the company?

■ **What formula or periodic valuation technique will you use** to determine the fair value of these shares upon redemption?

■ **How and when will the proceeds be paid?**

■ **If you and all of your partners are roughly the same age,** and the agreement provides for mandatory redemption upon death, then who will eventually assume control of the business? If it is the last surviving partner (and then his or her estate), have you unintentionally created a "survival of the fittest" policy?

■ **If your agreement** (or lack of an agreement) provides that the shares of each partner can be passed on to her or his spouse or heirs, can you get along with these people on a long-term basis? Do you want to separate ownership from control?

Understanding the Buy-Sell Agreement

The buy-sell agreement is a legal document that specifies how a company or its owners will redistribute ownership shares after one of the owners dies, becomes disabled, retires or otherwise leaves. The primary goal is to avoid conflict and confusion by keeping ownership and control in the hands of those individuals who will be responsible for managing the operations of the business. The ability of the remaining owners (or the company) to purchase the departing owner's shares must be provided for in some manner. This is typically accomplished through the purchase of a series of "key person" life insurance policies or some other reliable source, such as investment accounts specially designated for these purposes to ensure that cash will be available when the "triggering event" (such as a death or disability) occurs. The buy-sell agreement will also dictate, among other things, when an owner can transfer his or her shares and under what circumstances shares must be offered first to other shareholders/owners (or to the company)—known as "rights of first refusal." The agreement includes the procedures for making such an offer, payment terms or payment mechanism (lump-sum versus. deferred or installment payment) to the departing owner and procedures for resolving any disputes over valuation or non-payment. In a family-owned business, the restrictions on ownership and transfer of the shares can be very strict and in some cases may provide that only the lineal family members can be shareholders, either by initial issuance or upon transfer. Also consider the impact of a divorce and provisions in a pre-nuptial agreement when you prepare these ownership restriction provisions.

To assure that the departing owner or survivors and heirs receive full value on redemption, your agreement should spell out how the departing owner's shares will be valued, or direct that one or more outside appraisals be obtained when a triggering event occurs. Your buy-sell agreement should provide for periodic mandatory valuations; however, keep in mind that valuation is not an exact science, especially for small, closely held businesses.

When your business was first organized, you and the other co-founders agreed on how the business would be structured—partnership, corporation, etc. You might have also agreed on basic procedures for decision-making and governance, although these procedures may well have changed after a few years as conditions changed. You might also have had some discussion as to how and when the business would be dissolved or what would happen if a co-owner died or left the company. If you and your partners have not properly documented these discussions, then you may be headed for frustration, disappointment, and strained relationships unless you correct the situation as soon as possible. If you don't have a written agreement in place, or if your agreement is incomplete, use the following guidelines as a starting point and consult with your corporate attorney to have a written buy-sell agreement drafted. Even if you do have a comprehensive agreement, this is a good time to review its provisions. You may find the document needs updating due to a change in circumstances, the growth of your business or developments in your industry. In general, there are three basic types of buy-sell agreements:

Even if you have a comprehensive buy-sell agreement, this is a good time to review its provisions.

- **Cross-purchase agreements** are ideal for partnerships and corporations with small ownership groups (up to three people). The remaining owners directly purchase the departing owner's interest in the business, rather than doing it through the company.
- **Stock-redemption agreements** are simpler and easier to structure than cross-purchase agreements. This makes them best suited for corporations with four or more shareholders. The corporation buys back the shares of the departing owner, and the remaining owners see an increase in the value of their shares, not the number of their shares, as in a cross-purchase agreement.
- **Hybrid agreements** are combination arrangements that usually

---

Advantages of a Buy-Sell Agreement

A buy-sell agreement has many advantages for your business, including:

1. Future continuity. A buy-sell agreement helps assure the future continuation of the business. This security produces confidence and peace of mind not only for the firm's owners, but also for the firm's employees, customers, suppliers and creditors.

2. No unintentional ownership.

A buy-sell agreement eliminates the problem of unintentional owners. Survivors usually are unqualified to help run the business. They can even interfere in its operation.

3. Smooth redistribution of ownership. Because each owner joins in making the agreement, the plan can provide a built-in guarantee that each owner and his or her estate will be treated equitably regardless of who dies or leaves the business, or when.

---

put the priority for redemption with the corporation, but the shareholders have the option of directly redeeming a deceased owner's shares if the corporation is unwilling or unable to do so.

Dealing with Common Partnership Problems

Regardless of the reasons that originally brought you and your business partners together, there will inevitably be difficulties you'll have to overcome, just as with any relationship. Difficulties may result from internal conditions (such as lack of communication, jealousy or differing objectives), or external conditions (such as the influence of a spouse or key employee, competitive conditions or changes in the technology or marketplace). Perhaps one of the most challenging hurdles for a growing company to face is a dispute among its partners.

Partnership conflicts often involve a third party or outside circumstance that none of the partners can control, but that have a direct impact on the ability of each partner to continue growing the business. Basic agreements must be put in place to protect you and your partners from the outside world and from each other. However, contracts are not enough; the agreements must be supplemented with sound management and business practices, sensitivity to psychological and ego issues, and a clear strategic development plan. As you will learn from the partnership-problem scenarios that follow, no matter how optimistic you are about your business relationship with your partners, you need to be prepared to deal with difficulties among you in a way that won't stall the growth of your business.

THE "HIGH SCHOOL BEST FRIEND" OR "COLLEGE ROOMMATE" PARTNERSHIP. Old college roommates or high school best friends often start businesses together. But when disputes arise, the mix of a personal friendship with a business conflict can make the resolution of disputes especially complex.

THE "OBSOLETE" PARTNER. Often as a business grows, one or more of the co-founders may become unable to keep pace with the level of sophistication or business acumen the company now requires. He or she is no longer making a significant contribution to the business and in essence has become "obsolete." It's even harder when the obsolete partner is a close friend or family member. In this case, you may need to consider reducing this partner's responsibilities or severing the business relationship.

THE "CLASHING EGO" PARTNERSHIP. Entrepreneurs, as leaders with strong values and integrity, also often have extra large egos that tend to clash from time to time. Sometimes, the clash is short lived and easy to overcome, but at other times, it may cause an ongoing problem that cannot easily be resolved. The challenge becomes finding a balance between soothing wounded egos and doing what's best for the business.

THE PARTNERSHIP WITHOUT A COMMON GROUND. One common situation is that the co-founders are all slowly moving in different strategic directions with different visions for the company's future. At this point, communication can become strained and difficult because partners can't find a common ground. Some business owners simply lose the "fire in their belly" once the company reaches a particular stage of growth and when key goals and objectives have been met. When this happens, it's best for that particular partner to step down, be reassigned or find new challenges or markets to pursue.

THE "NOT-SO-SILENT" PARTNER. Few people whom I have met have ever gotten wealthy by being stupid or being silent, but entrepreneurs still want to believe there's such a thing as a "silent partner." Most silent partners are rarely silent and will go out of their way to interfere with the operations and management abilities of the operating partner.

THE "DIVERGENT LIFE PATHS" PARTNERSHIP. People tend to reach personal comfort levels or just plain "burn out" at differing stages of a company's growth. While one partner may be driven to take the business to new levels of growth, another may want to pursue a life on the tennis court. And frequently, as the business grows, so do the partner's families and nonbusiness commitments. A partner with young children may feel the pressure to spend more time at home, while the partner's absence from the business will significantly cut his or her ability to make sufficient contributions to the company's growth. Further, a growing family may bring income needs that the company is not able to meet.

IMPROPER BEHAVIOR BY A PARTNER. When a partner is involved in an illegal or unacceptable act that involves the company in any way, it can be very difficult to handle diplomatically. The issues—embezzlement, sexual harassment, employment discrimination, or other unacceptable or illegal acts—are sensitive, and the liability to the company is significant.

THE "TAKE THE MONEY AND RUN" PARTNER. Ordinary circumstances, such as the need to buy a home, or less-than-acceptable circumstances, such as the need to repay a gambling debt, can compel a partner to cash out of the business. Not only can this put a strain on the partners' relationship, it can also put a heavy strain on the company's funding.

THE REJECTED PARTNER. In a rapidly growing business, the exit strategy is often either the sale of the company to a third party or the registration of the company's stock in a public offering. Buyers of a company often want only one or two of the co-founders or partners. Many times the investment bankers who are handling an initial public offering (IPO) would prefer that one or more of the co-founders step down as a condition to the IPO being successful. I have even seen this scenario in venture-capital settings where two or three co-founders were asked either to leave or modify their positions as a condition of the venture capitalist closing the transaction. Naturally, such situations create tension and divided loyalties among partners.

Common Reasons for Partnership Conflicts

There are many reasons for conflicts between business partners. If you plan properly when you set up the partnership, many of them can be handled without threatening the survival of your business. Common reasons for partnership problems include:

In their zeal to fulfill a dream or goal, business partners often rush into business relationships with excitement and impatience, often overlooking a partner's character flaws or perhaps not getting to know a partner well enough to discover the flaws.

Just as with marriage, no one likes to consider the possibility of failure, and the negotiation of a business "prenuptial" agreement is seen as an unpleasant or negative view of the future of the relationship.

Many entrepreneurs in the early stages don't have the capital to properly hire lawyers to draft the types of shareholders or partnership agreements that are necessary to protect against certain kinds of problems and to provide predetermined solutions to these problems.

There are often significant disparities on how decisions are supposed to be made versus how they are actually made. Also, in rapidly growing closely held companies, decisions may not be properly documented or researched, and communication as well as key strategic decisions are made on an ad hoc basis.

Owners of small companies often find it hard to separate their roles as directors, officers, shareholders and key employees, because during the growth of a business, they often wear many hats.

Management systems are often not properly documented (either contractually or procedurally). Issues of control, authority and approvals are handled on an ad hoc basis with no formal guidelines.

Small companies often fail to provide for procedures in case of a "deadlock," when there are an even number of partners or directors.

The old adage "failure to plan is planning to fail" is often the case in the context of disputes among partners. The lack of a clear and concise strategic-development plan (not the boilerplate type that gets used to raise capital) often leads to confusion and problems among partners.

Entrepreneurs often tend to approach problem-solving on a reactive instead of proactive basis. By not understanding certain preventive-law techniques, such as legal audits, entrepreneurs fail to take advantage of another old adage, that "an ounce of prevention is worth a pound of cure."

Common Complaints of Business Partners

- Feeling that he or she is not getting his "fair share."
- Dissatisfaction with how his or her role has "evolved."
- Lack of trust in a business partner's competence or intentions.
- Personal and financial expectations not being met.
- Feeling excluded from decision-making.
- Being left out of the loop.

Entrepreneurs are often bad delegators, both among themselves as well as to key employees. This difficulty in delegation can lead to problems among partners and stifle the company's ability to truly "departmentalize."

Avoiding Common Partnership Conflicts

The best means of avoiding these problems is *prevention*. You and your partners must be willing to openly communicate, prepare for the worst, and detect problems before they mature. Here are some of the key measures you can take.

PERIODIC VALUATIONS OF THE COMPANY. While these are expensive, they are also critical and can provide a clear-cut and objective valuation of your company. Depending on your company's growth patterns and industry trends, the valuations should be done annually. Occasional financial and legal audits will help lend insight into the company's value and identify legal and financial problems before they mature.

PREPARE A SHAREHOLDERS AND/OR PARTNERSHIP AGREEMENT EARLY. It is also critical in the development stages of the business to address decision-making procedures on important issues. *These documents should be updated periodically to reflect changes in law or circumstances.* You can then take comfort in knowing that these agreements are in place well in advance of a dispute. Some of the decisions that might require unanimous approval in a shareholders agreement include:

- **changes to the company's Articles of Incorporation** and/or Bylaws;
- **increases or decreases** in the company's number of authorized shares of any class of stock;
- **the pledge of the company's assets** (real or personal), or the grant of a security interest or lien that affects these assets;
- **creating, amending or funding** a pension, profit-sharing or retirement plan;
- **signing any contract or agreement** deemed to be major; and
- **making major changes** in the nature of the company.

HAVE KEY-MEMBER INSURANCE POLICIES. These provide a source of capital for the buy-out of a partner's shares in the event of death or disability and will help avoid disputes that may arise out of such an event.

DRAW UP EMPLOYMENT AGREEMENTS FOR EACH PARTNER. These agreements should be separate and apart from the shareholders and partnership agreements. The employment agreement will provide for conditions of termination, which are especially critical in dealing with sensitive problems such as alcohol and drug abuse, sexual harassment, or employment discrimination. These agreements should also clearly set forth each partner's duties and decision-making authority.

If an employment agreement is reached in the early stages of your company's growth, then the possibility of a third-party investor, venture capitalist or investment banker setting forth these policies can be avoided. In short, taking a dose of preventive medicine can go a long way in saving you legal fees, anxiety and feeling as if you've wasted a productive effort.

CONDUCT PEER-TO-PEER PARTNER REVIEWS. These should be regularly scheduled and allow partners to review each other's performance in a candid manner. Each partner should buy into the format in advance, and criteria for review as well as the impact of a superior or poor review from a corporation-and ownership-perspective. These reviews help benchmark each founder's performance as well as get problems out into the open early on.

Managing the Inevitable Break-Up

If the business partners recognize that the working relationship is truly over and that all reasonable alternatives have been considered, the following strategies can provide for a smooth break-up.

STRATEGY #1: Once it has been decided that there are no solutions to the problems and discord among the partners, the clearest and most obvious choice is a repurchase of the disgruntled partner's (or partners') equity in the company (perhaps as a lump-sum or over time). The payment may be in cash, assets, contractual rights, intangibles, or a combination of those.

STRATEGY #2: Several companies have resolved disputes among partners by splitting the business by function, essentially spinning off different operating divisions of the company based on each partner's interest. If technology is involved, there can be cross-licensing arrangements among the various companies (or joint-venture agreements among the now separate companies). This strategy allows each partner to pursue his or her own interest and strategic objectives without losing some of the efficiencies and economies of scale created when the company was all under one roof. There may be other ways to divide and subdivide the company by function, product line, market, territory, target customers, etc. that you're unaware of. Ask yourself: How many different businesses am I really in?

STRATEGY #3: Selling certain key assets (or even the company) to a third party may allow a partner to transfer his or her interest to a separate company, providing a formal separation and an opportunity to pursue differing goals and objectives.

The Path Leading to Destruction of Partnership Relationships

1. The Seed of Discontent
(Goals and expectations are not met or begin to differ; lack of mutual trust and respect results.)

2. Avoidance
(Who, us? We don't have a problem!)

3. Ego's Swell & Burst
(Of course, the problem is that he or she doesn't see things my way!)

4. Battle Lines are Drawn
(We'd rather fight than resolve the problem.)

5. Emotion Overshadows Greed
(Emotion sets in and controls future of the business. Litigation ensues.)

STRATEGY #4: If there is a suspicion of fraud or embezzlement, consider a court-ordered accounting of the books and records of the company, which may lead to a corporate restructuring or court-ordered liquidation.

STRATEGY #5: Seeking dissolution of the company through a judicial decree may also be an alternative. The court would have to be convinced that the company should be dissolved because of a major event affecting the company (such as the insanity of a partner), because the company may involuntarily go out of business, or because the company is operating at a financial loss.

STRATEGY # 6: Consider arbitration, mediation, mini-trials and other alternative-dispute-resolution techniques that may be less expensive, less time-consuming and often less emotional than full-blown litigation.

STRATEGY #7: Setting up a field office may create certain operational and overhead inefficiencies, but in the event that one or more of the partners feels the need to relocate, the field office might be an effective way for the business relationship to continue. You're not actually breaking up the company, just putting some distance between partners who still want the business to stay intact.

STRATEGY #8: If the partners cannot reach an amicable solution, then formal litigation is inevitable. The partners should be prepared for a lengthy and expensive battle.

Advice to Consider Prior to the Break-Up

In over 15 years of advising rapidly growing companies, I've found the following tips to be useful when facing a dispute with a partner.

BE CREATIVE IN SEEKING AND STRUCTURING SOLUTIONS. It's short-sighted when partners merely repurchase the shares when other types of strategic or creative types of solutions would be a better choice.

BE CIVIL. The fact that you are ending your partnership does not mean that you will never have to deal with each other again, either socially or professionally—so don't burn any bridges.

BE REASONABLE AND REALISTIC REGARDING PRICE AND STRUCTURE. Regardless of whether you are the departing or remaining partner, it is important that the structure of the departure be clear, such as how and when the payments are going to be made, whether they are going to be made in cash or with other assets or key licensing agreements. Post-closing lawsuits are very difficult and complex and can be very costly to all parties involved and to your company. Consider an earn-out clause or some other right of participation or post-sale adjustment to help avoid a future dispute.

BE SENSITIVE TO THOSE AROUND YOU. It is important to recognize that the media, key vendors, key customers, creditors, and employees all must be treated with sensitivity when partners are having a problem. Do not lose sight of the impact of these disputes on company morale and leadership.

NEVER LITIGATE OVER MATTERS OF PRINCIPLE. Be sure that the potential rewards and remedies outweigh the many expenses and opportunity costs.

BE PATIENT IN YOUR BREAK-UP NEGOTIATIONS. Be sure to deal with the difficult issues. These could include notice to creditors, indemnification, and protection from post-break-up obligations and liabilities.

BE DISCIPLINED. Remember that these problems and their solutions are as much psychological as they are legal and as much strategic as they are contractual.

STAND FIRM. If you see a problem, don't avoid the need for confrontations or unpleasant negotiations. The longer you wait, the more intractable the problem will become.

Human Capital– A Critical Growth Driver

ECRUITING AND RETAINING QUALIFIED EMPLOYEES can be one of the most difficult aspects of managing a growing business. Entrepreneurial companies are competing not only with big firms that have greater resources, but also with each other. But many growing companies have improved their ability to compete for talented staff by offering benefits that bigger companies may not offer—such as an opportunity to participate in ownership and critical decision-making, flexible schedules, an informal work environment, less red tape, and an openness to new ideas and innovation. Creativity, flexibility and aggressive performance-based compensation are the most competitive tools available to small businesses.

There are many new human-capital solutions and strategies being considered and implemented by emerging-growth companies to solve recruitment and retention challenges—and there will always be something newer and more trendy. Current strategies—many facilitated by technological development—to attract staff to ensure that growth objectives are met include:

■ **"open-book management,"** a style of management that shares all key financial data with the employees so that they can better understand how their productivity has a direct impact on the company's performance;

- **the use of free agents;**
- **outsourcing critical functions,** including application service providers (ASPs) who host and support your software systems;
- **employee leasing;**
- **telecommuting** and flexible hours; and
- **many other strategies** designed to meet the needs of a changing workforce.

Emerging-growth companies have struggled to keep up with the rapidly changing demographic composition of the workforce, the need for highly skilled technical workers (which often leads to an increase in the need to recruit abroad and manage employer-sponsored immigration strategies), the demand for better balance of work and personal life and improved quality of life in the workplace, the need to truly respect and support diversity in the workplace and the challenge of staying competitive with larger employers competing for the same workforce. Shortages in the quality and quantity of labor can and will be one of the most significant hurdles in the way of a company's growth plans.

Recruitment Strategies for Emerging-Growth Businesses

Emerging-growth companies must customize their recruitment programs to find employees who may be a bit more patient in their compensation expectations or who will value noncompensation-based factors in evaluating different positions—factors such as leadership or management practices, corporate culture, flexible hours, training opportunities or special rewards and incentives. However, if you choose to offer noncompensation-based incentives to attract employees, proceed carefully and avoid offering an excessive amount of perks. Many dot.com companies in the late 1990's hired very young workers and devoted significant overhead to chill-out rooms, pool tables, vending machines, parties and retreats. This sometimes created an environment where little actual work got done and where some young workers were mislead into thinking that they could play Ping-Pong all day and still become millionaires through their stock options. Many of these companies went out of business and their employees were left looking for jobs.

Focus your recruitment efforts on sharing the company's medium-term growth objectives and career-advancement opportunities, its leadership style, training opportunities and respect for work/personal life balance. Emphasize any unique or general programs that are or may soon be in place that address quality-of-life issues, such as on-site childcare, affiliations with nearby health clubs, casual-dress policies or a willingness to support telecommuting. The candidates should understand and at least in part share the visions of the founder and the CEO of your company—which also means that this vision must be communicated early to all candidates.

Prepare and share job descriptions, and, where appropriate, modify them with the input of the new employee, so that everyone's expectations are clear and realistic from the outset.

As an emerging-growth company, your recruiting practices need to be very systematic. Prepare and share job descriptions, and, where appropriate, modify them with the input of the new employee, so that everyone's expectations are clear and realistic from the outset. It is also critical that new employees understand that your entrepreneurial growth company is not like big companies, and that the elements of their job descriptions and measurements of performance may change as different growth objectives are set and subsequently achieved.

The Role of Your Recruiting Team

The recruiting team for your emerging-growth company must be well versed in your company's objectives and strengths. For small companies, the recruiters will not be able to attract talented candidates with big salaries and signing bonuses, so they must be armed with a strong knowledge of your company's intangible strengths.

In reviewing and evaluating potential candidates, your recruiting team must have an excellent ability to identify workers who have strong communication skills, who are willing to be flexible and take responsibility, and who have a positive attitude and high energy levels. In some cases, these intangible assets may need to compensate for a lack of direct experience or academic credentials.

Tailor the interview to ensure that the candidate has qualities that would enhance his or her ability to be comfortable and productive in a culture of rapid evolution and change. Candidates who are naturally curious, enjoy problem-solving, and are creative and flexible will most quickly assimilate to the culture of an emerging-growth company.

Candidates who are naturally curious, enjoy problem-solving, and are creative and flexible will most quickly assimilate to the culture of an emerging-growth company.

Your recruiters shouldn't waste time asking questions about the information that's contained on the written résumé, but instead spend a great deal of time learning what really drives the candidate. A standard interview and sloppy reference check may be sufficient for hiring by a local dry cleaning shop or a Fortune 500 company (where a poor hire can be easily absorbed). But for an emerging-growth business, every hire is a critical hire, and a bad hire can be very costly.

Finally, the role of a good recruiter does not end when a candidate accepts a position with your company. It also involves follow-up and assurances until the employee actually starts working for your company and continues through the first few weeks on the job, which are critical to ensuring a smooth transition and integration into the company.

Beyond Conventional Recruitment Methods

Your recruiting team's approach to finding the right hires must be creative and aggressive. Merely relying on classified ads and employee-referral bonuses won't cut it. Even the use of headhunters and Web-based job sites won't meet your recruitment needs and hiring objectives. Many companies are turning to full-time, in-house recruitment teams that are totally focused on meeting the hiring needs of the company by participating in all possible hiring channels. Full-time recruiters can demonstrate their commitment and creativity by being focused on finding the best and brightest talent in non-traditional ways.

Some of the more savvy recruiting techniques include studying fellow traveler's luggage tags on airplanes to see if she or he works for a competitor, then striking up a conversation to see if the person would be interested in a position with your company. Similarly, a recruiter can strike up conversations at sporting events and parties when fellow attendees are wearing clothes or hats that bear the trademark of a competitor, to learn if they might make ideal candidates for your company. Successful recruiting is as much about marketing as it is about human-resources management, and demands constant networking, schmoozing and data gathering outside of the confines of your company's human-resources office.

Successful recruiting is as much about marketing as it is about human-resources management.

Alternatives to Permanent Hires

Up until this point, I have focused on the recruitment of traditional full-time employees. But what if even your well-planned recruitment program is not yielding results? Under what circumstances can or should your emerging-growth company consider free agents, or temporary workers, outsourcing, or employee leasing as either short- or long-term solutions to your human-capital challenges? As your company grows and its staffing needs grow, you will have a number of options to choose from to fill those needs. Carefully consider the short- and long-term implications of each option and its impact on the continued growth of your company.

Free Agents
Free Agents are independent contractors who, rather than making a long-term commitment to an employer, prefer the flexibility of working on specific projects or part-time for sev-

eral employers simultaneously. Free agents emerged as a solution for emerging-growth companies in 1999 and the practice of using them instead of hiring permanent staff has grown steadily since. Web sites and services such as FreeAgentNation .com, bCentral.com, guru.com, and PresenceWorks.com were established to match the human-resource needs of small and growing companies with free-agent talent. Although using free agents can be a very cost-effective and interesting solution to an emerging business's recruitment needs, it can also create ongoing concerns regarding issues such as loyalty, a genuine understanding of the company's objectives, protection of confidential information, quality control and disputes over ownership for the work that has been created.

The Outsourcing Alternative

Outsourcing is the practice of having outside vendors handle one or more of a business's operational, financial or management functions. Like the hiring of free agents, it has also become a popular solution for emerging-growth companies, especially in the information-technology (IT) areas, because of the pressure to keep up with emerging information technologies and the severe shortage of skilled IT workers. For example, rather than hiring permanent IT personnel, an emerging-growth company may turn to a vendor specializing in IT workers. This vendor acts as a middleman and provides IT workers for specific projects. Functions such as payroll, health-benefits management, accounting, insurance, training and office-administrative services can also be outsourced.

The use of an application service provider (ASP) is a common form of outsourcing that shifts the responsibility for installing, maintaining and updating a company's software systems into the hands of a "host," which is typically supporting that same software for a number of different companies. (ASPs will be covered in greater detail in Chapter 16.)

Although outsourcing can be a convenient and cost-effective staffing solution, it can also be very inefficient. A study by the MetaGroup in Stamford, Conn., estimates that in the year 2000 alone over $90 billion was wasted on poorly run outsourcing programs. Contributing to these excessive costs were vendors who sold either the wrong services or who sold "suite products and services" that their clients didn't want, need or know how to use properly (rather like being forced to buy an option package you don't need when you buy a new car).

Your company's Chief Financial Officer (CFO) and his or her team should carefully evaluate which functions should be handled externally. An internal specialist in the field must carefully evaluate outsourcing proposals to ensure that the solutions proposed by the vendor are the solutions your company really needs. Once you've selected a vendor, make sure that the outsourcing program is carefully managed and monitored to ensure that your company is truly getting value from the vendor. Finally, assign a point person to share new developments and relevant information with everyone within the company who may be affected by them.

Once you've selected a vendor, make sure that the outsourcing program is carefully managed and monitored to ensure that your company is truly getting value from the vendor.

Employee Leasing

Employee leasing is provided by a professional employer organization (PEO), which in essence becomes the growing company's outsourced human-resources department for some or all key functions. The PEO becomes a joint employer with the company, while contractually assuming substantial employer rights, responsibilities and risks.

According to the National Association of Professional Employer Organizations (NAPEO), when your company leases employees from a PEO, your company and the PEO contractually divide traditional responsibilities and liabilities. Typically, you retain full control over the operation of your business, and the PEO assumes responsibility for human-resource issues, such as payment of wages, benefits issues, and the reporting and payment of employment taxes out of its own account.

Before entering into an employee-leasing agreement, consider the following steps.

SET GOALS. Figure out what your company wants to accomplish through employee leasing. List these goals in order of importance.

SEEK LEGAL COUNSEL. Legal advice is crucial for determining the implications of the leasing arrangement on your legal liability. You need to know how much control of such legal issues as hiring and firing, hours or compensation you must give up to attain a certain degree of protection from liability and decide whether you are willing to give up this control before entering the lease arrangement.

ESTABLISH QUALIFICATIONS. Discuss your needs and obtain proposals from several leasing firms. Also examine the background of each leasing firm, and talk to the current and former clients of each firm about their experiences with the firm.

DETERMINE CHARGES AND SERVICES. Get bids from several companies. Each leasing firm's proposal should outline the specific services to be provided, the time frame for these services, and all deposits, charges and methods of payment. Startup costs and commitments should also be detailed. For example, if an account representative will spend time on-site to become familiar with operations, find out how long the representative will take and if there will be an additional charge. In addition, determine whether new job descriptions will be necessary and who will prepare them. Finally, find out the details of the leasing firms' employee-benefits package. All of these items should be in the contract that you sign with the leasing agency.

SPECIFY THE LEVEL OF SUPERVISION. Examine the number of field supervisors available relative to the number of leased workers on the company payroll. This ratio can vary substantially from one leasing firm to another and can affect the quality and the productivity of the work force you are leasing if the number is too low. Specify in the leasing agreement the frequency with which the field supervisor will visit your site—and make sure it is clear who the employees call if they have a grievance.

DEVELOP A RAPPORT WITH THE FIELD SUPERVISOR, IF THERE IS ONE, BEFORE A LEASING AGREEMENT IS SIGNED. This relationship is a sensitive one because of the "turf" issue. Have the leasing firm agree not to replace the field supervisor without your company's approval.

SPECIFY INSURANCE COVERAGE. Leasing companies provide a wide variety of insurance, including employee bonding, workers' compensation, general liability, professional liability and fiduciary responsibility. The legal liabilities in this area are complex, so have your company's insurance carriers review this portion of the agreement.

OBTAIN VERIFICATION. Insist that a CPA verify that the leasing firm has made all withholdings and payments as required by law and all employee-benefit contributions as specified in the agreement. Leasing firms that are members of the National Staff Leasing Association or the National Staff Network are already required to do this under their bylaws.

REQUIRE AN EMPLOYEE COMMUNICATIONS COMPONENT. Even if employees aren't really losing their jobs, the idea that they may be terminated from your company can still be unsettling for them. One way to overcome this fear is to have employees meet with current employees of the leasing company who have successfully made the transition.

The Role and Importance of Leadership in Preserving Human Capital Resources

Effective leadership is a key component in developing a successful human capital management strategy. Employees (as well as customers and shareholders) have the ability to "vote with their feet" if they do not agree with the vision, goals and values of the emerging company's leadership team. Today's leader of a growing company must be able to communicate a clear and consistent vision to the

---

Characteristics of Effective Leaders of Fast-Track Growth Companies

- Ability to make decisions quickly (and sometimes without the benefit of having all the key facts)
- Ability to overcome confusion and skepticism
- A sense of urgency to accomplish measurable goals
- Ability to delegate effectively and communicate at all levels in the organization
- Passionate (but not with rose-colored glasses)
- Ability to clearly and effectively communicate goals and vision
- Ability to inspire and motivate employees, shareholders, customers and market partners
- High tolerance for risk, along with an ability to admit mistakes and share praise and reward performance
- Keeps an ear close to the ground

---

employees and thus "walk the talk" when it comes to making decisions and formulating policies consistent with that vision. It is also critical that the leader has the ability to see the big picture *and* the minutia of the details. Like a good pilot, the emerging-growth company leader must be competent, credible and respected and must have the ability to fly the plane safely at ground level.

Today's leaders must have the ability to recruit, retain and develop talent within the company, understanding that loyalty and commitment are more conditional than ever before. The expectations of employees will continue to rise as the company grows, and the leaders of the company must keep pace or the willingness to follow will be lost. Employees at virtually all levels want to feel that they are having some input into the future direction of the company—which also creates trust and buy-in as the company heads down the path selected.

The Legal Challenges of Building Your Internal Team

O UR RAPIDLY DEVELOPING SERVICE- AND TECHNOLOGY-driven economy has made managing human resources more important than ever. Finding and keeping qualified personnel can be a significant challenge to small and growing businesses that compete daily with larger competitors. In an economy where skilled technical labor is at a premium and the dynamics of the employer-employee relationship change quickly, the owner of a growing company needs to stay abreast of trends in employee-retention strategies and developments in employment law.

While most companies have to surmount similar employment challenges, small and growing businesses face unique ones. It may be difficult for them to devote sufficient resources to areas such as recruitment and retention and legal compliance. This chapter is designed to assist small rapidly-growing businesses without a human-resources department with employment strategies, and offers guidelines for staying in compliance.

Employment-Law Basics

T he systems and procedures put into place by a company for the hiring, firing and treatment of employees involve a large body of federal and state labor and employment laws. Failure to understand and abide by these laws can be especially harmful to a small business because employee-related litigation can sap resources vital to business functions. The body of employment law continues to grow, and the courts and legislatures decide cases and issue legislation every year that can change the way you deal with personnel issues. However, the following federal statutes and regulations affecting employment are some of the most important ones, and most affect all businesses, regardless of whether they are small or big.

■ **Equal Pay Act of 1963** prohibits unequal pay based on gender.

■ **Title VII of the Civil Rights Act of 1964** prohibits discrimination based on race, color, religion, gender, sexual preferences, or national origin.

■ **Age Discrimination in Employment Act of 1967** (ADEA) prohibits discrimination against individuals age 40 or older.

■ **Rehabilitation Act of 1973** prohibits discrimination against disabled individuals by all programs or agencies receiving federal funds and all federal agencies.

■ **Immigration and Nationality Act** prohibits employers from discriminating on the basis of citizenship or national origin.

■ **Pregnancy Discrimination Act of 1978** prohibits discrimination against pregnant women.

■ **The Immigration Reform and Control Act of 1986** makes it unlawful for employers to recruit, hire or continue to employ illegal immigrants to the United States. The act also contains nondiscrimination provisions similar to the Immigration and Nationality Act.

■ **Americans with Disabilities Act of 1990** (ADA) prohibits discrimination against a qualified applicant or employee with a disability and applies to employers with 20 or more employees.

To fall within the ADA, a person's disability must substantially limit at least one "major life activity." HIV and AIDS are considered a disability. Ailments that can be controlled by medication, such as high blood pressure, or corrected with a device such eyeglasses or a hearing aid are not considered disabilities under the ADA. In addition, ADA prohibits discrimination based on a "relationship or association" with a disabled person, ensures access for the disabled and protects recovered substance abusers and alcoholics.

The ADA requires an employer to provide "reasonable accommodation" for the known disability of a qualified applicant or employee unless it would impose "undue hardship" on the employer's business. Small employers can often get assistance with funding accommodations from state rehabilitation agencies. There are also a number of tax incentives available to eligible small businesses to help offset the cost of ADA compliance.

■ **Civil Rights Act of 1991,** an expansion of the Civil Rights Act of 1964, gives employees the right to recover consequential monetary losses; damages for future lost earnings; nonpecuniary damages, such as pain and suffering, and punitive damages.

■ **Family and Medical Leave Act of 1993** (FMLA) requires employers to allow employees to take leave for medical reasons, the birth or adoption of a child or for the care of a child, spouse or parent who has a serious health condition. The leave may be unpaid (unless paid leave has been earned), for 12 workweeks in any 12-month period. During the leave, the employer is required to maintain any group health-care plan for the employee. An employee generally has the right to retain the same or equivalent position, pay, benefits, and working conditions when the leave ends. The FMLA applies to employers with 50 or more employees for each working day during each of 20 or more calendar workweeks in the current or preceding year.

Creating a Personnel Manual

As your business begins to grow, the personnel manual (or employee handbook) will play an important role in defining the relationship between you and your employees. It is vital to create a document that summarizes benefits, policies and procedures, and effectively communicates applicable guidelines for managing conflict. A

Sample Employee Manual Contents

Although every company's manual is different, most should contain some or all of the following:

- **mission statement;**
- **about the company** and its founders;
- **compensation and benefits,** which include:
  - office hours
  - overtime
  - vacation
  - maternity leave
  - sick leave
  - holiday pay
- **jury duty** and medical absences
- **overview** of employee benefits (health, dental, disability, etc.)
- **employment classification**
- **performance review,** raises and promotions
- **pension, profit sharing and**

retirement plans
- **eligibility** for fringe benefits
- **rewards, employee discounts** and bonuses
- **expense reimbursement policies**
- **standards for employee conduct,** including:
  - dress code
  - smoking
  - personal telephone calls, e-mail and visits
  - training and educational responsibilities
  - use of company facilities and resources
  - meals and breaks
- **safety regulations** and emergency procedures;

carefully crafted manual can facilitate your company's growth as well as reduce employee litigation. The personnel manual should reflect your company's culture, business objectives and business philosophy, and should be comprehensive enough to provide guidance to employees on all key policies. However, an overly complex or detailed manual may restrict management flexibility and lead to employee confusion and uncertainty.

A good manual provides a record of the company's hiring, compensation, promotion and termination policies and could be evidence in employee-related litigation. It is crucial to have your attorney carefully review the manual before it is given to employees (and before any material changes are made) to ensure that it complies with federal and local law. Some courts treat a personnel manual or employee handbook as if it were a binding contract between you and your employees. Find out

- **procedures for handling** employee grievances, disputes and conflicts;
- **employee duties** to protect intellectual property and confidential information;
- **term and termination** of the employment relationship
- **introductory period**
- **grounds for discharge**
- **employee termination** and resignation
- **severance pay**
- **exit interviews**
- **maintenance of employee records**
- **job application**
- **proof of right to work**
- **performance review** and evaluation report
- **benefit plan information**

- **exit interview information**
- **special legal concerns**
- **equal employment opportunity**
- **sexual harassment** and discrimination policy
- **Family and Medical Leave Act** policy
- **alcohol abuse** and drug use
- **career advancement opportunities**
- **charitable and political** contributions
- **garnishment of employee wages**
- **dealing with the news media** and distribution of press releases; and
- **employee acknowledgment** of receipt of manual (to be signed by the employee and placed in his or her permanent file)

what the law regarding employee handbooks is in your state and, depending on the state you are in, include a statement in the manual that explicitly states that the manual is not a contract, and management reserves the right to change the contents at any time. Employees should be required to sign and return a page acknowledging that they received, read and understand the manual.

The Hiring Process

Finding the right person for the right job can be an arduous task, and the myriad federal and local laws that must be followed during the interview and hiring process complicate it. Check the wording of all job postings to ensure there are no references to race, sex, religion, national origin or age, and remember to include the phrase "Equal Opportunity Employer" in your advertisement. Should you use a recruitment agency, send a written copy of your non-discrimination policy to the agency. Be certain to include minority universities, trade schools and publications in your recruitment whenever possible. You may also establish the practice of "posting positions" internally to give existing employees an opportunity to compete for the position.

Create a job application that will help you gather important information while complying with all applicable laws. Do not include questions that might disclose race, religion, age, or other similar "protected categories." Questions concerning disabilities must be very carefully phrased, and should be discussed with a lawyer. As your business grows you might need to designate an Equal Employment Opportunity (EEO) compliance officer to monitor employment practices and work with legal counsel to ensure all employment policies are followed, and that recent developments in the law are communicated to all employees.

Interviewers should be trained in the do's and don'ts of interviewing. Tailor the interview process to include questions designed to learn core work values while avoiding legally troublesome subjects, such as age and race. As a rule, avoid all protected-category topics during an interview. Fortunately, the most important issues for interviewers, such as the candidate's prior job experiences and prior challenges and opportunities, remain legally available for discussion.

Drafting Employment Agreements

Although formal employment agreements have traditionally been reserved for employees who are either senior management or serve key technical functions, these documents can be used for a wide variety of employees, and can serve as an important and cost-effective tool to safeguard confidential business information and preserve valuable human resources. A sound employee agreement, together with a well-developed compensation plan, can provide an economic and legal foundation for long-term employee loyalty. Also use employment agreements for free agents performing specific jobs, regardless of assignment duration. The following issues are essential provisions of an employment agreement.

LENGTH OF EMPLOYMENT. Will the job be temporary, fixed-term, or long-term? Consider the job responsibilities and your company's business plan, as well as potential mergers and acquisitions when deciding duration. Clearly state the start and end date, renewal options and grounds for termination of the arrangement by both parties.

DUTIES AND OBLIGATIONS. Include a summary description of the employee's duties and responsibilities. List tasks and objectives and consider creating a timetable for completion of assigned work projects.

COMPENSATION AND BENEFITS. The type of compensation will vary depending on the duties and skills of the employee. An agreement should include the timing of payments and conditions for bonuses. Applicable benefits may be explicitly stated and may include health insurance, company car, training, pensions, profit sharing, and retirement plans. Where the employee will simply be receiving the same benefits as other similar employees (such as vacation and sick leave), include a reference to these general company policies.

Using stock and stock options for employee compensation is an increasingly popular method of encouraging employee motivation, even for small businesses. These compensation mechanisms, however, can contain unexpected side effects for the employee and company. For example, there may be unexpected tax or profit- and loss-statement consequences. Under at least some rulings by the federal government, the value of stock options might need to be included in an employee's base pay, for purposes of computing that employee's overtime-pay rate. Finally, a termination decision, which is difficult in the best of circumstances, may become substantially more complicated when stock-related agreements need to be considered. Use a high degree of caution in this area, and consult a lawyer who is experienced both in the creation of employee stock-compensation agreements, and in the many problems that these agreements can cause.

NON-DISCLOSURE PROVISIONS. Trade secrets owned by a company are typically protected by trade-secret statutes. This protection may be enhanced with covenants that impose obligations on the employee not to disclose (in any form and to any unauthorized party) any information that the company regards as confidential and proprietary. This should include, among other things, customer lists, formulas and processes, financial and sales data, agreements with customers and suppliers, business and strategic plans, marketing strategies and advertising materials, and any other non-public information that gives the employer an advantage over its competitors. This covenant should cover the pre-employment period (interview or training period) and extend into post-termination. Broadly draft the covenant to favor your company. However, a non-disclosure covenant will be enforceable only to the extent necessary to reasonably protect the intellectual property at stake.

> **The non-disclosure agreement should cover the pre-employment period (interview or training period) and extend into post-termination. Broadly draft the covenant to favor your company.**

COMPETITION RESTRICTIONS. Many companies would like to be able to impose restrictions on their employees' rights to work for a competitor in any capacity after they leave the company. While the rules vary widely from state to state, courts generally have not looked favorably on such attempts to deprive individuals of their livelihood. Some courts have even set aside entire contracts on the basis of this section if the balance swings too far in favor of the employer. The courts require that any covenants against competition be reasonable as to scope, time, territory, and remedy for noncompliance and be necessary to protect the legitimate business interests and intellectual property of the company. Consult an attorney with a background in this area when you draft these provisions, which should always be tied to the actual work focus of the affected employee and should be actively enforced on a non-discriminating basis.

COPYRIGHTS AND OWNERSHIP OF INVENTIONS. The agreement should expressly assign to your company ownership of intellectual property that is developed by the employee during her or his employment with you. In the absence of a written agreement, the common-law principle of "shop rights" generally dictates that if an invention is made by an employee, and if it utilizes the resources of the employer, even if it is made outside of the scope of the employment, ownership is vested in the employer.

PROTECTION OF INTELLECTUAL PROPERTY. The agreement should contain provisions regarding non-disclosure and non-competition upon termination of employment. And when an employee leaves, these obligations should be reaffirmed during an exit interview that should be conducted in the presence of at least one witness. Inform the exiting employee of his or her continuing duty to preserve the confidentiality of your company's trade secrets and make him or her aware of specific information regarded as confidential. The interviewer should obtain assurances and evidence (including a written acknowledgment) that all confidential and proprietary documents have been returned and no copies retained. The new employer or future activity should be revealed, and, under certain circumstances, even notified of the prior employment relationship and the scope of post-employment restrictions. These steps put the new employer or competitor on notice regarding your company's rights and prevent the new employer from claiming that it was unaware that its new employee had revealed trade secrets. Finally, you should insist that the departing employee not hire co-workers after the termination of his or her employment with your company.

The 21st Century Workplace

Many growth businesses are experimenting with alternative workplace options, such as job-sharing, telecommuting, free agents, outsourcing, and employee leasing. The laws covering these arrangements are still very much "a work in progress." Hence, even though employers may feel pressured by employees to allow such arrangements, there are important practical and legal issues to consider. In a telecommuting arrangement, consider the following issues:

- **Think through accountability and supervision issues carefully.** How will you make sure that the employee is performing up to standards before performance problems become serious? If the employee is paid on an hourly basis, how will you keep track of time spent on work? How can you ensure accountability and productivity?
- **Who will pay for the equipment that an employee is using at home?**
- **To what extent do workplace laws and rules apply to the home office,** such as sexual harassment rules or OSHA?
- **Does your liability insurance cover claims arising from accidents at home?**

A variety of industries, particularly those specializing in high tech, have become extensive users of term-of-project employees, such as temporary workers, leased workers, and free agents. Although these employment alternatives may be viable human-resource solutions for companies that do not have the cash flow to pay for benefits such as health insurance or do not want to make a commitment to permanent employment arrangements, there are pitfalls that you should take steps to avoid.

For example, in 1999, a federal court determined that workers hired by Microsoft through a temp agency could qualify as "regular employees" and that they would be eligible for regular company benefits. In this case, the court ruled that a discount stock-purchase plan that was available to staff should be offered to temporary and contract employees as well. This decision could have broad implications for any business that employs temps on a long-term basis. Implications for you can include the fact that your "temporary" employees have rights to your expensive benefit plans, that you may not terminate them without good cause, or that they have earned vacation pay that you were not intending to extend to them. Be sure to consult with your lawyer for updates to the law in this area.

Workplace Privacy Issues

Developing technologies such as e-mail, the Internet and voicemail have created new legal and operational challenges for growing companies. An employer must strike a balance between an employee's "reasonable expectation of privacy" and an employer's "right to know." An overall concern is the growing company's ability to protect its intellectual property and confidential information (which is often its primary asset); therefore, information-technology systems must be designed to be secure against outside hacking as well as inside unauthorized access or use. There are several issues of concern.

PRIVACY. The courts have established that an employer has the right to monitor computer files, e-mail and voicemail; however, the courts also ruled that the systems for monitoring must be considerate of the employee's "reasonable expectation of privacy", although there they offered no clear legal definition of that phrase. You should create and publish a clear and concise policy that deals with these issues, from which your employees can shape their expectations. The absence of a policy leaves it open to the courts of each state to interpret what is reasonable.

Your policy must be based on a monitoring system that is within your legitimate business purposes. For example, monitoring and then taking disciplinary actions against an employee who spends every lunch hour looking at inappropriate pornography Web sites on company premises is clearly legitimate. But monitoring a secretary's occasional e-mail correspondence with her boyfriend, and using the information to time a request for a date with her, is not. (The latter situation can present a legal problem on more than one front because it can also trigger a claim of sexual harassment and invasion of privacy.)

Good employee-training programs on the appropriate uses of technology, and clear and concise policies that establish your right as employer to monitor electronic communications and reduce the employee's expectation of privacy, can help you avoid invasion-of-privacy litigation.

UNAUTHORIZED ACCESS. Growing companies must take steps to ensure that systems are in place to prevent unauthorized employee access to sensitive company data. Not only is this important for protecting your company's intellectual assets, it is also an important step for protecting the company from costly litigation. In the past few years, employers have been held liable for systems that easily allowed an internal or external hacker into personnel files or other sensitive databases, leading to unauthorized disclosures of embarrassing personal information, such as drug-test results, disciplinary actions, or other private matters. Even accidental disclosure of information can lead to employer liability in invasion-of-privacy claims. Be sure your data systems are protected with internal and external firewalls and encryptions.

DAMAGING DATA OR IMPROPER USE. Employers have been held liable when e-mail or voicemail systems were used to distribute offensive or inappropriate information, or when the company's computer systems were used to facilitate defamation or copyright infringement. Similarly, employees must be trained as to the type of information that should not be included in e-mail correspondence. As Microsoft painfully learned in the anti-trust case brought against it by the government, old e-mail, voicemail, computer files and other electronic records can be used against you in a formal legal dispute.

Clearly, although technology has been a boon for businesses of all sizes, it creates new legal challenges that, if not carefully managed, can create significant financial burdens.

Sexual Harassment

In 1964, the Supreme Court ruled that sexual harassment was actionable as a form of discrimination under Title VII of the Civil Rights Act of 1964. The Equal Employment Opportunity Commission (EEOC) defines sexual harassment as:

- **unwelcomed sexual advances,** requests for sexual favors and other verbal or physical conduct of a sexual nature;
- **where submission to or rejection of such conduct is used in making an employment decision** (such as a job offer, raise, or promotion).

This is also known as "quid pro quo" sexual harassment; or
■ **where such conduct has the effect of unreasonably interfering with an individual's work performance,** or creates an intimidating, hostile or offensive work environment. This is known as "hostile environment" harassment.

It is important to note that sexual harassment does not have to be overtly sexual in nature. Sexual harassment can include derogatory comments or hostile actions based on the victim's gender. Furthermore, the victim need not be the person to whom the sexual conduct is directed. If an employee's work environment or career advancement is adversely affected by sexual conduct toward a co-worker, sexual harassment may be present. Employers can also be liable for the actions of non-employees, such as outside vendors, where the employer knew of the harassment and failed to take corrective measures to remedy the situation.

The challenge of avoiding claims of sexual harassment in the workplace continues to be a major issue facing employers. Sexual-harassment claims by employees have resulted in multi-million-dollar verdicts in some cases. In one case, a jury rendered a $7.1 million verdict against a major law firm (the trial judge reduced the award to $3.5 million) when it found that a former partner of the law firm had been guilty of sexually harassing a newly hired paralegal, and that the firm had taken insufficient steps to rectify the problem and prevent its reoccurrence, in spite of the fact that it had been put on notice.

In another case, the D.C. Superior Court upheld a $5,000,000 jury verdict levied against a company for the conduct of one of its male supervisors. The award consisted of $187,000 in compensatory damages and $4,812,500 in punitive damages. The supervisor allegedly asked a male subordinate employee out on dates, commented on how the employee's pants fit, made inappropriate gestures toward his body, and engaged in other sexually suggestive conduct. After the employee complained to several supervisors, his hours were reduced and he was eventually terminated. The Court characterized the manager's conduct as "outrageous," "especially egregious," and "out of control." The Court also found that the employer "flagrantly ignored [the employee's] pleas for help."

Clearly, this is not an employment issue your company can afford to ignore. Courts have also held that, where an employer has an effective sexual-harassment prevention and complaint system in place, if an aggrieved employee does not make use of the complaint system, then the employee may be barred from bringing a lawsuit. This rule provides employers with a strong incentive to provide sexual-harassment training to all employees, and to make sure that there is a well-publicized complaint system in place.

As an employer, you have a duty to provide a workplace free from sexual harassment. To meet your responsibilities and to protect your company against sexual-harassment claims, you should undertake the following defensive measures:

- **Maintain and enforce** a written policy against sexual harassment.
- **Insist that all employees attend** mandatory training sessions on your company's sexual-harassment policy and be sure that they are aware of the consequences for violating the policy.
- **Maintain a complaint procedure** that allows the victim to file a complaint with a person other than his or her supervisor.
- **Investigate all complaints** thoroughly and confidentially.
- **Take appropriate action** following each and every investigation.

To avoid liability for a claim following an employee complaint of sexual harassment, have an officer of the company outside of the department concerned conduct a prompt investigation of the complaint, and make sure the investigation begins within days after you receive the complaint. The investigator should then adopt the following guidelines:

- **Carefully document when and how** the claim first came to the attention of the company.
- **Gather data to determine all relevant facts** concerning the conduct in question.
- **Keep all discussions and information** as confidential as possible.
- **Involve legal counsel early** in the fact-gathering process to protect against claims of disparagement or defamation.

Examples of Sexual Harassment

VERBAL

- **Calling a person** a hunk, doll, babe, or honey
- **Turning work discussions** to sexual topics
- **Asking personal questions** about social or sexual life
- **Asking about sexual fantasies,** preferences or history
- **Making sexual comments** about a person's clothing, body or looks
- **Making sounds** like kissing, howling, smacking lips, whistling, or cat calls
- **Telling lies** or spreading rumors about a person's sex life
- **Sexual comments** or innuendoes
- **Repeatedly asking** for a date from a person who is not interested

NON-VERBAL

- **Staring** at someone
- **Blocking** a person's path
- **Restricting,** hindering the other person's movements
- **Looking** a person up and down
- **Sexual or derogatory comments** about men or women on coffee mugs, hats, cartoons, posters, calendars, clothing, etc.
- **Making facial expressions,** such as winking, throwing kisses, or licking lips
- **Making sexual gestures** with hands or body movements
- **Letters,** gifts or materials of sexual nature
- **Invading a person's body space;** standing closer than appropriate or necessary for the work being done

PHYSICAL

- **Massaging** a person's neck, shoulders, etc.
- **Touching** the person's clothing, hair or body
- **Hugging,** kissing, patting, or stroking
- **Touching** or rubbing oneself sexually around or in the view of another person
- **Brushing** up against a person
- **Patting,** goosing, caressing, or fondling
- **Tearing,** pulling, or yanking a person's clothing
- **Exposing oneself**

Once the investigation is complete, you must then take prompt and effective action that is reasonably calculated to end the harassment and discipline the harasser. If the harassment occurred over an extended period of time, was severe, or the harasser had been disciplined previously for such conduct, then terminating the harasser may be appropriate.

However, if the conduct was less severe and other means may remedy the situation, such as transferring the harasser to a different department, you should probably not terminate an employee unless a second offense occurs. Giving the offender a second chance puts you in a better position to defend your action if the discharged employee subsequently sues you for wrongful discharge. If the employee is not transferred, monitor the situation to make sure the harassment does not recur. Even if the claim is not substantiated, you should determine whether preventive measures need to be taken to limit the risk of future complaints.

When the court decides a sexual-harassment case, it will analyze the investigation you made and the effectiveness of the remedial action taken.

When the court decides a sexual-harassment case, it will analyze the investigation your company made and the effectiveness of the remedial action taken. Typically, the court's determination of the effectiveness of your response is based on whether the remedial action ultimately succeeded in eliminating the harassment.

Sexual-harassment laws are still evolving and can be difficult for any business owner to grasp. Recent cases and guidelines do not draw clear distinctions between permissible behavior and illegal behavior that may subject your company to legal liability. The key to protecting your business against liability is to develop a stated policy regarding the type of conduct that will not be tolerated, to maintain an effective complaint procedure, and to enforce that policy consistently.

Guidelines for Firing of Employees

The decision to terminate an employee can be both emotional and frustrating. But it can also result in expensive litigation if it is not handled properly. These days, wrongful-termination lawsuits are not idle threats. When an employee wins a lawsuit for unfair termination, the remedies for unjust dismissal have ranged from modest "back-pay awards" to multi-million-dollar punitive-damages awards. For example, a federal magistrate in Wisconsin lowered a jury's award of $13,000,000 in compensatory and punitive damages to a mentally retarded and autistic man who was wrongfully terminated in violation of the Americans with Disabilities Act (ADA). Although the award was lowered to $300,000, the maximum allowed by federal law, the magistrate indicated that the jury wanted to send a message to the employer by imposing such a large award. The U.S. Equal Employment Opportunity Commission (EEOC) brought the lawsuit on behalf of a former janitor at a Chuck E. Cheese pizza restaurant. The employee was allegedly fired after a district manager of the employer stated that the employer does not hire "those kind of people."

To successfully defend against these types of claims, you must be prepared to demonstrate that employee performance evaluations, policies contained in personnel manuals and grounds for termination were applied in a consistent, nondiscriminatory fashion. You need to develop clear and uniform guidelines for final probation periods, opportunities to improve job performance, availability of training, and termination procedures. When employee termination becomes necessary for any reason, apply the following guidelines as a safeguard against lawsuits.

KEEP COMPREHENSIVE RECORDS ABOUT EACH EMPLOYEE, including any formal performance appraisal or informal warnings, comments or memos prepared by a supervisor to demonstrate the employee's poor work or misconduct. Use written evaluations and warning notices to provide an employee who has been performing poorly with plenty of advance notice of management's disappointment with his or her performance. In addition, keep witness statements, accident reports, customer complaints, and related documentation. If a case ever gets to litigation, these documents and records may be the only evidence available to support that there were valid reasons for terminating the employee.

ENSURE THAT YOU HAVE A PROPER BASIS FOR TERMINATION. Carefully review your personnel manuals, policy statements, memoranda, and related documents to ensure that no implied representation or agreement regarding the term of employment, severance pay, or grounds for termination has been made that is inconsistent with your company's intentions. Grounds for termination, which should be stated in the personnel manual, typically include:

- **discriminatory acts** toward employees or hiring candidates; physical or sexual abuse;
- **falsifying time records** or other key documents;
- **willful or negligent violation** of safety or security rules;
- **violation of company policies;**
- **unauthorized disclosure** of the company's confidential information;
- **refusal to perform work** assigned by a supervisor;
- **destroying or damaging** company property;
- **misappropriation** or embezzlement; or
- **drug abuse or gambling** on company premises.

It should also be made clear in the manual that these are examples only, and that other grounds for discipline or termination may exist.

ENSURE ALL ALTERNATIVES TO TERMINATION HAVE BEEN CONSIDERED. Even once a termination decision has been made by the immediate supervisor and the evidence supporting the cause collected, conduct an independent review of the proposed dismissal by a member of management at least one level above the direct supervisor of the employee. Strongly consider giving the employee an opportunity to cure the defect in performance.

The reviewer should take the time to meet the employee and hear his or her side of the story before making the final dismissal decision. This meeting should be in a quiet, confidential location, and should be undertaken in the presence of a witness. Place written records of these meetings in the employee's file. The reviewer should question the supervisor and the employee's co-workers to gather additional facts and to ensure that all company policies and procedures have been followed, especially those regarding performance appraisal and employee discipline.

CONDUCT AN EXIT INTERVIEW. Candidly and concisely explain the reasons for the employee's discharge during an exit interview. Emphasize to the employee that the reasons for termination are legitimate and are consistent with your company's past practices under similar circumstances. Also advise the employee what prospective employers will be told, and remind her or him of any non-compete covenants and his or her continuing obligation to protect your company's trade secrets.

PREPARE A COMPREHENSIVE RELEASE AND SEPARATION AGREEMENT. Give the employee several days to consider the release, and an opportunity to have it reviewed by legal counsel. The release-and-separation agreement should:

- **be supported by valid "consideration"** (some payment or agreement beyond what your company was already obligated to provide);
- **be signed by the employee** knowingly and voluntarily;
- **include the grounds for termination in the recitals** (the introductory pages of the agreement);
- **contain covenants against competition,** disclosure and litigation;
- **make sure the release protects all possible defendants in an employment action** (company, officers, directors, subsidiaries, etc.);
- **avoid commitments regarding references** to future employers; and
- **be checked carefully** against all applicable federal and state laws.

Employees are clearly one of the most valuable assets of an emerging-growth company. But if they are treated unfairly in the hiring or termination process, they can become a large liability. Employment agreements and personnel manuals are useful tools to define the rights and obligations of the employer and employee to each other. Further, careful documentation of employee performance, as well as a written record reflecting the race and sex of other persons dismissed or disciplined for the same or similar reasons can be invaluable in defending your company against unlawful-termination lawsuits. Also, when an employee is terminated, take care to document the race and sex of the individual replacing the discharged employee.

Employment Practices Liability Insurance

Many employers are receiving sales pitches from their insurance brokers that Employment Practices Liability Insurance (EPLI) is a "cure-all" for potential employee lawsuits. However, these policies often fall far short of what the sales pitches promise. For example, the areas of largest risk are typically not covered by these policies:

- **Most policies will not pay for any "punitive damage"** awards, but this is the single largest dollar risk of employee lawsuits.

- **Most policies will not pay for damages arising from "intentional misconduct,"** but most sexual-harassment and discrimination cases are viewed as intentional misconduct.

- **Most policies will not pay for claims of breach of contract,** but almost all employee lawsuits claim a breach of an express or implied employment contract.

- **Most policies will insist that a lawyer selected by the insurance company will be your lawyer,** even if you have a lawyer who already knows you and your company.

Ask tough questions of your insurance broker; make sure you understand all the limitations of a policy before you agree to pay for a policy that may ultimately afford you little protection.

Avoiding Defamation Claims

When your company needs to communicate information about employees to third parties, such as when asked for references, you must be careful to provide only verified and accurate facts. If you disclose untrue, offensive or objectionable private facts to a third party, you may be liable for a "defamation" suit. In a recent case, an employer was held liable for damages for stating that an employee was terminated for drug use, when the company's only evidence for this claim was a polygraph result that indicated only that the employee lied when responding to a question concerning drug use.

Most states grant certain persons, such as personnel directors, supervisors, employees participating in an internal investigation or unemployment-compensation commissions, a "qualified privilege" regarding negative information about employees. In such cases, negative information about an employee (or former employee) can be divulged on a need-to-know basis, as long as it is not communicated with a malicious intent. To avoid problems, your company may adopt a policy that, when responding to reference checks, company personnel may provide only the dates of a former employee's employment and his or her job title. Some companies have developed a limited-waiver-and-release form that departing employees can sign to approve the release of additional information, such as compensation.

Employee drug and alcohol abuse can cost companies lost productivity, threaten corporate security and increase liability.

Drug and Alcohol Abuse in the Workplace

Employee drug and alcohol abuse can cost companies lost productivity, threaten corporate security and increase liability. In an attempt to minimize these risks, many companies implement drug and alcohol testing programs. While some of these programs have proved to be helpful, most employers have not found the benefits of drug or alcohol testing to be worth the effort and expense—unless the company has specific, safety-sensitive jobs (such as truck drivers), or there is a reasonable suspicion that an actual problem exists. And although private-sector employees can often legally be subjected to drug and alcohol testing, using such testing raises many legal issues.

Because of the complexity of the legal issues involved, consult with a legal expert knowledgeable with the employment laws of your state before you draft and implement a drug and alcohol testing policy for your company. The following guide-

Sound Testing Procedures

- **Have a reputable, independent laboratory perform the testing,** using qualified and trained medical technicians or professionals, such as a pathologist, other physician, toxicologist or doctorate-level laboratory scientist.

- **The laboratory should have a strong track record,** credentials and quality-control procedures and should be subject to periodic testing for accuracy.

- **All work should be performed by the same laboratory** if possible, to ensure uniformity of tests and procedures.

- **You and the laboratory must determine in advance** and in writing what cutoff levels will result in a "positive" test finding, and you should advise employees of the applicable standards.

- **Make sure the lab has a policy of keeping part of all samples** that test positive, for purposes of later re-testing, if a test result is challenged.

- **Always submit positive test samples of employees** for immediate re-testing under an equally sensitive or more specific test.

- **The results of the second test** should always take precedence and be acted upon.

- **Random searches and tests of employees** are usually inadvisable except when compelling reasons justify their use. They should generally be limited to employees in positions posing a health or safely threat to others or to the employer.

- **Secure a consent form prior to all testing.** Those who refuse to sign the form or to submit to testing should be questioned regarding the reasons for refusal or suspended pending investigation.

- **Before testing, have employees list all medications** they've taken within the previous 30 days, and inquire whether the person has a drug or alcohol disability. The Americans with Disabilities Act (ADA) discrimination statute includes and protects drug and alcohol abusers who have recovered, because the courts have interpreted the statute to include such addictions within the definition of "disability."

lines will help you determine how best to apply such a policy.

- **Design your policy to address legitimate business concerns** and apply the policy in a non-discriminatory and private matter.

- **Identify circumstances** under which substance-abuse testing or searches will be done (random or upon reasonable suspicion).

- **Determine under what circumstances** urine samples would be taken under direct observation, and what steps should be taken to guard against alteration or substitution of a sample.
- **Employees, and possibly job applicants,** should be afforded the opportunity to explain or challenge positive test results.
- **Share test results only with the employee** or job applicant and to others only on a strict need-to-know basis.
- **Determine whether job applicants** will be allowed to reapply to your company, and designate a waiting period.
- **Document performance deficiencies consistently,** including witnessed observations of unusual behavior or incidents of wrong-doing that prompted testing in the first place.
- **If an employee who tests positive** is given a chance at rehabilitation, your company policy should explicitly state the conditions of the rehabilitation. Similarly, expressly state in company policy the conditions for employment after rehabilitation.
- **Issue a written policy expressly reserving the right** to search lockers, desks, and other company property, as well as an employee's property on company premises (including employee cars), where the employer has a reasonable suspicion that the property may contain unauthorized drugs or alcohol. Consider limiting random searches to employees in safety-sensitive jobs.
- **Before you implement the policy,** develop a plan for communicating the policy, both internally and externally, in a manner designed to gain the widest acceptance. A focus on safety concerns will increase employee acceptance of the policy.
- **To avoid litigation, train supervisors** to identify substance abusers and encourage them to report observed signs of impairment.
- **Be certain that your company's substance abuse policies** conform to all relevant laws and regulations.

- **Explain the penalties** for particular types of offenses.
- **Clearly state your policy in writing,** informing employees or applicants in advance of the penalties for violation of the rules, outlining the circumstances under which screening will be required, and explaining how the results will be used.

- **Adopt separate written policies** for job applicants and employees. If applicable, job candidates should be advised that they will be subject to drug and alcohol screening tests.
- **Define covered substances broadly,** to include narcotic and non-narcotic drugs, abused prescription drugs, and "designer" drugs.
- **If appropriate, apply different penalties to alcohol and drug abusers.** For example, alcoholics may be given an opportunity for rehabilitation but those who abuse illegal drugs might be automatically fired.
- **Train supervisors to recognize appropriate symptoms** and to administer the policy intelligently.
- **As the employer, bear the costs** of all drug and alcohol screening

The policy should prohibit the following conduct:

- **use, possession or sale of illicit drugs or alcohol** on the company premises, on company business, or during work hours (prohibition can extend to lunch and break time);
- **being under the influence of illicit drugs or alcohol** on company premises, on company business, or during working hours;
- **any possession, use or sale of alcohol or illicit drugs** off company premises adversely affecting the individual's performance, his or her or others' safety at work, or the employer's reputation;
- **switching or altering any urine sample** submitted for testing; and
- **refusing to submit a urine sample** for testing when required by management.

HIV/AIDS in the Workplace

There is a broad range of legal issues that an employer must consider when formulating policies dealing with HIV or AIDS. The laws of many states include people with HIV or AIDS within the definition of "disabled," thereby affording them protection under the Americans with Disabilities Act. Several states prohibit HIV/AIDS testing as a condition of employment, while others limit HIV/AIDS testing to those rare situations where the employer can show a legitimate reason for doing so.

To establish a legitimate reason, there must be some connection between HIV/AIDS and job performance and safety. An employer who tests for HIV/AIDS without a legitimate reason may be liable for an invasion-of-privacy claim by the job applicant or employee.

Through education and preparation, you can avoid many of the problems that can arise when an employee is infected with HIV. Consider the U.S. Surgeon General's guidelines for dealing with workplace HIV or AIDS issues:

- **Adopt an up-to-date HIV/AIDS education program** that discusses how HIV is transmitted and explains your company's policies regarding employees with HIV/AIDS.
- **Treat HIV/AIDS infected employees** in the same manner as other employees who suffer from disabilities or illnesses that are treated under company health plans and policies.
- **If their continued employment does not pose a safety threat to themselves,** other employees, or customers, allow HIV/AIDS infected employees to continue working as long as they are able to satisfactorily perform their jobs.
- **Make reasonable efforts to accommodate HIV/AIDS infected employees** by providing them with flexible work hours and assignments.
- **Keep confidential all information regarding HIV/AIDS** infected employees.

By educating your employees, you may be able to reduce the work disruption, legal implications, financial implications, and other effects that HIV/AIDS can have on your business. Due to the complexity and changing nature of HIV/AIDS, stay informed of the applicable laws in your state, and consult an employment attorney when handling workplace HIV/AIDS issues.

A Closing Thought

As your company continues on its fast-track growth path, it is important to protect your assets by being informed of and in compliance with the broad range of employment laws that govern your relationship with your employees. Take all necessary precautions to protect your company's financial assets, as well as such nontangible assets as its reputation. And because new laws on workplace issues are always being written and new decisions continue to be handed down by the courts, your education in this area will always be a work in progress.

Motivating and Compensating Your Team

A CRITICAL SET OF ASSETS FOR A RAPIDLY GROWING company is its human resources, as discussed in earlier chapters. To commit to the long-term growth of your company and stay focused on meeting your growth objectives, employees at every level must be properly motivated and compensated. As an emerging-growth company, it's critical that you find competitive advantages as you compete against your Fortune 500 counterparts in the effort to hire superior employees. Along with a carefully structured compensation package, you must also find the intangible motivators that ensure a highly productive workforce.

Creating a Culture That Fosters Motivated Workers

A s any experienced business leader will tell you, motivating people is far from an exact science. For some workers, money is the prime motivator, while for others it may be recognition, flexibility or career advancement. Regardless of each employee's specific performance motivators there are steps that your leadership team can take to boost and maintain morale that will serve as a motivator for all employees. These steps start with building a corporate culture:

- **that demands that personnel** at all levels are treated with respect and dignity;
- **that is relatively free** from egotistical behavior, red tape, nepotism and politics;
- **that encourages open communication** among employees at all levels;
- **that is committed to teamwork** and that values working together toward organizational goals, not striving to achieve selfish personal objectives;
- **where every employee feels valued;**
- **where employees feel secure in their positions** and their opportunities for advancement while never becoming complacent;
- **where teamwork** as well as individual performance are recognized and rewarded;
- **in which roles and performance targets** are clearly articulated to each employee, especially if your company has adopted a goal-based compensation system;
- **where each employee understand** how his or her role fits into meeting the overall objectives of the organization; and
- **where the employees trust the ability** of the company's leadership to make the right decisions.

Your management's approach to the development of employee-benefit and motivation programs can speak volumes by sending subtle messages about how your company views your employees. For example, an early-stage technology company recently replaced its free beer and pool tables program with free smoking-cessation programs, personal diet and fitness trainers and complementary car seats for families with newborn babies. The change not only sent a message regarding its concern for the welfare of its team, but also reflected that the company was in tune with the evolving needs of its workforce, which had shifted from those of young, single, party-loving GenXer's to those of married people with young families. At USAA, a rapidly growing insurance and financial-services company based in San Antonio, Texas, employee health programs are a way to convey a positive message to employees. The company's female employees are offered free breast-cancer screening tests via a mobile mammogram machine, and male employees are encouraged to take advantage of free prostate-cancer exams at the company's onsite infirmary. Other programs the company offers include five different child care assistance options, including an after-school educational program to cover children's after-school hours while their parents are still at work. As you strive to create programs for your employees, carefully consider their needs, as well as what your company's budget will permit.

Tips for Keeping Your Staff Motivated

Before turning to some strategies for structuring your company's benefits and compensation plans, here are some thoughts on motivating your workforce.

EMPLOYEES LIKE TO FEEL THAT THEY ARE WORKING WITH OTHERS, not for others. They do not enjoy being micromanaged and welcome the flexibility, autonomy and responsibility to make decisions for themselves and be accountable for the decisions that they make. Encourage your people to be proactive, not just reactive when it comes to problem solving and finding ways to enhance the company's performance, and reward them when their efforts yield real results.

WIN THE RESPECT OF YOUR TEAM. Most workers get caught up in the vision of the founder and the romantic heat of a company

---

Motivating Your Workforce: It takes more than money

Keeping your team motivated takes more than money and means finding the right mix of the following components:

- Culture of respect
- Strong leadership
- Constant innovation
- Empowering management styles
- Training
- Career advancement opportunities
- Base compensation
- Bonuses and benefits
- Opportunities for ownership

on a rapid ascent. But that passion can be fleeting, especially in a tight labor market, if the founder or leaders do not continue to share and communicate their vision and objectives and reward those who help the company meet those objectives.

DON'T USE THREATS, GUILT OR YELLING TO MOTIVATE YOUR TEAM. Fear will yield short-term results but is not likely to be an effective long-term motivator.

DO NOT BE AFRAID OF SOME DEGREE OF EMPLOYEE TURNOVER, provided that your turnover rates stay below industry standards. Aiming for a zero turnover rate may lead to complacency and mediocrity by keeping people in (or promoting them into) positions for which they are unqualified. A certain degree of turnover helps bring a new perspective and fresh ideas on how things are getting done and how they ought to be done.

TAKE THE TIME AND EFFORT TO REALLY ASK WHAT BENEFITS THE EMPLOYEES WANT and need to get the highest motivational results. Offer options that reflect the diversity in your workforce and avoid a "one-size-fits-all" approach. Carefully monitor what benefits your competitors are offering to ensure that your programs keep pace. Remember to focus on more than just cash; often it is the intangible factors that make the real difference.

TECHNOLOGY IS GREAT, BUT DON'T FORGET THE VALUE OF HUMAN INTERACTION. Many emerging-growth-company leaders are so dependent on e-mail, voicemail, cell phones and pagers that they don't spend enough face-time with their team. To really listen to feedback, new ideas, performance goals, etc., you need to meet with your staff in person.

THE WAY TO HOLD ON TO QUALITY PEOPLE IS NOT JUST TO PAY THEM WELL BUT ALSO TO TREAT THEM WELL. A positive, challenging, high-energy workplace where everyone is treated with respect can be very hard to leave, even for the promise of more money.

DO WHAT YOU SAY AND SAY WHAT YOU DO. Maintain open communication channels with your staff and keep the promises you make to them.

BIG BONUSES AND STOCK OPTIONS ARE IMPORTANT, BUT THEY ARE NOT THE ONLY THING. A pat on the back, a big smile, a congratulatory company-wide e-mail, or a small gift can go a long way in motivating and rewarding employees.

BE QUICK TO CELEBRATE AND SHARE ACHIEVEMENTS PUBLICLY but give criticism privately.

FINALLY, DON'T FOOL YOURSELF INTO THINKING THAT YOU HAVE WHAT IT TAKES TO MOTIVATE PEOPLE. Rather, people need to motivate themselves. Therefore, your role as an entrepreneur or leader of an emerging-growth company is to create a culture that inspires and empowers people to motivate themselves and properly rewards that self-motivation when results are achieved.

Compensating Your Employees for Win-Win Results

In your desire to build your business and maintain a strong and committed workforce, you must strike a balance between your personal success goals and those of your employees. You must avoid the appearance of achieving wealth at the expense of the rank and file, as well as the urge to "buy" your workers' loyalty with excessive and frivolous perks. At one extreme, a motivation and compensation plan that is structured with the objective of making the owners and investors in the company wealthy, while neglecting the needs of mid- and lower-level workers, will not win you favors with the majority of your staff. At the opposite extreme, if, like so many dot-coms have done, you lavish your staff with perks, such as rec rooms, free meals and liberal leave policies, topped off with six-figure salaries and stock options, you—like many of the dot-coms of legend—will quickly find yourself out of business. Although the latter arrangement may help you retain employees and attract an abundance of applicants, no company can sustain itself under such conditions and with that type of cost structure.

Developing Compensation and Benefit Programs

The development of compensation and benefit programs from 1997 to 2001 has been a rapidly moving target. In the late 1990s, there was a severe shortage of qualified and experienced upper- and middle-level management talent and technology-trained workers. As a result, many companies felt that they had to offer high-six-figure salaries, aggressive stock-option plans, country-club memberships, chauffeur-driven limousines, and corner-office suites with mahogany paneling and plush carpeting. But in early 2000 and 2001, as the economy slowed and stock prices fell, companies scaled back their lists of executive perks. Yet the need for qualified talent remained just as strong—putting even greater demands on the need to be creative and aggressive in structuring compensation and benefit programs.

> **Today's workers realize that not everyone will become an overnight millionaire from participation in stock-option programs. At the same time, they are looking for more than just cash as a motivator for joining a company.**

Today's workers realize that not everyone will become an overnight millionaire from participation in stock-option programs. At the same time, they are looking for more than just cash as a motivator for joining a company and helping it grow over the long-term. Your challenge as a growing company is to take the time to ask your employees (through interviews, periodic surveys, etc.) what they really want, develop the right mix of benefits, and then find a cost-effective way of delivering those benefits and services. Some companies have used non-cash incentives to keep employees focused and motivated. For example, Continental Airlines gives away six Ford Explorers every six months to six employees who are randomly selected from a pool of employees who had perfect attendance records for the previous six months. This is a cost-effective way to cut down on employee absences, boost morale, and deliver perks to deserving workers. (See the box on pages 116-117 for possible incentives your company can incorporate into its benefits.)

Many emerging-growth companies are recognizing that employees' lives are becoming busier and more complex, so they are providing services such as dry cleaning, travel services, and fitness centers at the workplace. Whether your company subsidizes these services or offers them at full cost, employees still view the conveniences as a timesaving benefit. For the employer, this is a cost-effective way to increase workplace productivity. Further proof that money isn't everything can be found in a recent study by Mercer Management Consulting Services, which surveyed the reasons why information-technology professionals stay at a given job. Among the top reasons were:

- **the opportunity to learn** and use new technology (training);
- **work environment** (culture);
- **autonomy** (management style);
- **challenging work assignments** (innovation);
- **career-development opportunities** (growth); and
- **high-quality supervision** (leadership).

Near the bottom of the list were the incentives provided under variable-pay arrangements.

Stock-Award and Stock-Option Plans

Broad-based employee stock-option plans remain a popular employee benefit. The National Center for Employee Ownership (NCEO), based in Oakland, Cal., estimates that between seven and ten million employees participated in stock-option programs in the year 2000. Among venture-backed high-growth companies in the technology industries, more than 85% offer stock-option plans to employees at virtually all levels, and more than 90% of Fortune 1000 companies offer stock-option plans as a long-term compensation incentive for executives.

Stock-option plans are essentially a contractual right to

Perks and Benefits an Emerging-Growth Company Might Offer

The following is an extensive list of incentives you can offer your employees. Take the time to find out which are most important to them, which are most cost-effective for your company, and work to develop the right package for your staff.

- Life and disability insurance plans
- Drug- and alcohol-abuse counseling programs
- Comprehensive health care insurance plans
- Onsite child care facilities or child care assistance subsidies
- Dental/eye care/pharmaceutical reimbursement plans
- Casual-dress policies
- Early eligibility for benefits
- Training costs and educational reimbursements (may be tied to grades)
- SERPs (Supplemental/Executive Retirement Plans)
- Seniority/tenure rollover from previous job
- Stock-option plans
- Loans or partial payments on housing costs
- Laptops/cell phones/pagers provided at little or no cost
- Signing bonuses
- Pension and profit-sharing plans
- Reimbursement of moving or relocation expenses
- Waiver or dilution of non-compete clauses
- Car allowances
- Aggressive 401(k) and 403(b) retirement plans (including rollover features with employer contributions and matches)
- Stipends toward residential living costs
- Executive/employee dining rooms with free or subsidized meals
- Transportation and commuting subsidies
- Executive mentoring of lower-level managers
- Employee innovation renewal programs
- Low/no interest consumer-loan programs
- Reserved parking spots or parking subsidies

purchase shares at a fixed price for a certain period of time. The fixed price is known as the strike price, and the period of time is known as the vesting schedule; that is the period of time during which the employee or executive is eligible to actually exercise the option rights. Vesting periods typically run three to five years before all or part of the options can be exercised; however, in a competitive marketplace, vesting periods can be more aggressive.

- Flexible work arrangements and job-sharing programs
- Outplacement services
- Free transportation home when working late
- Flexible work hours
- Charitable contribution funds and directed-giving programs
- Elder-care assistance programs
- Golden parachutes (e.g., change-in-control agreements that provide for big severance packages if the company is involved in a merger or acquisition); includes "gross-up" payments to cover tax liability)
- Telecommuting options (allowing work from home)
- Prepaid legal services plans
- Onsite facilities for doctor appointments
- Aggressive vacation policies (including a vacation stipend)
- Aggressive family and health leave policies
- College-tuition subsidy program (for employees or their dependents)
- Inexpensive take-home meals
- Financial-planning, estate-planning and retirement-planning seminars
- Onsite health and fitness facilities (or arrangements for discounts with a nearby facility)
- Group home- and automobile-insurance programs
- Adoption-assistance programs
- Executive and management-training retreats
- Onsite executive concierge, massage, custom-tailors, dry cleaning, shoe shines or spa/salon services
- Access to the corporate jet, vehicles or apartments
- Tickets to local sporting events and theatre
- Stress/time management and wellness seminars
- Half-day Fridays (summers only)
- First-class air-travel upgrades
- Employee appreciation days, picnics and ice-cream socials
- Be CEO for a day/spend a day with the CEO program

Volatile capital markets can force emerging-growth companies to restructure their plans to reflect market conditions. This is because the strike price for the purchase of the shares, which is typically set at the time the employee or executive joins the company, may be well above what the shares are trading for in the public markets. Or, for a privately-held company, the strike price may be at a higher valuation than the company can justify. For example, Real Networks, whose shares fell 89% in 2000, allowed its employees to exchange their existing stock options for new ones that would reflect a downwardly adjusted strike price. Many other technology firms, such as Sprint, WebMethods, Advanced Micro Devices, Inc. and Amazon.com, followed in this path in late 2000 and in 2001 to avoid stock-price volatility, creating a situation where managers and employees no longer wanted stock options in lieu of cash compensation.

Understanding Specific Stock-Award and Stock-Option Plans

The following is a summary of stock-option and -award plans. Because of the stringent requirements, discuss and implement such plans with the assistance of your lawyer, accountants and financial advisers.

STOCK BONUS AWARD PLANS. In lieu of paying executive bonuses in the form of cash, your company may opt to pay the award in the form of company stock. In some circumstances, an award of company stock can have a greater motivational impact and build long-term loyalty. Cash is sometimes included along with the stock award to cover the income-tax liability that will accrue to the employee from the receipt of stock. The value of the stock award will be subject to income-tax withholding and employment taxes. Since the stock award is a form of compensation, your corporation will be entitled to a tax deduction equal to the value of the stock award.

INCENTIVE STOCK OPTIONS (ISOs). ISOs qualify for special tax treatment. An ISO is a right granted by an employer to an executive, allowing him or her to a specified number of shares during a specific period at a fixed price. The fixed price (also known as the strike price) is the market price of the stock (or the value of the stock, if the stock is not regularly traded) at the date the ISO is granted. The executive can delay the purchase of the stock (that is, the "exercise" of the ISO) for a period of up to ten years, during which time the stock will presumably increase in value. The executive can then purchase the stock at what is likely to be a bargain price at the time of purchase. As long as certain prescribed holding-period requirements are met, the executive does not recognize any taxable income at the time the ISO is granted or at the time it is exercised. The holding-period requirements mandate that, upon exercising the ISO, an executive must hold the stock for two years after the award or grant date of the ISO or one year after the exercise of the ISO. When the executive finally sells the stock, he or she must pay capital gains on the difference between the strike price and the price when the stock is sold. Your corporation receives no deduction in this case, but does if the stock is sold before the holding period is up, as explained next.

Upon the exercise of a non-qualified stock option, the executive will recognize taxable income at ordinary-income rates equal to the difference between the amount paid for the shares and the fair market value at the date of exercise.

If an executive sells the stock within two years of the ISO's grant date or within one year of the exercise date, that is called a disqualifying disposition. The executive will have to recognize ordinary income as a result of the sale of the shares in an amount equal to the difference between the strike price and the sale price of the shares. The difference between the strike price and the fair market value at exercise is ordinary income, and the increase in value from exercise to disposition is a capital gain. When a disqualifying disposition occurs, your corporation will be entitled to a deduction equal to the amount the executive is required to recognize as ordinary income.

NON-QUALIFIED STOCK OPTIONS (NQSOs). These plans do not ordinarily result in recognition of taxable income when they are granted unless the option is immediately transferable; are immediately exercisable in full; are not subject to restrictions that would offset the fair market value of the option; and have a readily ascertainable fair market value. If NQSOs do not satisfy all of these conditions (which is the usual case), federal income tax is not applicable at the time of grant. Upon the exercise of an NQSO, however, the executive will recognize taxable income at ordinary-income rates equal to the difference between the strike price (amount paid for the shares) and the fair market value at the date of exercise. The taxable-income amount is subject to income-tax withholding and employment taxes.

A subsequent sale of the shares will result in capital gains to the executive. His or her basis for purposes of reporting gain or loss will be the fair market value of the shares on the exercise date.

Your corporation incurs no expense (other than administrative costs) in granting NQSOs and receives a tax deduction for compensation expense incurred equal to the amount the executive is required to recognize as ordinary income. This deduction is not recognizable at the time of the grant of the NQSO, but at the time the executive recognizes taxable income from the exercise of the stock option.

STOCK APPRECIATION RIGHTS (SARs). Upon exercise, SARs entitle the employee to receive in cash the difference between the strike price and the fair market value of the stock, occasionally accompany the grant of stock options. SARs enable the holder of the option to realize the increase in market value of the stock without paying an exercise price. The plan under which SARs are granted may authorize the differential in stock value to be paid to the employee in cash, corporation stock or in a combination of the two, and may give your employee the right to choose the form of payment.

SARs may be granted in connection with the grant of NQSOs or ISOs, but if granted in connection with an ISO, then the SARs must meet the following requirements:

- **they must expire no later** than expiration of the ISO;
- **they must not exceed** the number of shares subject to the ISO;
- **they must be for no more than 100% of the spread** or difference on exercise of the ISO and may be exercised only when there is a spread or difference; and
- **they must be subject to the same conditions** of non-transferability as the ISO itself.

SARs may take the form of units of phantom stock, entitling the holder to a form of deferred compensation. In either case, SARs may be subject to vesting restrictions based on continued employment, performance goals and other factors. Upon the exercise of an SAR, the executive will be deemed to have received taxable compensation subject to income-tax withholding and employment taxes, and your corporation will be entitled to a tax deduction in the amount of the executive's taxable compensation.

For financial-reporting purposes, the income statement of the corporation must be adjusted on a quarterly basis to reflect the difference between the fair market value of the corporation's stock at the end of each quarter and the exercise price of the outstanding stock options where SARs are attached. As a result, a corporation that may be highly profitable and whose stock is rising may experience significant charges against earnings because of a rising stock price.

> **A principal advantage of a restricted-stock plan to an executive is that it provides considerable tax flexibility by permitting the individual to select the date of grant (as opposed to the date of vesting) for reporting taxable income.**

RESTRICTED STOCK. Restricted stock is generally the common stock of a corporation, issued to an executive in connection with the performance of services to the corporation. The shares are generally issued without cost or for a nominal price. The executive's right to unconditional ownership in some or all of the shares of the stock (vesting) may be subject to the executive's continued employment by the corporation for a certain period, satisfaction of performance goals and other criteria. In addition, the stock may vest over a period of time according to a prearranged schedule. The plan or agreement typically requires forfeiture of non-vested shares when the participant leaves the company (or fails to achieve performance goals) during the restricted period.

A principal advantage of a restricted- stock plan to an executive is that it provides considerable tax flexibility by permitting the individual to select the date of the grant (as opposed to the date of the vesting) for reporting taxable income. Your corporation is entitled to a tax deduction equal in amount to the taxable income recognized by the executive.

Some employers believe that the psychological benefit of immediate stock "ownership" and the possibility of substantial appreciation are perceived by the executive as more tangible and are therefore more of an incentive than other forms of executive compensation. In addition, because the "ownership" is more real, the forfeiture provisions may tend to act as a stronger deterrent to the voluntary termination of employment by the executive.

PHANTOM-STOCK PROGRAMS. The term "phantom stock" is typically used to describe a long-term incentive program based on phantom, rather than real, shares of corporate stock. Phantom-stock plans make use of units of corporate shares that might otherwise be granted to executives. The value of these units typically equals the appreciation in the market value of the underlying stock between the time they are acquired by the executive and their settlement date. The settlement usually occurs at retirement, termination of employment, or some other fixed date. At settlement, the award may be payable as a lump sum or in installments over a period of ten to 15 years. Occasionally, phantom-stock plans allow participants to determine their own settlement dates.

Phantom-stock units can be settled in cash, stock, or some combination of the two. Furthermore, dividend equivalents are sometimes paid or accrued on phantom stock. From the executive's point of view, the advantages of a phantom-stock plan include:

- **They offer possibilities for gains** if the corporation's stock increases in value.
- **Unlike stock options,** they require no investment on the part of the individual.
- **No tax is owed** until the phantom units are settled in cash or stock.

The disadvantages are:

- **There is little flexibility** regarding the form or timing of payment, since such terms are typically stipulated by the plan.
- **There are no opportunities** for favorable capital-gains treatment.

From the corporation's perspective, the advantages of phantom-stock plans are that they:

■ **align the interests of management** with those of shareholders;

■ **provide equity-based incentives** without the actual use of stock;

■ **permit tax deductions** for award settlements; and

■ **facilitate stock ownership,** if awards are paid in stock.

And the disadvantages include:

■ **potentially fluctuating and unbounded charges** to earnings for financial-statement reporting purposes, similar to those described for SARs, unless appreciation under the plan is capped;

■ **costs that may not relate to executive performance;** and

■ **some executives may view phantom-stock plans** as having little "actual value."

ESOPs as a Motivation and Compensation Tool for Owners of Emerging-Growth Companies

The Employee Stock Ownership Plan (ESOP) has been established by many corporations to provide employees with ownership of the corporation's stock through tax-deductible contributions made by the employer. ESOPs are also utilized to acquire a portion (or all) of a corporation's outstanding stock from its stockholders, resulting in employee-controlled ownership of the business through a tax-advantaged trust.

The company stock that ESOPs purchase and then allocate to individual employees' accounts can be acquired in various ways. Under some plans, the employer contributes securities or cash every year to the ESOP so it can buy company stock. Most ESOPs, however, obtain bank loans to buy the stock, and the employer may use the proceeds of the stock purchase to expand the business or, in the case of a small company, to fund the owner's personal retirement nest egg. In addition, ESOPs provide the principal business owner some important tax advantages—in addition to the ability to deduct the full payments (principal and interest) on loans obtained through the ESOP.

An ESOP itself may also borrow the money, typically from a bank, to buy the business owner's stake in the company. If, after buying stock from the owner, the ESOP owns at least 30% of the company, the owner may defer capital-gains taxes if the proceeds are invested in other securities, such as stocks and bonds. No capital-gains tax is paid until those investments are sold.

Apart from tax advantages, the most impressive aspect of an ESOP is the potential for productivity gains brought about by increased employee motivation.

Risks in Creating an ESOP

An ESOP can be prohibitively costly for small companies; for those with high employee turnover (such as fast-food outlets and gas stations); or for companies that rely heavily on contract workers (such as real-estate agencies, temporary services or construction companies), who would be barred from participating under applicable IRS guidelines. ESOPs may also pose too many problems for businesses with chronically uncertain cash flow.

An ESOP is contractually obliged to repurchase stock from employees who leave the company or retire, and over time that obligation can cause big headaches if the money isn't available. In addition, an ESOP can be a catastrophe if the company creates one without a commitment to employee participation in management of the company. Employee owners come to expect participation, and if they are shunted aside, they become resentful and management finds that it has created a monster.

From the employee's perspective, an ESOP also poses certain risks. A primary concern is that most of an employee's retirement nest egg is invested in the stock of one small company. If the company goes bankrupt, the employee's ESOP stock holdings may be worthless. However, of the roughly 10,000 ESOPs created over the past 20 years, only 1% has had to file for bankruptcy. There are two general categories of ESOPs:

- **A leveraged ESOP uses borrowed funds** (either directly from the company or from a third party lender based on the guaranty of the company, with the securities of the employer as collateral) to acquire the employer's securities. The ESOP will repay the loan from contributions by the employer and the employees, as well as from any dividends that may be paid on the employer's securities.
- **A non-Leveraged ESOP uses a stock-bonus plan** (or contribution stock-bonus plan with a money-purchase pension plan) that purchases the employer's securities with funds from the employer (not provided by a third party lender) that would have been paid as some other form of compensation.

Legal Considerations in Structuring an ESOP

ESOPs, like all deferred compensation plans, must meet certain IRS minimum requirements. Failure to meet these requirements will result in the employer's contributions not being tax deductible, thereby defeating many of the tax advantages of the ESOP as well as the strategic objectives of the seller. These requirements include:

- **establishing a trust** in order to make contributions and administer the plan. The trust must be for the exclusive benefit of the participants and their beneficiaries.
- **structuring the ESOP so that it is not "top-heavy"** in the allocation of assets and income distribution. The plan must not discriminate in favor of officers, major shareholders or highly compensated employees. For example, a coverage test may require that at least 70% of all non-highly compensated employees must be covered by the plan.
- **the ESOP must benefit no fewer than the lesser of 50 employees** or 30% of the company's employees.
- **the ESOP will invest primarily** in the securities of the sponsoring employer. Although there are no strict guidelines, it is assumed that the ESOP portfolio will include at least 50% to 60% of the employer's securities at any given time. Remaining assets of the ESOP trust should be invested in prudent securities that offer liquidity and diversification of the portfolio.

■ **vesting in compliance with one of the minimum vesting schedules** set forth by the IRS. The plan must adopt either five-year cliff vesting (employee must be fully vested after five years of service but need not be vested at all before that time) or seven-year scheduled vesting (20% is fully vested after three years, and an additional 20% is vested per year until 100% vesting is reached after seven years).

■ **establishing voting requirements** that conform to IRS rules. Voting rights may be vested in the trust's fiduciary agents, except under certain circumstances where rights must be "passed through" to the plan's participants. Generally, passing through becomes an issue when the vote will involve mergers, consolidations, reorganizations, recapitalizations, liquidations, major asset sales and the like. Voting rights "in toto" may be passed through to employees at the discretion of the employer in structuring the plan. Failure to fully "pass through" these rights may raise personnel and productivity problems, because if the employees do not feel like true owners, they may become cynical about the ESOP, thereby defeating a major incentive for adopting it.

■ **complying with IRS rules** regarding the distribution of ESOP benefits and assets. The plan must provide for a prompt (within one year) distribution of benefits to the beneficiary following retirement, disability or death. The nature and specific timing of the distribution will depend in part on the cause for separation from service with the company as well as whether the sponsoring employer is closely held or publicly traded.

■ **contributing based** on a specific percentage of payroll. This could take the form of a money-purchase pension plan (in which a contribution is required based on a percentage of the employee's pay), or may be based on some other formula, such as a percentage of profits, as is the case with some profit-sharing plans. This latter form provides for maximum flexibility in that contributions are completely at your discretion. Each year you make a determination of the appropriate amount of contribution. The plan provides for a minimum contribution sufficient to permit the plan to pay any principal and interest due with respect to a loan used to acquire employer securities. The employer's contribution may be made in cash or other property, including employer's securities. In the event that you contribute your own securities, you may obtain a so-called cashless deduction. You are entitled to deduct the fair market value of the securities so contributed, and the contribution involves no cash outlay on your part.

■ **providing "adequate consideration"** in connection with the purchase of employer stock in an ESOP. This requires that some method for valuation of the shares must be available. For publicly traded companies, this is generally not a problem, because the prevailing market price is a sufficient indication of value. For privately held companies, however, value must be determined by the fiduciary agents of the plan acting in good faith. This will generally require an independent appraisal, initially upon the establishment of the ESOP, and at least annually thereafter.

Legal Documents Needed in the Establishment of an ESOP

There are many legal documents that must be prepared in the organization and implementation of an ESOP. These documents will be prepared by your lawyer, but only after receiving input from all key members of your ESOP team (such as financial and human-resources staff, accountants, investment bankers, commercial lenders, the designated trustee, the designated appraisal firm, etc.). Preliminary analysis should include:

■ **impact on dilution,** ownership, control and earnings of the company;

■ **type of securities to be issued** (common *versus* preferred);

■ **tax deductibility** of contributions and related tax issues;

■ **registration of the securities,** where required, under federal and state securities laws;

■ **employee motivation** and productivity-improvement analysis;

■ **current and future capital requirements** and growth plans of the company;

■ **interplay of the ESOP** with other current or planned employee benefit plans; and

■ **timetable for planning,** organization and implementation of the ESOP.

The ESOP Plan and ESOP Stock Purchase Agreement

The primary issues to be addressed by each of these documents are:

The ESOP Plan
(in which a trust agreement is self-contained)

1. Designation of a name for the ESOP
2. Definition of key terms (e.g., "participant," "year of service," "trustee")
3. Eligibility to participate (standards and requirements)
4. Contributions by employer (designated amount of formula; discretionary)
5. Investment of trust assets, primarily in employer securities (plans for diversification of the portfolio; purchase price for the stock; rules for borrowing by the ESOP, etc.)
6. Procedures for release of the shares from encumbrances (formula to be applied as ESOP obligations are paid down)
7. Voting rights (rights vested in the trustees; special matters trigger-ing employee voting rights)
8. Duties of the trustee(s) (accounting, administrative, appraisal, asset management, record keeping, voting obliga-tions, preparation of annual reports, allocation and distribu-tion of dividends, etc.)
9. Removal of trustee(s)
10. Effect of retirement, disability, death and severance of employment
11. Terms of the "put" option (for closely held companies)
12. Rights of first refusal upon transfer
13. Vesting schedules

ESOP Stock-Purchase Agreement
1. Appropriate recitals
2. Purchase terms for the securities
3. Conditions to closing
4. Representations and warranties of the seller
5. Representations and warranties of the buyer
6. Obligations prior to and following the closing
7. Termination
8. Legal opinion (exhibits, attachments and schedules)

Once these and other factors have been considered, and strategic decisions made, you may instruct your counsel to pre-pare the necessary documentation. In a leveraged ESOP, the documents may include:

- **an ESOP plan;**
- **ESOP trust agreement,** which may be combined with the plan;

- **ESOP loan documentation,** which includes the loan agreement and note guaranty. You may get more than one set—one from the lender, and one for you to give to the ESOP when you make a "mirror-image" loan to the plan;
- **the ESOP stock-purchase agreement,** which allows for stock to be purchased from the employer or its principal shareholders;
- **corporate charter amendments** and related board resolutions; and
- **legal opinion** and valuation reports.

Raising Equity Capital for an ESOP Transaction

There are a wide variety of private-equity and venture-capital firms that specialize in providing the equity capital needed to structure an ESOP and to finance the partial sale of the company to the ESOP. As with all sources of equity capital, the fund managers will require that you and your employee group prepare a business plan.

American Capital Strategies Inc. provides equity financing for ESOPs and management buy-out (MBO) transactions. ACS has provided capital or participated in more than 30 ESOP transactions and only three have been subsequently unsuccessful (on a post-closing basis). In a typical transaction, the employee group will have majority ownership of the company, but ACS will protect its investment and minority stake with control of the board of directors, a series of covenants affecting operations and performance and perhaps wage-and-benefit concessions.

Although you may increase employee motivation and loyalty through ownership in your company, whether through stock awards and options or ESOPs, these plans must be implemented with careful planning and a genuine understanding of the needs and wants of your employees. In addition to seeking sound legal and accounting advice, be sure to take the time to get the feedback of current employees and to address their concerns.

Guidelines for Establishing a Board of Directors and Advisory Board

THE QUALITY OF YOUR COMPANY'S MANAGEMENT team and the staff selected by that team are critical to your growing company's long-term success and to meeting growth objectives. Chapters thus far have focused on recruiting, retaining and compensating the team and avoiding legal problems related to the expansion of your human-capital resources. But to whom does your senior management turn for coaching, mentoring, advice and guidance? Who provides executives with the general policy and direction around which a specific growth plan is built and executed? It can get very lonely at the top, and the CEO must feel that there are objective and trusted advisers that he or she can turn to for advice. For most growing companies, the answer is two-fold: a formal board of directors, and an informal advisory board (or series of boards for specific purposes). People often confuse these two types of boards, but each plays a different role for your company, and they have different responsibilities.

The Board of Directors

Virtually all state corporate laws mandate that a board of directors be established for both publicly owned and privately held corporations. The board owes very specific fiduciary duties to the shareholders of a corporation. The basic governing structure is that the shareholders elect the board's directors, who in turn appoint the officers. The role of the directors is to set broad goals and policy objectives for the company to benefit and protect the interests of the shareholders, and it is incumbent on the officers to develop and implement plans to meet these goals and objectives. A strong board of directors has broad-based business

> **The role of the directors is to set broad goals and policy objectives for the company to benefit and protect the interests of the shareholders.**

experience, strong industry knowledge, adequate time to devote to truly understanding the company's key challenges and weaknesses, the objectivity to challenge decisions made by the management team, and is well connected. In addition, a good board of directors maintains an objective view of the company and its position in its industry, and is not easily discouraged if the company gets off course.

Board members should take their responsibilities very seriously, especially when it comes to critical duties (such as board-meeting preparation and attendance and maintaining confidentiality) and should not be pursuing personal agendas. Each board member and the board as a whole must be constantly guided by the question, What is in the best interest of our shareholders?

Formal Responsibilities of the Board of Directors

There are certain legal duties imposed on a director that must be met in connection with the candidate's service on the board. Each act or decision of the board must be performed in good faith and for the benefit of the corporation. The legal obligations of the directors fall into three broad categories: a duty of care, a duty of loyalty, and a duty of fairness.

DUTY OF CARE. The directors must carry out their duties in good faith with diligence, care and skill in the best interests of the corporation. Each director must actively gather information to make an informed decision regarding company affairs and in formulating company strategies. In doing so, the board member is entitled to rely primarily on the data provided by officers and professional advisers, provided that the board member has no knowledge of any irregularity or inaccuracy in the information. There have been instances in which board members were held personally responsible for misinformed or dishonest decisions made in bad faith, such as the failure to properly direct the corporation or where the board knowingly authorized a wrongful act.

The duty of loyalty requires that each director exercise his or her powers in the interest of the corporation and not in his or her own interest or in the interest of another person or organization.

DUTY OF LOYALTY. The duty of loyalty requires that each director exercise his or her powers in the interest of the corporation and not in his or her own interest or in the interest of another person or organization. The duty of loyalty has a number of practical implications: A director must avoid any conflicts of interest in dealings with the corporation and has a duty not to personally usurp what is more appropriately an opportunity or business transaction to be offered to the corporation. For example, say an officer or director of the company was in a meeting on the company's behalf and a great opportunity to obtain the licensing or distribution rights for an exciting new technology was offered. It would be a breach of the duty of loyalty for the director to try to obtain these rights individually and not first offer them to the corporation.

DUTY OF FAIRNESS. The last duty a director has to the corporation is that of fairness. For example, duty-of-fairness questions may come up if a director of the company is also the owner of the building in which the corporate headquarters are leased and the same director is seeking a significant rent increase for the renewal term. It would certainly be a breach of the duty of fairness to allow the director to vote on this proposal. The central legal concern under such circumstances is usually that the director may be treating the corporation unfairly in the transaction, because the director's self-interest and gain could cloud her or his ability to make an objective decision. When a transaction between an officer or director and the company is challenged, the individual will have the burden of demonstrating the propriety and fairness of the transaction. If any component of the transaction involves fraud, undue overreaching or waste of corporate assets, it is likely to be set aside by the courts. For the director's dealings with the corporation to be upheld, the "interested" director must demonstrate that the transaction was approved or ratified by a disinterested majority of the company's board of directors.

For each member of the board of directors to meet his or her duties of care, loyalty and fairness to the corporation, the following general guidelines should be adhered to. (Many of these guidelines, in a modified format in some cases, can also be used to govern the selection and operation of the company's advisory board.)

THE DIRECTORS SHOULD BE FURNISHED with all appropriate background and financial information relating to proposed board actions well in advance of a board meeting. An agenda, proper notice and a mutually convenient time, place, and date will ensure good attendance records and compliance with applicable statutes regarding the notice of the meetings.

A VALID MEETING OF THE BOARD OF DIRECTORS may not be held unless a quorum is present. The number of directors needed to constitute a quorum may be fixed by the articles or by-laws, but is generally a majority of board members.

WORK WITH YOUR LAWYER to develop a set of written guidelines on the basic principles of corporate law for officers and directors. Keep the board informed about recent cases or changes in the law.

WORK CLOSELY WITH YOUR LAWYER. If the board or an individual director is in doubt as to whether a proposed action is truly in the best interests of the corporation, consult your lawyer immediately—not after the transaction is consummated.

KEEP CAREFUL MINUTES of all meetings and comprehensive records of the information upon which board decisions are based. Be prepared to show financial data, business valuations, market research, opinion letters, and related documentation if the action is later challenged as being "uninformed" by a disgruntled shareholder. Well-prepared minutes will also serve a variety of other purposes. These include written proof of the directors' analysis and appraisal of a given situation, proof that parent and subsidiary operations are being conducted at arm's length and as distinct entities, or proof that an officer had authority to engage in the transaction being questioned.

BE SELECTIVE IN CHOOSING CANDIDATES for the board of directors. Avoid the consideration or nomination of someone who may offer credibility but is unlikely to attend any meetings or have any real input to the management and direction of your company. It is often the case that the most high-profile business leaders are spread too thin with other boards and activities to add any meaningful value to your growth objectives. Such a passive relationship will only invite claims by shareholders for corporate mismanagement. Avoid inviting a board candidate who is already serving on more than five boards or so, depending on his or her other commitments. Similarly, don't accept an invitation to sit on a board of directors of another company unless you're ready to accept the responsibilities that go with it.

IN THREATENED TAKEOVER SITUATIONS or friendly offers to purchase the company, be careful to make decisions that will be in the best interests of all shareholders, not just the board and the officers. Any steps taken to defend against a takeover by protecting the economic interests of the officers and directors (such as lucrative "golden parachute" contracts that ensure a costly exit) must be reasonable in relation to the threat.

ANY BOARD MEMBER WHO INDEPENDENTLY SUPPLIES goods and services to the corporation should not participate in the board discussion or vote on any resolution relating to his or her dealings with the corporation. This will avoid conflict-of-interest claims. A "disinterested" board must approve proposed actions after the material facts of the transaction are disclosed and the nature and extent of the board member's involvement is known.

PERIODICALLY ISSUE QUESTIONNAIRES to officers and directors regarding possible self-dealings or conflicts of interests with the corporation. Provide incoming board members and newly appointed officers with a more detailed questionnaire. Always circulate these questionnaires among the board prior to any securities issuances (such as a private placement or a public offering).

DON'T BE AFRAID TO GET RID OF an ineffective or troublesome board member. Don't let the board member's ego or reputation get in the way of a need to replace that member with someone who is more committed or can be more effective. It may be best to avoid having close friends on the board of directors, as they may be difficult to terminate.

MAINTAIN THE QUALITY OF THE BOARD and measure it against the growth and maturity of your company. Emerging businesses tend to quickly outgrow the skills and experiences of their initial board of directors. Try to recruit and maintain board members who bring strategic benefits to your company, but whose other duties don't prevent them from being effective because of potential conflicts of interests. This is especially true for your outside team of advisers, such as lawyers and auditors, who may not be able to render objective legal and accounting advice if they wear a second hat as a member of the board. These professionals may be able to serve on you advisory board, instead, without a possible conflict of interest.

BOARD MEMBERS WHO OBJECT to a proposed action or resolution should either vote in the negative and ask that such a vote be recorded in the minutes of the meeting, or abstain from voting and promptly file a written dissent with the secretary of the corporation.

Following these rules can help ensure that your board of

directors meets its legal and fiduciary objectives to your company's shareholders and also provides strong and well-founded guidance to your company's executive team to help ensure that growth objectives are met.

The Advisory Board

An advisory board is not governed by state corporate laws, does not owe the same levels of fiduciary duties to the shareholders (and generally cannot be held responsible for their acts or recommendations), and can be much more informal. An advisory board can be assembled for general purposes, or a series of advisory boards could be set up for very specific purposes (such as conducting a technical review, creating a marketing strategy, reviewing recruitment and compensation guidelines, or research and development).

An advisory board can also be an excellent way to get outside expertise on certain matters without severing existing relationships. For example, you may want access to a highly respected business lawyer but may be reluctant to fire your current law firm. Asking that lawyer to serve on your advisory board can be a good compromise. A fast-track growth company will often set up an advisory board in connection with the capital-formation process. This demonstrates to prospective investors in the business plan that the officers of the company have access to a credible and objective source of advice. However, prospective investors will put varying weights on the strength and composition of the board of advisers in making their final investment decisions, and will often want direct access to the advisory-board members as part of their due-diligence process and to ascertain the depth of their commitment.

Unlike recommendations made by the board of directors, management can reject an advisory board's recommendations. Also, because members of the advisory board do not owe the same duties to your company and its shareholders, they can be used in mediating disputes among the officers or between the officers and the directors. They can also be used in identifying potential candidates for the board of directors

continued on page 145

Form of Advisory-Board Member Agreement

This Advisory Board Member Agreement (this "Agreement") is entered into as of [_____, 20____] by and between [_____] (the "Adviser") and Emerging-Growth Company, a [_____] corporation (the "Company").

WHEREAS, the Company has established a Board of advisers (the "Advisory Board") which advises the Company's Board of Directors (the "Board") and executive officers on matters involving [_____];

WHEREAS, the Company has invited the Adviser to serve as a member of the Advisory Board and to serve in such capacity until the earlier of (i) the expiration of the Term (as defined below); or (ii) the Adviser's earlier removal, resignation or death;

WHEREAS, it is a condition to the Adviser's assuming the position of adviser that he, and the Company, execute and deliver this Agreement, in order to delineate the general scope of his duties, to ensure the confidentiality of information presented to the Adviser and to protect the relationship of the Company with its employees and customers.

NOW THEREFORE, in consideration of the foregoing premises, and the mutual covenants contained herein, and for other good and valuable consideration, the receipt and sufficiency of which are hereby acknowledged, the parties hereto agree as follows:

ADVISORY BOARD. The Company hereby appoints the Adviser to its Advisory Board for a period of [_____] beginning on the date hereof and the adviser hereby accepts such appointment; provided that: (i) such appointment shall automatically terminate upon the adviser's death, and (ii) the Company shall be entitled to remove the adviser from the Advisory Board, and the Adviser shall be entitled to resign from the Advisory Board, in either case at any time and for any reason or no reason (that period of time which the Adviser serves as a member of the Advisory Board is hereinafter referred to as the "Term"). In connection with the Adviser's appointment to the Advisory Board and during the Term, the Adviser agrees (i) to meet with the Board or executive officers as called upon from time to time and to advise the person(s) calling such meeting on the [_____] and (ii) to attend regular meetings of the Advisory Board, as may be scheduled or called by the Board or Chief Executive Officer of the Company (the "CEO").

COMPENSATION AND REIMBURSEMENTS. In consideration hereto , and in consideration of the Adviser's Agreement to serve as an adviser on the Company's Advisory Board, the Company: subject to the approval of the Board, shall grant to the Adviser a non-qualified stock option (the "Option") under the Company's 2001 Stock Incentive Plan (the "Plan") to acquire an aggregate of [_____] shares of Common Stock of the Company, [$_____] par value per share, vesting quarterly over a [_____]-year period and exercisable over a five-year period in accordance with the terms and conditions of the Plan and a Non-Qualified Stock-Option Agreement by and between the Company and the Adviser (the "Stock Option Agreement"); shall reimburse the Adviser for all reasonable expenses incurred in attending meetings of the Advisory Board and in performing any other duties requested of him by the Company in accordance with the Company's reimbursement policies.

CONFIDENTIALITY.

Company Information. The Adviser acknowledges that as a member of the Advisory Board, the Adviser will have access to the Company's trade secrets, confidential information, data or other proprietary information, including without limitation information relating to existing products, new products, processes, know-how, designs, specifications, inventions, formulas, methods, developmental or experimental work, improvements, databases, software programs (including source code and object code software source documentation), flow diagrams, development tools, unpublished patent applications, business plans, budgets and unpublished financial information, licenses, prices and costs, suppliers and customers, and information regarding the skills and compensation of employees of the Company (collectively, "Confidential Information"). The Adviser hereby agrees at all times during the Term, and thereafter, to hold in strictest confidence the Confidential Information, and not to use, except for the benefit of the Company, or to disclose to any person or entity the Confidential Information, without the written authorization of the Board and CEO. The confidentiality obligation set forth in this Section 3 shall not apply to Confidential Information that has entered the public domain, other than as a result of the Adviser's breach of this Agreement, or that is required by law to be disclosed; provided that, prior to such legally required disclosure, the Adviser will consult with the Company so that the Company may seek an appropriate order.

Current and Former Employer Information. The Adviser agrees that, during the Term, the Adviser will not improperly use or disclose any confidential or proprietary information or trade secrets of any current or former employers or companies, if any, and will not bring onto the premises of the Company any unpublished documents or any property belonging to any current or former employers or companies unless: (i) consented to in writing by said employ-

(continued on the next page)

Form of Advisory-Board Member Agreement (continued)

ers or companies; and (ii) a copy of such written consent is transmitted to the Board prior to any such use or disclosure otherwise prohibited by this Section 3(b).

Third-Party Information. The Adviser acknowledges that the Company has received and in the future will receive from third parties their confidential or proprietary information subject to a duty on the Company's part to maintain the confidentiality of such information and, in some cases, to use it only for certain limited purposes. The Adviser agrees that he owes the Company and such third parties, both during the Term and thereafter, a duty to hold all such third-party confidential or proprietary information in the strictest confidence and not to disclose it to any person, firm or corporation (except in a manner that is consistent with the Company's agreement with the third party) or use it for the benefit of anyone other than the company or such third party (consistent with the Company's agreement with the third party), unless expressly authorized in writing to act otherwise by an officer of the Company.

NON-SOLICITATION. The Adviser, during the Term and for a period of one (1) year thereafter, shall not directly or indirectly, solicit or encourage any employee or any other person or entity who is a customer or supplier of the Company to terminate, or otherwise interfere in, its then-current relationship with the Company.

ASSIGNMENTS OF INVENTIONS. The Adviser shall disclose promptly to the Company any and all conceptions and ideas for inventions, improvements, discoveries and works, whether or not patentable or copyrightable, which are conceived or made by the Adviser alone or jointly with another during the Term or within six (6) months thereafter and which are related to [_____], the current or future products of the Company or any of its affiliates or subsidiaries, or which the Adviser conceives as a result of his or her activities as an Adviser (collectively, "Proprietary Rights"), and the Adviser hereby assigns and agrees to assign all his or her interests therein to the Company or its nominee. All copyrightable Proprietary Rights shall be considered to be "works made for hire." Whenever requested to do so by the Company, the Adviser shall execute and deliver to the Company any and all applications, assignments or other instruments and do such other acts that the Company shall request to apply for and obtain Letters of Patent of the United States or any foreign country or to otherwise protect the Company's interest therein. In the event the Company is unable for any reason, after reasonable effort, to secure the Adviser's signature on any document needed in connection with the actions specified in this Section 5, the Adviser hereby irrevocably designates and appoints the Company and its duly authorized officers and agents as his or her agent and attorney-in-fact, to act for and on his or her behalf to execute, verify and file any such documents and to do all other lawfully permitted acts to further the purpose of this Section 5 with the same legal force and effect as if executed by the Adviser.

NO CONFLICTING EMPLOYMENT; NO CONFLICTING OBLIGATIONS. During the Term, the Adviser shall not, without the Company's express written consent, engage in any other employment or business activity directly related to the business in which the Company is now involved or becomes involved, nor engage in any other activities which conflict with his obligations to the Company as an Adviser. The Adviser hereby represents, warrants and covenants that his assuming and maintaining the position of Adviser on the Company's Advisory Board does not and will not, during the Term, breach any agreement to keep in confidence information acquired by the Adviser in confidence or in trust prior to and after assuming such position.

RETURN OF COMPANY DOCUMENTS. The Adviser agrees that upon expiration of the Term, for whatever reason, he will (or his personal representative or executor will, in the case of his incapacity or death) deliver to the Company and will not keep in his possession (or in the possession of any representative or executor, or recreate or deliver to anyone else) any and all devices, records, data, notes, reports, proposals, lists, correspondence, specifications, drawings, blueprints, sketches, materials, equipment, other documents or property, together with all copies thereof (in whatever form or media) belonging to the Company, its successors or assigns or relating to the Confidential Information.

NOTIFICATION. The Adviser hereby consents to the Company's notification, during and at any time after the expiration of the Term, of any employer or other applicable third party of his rights and obligations under this Agreement.

LEGAL AND EQUITABLE REMEDIES. The Adviser acknowledges and agrees that the Company would be damaged irreparably in the event any of the provisions of this Agreement are not performed in accordance with their specific terms or otherwise are breached. Accordingly, the Adviser agrees

(continued on the next page)

Form of Advisory-Board Member Agreement (continued)

that the Company shall be entitled to an injunction or injunctions to prevent breaches of the provisions of this Agreement and to enforce specifically this Agreement and the terms and provisions hereof in any action instituted in any court of the United States or any state thereof having jurisdiction over the parties hereto and the subject matter hereof, in addition to any other remedy to which it may be entitled, at law or in equity.

RELATIONSHIP TO THE COMPANY. The Adviser is retained only for the purposes and to the extent set forth in this Agreement and it is expressly understood and agreed by the Adviser and the Company that the Adviser shall serve the Company solely as an independent contractor and not as an employee. The Adviser shall not have any authority to enter into agreements or commitments on behalf of the Company, except as expressly set forth in a writing executed and delivered by the President of the Company as directed by the Board, and the Adviser shall not be entitled to receive any payments from the Company by way of compensation, expenses, reimbursements or otherwise, except for the compensation and reimbursements to be paid by the Company as set forth in Section 2 above. Nothing contained herein shall be construed as making the Adviser an affiliate, owner or employee of the Company.

PUBLICITY. The Adviser will not originate any publicity, news release or other public announcement, written or oral, relating to this Agreement without the Company's prior written consent. Neither the Adviser's name nor that of the Company will be used in any advertising, promotional or sales literature, or other publicity without the prior written approval of the party whose name is to be used; provided, however, that the Adviser hereby consents to the use in any Registration Statement or pre- or post-effective amendment thereto, filed by the Company, with the Securities and Exchange Commission, the National Association of Securities Dealers, Inc., the NASDAQ National Market System, or any other national securities exchange or automated quotation system, or in any other document related thereto, of the Adviser's name and to any other disclosure relating to the Adviser's relationship with the Company or of any agreements between the Adviser and the Company.

TERMINATION. Subject to the provisions of Section 13 below, this Agreement shall terminate upon expiration of the Term.

SURVIVAL. All terms of this Agreement shall survive the assignment of this Agreement by the Company to any successor in interest or other assignee.

The obligations of the Adviser under Sections 3, 4, 5, 7 and 11, the rights of the Company under Sections 5, 8, 9 and 11, and the provisions of this Section 13, shall survive the termination or expiration of this Agreement.

MISCELLANEOUS. Notices. All Notices required or permitted under this Agreement shall be in writing and shall be addressed to the other party at the address set forth below or at such other address or addresses as either party shall designate to the other in accordance with this Section 14(a). All Notices shall be sent by registered or certified mail, return receipt requested, or by Federal Express or other comparable courier providing proof of delivery and shall be deemed date given and received (i) if mailed, on the third business day following the mailing thereof, or (ii) if sent by courier, the date of its receipt.

If to the Company:_____

With a Copy to:_____
(Company's attorney)

If to the Adviser:_____

With a Copy to: _____
(Adviser's attorney)

Governing Law; Consent to Personal Jurisdiction. This Agreement will be governed by and construed according to the internal laws of _____, without regard to the conflicts of law principal thereof. The Adviser hereby expressly consents to the personal jurisdiction of the state and federal courts located in _____ for any lawsuit filed in such court against the Adviser by the Company arising from or relating to this Agreement.

Entire Agreement. This Agreement sets forth the final, complete and exclusive agreement and understanding between the Company and the Adviser relating to the subject matter hereof and supersedes all prior and contemporaneous understandings and agreements relating to its subject matter. No modification of or amendment to this Agreement, nor any waiver of any rights under this Agreement, will be effective unless in writing signed by each of the parties hereto.

(continued on the next page)

Form of Advisory-Board Member Agreement (continued)

Severability. Any term or provision of this Agreement that is invalid or unenforceable in any situation in any jurisdiction shall not affect the validity or enforceability of the remaining terms and provisions hereof or the validity or enforceability of the offending term or provision in any other situation or in any other jurisdiction.

Successors and Assigns. This Agreement will be binding upon the Adviser's heirs, executors, administrators and other legal representatives and will be for the benefit of the Company, its successors and its assigns.

Waiver. No waiver by the Company of any breach of this Agreement shall be a waiver of any preceding or succeeding breach. No waiver by the Company of any right under this Agreement shall be construed as a waiver of any other right. The Company shall not be required to give notice to enforce strict adherence to all terms of this Agreement.

Understand Entire Agreement. THE ADVISER REPRESENTS AND WARRANTS THAT HE HAS READ AND UNDERSTANDS EACH AND EVERY PROVISION OF THIS AGREEMENT AND FURTHER UNDERSTANDS THAT HE IS FREE TO OBTAIN ADVICE FROM LEGAL COUNSEL OF HIS CHOICE, IF DESIRED, IN ORDER TO INTERPRET ANY AND ALL PROVISIONS OF THIS AGREEMENT AND HAS FREELY AND VOLUNTARILY ENTERED INTO THIS AGREEMENT.

IN WITNESS WHEREOF, the parties hereto have executed, or caused to be executed, this Agreement as of the date first above written.

ATTEST: _____
(Secretary)

THE COMPANY
By: _____
Title: _____

ATTEST: _____
(Secretary)

THE ADVISER:
By: _____
Title: _____

(or be recruited for seats on the board).

The rules governing the board of advisers are not mandated under corporate law; therefore, it is critical to be very clear regarding your expectations of each advisory board member, as well as how members will be compensated for their efforts. The best way to clarify these objectives and rewards and avoid conflict about them is to prepare an advisory board member agreement (see the box on pages 138 through 144).

In the early stages of your company's development, the rewards to advisory-board members should be structured in a way that encourages a long-term commitment and proactive, not merely reactive, contributions to your company's growth plans.

Tips for Hiring Effective Outside Advisers

CRITICAL SUCCESS FACTOR FOR FAST-TRACK GROWTH companies is the need to build a team of lawyers, accountants, and consultants, as well as other external professional advisers in a wide variety of business disciplines (such as marketing, sales, finance, strategic planning, and computer systems). The relationship with this team of advisers must be carefully managed to ensure cost efficiency, compatibility among team members and that tasks and problems are assigned to an adviser with the appropriate background and expertise.

Identifying Your Company's Needs

As a general rule, when you hire professional service providers and business consultants, you'll be doing so to fill a particular need, such as:

- **expert advice in a particular field of knowledge;**
- **a readily available pool of human resources** when you can't hire full-time employees;
- **identification and solution of specific problems** or barriers to growth;
- **stimulation or implementation of new ideas,** technology or programs;

- **a sounding board** (or even a shoulder to cry on);
- **access to contacts and resources** (through their Rolodexes); and
- **insights on the successes and failures** of other companies similarly situated.

Once your company's particular need or specific project or problem has been identified, there are certain key questions you must address during the selection process, such as:

- **How does the background,** education and experience of the particular adviser relate to the task or problem you need to resolve?
- **How much does the professional adviser charge for services?** What billing options, if any, are available? Will the firm accept any creative payment options, such as equity for services (see below), deferred fees, reduced rates or project-specific discounts or contingencies? Do rates vary among various members of the firm? How much will it cost to accomplish this specific project to resolve the problem?
- **What is the expertise of the staff members** who will be assigned to your project? Will you be able to get access to other members of the firm with specialized expertise on an as-needed basis?
- **What is the firm's anticipated timetable** for completing the work? What progress reports will you be given? What input will your company's management team have to give to the service provider?
- **What references can the service provider offer?** Who are their clients? Does the firm have any actual or potential conflicts of interest? How does your company compare to the firm's existing client base?

In addition, there are certain myths regarding the use of outside advisers that must be dispelled prior to the commencement of your relationship with them. The more common myths include:

- **The need for an outside consultant** is a sign of your management team's inability, business weakness or failure;
- **Consultants never really understand** the special demands and problems of a company;

■ **Consultants are just too expensive,** especially for what you get in return—a lot of advice about things you already know; and

■ **If these consultants know this industry so well,** then why aren't they running their own companies?

You must understand the exact reason why your company is retaining the adviser, and ask the right questions before hiring one. This will enable you to enter into the relationship with the proper attitude.

The rest of this chapter is devoted to the dynamics of the lawyer-entrepreneur relationship; however, you will find these insights and observations to be equally applicable to relationships with accountants, business consultants, bankers, advertising agencies, and other key advisers.

Finding the Right Lawyer for Your Growing Business

As your company grows, it is likely to undergo a variety of changes in its structure; in the products and services it offers; the markets it serves; and in its capital requirements. Each change will raise a host of legal issues that must be carefully considered prior to implementing a strategy to achieve the next level of growth. As a result, your outside legal counsel should serve as a key member of your external team of advisers and serve as an active participant in the development of your company. The lawyer should be at a firm that is committed to the successful execution of your business-growth plan and be prepared to meet your needs at each stage of your company's growth. When an experienced lawyer is made an integral part of the management team, you will enjoy several benefits, including:

■ **a genuine understanding of the legal hurdles** and requirements raised by a particular proposed strategy or transaction prior to implementation or closing;

■ **an identification of the optimal legal structure** and alternatives for achieving your objectives; and

■ **the cost-savings that result from having a lawyer** who truly understands your basic goals as well as the internal politics and trends affecting your industry.

The costs of having legal counsel participate in the growth-planning and decision-making process will be far outweighed by these benefits.

Entrepreneur-lawyer relationships have changed significantly in recent years. The strength of a personal relationship is no longer enough to sustain a long-term working relationship; nor is the ability to draft an effective contract the measure of a good advocate. Entrepreneurs do not maintain loyalty to their lawyers or other advisers the way they once did. They are more willing than ever to leave a long-term relationship if true insight, efficient performance and other value-added services are not consistently delivered. As the pace of business has become ever faster, the tolerance for mistakes, missed deadlines, exceeding budgets or a lack of business acumen on the part of a business lawyer has decreased.

In this highly competitive legal-services marketplace, the law firms that compete effectively for the business of entrepreneurs are ready to deliver services in a manner that is cost-effective, strategy-driven, takes advantage of all available technologies, and focuses on problem-solving and creative solutions. Today's business lawyers must be knowledgeable as to how technology and the Internet are affecting the growth of small companies, have strong strategic-planning skills and be willing to use their connections to sources of capital and other helpful contacts to benefit their clients. They must be ready to assume the role of trusted adviser and sounding board and offer the resources and experience to have the comfort and the confidence to avoid the need to "oversell" services or to "overbill" for tasks performed.

Selecting Your Business Lawyer

The process of selecting, retaining, and knowing how and when to use a lawyer is among the more important business decisions that an entrepreneur must make, both initially and throughout the growth of the company. Yet, most entrepreneurs express frustration, dissatisfaction and confusion when asked about the law-firm selection and retention process. Among their chief complaints are: high fees, failure to meet deadlines, lack of business savvy, inaccessibility, inability to cut through red tape, inexperienced staff, and a general inability to understand the business ramifications of legal decisions. As a result, lawyers are often viewed as a necessary evil who do not always make the desired contribution to the growth of a business.

The key to a successful attorney-entrepreneur relationship is knowing how to select a lawyer and when to seek his or her advice.

Some entrepreneurs' approach to overcoming the difficulty of finding satisfactory legal counsel is to take matters into their own hands; however, this strategy often backfires and creates even larger legal problems. The key to a successful attorney-entrepreneur relationship is knowing how to select a lawyer and when to seek his or her advice.

The days when your divorce lawyer could also handle a complicated corporate transaction are long gone. Because of the increasing complexity of the law and the ever-growing specialization of the legal profession, the division of assets in your family in a divorce or in estate planning, and the division of assets in your corporation in a merger, acquisition or shareholders agreement must be handled by two very different types of lawyers. Although it is more than likely that the lawyer who prepared your will could also assist in the performance of routine corporate tasks during the formation of your company, as the business expands and its legal needs become more complex, you may quickly find that you've outgrown a general practitioner. You must periodically assess whether your current lawyer or law firm is fully meeting your company's legal needs.

You are likely to have varying personal preferences with respect to the age, experience and interests of the lawyer you hire. However, be sure to weigh carefully the advantages and disadvantages of selecting a lawyer who fits a particular requirement that you set. For example, you may determine that an older, more seasoned lawyer is a top priority. However, the reality may be that an older lawyer with time constraints will assign the project to one who is younger, and less experienced. Not only will you not be getting the experience you sought, but your expenses may also be increased because, although his billable rates are lower, the inexperienced lawyer may take much longer to finish the project assigned to him. Similarly, age and reputation should be viewed with a grain of salt. A lawyer practicing for three years who has devoted all of his or her attention to a given area of law will probably know more about that area of law than would a general practitioner with 30 years experience. Regardless of what your priorities are, the following are criteria that you should use in selecting legal counsel.

RESPONSIVENESS. Your lawyer must be able to meet your timetable for accomplishing a particular transaction or implementing a particular strategy. A lawyer with all the expertise in the world on a given legal topic is of no use to your company if the knowledge can't be communicated in a clear and timely fashion. Make sure that deadlines are discussed and that the lawyer has access to the necessary resources to meet those deadlines.

BUSINESS ACUMEN. A common complaint among business clients is that their lawyers fail to comprehend the business ramifications of legal decisions. Although small companies need an independent and objective legal adviser, they also need a lawyer with business acumen, management and marketing skills, and a genuine understanding of the industry in which the company operates. Lawyers who lack the ability to understand the impact of the law on your business goals and objectives should not make legal decisions and strategies.

REPUTATION. You will obviously want to hire a law firm with a good reputation in the business community and lawyers you can trust with your growth plans. However, reputation goes beyond a series of names on a door or letterhead. In considering the references of any lawyer you might hire, look closely at the foundation on which the reputation has been built. Avoid lawyers who have built a reputation solely on the basis of heavy networking, but who have little actual experience with businesses in your industry. Rather, focus on the quality of the service, the depth of expertise and the business acumen that will allow them to be an effective sounding board.

PHILOSOPHY AND APPROACH. You need to understand a lawyer's or firm's overall philosophy and approach. Are they more inclined to be "deal makers" or "deal breakers"? Are they truly trusted advisers or just a necessary evil? Do they understand the importance of value-added relationships (e.g. bringing more to the table than just good documents or accurate advice)? Are they an asset or a liability to your company's growth and its ability to meet or exceed its business plan?

REPRESENTATIVE CLIENT BASE. A lawyer's list of clients may read like a *Who's Who* of the Fortune 500, but this does not necessarily mean that he or she will understand the legal needs of your growing company. As it has often been said, "A Small Business Is Not a Little Big Business." Yet many corporate lawyers assume that because they have handled a $500 million acquisition, they can understand the legal needs of the parties to a $500,000 transaction. Although some of the legal planning and documentation may be similar, the business goals and philosophies of the parties are likely to be very different. Also evaluate the lawyer's client base to determine whether there are any actual or potential conflicts of interest, complementary resources or whether the lawyer has experience in prior matters that are relevant to your company.

BILLING RATES AND POLICIES. When your resources for legal expenses may be scarce, managing legal costs is of especially great concern. The good news is that increasing competition among lawyers for early- and mid-staged business clients demonstrating growth potential has created a certain amount of flexibility in billing policies. At the same time, however, lawyers at firms of all sizes expect to be paid for quality services rendered within a client's deadline. Therefore, it is important that you are clear about the billing rates and policies before any legal work is begun. One effective means of controlling billing rates and policies (as well as defining related rights and obligations of the lawyer and the client) is the use of a retainer agreement. A retainer agreement is for the protection of both parties because it resolves any mystery about the relationship before any work commences and can be used to establish working budgets that establish cost ranges for specific projects. The components of a well-drafted retainer agreement include:

- **nature of the services** to be provided;
- **compensation** for services rendered;
- **use of initial retainers** or contingent fees;
- **reimbursement** of fees and expenses;
- **conditions for withdrawal** or termination of counsel;
- **counsel's duty** to provide status reports;
- **time limitations** or timetables for completion of work;
- **ceilings or budgets** (if any) for legal fees; and
- **any special provisions** needed in the agreement as a result of the nature of the project (e.g., rules governing media relations, court appearances, protocol, etc.).

EFFICIENCY. You should quickly get out of the habit of relying on legal counsel for basic tasks, such as routine corporate, securities or tax filings, which can be performed in-house at a far lower cost. It is the responsibility of counsel to train a legal-compliance officer within your growing company who will be responsible for recurring legal and administrative tasks. Also, carefully monitor how the lawyer handles projects in order to ensure that assignments are being completed in an efficient and cost-effective manner. For example, tasks that could be performed by a more experienced lawyer in one day at $350 per hour should not be assigned to a more junior associate who will take three days at $175 per hour. Finally, a good lawyer will be the first to tell you when a matter may be outside his or her area of expertise or jurisdiction, at which point another member of his or her firm should be brought in or special counsel should be retained.

KNOWLEDGE AND SKILLS. The type of knowledge and skills that you should look for in a lawyer will naturally be influenced by the specific tasks, assignment or transaction for which you need assistance. If the task involves an adversarial dispute, then a skilled litigator will certainly be more useful than a transactional lawyer will. Conversely, a litigator may be very inappropriate for a complex business deal where the skills of a more diplomatic lawyer would be more effective in negotiating and closing the transaction.

CREATIVITY. The identification and analysis of alternative methods of structuring a transaction or achieving an objective are among the most important tasks that a lawyer performs for an emerging-growth company. The ability to develop creative legal solutions to a client's problems or disputes is clearly one trait that should be sought when selecting legal counsel.

Controlling Your Company's Legal Costs

As businesses grow, an increasingly larger portion of their annual budget must be allocated for the cost of legal services. As a result, many business owners have attempted to control this expense either by avoiding lawyers or by avoiding the invoices sent by them. Neither strategy is effective. Completely ignoring lawyers is likely to result in problems that far outweigh the cost of retaining competent counsel. Similarly, ignoring the legal invoices will lead to tension in the relationship, resentment by counsel toward tasks assigned by the client, or even litigation. The best way to control the cost of legal services is to work with legal counsel in an efficient manner, as follows:

- **Be prepared before a call or meeting with your lawyer.** Gather all facts and review all documents before a telephone call or conference and develop a specific agenda and list of questions.
- **Clearly define your goals and objectives.** Many entrepreneurs don't clearly tell (and lawyers don't ask) their goals and objectives for a given transaction or strategy. If counsel understands your key objectives and negotiating parameters, then your company is likely to get much better value for its legal dollars.
- **A designated legal-compliance officer within your company** should be able to handle the basic forms, correspondence, renewal filings, etc.
- **Do not let executed contracts collect dust.** Most contracts must be

consulted periodically. Failure to understand or perform obligations under a contract will usually lead to litigation.

■ **Request that your lawyer set a ceiling on fees for a given project or transaction.** Lawyers experienced in an area of law should be able to predict the amount of time it will take to accomplish a specific task, absent any special problems, facts or circumstances.

■ **Monitor administrative and incidental expenses.** Ask your lawyer about travel, photocopying, postage and related expenses. If these extra fees are too steep for your budget, ask your lawyer to make alternative arrangements for these services.

■ **Review all bills and invoices carefully.** Insist on an itemized account statement that adequately explains all charges. Be certain that your company is paying only for services that were truly necessary and actually rendered.

■ **Do not pay for the training of an inexperienced lawyer.** Although virtually every legal matter will entail a certain amount of legal research, this does not mean that your company should have to foot the entire bill to train a lawyer who is handling a matter of a particular nature for the first time. Check the bills carefully to monitor exactly which lawyers or paralegals are working on your behalf.

■ **Take a pro-active role in the preparation and negotiation of legal documents.** Insist on participating in the process of identifying alternatives and developing solutions. Request that periodic progress reports be provided to managers who are responsible for the given project or transaction.

■ **Establish guidelines as to who may communicate with legal counsel and for what purposes.** As your company grows, it is likely that a larger number of people will come into contact with legal counsel. If not properly controlled, this will result in mixed signals from your company to the lawyer, unnecessary or duplicate tasks being assigned, or personal matters being handled at your company's expense.

Exchanging Equity for Services

The affordability of securing expert advice from professionals, including law firms, has always presented challenges to early-stage enterprises. The traditional cash-for-services model remains the predominant method of compensating law firms. Recently, however, entrepreneurs have begun to pay for legal services, either in whole or in part, by transferring equity interests in the new companies to law firms.

What follows is a checklist of the key issues and questions that an entrepreneur should consider before transferring equity to a law firm as payment for legal services.

WILL THE LAW FIRM ACCEPT EQUITY? A logical question to ask a law firm before retaining its services is whether the firm would consider accepting some equity in your enterprise as compensation. Some law firms will not accept stock as payment for services as a matter of policy, while others may insist on traditional payment for their services but be willing to make a direct investment in your company either through individual partners or via an internal venture fund. If you receive an affirmative answer, you might also want to ask the law firm how it has structured fee arrangements in the past, and how frequently it has agreed to such alternative-fee arrangements. Each client's arrangement will be structured differently, and no current benchmark exists among the legal industry mandating that a specific percentage of fees should be paid in the form of equity, or in cash.

HOW CAN I CONVINCE THE LAW FIRM TO ACCEPT EQUITY? Perhaps the most difficult challenge facing any entrepreneur who wishes to pay either all or a portion of the company's fees in the form of equity, lies in convincing the law firm that the equity transferred has a cash value equivalent to the legal services performed. Because enterprises at the earliest stages of development face the realistic prospect of eventual failure, it is incumbent upon the entrepreneur to arrive at a fair value for the equity being exchanged for services, which is typically supported by the company's business plan or the company's performance to date.

SHOULD I PAY WITH STOCK OR STOCK OPTIONS? The client must also decide whether to offer actual stock or stock options as payment, a decision that will often have tax implications for the law firm. As a general matter, taxes are deferred on stock options until the options are exercised, while the receipt of stock requires the recipient to report income immediately. Additionally, if you offer stock options, the law firm may demand certain terms, such as a required payout if various conditions occur before the law firm exercises its options.

WILL THE LAW FIRM HAVE A CONFLICT OF INTEREST? Entrepreneur clients should also be aware of the potential conflicts of interest that might arise when a law firm becomes an owner of the enterprise. The law firm's role as objective counselor and adviser to your company can potentially conflict with the law firm's role as a financial stakeholder in the enterprise. A committee of the American Bar Association takes the position that there is nothing illegal or unethical about law firms accepting equity as payment for legal services rendered. According to the committee, however, any such transaction between the law firm and the client must be fair and reasonable to the client; the terms of the transaction must be fully disclosed to the client; the client must consent in writing to the arrangement; and the client must be given a reasonable opportunity to seek a second legal opinion on the matter. The ethical guidelines on this issue are still a bit unclear and few cases exist on this issue that are helpful in structuring the arrangement to avoid conflicts

DO I WANT THE LAW FIRM EXERCISING CONTROL OVER MY BUSINESS? Entrepreneurs must also evaluate the implications on management before transferring an ownership interest in the enterprise to a law firm. Although some entrepreneurs might welcome the prospect of outsiders holding some decision-making power, others might not be comfortable with such an arrangement. Before agreeing on any fee structure with a law firm that involves the transfer of equity, carefully evaluate how the transfer might affect both day-to-day management and the overall business philosophy of your enterprise. Another difficult example is where a transaction may be pending, such as a round of venture-capital financing or an acquisition, where the law firm will be performing legal services but may also be influenced by its own pecuniary interests in the outcome of the transaction. This cloud on objectivity is not likely to be helpful to your company or its shareholders.

IS TRANSFERRING EQUITY A GOOD BUSINESS DECISION? Avoiding the payment of cash for legal services might seem quite tempting at first, because it helps preserve needed funds for operations and other purposes. However, you must consider the long-term implications of such a decision. If the transfer of equity to a law firm would mean compromising core principles of your enterprise, or putting at risk the health and potential growth of your company, soul-searching and self-assessment may be in order. You must look at both the short-term and the long-term consequences before deciding to transfer equity to a law firm.

The relationship between the entrepreneur and the lawyer must be one of synergy, ongoing communication, mutual respect and understanding, and trust and confidence. A shared goal of planning, implementing and monitoring actions will ensure that business objectives come to fruition in a cost effective and trouble free manner. The best interest of the company—its employees, shareholders, assets, products and services, and future—must be placed as the highest priority by legal counsel. Selecting the right lawyer and other key professionals to help your company grow is crucial to its long-term success.

Preventive Law

A concept known as preventive law has become very popular among rapid-growth companies and their legal counsel. Preventive law is a "two-way street" approach to the lawyer-entrepreneur relationship that redefines the nature and purpose of that relationship. Under this approach, legal counsel must be pro-active instead of reactive in identifying potential problems, and the owners and managers (and where applicable, the in-house legal counsel) of the company must work with their outside lawyers to recognize legal issues before they mature into more serious problems or conflicts.

Preventive law dictates that certain periodic steps are taken that enable legal counsel to properly assess the legal health of the rapidly growing company and prescribe a set of strategies and solutions for any problems identified in the check-up. This legal check-up is often referred to as a "legal audit."

Understanding the Legal Audit

In a legal audit, your growing company's management team meets with outside legal counsel in order to:

- discuss strategic plans and objectives;
- review key documents and records; and
- analyze and identify current and projected legal needs of your company.

The legal audit also lays the groundwork for the establishment of an ongoing legal compliance and prevention program to ensure that your growing company's goals, structure and ongoing operations comply with the latest developments in business and corporate law. Finally, the legal audit helps managers identify the legal issues triggered by changes in strategies, goals or objectives and allows the planning of legal tasks that must be accomplished as a result of the issues identified.

A comprehensive legal audit will examine a wide range of issues that may be as mundane as whether or not the company is qualified to do business in foreign jurisdictions, or as complex as an analysis of the company's executive-compensation and retirement plans, to ensure consistency with current tax and employment law regulations. The topics that must be addressed in a legal audit include:

- choice and structure of the entity;
- recent acts of the board of directors and documentation (or lack thereof) relating to those decisions;
- protection of intellectual property;
- forms and methods of distribution and marketing;
- pending and threatened litigation;
- estate planning;
- insurance coverage;
- hiring and firing practices;
- employment agreements;
- securities law compliance;

- **antitrust and related trade regulations;**
- **product liability and environmental law; and**
- **a review of sales and collection practices.**

The extent and complexity of your company's legal audit will vary depending on the size and stage of growth of the company, the type of business you're in (service *versus* manufacturing), the number of shareholders and employees you have, the extent to which your company does business in a regulated industry, and a host of other factors.

A legal audit may be performed on a periodic basis as part of an ongoing compliance program or may be performed in connection with a specific event, such as a financial audit, or in connection with a specific transaction, such as an acquisition or securities offering. There are also specialized legal audits in specific areas such as tax, labor and employment, estate planning/asset protection, government contracts, franchising compliance, and environmental law audits.

The Legal-Audit Process

THE PRELIMINARY QUESTIONNAIRE. The legal audit should begin with a comprehensive questionnaire for your company's management team to review and address prior to the arrival of the team of lawyers who are to conduct the audit. In the case of smaller companies, a simple checklist of issues or a formal agenda will be more than sufficient to prepare for the initial conference. (See pages 163 through 170 for a closer look at the legal-audit questionnaire.)

THE INITIAL CONFERENCE. Once the documents and related materials requested in the questionnaire have been assembled and problem areas preliminarily identified, schedule a meeting between audit counsel and the designated officers of your company who are well-versed in the various aspects of its operations. Related members of the management team, such as the company's outside accountant and other professionals that play key advisory roles to the company, should be present during at least the portion of the audit that relates to their area of expertise. This initial series of conferences is basically an information-gathering exercise to familiarize the legal auditor with the most current information about all aspects of your company. The audit team should also perform some onsite observations of your company's day-to-day operations. The legal-audit team should also review the company's current financial statements and spend some time with your company's accounting firm.

IMPLEMENTATION OF THE POST-AUDIT RECOMMENDATIONS. Once the legal-audit team has issued its post-audit evaluation to your company's management team, the recommendations of the report can be implemented. The steps that follow will vary, depending on the growth planned by your company as well as the specific findings of the report. At a minimum, schedule meetings with key personnel to review and discuss the post-audit recommendations; prepare internal memos to inform rank-and-file employees; conduct employee seminars to educate employees about proper procedures and compliance; and in certain cases, develop handbooks and operations manuals for guidance of the company's staff. If significant problems are discovered during the audit, counsel should be careful as to what is included in the final written report to avoid potential adverse consequences down the road under the federal or state rules of evidence. In addition, establish a "tickler system" for periodic reporting and key dates or deadlines, as well as a time set for the next legal audit.

The failure to have an independent legal audit performed by qualified legal counsel can have a significant adverse impact on a company. The risks of non-compliance with the many laws and regulations include:

- **Failure to keep proper books and records** or mixing personal assets with business assets, which could lead to litigation by co-owners or to an ability by third parties to "pierce the corporate veil," thereby removing the limited-liability protection of a corporation, or LLC;
- **Failure to obtain all proper permits and licenses,** which could lead to fines and penalties (and in come cases even closure of the business) by governmental agencies;

■ **Failure to comply with certain laws and regulations,** which may lead to problems under federal law with agencies such as the IRS, the EEOC, the EPA, and even the SEC;

■ **Failure to have employment applications,** personnel handbooks and general employment policies reviewed periodically, which could give rise to governmental and civil liability;

■ **Failure by the directors of the company** to keep accurate records and minutes of its decision-making procedures (e.g., proving that directors are exercising informed judgment), which could subject the company and its board to liability from its shareholders and investors; and

■ **Failure to monitor the company's reporting requirements,** which may put it into default with lenders or investors.

The Legal-Audit Questionnaire

The purpose of the legal-audit questionnaire is to give your outside legal advisers as comprehensive a picture of your company as possible, thereby enabling them to tailor their assistance to your company's specific needs. The following topics should be covered in the legal-audit questionnaire.

CORPORATE MATTERS. Under what form of ownership is the company operated? When was this decision made? Does it still make sense? Why or why not? Have all annual filings and related actions such as state corporate annual reports or required director and shareholder meetings been satisfied? What are your company's capital requirements in the next 12 months? How will you raise this money? What alternatives are being considered? What issues are triggered by these strategies? Have you considered applicable federal and state securities laws in connection with these proposed offerings?

Will key employees be offered equity in your enterprise as an incentive for performance and loyalty? Is such equity available? Have the adoption of such plans been properly authorized? Will the plan be qualified or non-qualified? Up to what point? Has anyone met with your key employees to ascertain their goals and preferences? Have all necessary stock-option plans and employment agreements been prepared and approved by the shareholders and directors of the company?

Will any of the founders of the company be retiring or moving on to other projects? How will this affect the current structure? If your company is a corporation, was an election under Subchapter S ever made? Why or why not? If the entity is an "S corporation," does it still qualify? Is such a choice unduly restrictive as your company grows (e.g., hampering ability to attract foreign investment, allowing taxation of undistributed earnings, etc.)? If the entity is not a Subchapter S corporation, could it still qualify? Is this a more sensible entity under the applicable tax laws? Or should a limited liability company (LLC) be considered as an alternative?

Have all necessary stock-option plans and employment agreements been prepared and approved by the shareholders and directors of the company?

Have by-laws been prepared and carefully followed in the operation and management of the corporation? Have annual meetings of shareholders and directors been properly held and conducted? Have the minutes of these meetings been properly and promptly entered into the corporate record book? Have transactions "outside the regular course of business" been approved or ratified by directors (or where required by shareholder agreements or by-laws) and resolutions been recorded and entered into the corporate records? Are there any "insider" transactions or other matters that might constitute a conflict of interest? What checks and balances are in place to ensure that these transactions are properly handled?

Have quorum, notice, proxy and voting requirements been met in each case under applicable state laws? To what extent does your company's organizational and management chart reflect reality? Are customers and suppliers properly informed of the limits of authority of your employees, officers or other agents of the company?

BUSINESS-PLANNING MATTERS. Has a business and management plan been prepared? Does it include information about your company's key personnel; strategic objectives; realistic and well documented financial statements; current and planned products and services; market data, strategy and evaluation of competition; capital structure and allocation of proceeds; capital-formation needs; customer base; distribution network; sales and advertising strategies; facility and labor needs; risk factors; and realistic milestones and strategies for the achievement of these plans and objectives? How and when was the business plan prepared? Has it been reviewed and revised on a periodic basis or is it merely collecting dust on a manager's bookshelf? Has it been changed or supplemented to reflect any changes in your company's strategies, plans or objectives? To whom has the plan been shown? For what purposes? Have steps been taken to preserve the confidential nature of the document? To what extent have federal and state securities laws been reviewed to prevent violations due to the misuse of the business plan as a disclosure document?

How and when was the business plan prepared? Has it been reviewed and revised on a periodic basis or is it merely collecting dust on a manager's bookshelf?

COMPLIANCE WITH GOVERNMENTAL AND EMPLOYMENT-LAW REGULATIONS. Have you filed all required federal and state tax forms (i.e., employer's quarterly and annual returns, federal and state unemployment-tax contributions, etc.)? Are you meeting federal and state record-keeping requirements for tax purposes? Have you established all payroll and unemployment-tax accounts? Has the company been qualified to do business in each state where such a filing is required? Have you obtained all required local business permits and licenses? Are the company's operational policies in compliance with OSHA, EEOC, NLRB, and zoning requirements? Has the company ever had an external environmental-law compliance audit performed? Has the company developed smoking, substance-abuse testing, child-labor laws, family leave or child care policies and programs that are in compliance with federal, state and local laws? Have you made modifications to the workplace in compliance with the Americans with Disabilities Act? Have you taken steps to ensure compliance with applicable equal-employment opportunity, affirmative action, equal pay, wage and hour, immigration, employee benefit, and worker's compensation laws? When is the last time the company consulted these statutes to ensure that current practices are consistent with applicable laws? Has the company prepared an employment manual? When is the last time it was reviewed by qualified counsel?

EMPLOYEE BENEFIT PLANS. Has your company adopted a medical-reimbursement plan? Group life insurance? Retirement plans? Disability plans? If not, should such plans be adopted? If yes, have you made all amendments to the structure and ongoing management of these plans to maintain qualification? Have you filed annual reports with the U.S. Department of Treasury, and are your pension and profit-sharing plans filed with U.S. Department of Labor? Have you made any changes in the administration of these plans? Have there been any recent transactions between the plans and the company, its trustees or its officers and directors?

CONTRACTUAL MATTERS. On which material contracts is the company directly or indirectly bound? Did you draft these agreements in compliance with applicable laws, such as your state's version of the Uniform Commercial Code? Is your company still able to meet its obligations under these agreements? Is any party to these agreements in default? Why? What steps have been taken to enforce the company's rights and/or mitigate damages? To what extent are contractual forms used when selling company products and services? When is the last time these forms were updated? What problems have these forms triggered? What steps have you taken to resolve these problems? Are employees who possess special skills and experience under an employment agreement with your company? When was the last time the agreement was reviewed and revised? What about sales representatives? Are they under some form of a written agreement and commission schedule? Has the scope of their authority been clearly defined and communicated to the third parties with whom they deal? To what extent does your company hire independent contractors? Have you prepared agreements with these parties? Have you included the intellectual-property issues, such as "work for hire" provisions, in these agreements?

PROTECTION OF INTELLECTUAL PROPERTY. To what extent are trademarks, patents, copyrights and trade secrets among the intangible assets of your business? What are the internal company procedures for these key assets? What agreements (such as ownership of inventions, nondisclosure and noncompete) have you struck with key employees who are exposed to the company's intellectual property? What procedures are in place for receiving new ideas and proposals from employees and other parties? What steps have been taken to protect the company's "trade dress," where applicable? Have you registered trademarks, patents and copyrights? What monitoring programs are in place to detect infringement and ensure proper usage by third parties? Are documents properly stamped with copyright and confidentiality notices? Have you contacted your counsel to determine whether any new discovery is eligible for registration? Does your company license any of its intellectual property to third parties? Has experienced licensing-and-franchising counsel prepared the agreements and disclosure documents?

RELATIONSHIPS WITH COMPETITORS. How competitive is your industry? How aggressive is your company's approach toward its markets and competitors? What incentives does your company offer to attract and retain customers? To what professional and trade associations does your company belong? What type of information is exchanged? Does the company engage in any communication or hold any cooperative agreement with a competitor regarding price, geographic territories or distribution channels that might constitute an antitrust violation or an act of unfair competition? Has your company established an in-house program to educate employees about the mechanics and pitfalls of antitrust violations? Has an antitrust action ever been brought or threatened by or against your company? What were the surrounding facts? What was the outcome? Have you recently hired a former employee of a competitor? How was he or she recruited? Does this employee use skills or knowledge gained from the prior employer? To what extent have you notified the prior employer? What steps are being taken to avoid a lawsuit involving misappropriation of trade secrets or interference with contractual regulations? Does the company engage in comparative advertising? How do you generally treat the products and services of the competitor? Are any of your trademarks or trade names similar to those of competitors? Have you been involved in any prior litigation with a competitor? Threatened litigation?

FINANCING MATTERS. What equity and debt financing have you obtained in the past three years? What continuing reporting obligations or other affirmative or negative covenants remain in place? What triggers a default and what new rights are created to the investors or lenders upon default? What security interests remain outstanding?

MARKETING AND DISTRIBUTION ISSUES. Has your company clearly defined the market for its products and services? Who are the key competitors? What are their respective market shares, strengths, weaknesses, strategies, and objectives? What new players are entering this market? What barriers exist to new entry? What is the saturation point of this market? What are the key distribution channels for bringing these products to market? Have you addressed all necessary agreements and regulations affecting these channels (i.e., labeling and warranty laws, consumer-protection laws, pricing laws, distributorship agreements, etc.)? If your company is doing business abroad, have you carefully reviewed all import and export regulations? Has a system been established to ensure compliance with the Foreign Corrupt Practices Act? Are you considering franchising as a method of marketing and distribution to expand market share? To what extent can all key aspects of your company's proven success be reduced to an operations manual and taught to others in a training program? To what extent are competitors engaged in franchising? If franchising is appropriate for distribution of your company's products or business, has an experienced franchise legal counsel prepared all necessary offering documents and agreements? What initial franchise fee will be charged? What ongoing royalties will be charged? Are these fees competitive? What ongoing programs and support will you give to franchisees? What products and services must the franchisee buy from your company? Under what conditions may one franchise be terminated or transferred? Are any alternatives to franchising being considered? Has your company looked at dealer termination, multi-level marketing or pyramid laws?

If your company is doing business abroad, have you carefully reviewed all import and export regulations?

Legal audits offer an inexpensive, yet comprehensive method of making sure that the small and growing company's plans and objectives are consistent with developments in the law. The process helps to identify problem areas, maintain legal compliance, offer legal solutions and alternatives for the achievement of the company's short- and long-term business objectives, and forces your company's leaders to re-evaluate the company's strategies in light of the legal costs, risks and problems that have been identified in the audit.

Legal regulations and considerations govern nearly every aspect of business development and growth directly or indirectly. You must be familiar with the legal constraints and projections relevant to your particular enterprise, and each manager in your company must understand the legal costs, benefits and risks of each management, marketing and financial decision he or she makes.

The selection and retention of legal counsel that can meet your growing company's evolving legal requirements is crucial to its long-term success. The interview and selection process should include a careful analysis of the lawyer's reputation, billing policies, experience, understanding of rapid-growth companies, efficiency, and responsiveness. Once you have selected a lawyer, he or she should serve as a key member of your company's management team responsible for strategic planning, implementation and ongoing evaluation.

The Capital Requirements for Business Growth

Key Components of a Capital-Formation Strategy

V IRTUALLY ALL TYPES OF FAST-TRACK GROWTH strategies, especially the organic-growth strategies such as internal expansion or mergers and acquisitions, will require capital for successful implementation. Your ability to develop a viable capital-formation strategy for your company will ultimately determine the company's long-term success. In an environment where the capital markets are tightening, it is more important than ever that your company and its business-growth plans focus on solid revenues, real profits, strong customer relationships, and technology that provides a genuine competitive advantage. This chapter offers an overview of the development of a capital-formation strategy, with an emphasis later in the chapter on budgeting and forecasting for successful capital formation.

You would have to have be doing your best Rip Van Winkle imitation not to have realized that 2000 and 2001 were very volatile years from an economic, political and technological perspective. And we all face at least the next few years with some genuine fears and concerns: Are we on the edge of a recession? What will the Bush administration do to foster the needs of small and growing companies? Which companies will survive the dot-com shakeout? Will global markets remain strong? We'll learn a lot more about the answers to these questions as time passes, but until then, here are a few of my observations and predictions.

Capital-Formation Trends Affecting Small and Growing Businesses in the Foreseeable Future

THE NEXT FEW YEARS WILL BE VERY DARWINIAN. Unlike the past few years, only smart and strong companies did well in 2001 and will prosper in the years ahead. There is simply not enough fat in capital markets or the workforce to take the weak along for the ride. There has been a definite return to reality, a refocusing on business fundamentals. There will be more emphasis on protecting and building on what you have, rather than focusing on rapid growth. Entrepreneurs must be flexible and highly responsive to market changes and customer needs, and should be extra careful in the management and use of precious resources. The party is not over but the bouncer at the door just got a lot bigger and is being more selective about who gets in to the party—and who stays in!

GROWTH MUST BE STRATEGIC AND CREATIVE. The capital markets for small and midsize companies now and over the next few years will not be as accessible or as affordable as they were in 1999 and early 2000. Therefore, your plans to grow your business must be more strategic and more creative than ever before, with a greater focus on partnering, licensing, alliances and even domestic and international franchising.

VALUATIONS MUST BE REALISTIC. If you are lucky enough to raise capital for your growing company in the near future, don't expect the sky-high valuations that entrepreneurial companies enjoyed during the last 1990s. Venture investors have returned to ground level and realize that many of their investments will not qualify for an initial public offering twelve months later! Therefore, be prepared to give up more ownership for smaller amounts of capital and possibly even more control if you need to raise equity capital. The capital markets are now focused on very specific opportunities, not large-scale sectors or trends. There is no forgiveness or room for mediocrity just because your company is in a "hot sector." You need to extend your time horizons and narrow your expectations. The markets want to see real value created prior to the next round of capital infusion. Your window to the next round will be larger as a result of this emphasis on real accomplishment. You need to be more creative and aggressive in your search for capital, turning over new stones such as strategic financing from customers, vendors or corporate venture capitalists, three sources that are expected to grow significantly over the next few years.

YOU WILL NEED TO HIRE THE STRONG-WILLED AND THE PATIENT. It has always been difficult for emerging-business owners to compete with their larger competitors to recruit and retain qualified personnel. The early-state business owner's most recent "secret weapon" to attract human capital has been the promise and potential upside of stock options. But qualified workers have been sufficiently burned by worthless options, failed IPOs and dilutive mergers so that these plans may no longer serve as an effective carrot. To combat this trend, take the extra time to look for potential employees who are not as focused on the "rapid rise to riches" and may be willing to trade a friendly and flexible atmosphere for the higher salaries offered by your larger competitors.

MAKE TECHNOLOGY YOUR FRIEND. You will need to use the Internet and available communications technologies more strategically than ever to survive in the highly competitive business environment that this first decade of the new millennium is bringing. The entrepreneurship boom of the '90s means that more companies of all sizes will be competing for the same customers and available market share. It will be critical that you take advantage of Internet-based resources to gather competitive data, generate new leads, find opportunities for cost-savings, and learn new information that will help you manage your business and level the playing field in competing against larger companies.

"BEST TO MARKET" BEATS "FIRST TO MARKET." Ray Kroc did not invent the cheeseburger anymore than Steve Jobs invented the computer or Fred Smith invented the mail-delivery system. But all three were visionaries regarding the potential of these products and services, and they built their companies around these opportunities. They were aggressive, creative, and persistent, and they had an ability to convince others to buy into their vision and share their dream, on a foundation of trust, integrity and substance. All three of these entrepreneurs brought new applications to existing industries and then trained their customers to become comfortable with the new paradigms that they had created. Suddenly, almost overnight, having a meal in three minutes, a personal computer at your desk and a package delivered overnight became not the exception, but the rule. These men set a new standard that everyone else had to emulate and improve upon. That's what great entrepreneurs do—they get an entire industry to jump higher, run faster and move farther, by raising the bar each time that everyone else starts to get comfortable or complacent.

So what will it take to raise capital and manage growth in this volatile environment? To continue to flourish, your emerging-growth company needs to put (and keep) in place the following:

- **a strategy and commitment** to protecting and leveraging your company's intellectual property;
- **an experienced and mature management team** that knows how to actually *make* money, not just raise money;
- **a business model that will produce sustainable and durable revenue streams** (for example, targeted customers who can actually pay for what they buy from you);
- **a genuine understanding of the strengths, weaknesses** (and likely next moves) of your competitors;
- **a corporate culture that is more focused on financial performance** and financial tables than pool tables and chill-out rooms; and
- **a leadership vision that is more focused** on keeping your eyes on the road rather than searching for the next exit strategy.

The Key Elements of a Capital-Formation Strategy

All capital-formation strategies (or, put simply, ways of raising money) revolve around a balancing of four critical factors: *risk, reward, control* and *capital* itself. You and your source of venture funds will each have your own ideas as to how these factors should be weighted and balanced. Once a meeting of the minds takes place on these key elements, you'll be able to do the deal.

RISK. Venture investors need to mitigate their risk, which you can help them accomplish by having a strong management team, a well-written business plan and the leadership to execute the plan.

REWARD. The rewards desired by the venture investor may vary depending on the type of investor you are working with. Your objective, however, is to preserve your right to participate in a significant share of the growth in the value of your company as well as any subsequent proceeds from the sale or public offering of the company.

CONTROL. It's often said that the art of venture investing is "structuring the deal to have 20% of the equity with 80% of the control." While that may be a bit of hyperbole, depending on the venture firm's philosophy and its lawyers' creativity, there are many different tools available to venture investors to exercise control and reduce risk. Only you can dictate which levels and types of controls are acceptable, but remember that the higher the risk of the deal, the higher the degree of control the investor will demand.

CAPITAL. Negotiations with venture investors often focus on how much capital they will provide, when they will provide it, what types of securities they will purchase (preferred stock, convertible notes, or debt with warrants, for example) and at what valuation, what special rights will attach to the securities and what mandatory returns will be built into the securities. Before approaching a venture capitalist, carefully consider how much capital you really need, when you will need it, and whether there are alternative sources for that capital.

Regardless of your industry sector, the state of the economy, or any other variable, in addition to balancing these four components in a manner satisfactory to your investor, you must also present prospective investors with the following:

■ **a focused and realistic business plan** that is based on a scalable and defensible business and revenue model;

■ **a strong and balanced management team** with an impressive individual and group track record;

■ **wide and deep targeted markets,** rich with customers who want and need (and can afford) your company's products and services; and

■ **some sustainable competitive advantage** that can be supported by real barriers to entry (the best barriers are those created by proprietary products or brands that are owned exclusively by your company).

Finally, there should be some sizzle to go with the steak. This may include excited and loyal customers and employees, favorable media coverage, nervous competitors who are genuinely concerned that you may be changing the industry, and a clearly defined exit strategy that allows your investors to be rewarded for taking the risks of investment within a reasonable period of time.

Understanding the Different Types of Investors

Most investors fall into at least one of the following categories: emotional investors, who invest in you out of love or because of a relationship; strategic investors, who invest in the synergies offered by your business (although financial return may be a factor, the primary motivation for such investors is non-financial and may be based on a strategy to grow their own businesses through access to your resources); and financial investors, whose primary or even exclusive motivation is a return on capital, and who invest in the financial rewards that your business plan (if properly executed) will produce.

Your approach, plan and terms may vary depending on the type of investor you're dealing with, so it's important for you to understand a prospective investor's objectives well in advance. Your goal is to meet those objectives without compromising the long-term best interests of your company and its shareholders. Achieving that goal is challenging, but can be easier than you might think, if your team of advisers has extensive experience in meeting everyone's objectives to get deals done properly and fairly. The more preparation, creativity and pragmatism your team shows, the more likely that the deal will get done on a timely and affordable basis.

The more preparation, creativity and pragmatism your team shows, the more likely that the deal will get done on a timely and affordable basis.

Understanding the Different Sources of Capital

You have two basic choices in your search for capital to grow your company: debt or equity. Defining your "optimal capital structure"—a proper balance between the two—is a challenge, as is finding these sources of capital at affordable rates. The guidelines for determining affordability vary depending on whether you're pursuing debt or equity. For debt, affordability refers to the term, interest rate, amortization, and the penalties for nonpayment. For equity, affordability refers to worth (known as valuation), dilution of the shares or control held by the current owners, as well as any special terms or preferences (such as mandatory dividends or redemption rights).

Sources of Debt Financing

For small or growing companies, there is a wide variety of sources for debt financing. The following are some of the most common.

COMMERCIAL BANKS. Small companies are much more likely to find an attentive audience with a commercial loan officer after the start-up phase has been completed. In determining whether or not to extend debt financing (essentially, make a loan) to your business, bankers will first look at your general credit rating, collateral, and your ability to repay. Bankers will also closely examine the nature of your business, your management team, competition, industry trends, and the way you plan to use the proceeds. A well-drafted loan proposal and business plan will go a long way toward demonstrating your company's credit-worthiness to the prospective lender.

COMMERCIAL-FINANCE COMPANIES. Many companies who seek debt financing but are rejected by banks turn to commercial-finance companies for credit. These companies usually offer debt financing at considerably higher rates than an institutional lender, but they might provide lower rates if you pay for other services they offer, such as payroll and accounts-receivable management. Because of fewer federal and state regulations, commercial-finance companies generally have more flexible lending policies and more tolerance for risk than do traditional commercial banks. However, commercial-finance companies are just as likely as commercial banks to reduce their risk with higher interest rates and more stringent collateral requirements for loans or credit to undeveloped companies.

STATE AND LOCAL GOVERNMENT LENDING PROGRAMS. In an effort to foster economic development, many state and local governments provide direct capital or related assistance through support services or even loan guarantees to small and growing businesses. The statutes authorizing the creation of the development agency usually regulate the amount and terms of the financing.

TRADE CREDIT/CONSORTIUMS. Many growing companies overlook an obvious source of capital or credit when exploring their financing alternatives: suppliers and customers. Suppliers have a vested interest in the long-term growth and development of their customer base and may be willing to extend favorable trade-credit terms or even provide direct financing to help fuel a good customer's growth. Similar principles apply to customers who rely on the company as a key supplier of resources. The consortium is an emerging trend in customer-related financing. Under this an arrangement, a select number of key customers finance the development of a particular product or project in exchange for a right of first refusal or territorial exclusivity for the distribution of the finished product. Carefully examine applicable federal and state antitrust laws before structuring a consortium.

> **Many growing companies overlook an obvious source of capital or credit when exploring their financing alternatives: suppliers and customers.**

LEASING COMPANIES. Leasing can provide a variation on debt financing if your company is looking for capital to purchase equipment. Leasing typically takes one of two forms:

- **Operating leases usually include both the asset and a service contract** over a period of time (which is typically less than the actual useful life of the asset). The total payments under the operating-lease contract aren't sufficient to cover the full value of the equipment, which usually means lower monthly payments for you. If negotiated properly, the operating lease will contain a cancellation clause, which gives you the right to cancel the lease (with little or no penalty). This would provide you with more flexibility in the event that sales decline or the equipment leased becomes obsolete.
- **Capital leases differ from operating leases** in that they usually don't include any maintenance services and involve your use of the equipment over the asset's full useful life.

Sources of Equity Capital

In your search for equity financing, you may be able to tap one or more of the following sources.

continued on page 184

The Capital Formation "Reality Check" Strategic Pyramid

There are dozens of different ways to raise capital for your growing business. However, some strategies will be more likely to succeed than others based on your stage of growth as well as the current trends within your industry. There are also certain traditional "stepping stones" that are usually followed. As you move up the strategic pyramid at right, there are fewer choices for raising capital, and the criteria for qualifying become more difficult to meet, thereby reducing your chances of rising to that level. It is also important to bear in mind that each source of capital on each rung may judge you on the quality and success of the deal made on the prior rung. In other words, angels may judge you by the extent of your own commitment, venture capitalists (VCs) may judge you by the extent of the commitment and reputation of the angels that you attract and investment bankers may judge you by the track record of the venture capitalists that commit to your deal.

1. Your own money/resources (credit cards, home-equity loans, savings, 401(k) loans, etc.). A necessary precursor for most venture investors. (Why should we give you money if you're not taking a risk?)

2. The money/resources of your family, friends, key employees, etc. Investments based on trust and relationships.

3. Small Business Administration/ microloans/general small-business commercial lending. Very common but requires collateral (tough in intangible-driven businesses).

4. Angels (wealthy families, cashed-out entrepreneurs, etc.). Found by networking/or on the Internet/ smaller angels versus super angels. Rapidly growing sector of venture-investment market, but avoid taking money from someone who can't afford to lose it.

5. Bands of angels that are already assembled. Syndicates, investor groups, private investor networks, pledge funds, etc. Find out what's out there in your region and get busy networking.

6. Private Placement Memoranda (PPM) under Regulation D. Groups of angels that you assemble. You need to understand federal and state securities laws, have a good hit list and know the needs of your targeted group.

7. Larger-scale commercial loans. You'll need a track record, a good loan proposal, a banking relationship and some collateral.

8. Informal VC. strategic alliances, Fortune 1000–Corp. VCs, global investors, etc. Synergy-driven: more patient, more strategic. Make sure you get what was promised.

9. Early-stage venture capital/ seed-capital funds (SBICs). A small portion (less than 15%) of all VC funds; very competitive, very focused niche—typically more patient, and has less aggressive return-on-investment (ROI) needs. These are typically called "A" round investors and you should aim to raise enough money at this stage to bring your product or service to the marketplace.

10. Institutional venture-capital market. Usually 2nd- or 3rd-round money. You'll need a track record or very hot industry. They see hundreds of potential deals and make only a handful each year.

11. Big-time venture capital (VC). Large-scale institutional VC deals (called "B"- and "C"-round investors, to sustain growth as well as prepare for IPO or merger and acquisitions [M&A] exit strategies).

12. Initial Public Offerings (IPOs). The grand prize of capital formation.

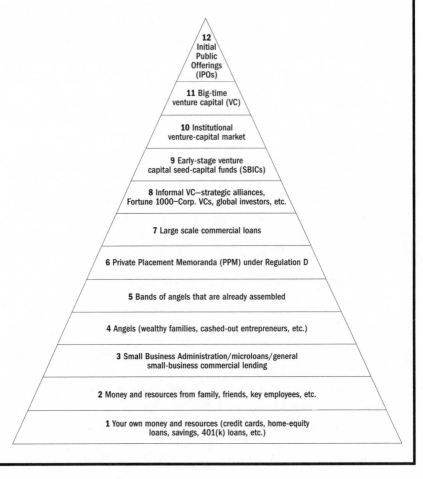

PRIVATE INVESTORS. Many early-stage companies receive initial equity capital from private investors, either individually or as a small group. These investors are called "angels" or "bands of angels"—and are a rapidly growing sector of the private-equity market.

INSTITUTIONAL VENTURE-CAPITAL FIRMS. Perhaps the best-known source of equity capital for entrepreneurs in recent years has been the traditional venture-capital firm. These formally organized pools of venture capital helped create Silicon Valley and the high-technology industry, our nation's fastest-growing business sector. However, these funds do very few deals each year, in comparison with the total demand for growth capital, so be ready for look to other sources. (Venture-capital firms will be covered in greater detail in Chapter 12.)

MERGERS AND ACQUISITIONS (M&AS). Merger with or acquisition by a cash- or asset-rich company can provide a viable source of capital for your growing company. This kind of transaction triggers many legal, structural and tax issues that the seller of a business must consider. The number of deals in the middle-market merger-and-acquisition sector may be increasing due to the impact of consolidation on technology; the "trickle-down" of the mega-mergers of the late 1990s; and the need for midsize companies to remain competitive in an age of mostly megacompanies and small niche players. (Mergers and acquisitions are the focus of Chapter 15.)

STRATEGIC INVESTORS AND CORPORATE VENTURE CAPITALISTS. Many large corporations have established venture-capital firms as operating subsidiaries that look for companies to invest in, not only to achieve financial returns but also to realize strategic objectives, such as access to the technology that another company has developed. Examples include Intel, Motorola, AOL, MCI/Worldcom and Oracle, which all have a track record of making venture-capital-style investments in companies that can help them achieve their own strategic objectives.

One area of concern among corporate venture capitalists is the tendency toward unrealistic valuations. In the past, many early-stage companies went to strategic investors too early, received very high valuations and then had trouble raising additional funds given the benchmark of the new, higher valuation. Nobody wants to buy into a cow that is pumped full of water!

OVERSEAS INVESTORS. There are a wide variety of overseas investors, foreign stock exchanges, banks and leasing compa-

---

Choosing the Right Source of Capital

Choosing between getting a loan or selling part of your business to an equity investor is often a difficult decision to make. In general, loans are better for businesses if the cash flow allows for realistic repayment schedules and the loans can be obtained without jeopardizing personal assets. On the other hand, equity investments are often preferred to finance start-up ventures because of their flexible repayment schedules. With either alternative, however, you should be aware of the trade-offs you may have to make.

LOANS
Advantages
- Lender has no profit participation or management say in your business. Your only obligation is to repay loan on time.
- Interest payments (not principal payments) are a deductible business expense.

EQUITY
Advantages
- You can be flexible about repayment requirements.
- Investors may be partners and often offer valuable advice and assistance.
- If your business fails or goes bankrupt, you probably will not have to repay your investors.

Disadvantages
- You may have to make loan repayments when your need for capital is greatest, such as during your company's start-up or expansion.
- You may have to assign a security interest in your property to obtain a loan, thereby placing personal assets at risk.

Disadvantages
- Equity investors require a larger share of the profits.
- Your partners and shareholders have a right to be informed about all significant business events and a right to ethical management. They may sue you if they feel that these rights are compomised.

---

nies that are interested in financing transactions with U.S.-based companies. Be sure to consider cultural and management-style differences before you engage in any international-financing transaction.

INTERMEDIARIES. Many growing companies begin their search for capital with the assistance of an intermediary, such as an investment banker, broker, merchant banker or financial consultant. These companies and individuals aren't direct suppliers of equity capital, but can assist you in obtaining financing through commercial lenders, insurance companies, personal funds or other institutional sources. Investment bankers will also arrange for equity investment by private investors, usually in anticipation of a subsequent public offering of the company's securities.

How Much Money Do You Really Need?

One mistake entrepreneurs often make in their search for capital is to raise too little or too much. If you misbudget or misjudge your actual capital needs or fail to demonstrate creativity in exploring alternative ways of obtaining capital, you run the risk of losing credibility with prospective investors. If you ask for too little and subsequently need to request additional capital, the process will be more stringent and the cost will usually be much higher. If you ask for too much (even though some experts say you can never have too much capital in an early-stage enterprise), it may be a turn-off to a prospective investor and could lead to waste. Even worse, an overly large equity investment will dilute your ownership and control more than is necessary.

Investors often provide capital in stages rather than in a lump sum. These stages (or "tranches") are often tied to specific business-plan milestones or performance objectives, such as revenues, profits, customer levels, recruitment of team members or obtaining regulatory approvals. Breaking the invest-

---

Do You Have the Right Investor? A Few Key Tips

1. Always look for the smartest and best-connected capital you can find—the dividends will far exceed the cash. Avoid dumb or passive money at all costs.

2. When things go wrong, do your investors ask: "Why did *you* do that?" or do they ask: What can *we* do now to solve the problem?" The better investors will always view it as *our* problem—not as an us versus them issue.

3. Avoid strategic investors whose growth plans on strategic issues may be inconsistent with yours. Get a handle on where *they* are heading and as to how their plans fit with yours.

4. Will your current investors help you attract new investors at increased valuations? Do they have the Rolodex and reputation to bring new investors to the table when additional capital is required?

---

ment into tranches protects the investor against capital mismanagement and waste and protects you against premature dilution of ownership or loss of capital. Your natural inclination may be to request that all of the necessary capital be invested in a lump sum (to reduce the chances that future conditions will prevent you from receiving all the money you need). But bear in mind that there may be some real advantages in allowing for a staged investment.

Budgeting and Forecasting

Before you can consider specific equity and debt capital-formation strategies, which we discuss in Chapters 12 and 13, it is critical that you are able to develop strong budgets, forecasts and allocation-of-proceeds statements that support your business-growth strategy. All sources of capital, regardless of whether they are venture capitalists or commercial lenders, will want to know that you and your management team have taken the time to determine the amount of capital needed to implement the growth strategy you have selected. They'll also want to know the impact that the capital infusion will have on your company from a cash-flow and net-worth perspective.

The best place to demonstrate that your team has thought

through the financial components of the capital required to implement the growth strategy is in the budgets/allocation of proceeds and the financial-projections sections of your business-growth plan.

BUDGETS AND ALLOCATION OF PROCEEDS. In this section of your business-growth plan you should address how much money you will need to implement your company's business-growth strategy and why. You should also demonstrate when the various capital levels will be required, to allow investors to invest in stages. Also state here how you will use the money and why you believe that this expenditure is necessary for a company at your stage. This section should offer at least three different scenarios reflecting different funding levels, from low to high, because it is unlikely that you will raise the exact amount of the money you require.

FINANCIAL PROJECTIONS/FORECASTS. Financial projections or forecasts demonstrate to prospective lenders or investors that your team has thought through the impact that the infusion of capital will have on your company's financial performance and growth plans. They predict what the company's sales, costs, profits and net worth will be at various points in the future if the capital is raised and the growth strategy is successfully implemented.

While underlying detail should be available for further discussion, financial forecasts should include high-level figures, not line-item detail, department by department. You should present five-year projections, monthly for at least the first year (but not for more than two) and quarterly or annually for the remaining years. Present the financial projections in at least three scenarios—worst case, expected case and best case—to demonstrate that you and your advisers have conducted sensitivity analysis for the forecasting process. Your financial forecast should include all the elements listed in the box above.

As supporting documentation for the financial projections, include notes detailing assumptions, payment policies, receivables policies, depreciation utilized, and any other information

---

Elements to Include in a Financial Forecast

PROFIT AND LOSS STATEMENT
1. Units sold
2. Reserves
3. Cost of goods sold
4. Operating expenses
5. Net income (loss)

CASH BUDGETS
1. Beginning cash
2. Cash from operations
   Sales
   Interest
3. Cash from other sources
   Investors
   Lenders
4. Cash uses
   Capital expenditures
   Cash operating expenses
   Interest expense
5. Ending cash

BALANCE SHEET
1. Current assets
   Cash, investments
   Receivables
   Inventory
   Other
2. Fixed assets
   Machinery and equipment
   Accumulated depreciation
3. Total assets
4. Current liabilities
   Accounts payable
   Notes payable
   Other
5. Long-term liabilities
   Notes to officers
   Term debt
   Other
6. Equity
   Paid in capital
   Retained earnings (loss)
7. Total liabilities and equity

---

used in generating the figures. Essentially, you are identifying the key facts that you relied on to arrive at these numbers.

Tips for Preparing Accurate Budgets and Forecasts

The key to developing effective forecasts and budgets is to have clear and detailed footnotes that explain your underlying assumptions and the variables that affect these assumptions. Explain what key factors and sources of data you relied on in arriving at your assumptions. If you can't back up the numbers, prospective investors and lenders will not take your proposal seriously and will be unlikely to do the deal. (See the box on page 192 for a sample statement of assumptions.)

Do not underestimate cost projections, which is something emerging-growth companies often do, especially in the area of personnel expenses. Be sure to include all costs associated with human resources, such as headhunter fees, benefits, and office space, not just salaries and projected bonuses.

Understand your key growth drivers and the variables that affect actual performance. If your chief revenue driver is people, for instance, do your projections match up with your current level of staff? Are you sure you will be able to attract and retain additional personnel as you grow? Your strategy must match the numbers.

Understand the financial and cash-flow needs of the prospective lender or investor. For commercial lending, do your projections and cash flow match up with the schedule of debt-service payments? Don't force-fit your projections into a third party's perceived cash-flow needs or their expected rates of return. Your numbers will either meet their needs or they won't. In fact, realistic projections will often help you narrow the field of prospective lenders or investors because your company's timing for creating positive cash flow will help you select the appropriate source of capital.

Know the numbers for your competitors and industry overall. Does your forecast fit with applicable and relevant key industry ratios? Why or why not? Where are you stronger than the norm? Where are you weaker? Why? Investors and lenders who regularly provide capital to your industry will be very familiar with these numbers, and you need to be as well.

The contents of the business-growth plan and the growth strategy you present must consistently match up with your stated capital needs and projected cash flow. These are often called the "critical linkages" between the body of the plan and the forecasts that must fit smoothly together. For example, the sales forecast should fit with the marketing budget; the new-product development must fit with the research-and-development budget. A sophisticated investor will quickly spot gaps between the words and the numbers. There must also be agreement among your senior team members regarding key milestones and capital needs; resolve any major differences of opinion well before you meet with prospective sources of capital.

Don't rely too heavily on outside advisers or software programs when preparing budgets and forecasts. The prospective lenders and investors want to know how you arrive at these conclusions, not how some consultant or software program got there. Use your advisers as editors and for feedback, but not as primary drafters of your budget and forecasts.

Give yourself plenty of working capital as a cushion so that you do not run out of cash too soon. It is very costly to go back to the source of capital for additional funds prematurely or in between expected rounds.

Don't overload the prospective investor or lender with too much information. Although most business-growth plans fall short of adequately explaining their assumptions, others go too far, providing unnecessary detail. Focus on providing only the information needed or requested by the lender or investor.

When you budget your financial models, demonstrate that management will stay focused on controlling costs during the growth phase, so that as sales increase, expenses increase at a slower rate. Many companies have experienced the classic "sideways V," where sales go up but profits go down.

The ability to contain and control costs, keep debt low on the balance sheet, experience rapid sales growth, increase profit margins, build multiple reserve streams and strong earnings, and position your company for additional rounds of capital at higher valuations are all critical drivers for continued business growth. All will depend on the systems and procedures you put in place to measure and monitor performance. Your financial projections must demonstrate to potential investors and lenders that your team will be constantly reviewing this data and fine-tuning your operations to achieve maximum growth and profitability.

Sample Statement of Assumptions

Financial projections:

■ Management believes that the initial funding of $2.5 million will be adequate to carry the company through initial profitability. It is anticipated that receivables and inventory financing from commercial bank sources will be available in the second quarter of year two.

■ The company anticipates being able to sustain a gross margin in the 40% range, which approximates industry average. On a net basis, it will turn, approximately, 9% to 11% of sales to the bottom line beginning in its third year.

■ Management has taken what it believes to be an extremely conservative approach in formulating its pro forma financial; no debt financing is shown until year two, and lease financing is not proposed as an option. Management is vigorously pursuing both avenues at this stage and fully expects to arrange at least modest credit facilities in the short term.

Assumptions underlying financial projections:

■ Founders contribute $70,000 cash to the company in month one (accomplished).

■ Founders defer salaries and out-of-pocket expense of $42,500 indefinitely (accomplished).

■ Depreciation is calculated on all fixed and capital assets assuming five-year lives and straight-line computation.

■ Receivables are 30 days in duration (industry standard is 30 days).

■ Payables are 30 days (industry standard is 50-65 days), do not begin until month thirteen, and equal only 50% of inventory costs during the period (trade support is expected much sooner).

■ Inventories turn an average of seven times per year (on top of a fixed base of $40,000).

■ Salaries through month 18 are approximately 50% to 75% of industry standard (higher at lower personnel levels in the company).

■ Interest is earned at 8% per annum.

■ Interest is paid at 13% per annum.

■ Cash purchases are the sum of the period's cost of goods sold, 50% of inventory purchases, and capital acquisitions.

■ Minimum cash on hand is $20,000 (under bank line when cash flow is negative for the period).

■ Detailed budgets underlying the financial projections are available for further review and discussion.

Strategies for
Raising Equity Capital

V IRTUALLY ALL TYPES OF FAST-TRACK GROWTH COM-
panies raise some amount of equity capital to continue to fuel their expansion. Further, they typically require multiple rounds of equity to reach
all of their performance targets prior to being
acquired or going public. The two most common ways that a
rapidly growing company raises equity capital are through a
private-placement memorandum offering (PPM offering) or by
raising capital from a venture capitalist, either a stand alone
venture-capital fund or the venture-capital investing arm of a
large corporation. This chapter provides an overview of these
two strategies. (For more information on raising capital at the
earlier stages of a company's development or a more detailed
discussion of capital-formation strategies, see my book, *Raising
Capital*, also published by Kiplinger Books.)

Private Placement Offerings

P rivate placements generally include any type of securities
offering by a small or growing company. Unlike the sale
of other, more public types of offerings, private placements need not be registered with the Securities and Exchange
Commission (SEC), therefore making private placements an

easier road to travel to obtain capital. With loan criteria for commercial bankers and investment criteria for institutional venture capitalists tightening, the private-placement offering remains one of the most viable capital-formation alternatives available. To determine whether a private placement is a sensible strategy for raising capital, you must have a fundamental understanding of federal and state securities laws affecting private placements (an overview is provided later in this chapter), be familiar with the basic procedural steps that need to be taken before such an alternative is pursued, and have a team of qualified legal and accounting professionals. For a growing business, the advantages of a private placement include:

- **reduced transactional and ongoing costs** because of its exemption from many of the extensive registration and reporting requirements imposed by federal and state securities laws;
- **the ability to structure a more complex and confidential transaction,** because the deal is usually made with a small number of sophisticated investors; and
- **a more rapid penetration into the capital markets** than with a public offering of securities requiring registration with the SEC.

Federal Securities Laws Applicable to Private Placements

As a general rule, Section 5 of the Securities Act of 1933 (the Securities Act) requires that you file a registration statement with the SEC before you can offer to sell any security in interstate commerce unless an exemption is available under Sections 3 or 4 of that act. The penalties for failing to register or for disclosing inaccurate or misleading information are quite stringent. In addition to the considerable time and expense you will have to put in to register under Section 5, you must also be prepared to assemble a network of underwriters and brokers to make a market for your security. As an issuer or offeror registering under Section 5, your company is also subject to strict periodic reporting requirements. The most commonly recognized transactional exemption to Section 5 is a private placement.

To qualify for a private placement, you must work with legal counsel to structure the transaction within one of the various categories of exemptions available. These include Section 4(2), considered the broad private-offering exemption, designed for "transaction(s) by an issuer not involving any public offering"; Section 3(a) (11), an intrastate exemption; and Regulation D, the most commonly selected regulation that fast-track growth companies rely on in seeking a transactional exemption from registration. Regulation D offers three options: Rules 504, 505 and 506.

Rule 504 permits offers and sales of not more than $1 million during any 12-month period by any issuer that is not subject to the reporting requirements of the Securities Exchange Act of 1934 (the Exchange Act). The aggregate offering price for an offering under this rule may not exceed $1 million, less the aggregate price for all securities sold in the 12 months before the start of and during the Rule 504 offering; rely on any exemption based on Section 3(b) of the Securities Act; or violate Section 5 of the Securities Act.

> **To qualify for a private placement, you must work with legal counsel to structure the transaction within the various categories of exemptions available.**

Rule 504 places virtually no limit on the number or the nature of the investors that can participate in the offering. The issuer may use general advertising and solicitation, and there are no restrictions on resales of securities. Even though no formal disclosure document (also known as a prospectus) needs to be registered and delivered to offerees under Rule 504, I strongly recommend that you do so to avoid potential problems with unqualified or unsophisticated investors who may later claim not to have known what they were investing in. There are also many procedures that you must understand and follow. An offering under Rule 504 is subject to the general anti-fraud provisions of Section 10(b) of the Exchange Act and that section's Rule 10b-5. This specifies that all documents or other information you provide to prospective investors must be accurate and not misleading by virtue of their content or omissions in any material respect.

The SEC also requires that its Form D be filed for all offerings under Regulation D within 15 days of the first sale. Finally, if you are seeking to raise capital under Rule 504, examine applicable state laws very carefully, because although many states have adopted overall securities laws similar to Regulation D, many of these laws do not include an exemption similar to 504. As a result, you may need to prepare a formal memorandum, which is discussed later in this chapter.

Rule 505 has many of the same filing requirements and restrictions imposed by Rule 504 (such as the need to file a Form D), in addition to an absolute prohibition on advertising and general solicitation for offerings. Any company that is subject to the "bad boy" provisions of Regulation A—which applies to persons who have been subject to certain disciplinary, administrative, civil or criminal proceedings, or sanctions that involve the company or its predecessors—is disqualified from being a 505 offeror.

Many companies select Rule 505 over Rule 504 in part because its requirements are consistent with many state securities laws. Perhaps more important for the rapidly growing company, Rule 505 allows an issuer that is not an investment company to sell up to $5 million of its securities in a 12-month period to an unlimited number of accredited investors. (For purposes of Regulation D, an accredited investor is a person or a company that is considered to be able to withstand the economic risks involved in securities transactions. Individuals are considered to be accredited if they fall into at least one of eight categories set out in Rule 501(a) of Regulation D. Individuals whose net worth, or joint net worth with a spouse, exceeds $1 million at the time of purchase, or who had an individual income in excess of $200,000 in each of the last two years, or joint incomes in excess of $300,000, and who have a reasonable expectation of reaching the same income level in the current year are considered accredited investors pursuant to Rule 501(a), as are directors, executive officers or general partners of an issuer.) Rule 505 also permits sale of securities to up to 35 non-accredited investors, regardless of their net worth, income or "sophistication" (see the discussion under Rule 506).

Rule 506 is similar to Rule 505; however, under this rule there is no restriction on the dollar amount of securities your company may offer to an unlimited number of accredited investors and up to 35 non-accredited investors. If you require large amounts of capital, this exemption is the most attractive.

The key difference under Rule 506 is that any non-accredited investor must be "sophisticated." In this context, a sophisticated investor is one who does not fall into any of the eight categories specified by Rule 501(a), but whom the issuer believes to "have knowledge and experience in financial and business matters that render him capable of evaluating the merits and understanding the risks posed by the transaction" (either acting alone or in conjunction with the purchaser representative).

> **If you require large amounts of capital, Rule 506 is the most attractive of the Regulation D exemptions.**

If the purchaser employs a purchaser representative, the representative must be unaffiliated with the issuer, knowledgeable in business matters and be acknowledged by the purchaser in writing. The best way to remove any uncertainty over the sophistication or accreditation of a prospective investor is to request that he or she complete a comprehensive confidential offeree questionnaire before you sell them securities. Rule 506 eliminates the need to prepare and deliver disclosure documents in any specified format, if exclusively accredited investors participate in the transaction. As with Rule 505, there is an absolute prohibition on advertising and general solicitation. States cannot impose their registration requirements on securities issued pursuant to Rule 506, but can demand only notification that the securities are going to be sold under Rule 506.

State Securities Laws Applicable to Private Placements

Regulation D was designed to provide a foundation for uniformity between federal and state securities laws, an objective that has yet to be fully met on a national level. Full compliance with the federal securities laws is only one level of regulation that you must take into account when you develop plans and strategies to raise capital through securities offerings. Whether or not an offering is exempt under federal laws, you may still be required to register the securities in the states in which they will be sold under applicable state securities laws, also known as "Blue Sky" laws. Obviously, you must consider the expenses and requirements for compliance with both federal and state laws.

Overall, there are a wide variety of levels of review among the states, ranging from very tough merit reviews (designed to ensure that all offerings of securities are fair and equitable) to very lenient notice-only filings (designed primarily to promote full disclosure). A comprehensive discussion of the state securities laws is beyond the scope of this chapter, but be aware that every state has a statute governing securities transactions and securities dealers. Carefully check the securities laws of each state where you will make an offer or sale before you distribute the offering documents to determine:

- **whether the particular limited offering exemption selected** under federal law will also apply in the state;
- **whether pre-sale or post-sale registration** or notices are required;
- **whether special legal disclaimers or warnings ("legends")** or disclosures must be made in the offering documents;
- **what the available remedies are to an investor** who has purchased securities from a company that has failed to comply with applicable state laws; and
- **who may offer securities for sale** on behalf of the company.

Private Placements and the Internet

While the SEC has accepted some aspects of the Internet, it has not yet supported its use in private offerings. Recently, some experts have argued that the SEC should recognize that the Internet affects, and will continue to affect, the way business is done and therefore should modify its rules to allow issuers to take advantage of the Internet's capabilities. As the law stands now, the SEC has determined that placing offering materials on the Internet would be inconsistent with Rule 502(c), which prohibits the use of general solicitation.

There have been numerous suggestions as to how the SEC could change its rules regarding solicitations on the Internet, ranging from abolishing the application of Rule 502(c) to the Internet to using its exemption authority to carve out a new exemption for private offerings over the Internet. Some experts have even suggested that the SEC create a central Web site for listing private offerings made pursuant to an amended Rule 506. If the SEC were to repeal its general solicitation ban with regard to the Internet, both private investors and small issuers would benefit. Investors would be able to have access to information more easily, and issuers would be able to reduce the costs associated with offerings. Further, with a central Web site, the SEC would be able to monitor private offerings for fraud.

Preparing the Private Placement Memorandum

Work with your lawyer to prepare the documents and exhibits that will constitute your company's private placement memorandum (known as the PPM). Describe your company's background in your PPM, as well as the risks to the investor and the terms of the securities being sold. There are several factors to consider in determining the exact degree of disclosure that your documents should include, such as:

- **the minimum level of disclosure** that must be made under federal securities laws (which depends, in part, on the exemption from registration you are relying on);
- **the minimum level of disclosure** that must be made under an applicable state's securities laws (which depends on the state or states in which you are offering or selling the securities);
- **the sophistication and expectations** of the targeted investors (e.g., some investors will expect a certain amount of information to be presented in a specified format regardless of what the law may require); and
- **the complexity or nature of your company** and the terms of the offering. It may be advisable for you to prepare detailed disclosure documents regardless of whether or not you are required to do so to avoid future liability for misstatements, fraud or confusion, especially if the nature of your company and the terms of the offering are very complex.

Once you and your lawyer have dealt with these factors, consider the costs of preparing a more comprehensive prospectus than may be required against the benefits of the additional protection such a document would provide to your company. The key question you and your legal advisers should answer is: What is the most cost-effective vehicle for providing the targeted investors with the information they require and that both applicable law and prudence dictate they must have?

The specific disclosure items you should include in the PPM will vary under federal securities laws and applicable state laws depending on the size of the offering and nature of the investors. The text of the PPM should be descriptive, not persuasive, allowing prospective investors to reach their own conclusions as to the merits of the securities your company is offering. Use the following checklist to determine what should be included in your PPM.

INTRODUCTORY MATERIALS. These introduce the prospective investor to the basic terms of the offering. A cover page should include a brief statement about your company and its core business, the terms of the offering (often in table form), and all required legal disclaimers and warnings (sometimes referred to as the legends) required by federal and state laws. Following the cover page, include a summary of the offering, which serves as an integral part of the introductory materials and as a cross reference for the reader. The last two parts of the introductory materials are usually a statement of the investor-suitability standards, which includes a discussion of the federal and state securities laws applicable to the offering and the definitions of an accredited investor as applied to the offering.

DESCRIPTION OF YOUR COMPANY. This section of the PPM should include a discussion of your company's history, including its affiliates and predecessors; its principal officers and directors; products and services; management and operating policies; performance history and goals; competition; trends in the industry; advertising and marketing strategy; suppliers and distributors; intellectual-property rights; key real and personal property; customer demographics; and any other material information that is important for the investor to know.

RISK FACTORS. Although this is usually the most difficult section to write, it's clearly considered one of the most important to the prospective investor. Its purpose is to outline all of the factors that make your offering or projected business plan risky or speculative. Naturally, the exact risks to the investors posed by the offering will depend on the nature of your business and the trends within your industry.

> **Although the risk section is usually the most difficult section to write, it's clearly considered one of the most important to the prospective investor.**

CAPITALIZATION OF THE ISSUER. Explain in this section your company's capital structure both before and after the offering. For the purposes of this section in the PPM, you must disclose all authorized and outstanding securities (including all long-term debt).

MANAGEMENT OF YOUR COMPANY. Include a list of the names, ages, special skills or characteristics of and biographical information on, each officer, director or key consultant employed by your company; compensation and stock-option arrangements; bonus plans; special contracts or arrangements; and any transactions between your company and individual officers and directors (including loans, self dealing, and related types of transactions). Also disclose here the role and identity of your company's legal and accounting firms, as well as any other experts retained in connection with the offering.

TERMS OF THE OFFERING. Describe the terms and conditions of your offering, the number of shares and the price. If you are offering your company's securities through underwriters, brokers or dealers (to the extent permitted by federal and state laws), then you must disclose the name of each distributor as well as the terms and nature of the relationship between you and each party; the commissions to be paid; the obligations of the distributor (e.g., guaranteed or best-efforts offering); and any special rights, such as the right of a particular underwriter to serve on the board of directors, any indemnification provisions or other material terms of the offering. (Base the terms and structure of your offering on a series of preliminary and informal meetings with possible investors—without those discussions qualifying as a "formal offer" as that term is defined by the securities laws—as well as research on current market conditions and recently closed, similarly situated offerings.)

ALLOCATION OF PROCEEDS. In this section of the PPM, you must state the principal purposes for which you will use the net proceeds, along with the approximate amount you intend to use for each purpose. Give careful thought to this section because any material deviation from the use of funds as described in the PPM could trigger liability. If you and your advisers have not prepared an exact breakdown, then try to describe why you are raising additional capital and what business objectives you expect to pursue with the proceeds.

DILUTION. In this section, include a discussion of the number of shares outstanding prior to the offering, the price paid for them, the net book value, the effect on existing shareholders of the proposed offering, as well as dilutive effects on new purchasers at the completion of the offering. Often the founding shareholders (and sometimes their key advisers or the people who will help promote the PPM) will have acquired their securities at prices substantially below those in the prospective offering. As a result, the book value of shares purchased by prospective investors pursuant to the offering will be substantially diluted.

DESCRIPTION OF SECURITIES. Explain here the rights, restrictions and special features of the securities you are offering, and any applicable provision of the articles of incorporation or by-laws that affect their capitalization (such as preemptive rights, total authorized stock, different classes of shares or restrictions on declaration and distribution of dividends).

FINANCIAL STATEMENTS. The statements you must provide will vary depending on the amount of money you intend to raise, applicable federal and state regulations, and the nature of your company and its stage of growth. Provide an explanation of these financial statements and an analysis of your company's current and projected financial condition.

EXHIBITS. Append as exhibits your company's articles of incorporation and by-laws, key contracts or leases, brochures, news articles, marketing reports, and résumés of the principals. Lawyers and accountants typically examine these documents during the due-diligence process.

Subscription Materials

Once prospective investors and their advisers have made a decision to provide capital to your company in accordance with the terms of your PPM, there are a series of documents that investors must sign as evidence of their desire to subscribe to purchase your securities as offered by the PPM. The various subscription materials that should accompany the PPM serve several purposes. The two key subscription documents are:

Offeree or purchaser questionnaire, which is developed to obtain certain information from prospective offerees and serves as evidence of their level of sophistication as investors. You may also wish to attempt to obtain information regarding the prospective purchaser's background, citizenship, education, employment, investment and business experience.

Subscription agreement is the contract between your company and the purchaser (investor) for the purchase of the securities. It should, therefore, contain acknowledgments of:
- **the receipt and review by the purchaser** of the information you provided about your company and the offering;
- **the restricted nature of the securities to be acquired** and the fact that the securities were acquired under an exemption from registration;
- **any particularly significant suitability requirements,** such as the amount of investment or passive income, tax bracket, and so forth, that may be crucial to the purchaser's ability to obtain

the benefits of the proposed investment;

■ **an awareness of specific risks** disclosed in the information you furnished; and

■ **the status of the purchaser representative** (if one is used).

The purchaser should reconfirm in the subscription agreement the accuracy and completeness of the information that was provided in the offeree or purchaser questionnaire; the number and price of the securities she or he is purchasing and the method of payment. The purchaser should further agree to any special elections that may be contemplated (such as S-corporation elections or accounting methods). The subscription agreement often contains the purchaser's agreement to indemnify the issuer against losses or liabilities resulting from any misrepresentations on the part of the prospective purchaser that would void or destroy the exemption from registration that the issuer is attempting to invoke. The purchaser should also acknowledge in the agreement that she or he has the authority to execute the agreement.

Understanding Venture-Capital Transactions

The term "venture capital" has been defined in many ways, but it refers generally to relatively high-risk, early-stage financing of young emerging-growth companies. The professional venture capitalist is usually a highly trained finance professional who manages a pool of venture funds for investment in growing companies on behalf of a group of passive investors.

Owners and managers of fast-track growth companies often have mixed views toward the institutional venture-capital industry. They welcome the money and management support they desperately need for growth, but fear the loss of control and restrictions that are typically placed on a company by the investors. To achieve balance between the needs of the venture capitalist and the needs of your company, you must understand the process of obtaining venture-capital financing. You must also understand that the days of venture capitalists assigning lofty valuations to poorly prepared, three-page business plans are also long gone. There has been a definite return to fundamentals, a return to the old rules, with an emphasis on real customers, achievable revenues, sustainable profits and a genuine competitive advantage.

Three Types of Venture Capitalists
In general, there are three different types of traditional institutional pools of venture capital, though in recent years the lines between the three may be blurring. These include:

PUBLIC AND PRIVATE INSTITUTIONAL VENTURE-CAPITAL FIRMS. These firms are typically organized as limited partnerships that seek capital from venture investors, trusts, pension funds and insurance companies, among others. They in turn manage and invest that capital in high-growth companies. Venture-capital firms tend to specialize in particular niches, either by industry, territory or a business's stage of development. Their investors expect a certain success rate and return on investment (ROI), which is critical to the firm's track record and its future ability to attract additional capital.

SBIC/MESBIC. The Small Business Investment Act, enacted in 1958, established a national program for licensing privately owned small-business investment companies (SBIC). Minority-Enterprise SBICs (MESBICs) were added by a 1972 amendment to the Act. Although the SBIC program has experienced some difficulty, it remains an integral part of the organized venture-capital community. The program allows the Small Business Administration (SBA) to grant licenses to certain types of venture-capital firms that are eligible to borrow money from the federal government at attractive rates in exchange for certain restrictions on deal structures as well as the types of businesses for which the SBIC can provide capital.

CORPORATE VENTURE-CAPITAL DIVISIONS. These include venture-capital divisions established by large corporations such as Intel, Nokia and Motorola. The purpose of these divisions is generally to fund small companies that have technology or resources that the larger corporation wants or needs, thereby allowing it to have access to the technology or resources. The investment is often structured more like a quasi-joint venture, because corporate venture-capital often brings not only money to the small company, but also access to the resources of the large company. Corporate venture-capital efforts typically revolve around the corporation's goals of incubating future acquisitions, gaining access to new technologies, obtaining intellectual-property licenses, providing work for unused capacity, bringing technological and entrepreneurial thinking to current corporate staff, and breaking into new markets.

The Importance of Preparation

Careful preparation is essential for you to obtain an initial meeting with the institutional venture capitalist. There should be three central components to your preparation process: business and strategic planning, effective networking,; and narrowing the field.

You will need a well-written business plan and financing proposal for your company to be taken seriously by any sophisticated source of capital. Effective networking means getting the business plan into the hands of the appropriate venture capitalists by using professional advisers, commercial lenders, investment bankers and consultants who have the contacts and the know-how to get this done.

The average venture-capital firm sees thousands of business plans per year, provides a return phone call to only a few dozen candidates and may actually close only four to six deals. In addition, many venture-capital firms are more focused on providing capital to struggling members of their existing portfolios, rather than taking on new challenges by providing capital to new candidates.

Clearly, chances for survival in this competitive process depends on finding a way to stand out from the crowd. Most venture capitalists have certain investment preferences regarding which companies they will include in their investment portfolio. These preferences may be based on the type of industry, geographic location, projected rates of return, stage of development or amount of capital required. Rather than waste precious resources by blindly sending business-growth plans to any and all venture capitalists in your region, research the venture-capital industry to match the characteristics of the proposed investment with the investment criteria of the targeted firm. Try to narrow your search to those venture-investment firms that already have a core understanding of the dynamics of your industry. When you find investors who share your vision and know your target markets, then the only decision criterion left to be met is whether you have the right team to be competitive, saving you several hurdles and lots of time.

The average venture-capital firm sees thousands of business plans per year, provides a return phone call to only a few dozen candidates and may actually close only four to six deals.

If your business-plan submission survives the rigid initial review of most institutional venture-capital firms, then the key to your first meeting and success thereafter is PREPARATION! As the saying goes, "You never get a second chance to make a first impression." The venture capitalist's invitation to have a meeting with you is often a second step following their preliminary review of your business-growth plan, but it is a precursor to the actual commitment of a term sheet. Therefore, it is critical that your presentation and handling of their questions goes very well, or there will be no subsequent steps. Include the following steps in your preparations.

HAVE MANY DRESS REHEARSALS. The rehearsals will help you survive the first meeting and get to the next one. Rehearse your presentation many times, using a moot court made up of different audiences who will ask different questions, replicating the actual meeting that you'll have with the managers of the venture-capital firm. Make sure your rehearsal audiences (including lawyers, accountants, business-school professors, and other entrepreneurs who have raised venture capital) have the background and the training to ask the right questions (including the tough ones) and evaluate your responses critically. Do your homework and learn what the venture-capital firm's "hot buttons" are so that you can address key issues in your presentation. Be prepared for the tough questions and don't be scared, intimidated or upset when the really hard ones come at you. If the venture-capital firm's team doesn't ask tough questions, then they are not engaged in your presentation, which in turn means there probably will not be a deal.

FIND A MENTOR. It's always helpful to have a venture-capitalist coach or mentor who has either raised venture capital or served as an adviser on or negotiated a venture-capital transaction. The mentor or coach can help you stay focused on the issues that are important to the venture capitalists so your presentation will not be a waste of their time. The mentor can reassure you during the difficult and time-consuming process, and teach you to remain patient, optimistic and level-headed about the risks and challenges that you face.

KNOW YOUR DASHBOARD. Most venture capitalists will want to know that *you* know the five or six key business matrices that your team will use to measure and monitor your company's performance. These matrices are known as the executive's "dashboard," referring to the gauges you need to keep an eye on to make sure that your car stays on track, has all of the necessary fuel and fluids, does not go too fast or too slow, does not overheat, etc.—all applicable by analogy to the proper management and fast-track growth of a business.

PREPARE A DETAILED GAME PLAN. Prepare a specific presentation that isn't too long or too short (usually 15 minutes is about right). Don't attempt to read every word of your business plan or put every historical fact about your company on a slide presentation. Keep the presentation crisp and focused, and be prepared to answer questions and to defend your key strategic assumptions and financial forecasts. Remember that every minute counts. Even the small talk at the beginning of the meeting is important because the seasoned venture capitalist is sizing you up, learning about your interests and looking for the chemistry that is key to a successful relationship.

MAKE YOUR TEAM AVAILABLE TO MEET THE VENTURE CAPITALIST. Don't overlook the personal component of the evaluation. Any experienced venture capitalist will tell you that, at the end of the day, the decision to invest depends on the strength of the people who will be there day to day to execute and manage the future of the company. The venture capitalist will look for a management team that's educated, dedicated and experienced (and ideally has experienced some success as a team prior to this venture). The team should also be balanced, with members' skills and talents complementing each other so that all critical areas of business management are covered—from finance to marketing and sales to technical expertise.

HAVE PASSION BUT DON'T OVERLOOK THE RISKS. The experienced venture capitalist wants to see that you have a passion and commitment to your company and to the execution of the business plan. However, he or she does not want to be oversold or have to deal with an entrepreneur who is so enamored of an idea or plan that he or she can't grasp its flaws or understand its risks. Many entrepreneurs fail to make a good impression in their initial meeting with venture capitalists because they can't strike a balance between enthusiasm and realism.

Demonstrate your personal commitment to the project. All venture capitalists will size up your personal commitment to your business and its future. Generally, venture capitalists won't invest in entrepreneurs whose commitment to the business is only part-time or whose loyalty is divided. In addition to fidelity to the venture, investors want to see a high energy level, a commitment to achievement as well as leadership, self-confidence, and a creative approach to problem solving. You will also have to demonstrate your personal financial commitment by investing virtually all of your own resources in a project before you ask others to part with their resources. Remember, any aspect of your personal life, including your finances, may be of interest to the venture capitalist in the interview and due-diligence process. Don't get defensive or be surprised when the range of questions are as broad as they are deep—venture capitalists are merely trying to predict the future by learning as much as possible about your past and current situation.

KEEP AN OPEN MIND AND HAVE AN HONEST EXCHANGE OF INFORMATION. One sure deal killer for venture-capital firms is finding out that you're hiding something from your past or downplaying a previous business failure. Seasoned venture capitalists can and will learn about any skeletons in your closet during the due-diligence process, and will walk away from the deal if they find something that you should have disclosed to them at the outset. A candid, straightforward channel of communication is critical. And in an environment with the pools of venture capital shrinking and the standards rising, be ready for even more extensive rounds of due diligence and information requests from the venture-capital firm and their team of advisers.

Being straightforward about a previous business failure may work to your advantage in more than one way, because it may be viewed as a sign of experience—provided that you can demonstrate that you've learned from your mistakes and figured out ways to avoid them in the future. Similarly, you must demonstrate a certain degree of flexibility and versatility in your approach to implementing your business plan. The venture capitalists may have suggestions on the strategic direction of the company and will want to see that you are open-minded and receptive to their suggestions. If you're too rigid or too stubborn, they may view this as a sign of immaturity or see you as a person with whom compromise will be difficult down the road. Either one of these can be a major deal turn-off and cause the investors to walk away. For example, the technology downturn and general economic slowdown in late 2000 and 2001 forced many venture-backed companies to revisit their business-growth plans and revenue models. The better ones had "market-driven epiphanies" and successfully morphed into profitable (or soon to be profitable) companies, while the more stubborn companies continued to struggle or folded.

HAVE A BIG MARKET AND A BIG UPSIDE. A venture capitalist who suspects that your product or service has a narrow market, limited demand and thin margins will almost always walk away from the deal. Make sure your business plan and your presentation adequately demonstrate the size of your potential market(s) and the financial rewards and healthy margins that strong demand will bring to your company's bottom line. If your target market is too mature with established competitors, then the venture capitalist may feel the opportunity is too limited and will not produce the financial returns that they expect. Venture capitalists generally look for a company that has a sustainable competitive advantage, demonstrated by a balanced mix of products and services that meet a new need in both domestic and overseas markets. Remember that most venture capitalists want a 60% to 80% return for seed and early-stage or post-launch deals and at least a 25% to 35% return on later-stage or "mezzanine level"

Venture capitalists want deals in which both the investors and the entrepreneurs can enjoy the upside and where the scale is not weighted in favor of one over the other.

investments. When the average investor can double his or her money with investments in lower-risk companies like General Electric and Home Depot, then your business plan and presentation must clearly demonstrate that the venture capitalists' money will be better served in your company.

KNOW WHAT REALLY MOTIVATES THE VENTURE CAPITALISTS. David Gladstone, a seasoned venture capitalist and author of the *Venture Capital Handbook*, writes: "I'll back you if you have a good idea that will make money for both of us." That sentence captures the essence of the venture capitalist's decision-making process. You must have a good idea—one that's articulated in a business plan that realistically expresses the risks and opportunities and how your management team will influence the odds of success and survival. But the idea must also make money for both you and your investors. Venture capitalists want deals in which both the investors and the entrepreneurs can enjoy the upside and where the scale is not weighted in favor of one over the other. In addition, they seek out deals where, in exchange for providing capital and wisdom, they will have some control over the deal, the governance of the company, and protection in the documents to ensure that their investment and ability to participate in the growth and success of the company are protected.

HAVE AN EXIT STRATEGY. Investors aren't looking for a long-term marriage; they will want to know how you intend to get their original investment and return on capital back to them within four to six years. Your business plan and oral presentation should include an analysis and an assessment of the three most common exit strategies—namely, an initial public offering, a sale of the company, and a redemption of the venture capitalists' shares of the company by the company directly. Other exit strategies include restructuring the company, licensing the company's intellectual property, finding a replacement investor or even liquidating the company. But remember that focusing too much on an exit strategy may send the wrong signal to the prospective venture investor—that you are impatient, naïve, or not focused on building a truly great company.

Key Factors Influencing the Venture Capitalist's Investment Decision

Regardless of a company's stage of development, primary products and services, or geographic location, there are a number of variables that all venture-capital firms will consider in analyzing any business plan presented for consideration. These variables generally fall into four categories—management team, products and services, markets, and return on investment. You and your team must be prepared to answer the following questions regarding these variables:

MANAGEMENT TEAM
- **What are the background, knowledge, skills and abilities** of each member of your management team?
- **How is this experience relevant** to your proposed business plan or project?
- **How are risks and problems identified,** managed and eliminated by the members of your management team?

■ **To what extent does each member of your management team** exhibit certain entrepreneurial personality traits, such as self-confidence, leadership skills, tenacity, drive and unbounded energy?

PRODUCTS AND SERVICES

■ **At what stage of development are your products and services?** What is the specific opportunity that you have identified? How long will this window of opportunity remain open? How will you exploit this opportunity?

■ **To what extent are your products and services unique,** innovative and proprietary? What steps have you taken to protect these proprietary features?

■ **Do you control the means of producing the products** and services or are you dependent on a key supplier or licensor?

■ **Do your products or services represent a technological breakthrough** or are they more low-tech with less risk of obsolescence?

MARKETS

■ **In what stage of its life cycle** is the industry in which your company plans to operate?

■ **What is the size and projected growth rate** of the market your business is targeting?

■ **Through what marketing, sales and distribution methods** will you bring your products and services to the marketplace?

■ **What are the strengths of each of your direct,** indirect and anticipated competitors? What are their weaknesses?

■ **If the development of your products and services** will create new markets, what are the barriers to entry in these markets?

■ **Who is the typical consumer of your company's products and services?** How have consumers responded to your products or services so far?

RETURN ON INVESTMENT

■ **What is your current and projected valuation and performance** in terms of sales, earnings and dividends? To what extent have you substantiated these budgets and projections? Have you over- or underestimated the amount of capital you'll require?

Key Elements of a Successful Presentation to the Venture Capitalist

TEAM

- is able to adapt
- knows the competition
- is able to manage rapid growth
- can manage an industry leader
- has relevant background and industry experience
- shows financial commitment to company, not just sweat equity
- must be strong with a proven track record in the industry

PRODUCT OR SERVICE

- must be real, and it must work
- should be unique
- should be proprietary
- should satisfy a well-defined need in the marketplace
- must show potential for expansion into new products or services, to avoid being a one-product company
- must be usable
- must solve a problem or significantly improve a process
- can be manufactured or produced in mass quantities to allow for cost-savings through economies of scale

MARKET BUSINESS PLAN

- should have current customers and the potential for many more
- should project rapid market growth (25% to 45% per year)

- should have market potential in excess of $250 million
- should show where and how you are competing in the marketplace
- should show possibility of being a market leader
- should outline any barriers to entry
- must tell the full story, not just one chapter
- must define the building of a company, not just a product
- must be compelling
- should contain a strong and well-written executive summary
- should show the potential for rapid growth and knowledge of your industry, especially competition and market vision

RETURN ON INVESTMENT

- should have milestones for measuring performance
- should plan to meet or exceed the milestones given
- should address all of the key areas
- should detail projections and assumptions realistically
- Shows excitement and color
- must show superior rate of return (30% to 40% per year) with a clear exit strategy

■ **How much money and time have you**—and your managers— already invested? How much more time and money are you willing to commit before realizing a return on your own personal investments? How well are you managing your current assets and resources?

■ **How much capital will you require now** and at later stages to bring your business plans to fruition? What types of securities are you offering? Will additional dilution be necessary to meet your growth objectives? To what extent?

■ **What is the projected return on the proposed investment?** How will this projected return be affected if you fail to meet your business plans or financial projections? What rights, remedies and exit strategies will investors be able to use if problems arise?

In addition to addressing these questions in the business plan and being ready to explain any part of them in a meeting with venture capitalists, there are also certain negative factors that you should avoid at all costs because they often disqualify what might be an otherwise workable deal. These include:

■ **placing unqualified family members** in key management positions;

■ **projections that provide for excessive management salaries,** company cars and other unnecessary executive benefits;

■ **an unwillingness to provide a personal guaranty** for debt financing;

■ **an incomplete or overly slick business plan;** or

■ **a business plan that projects overly optimistic** or unrealistic goals and objectives.

Negotiating and Structuring the Venture-Capital Investment

The overview of the proposed structure of the deal will be reflected in the term sheet. The issuance of the term sheet usually reflects that the business and strategic due diligence has been completed and that the venture-capital team is prepared to move forward, subject to the legal due diligence and the negotiation of the definitive documents. The term sheet will also reflect any special due-diligence concerns or specific performance conditions that the venture investor may want to impose on your company. In negotiating term sheets with venture investors, choose your battles wisely and don't get overemotional during the process.

The negotiation and structuring of most venture-capital transactions will depend in part on industry standards, legal boilerplate or structural rules-of-thumb, but will also reflect the need to strike a balance between your needs and concerns and the venture capitalist's investment criteria and assessment of the risks attached to your company's ability to meet its plans. Negotiation regarding the structure of the transaction will usually revolve around the types of securities involved, the principal terms of the securities and the special provisions to ensure the venture capitalist's ability to participate in the upside and protect against the downside. The type of securities ultimately selected by investors and the structure of the transaction usually falls into one of the following categories.

PREFERRED STOCK. This is the most typical form of security issued in connection with a venture-capital financing of an emerging-growth company. This is because of the many advantages that preferred stock offers an investor—it can be converted into common stock, and it has dividend and liquidation preference over common stock. It also has anti-dilution protection, mandatory or optional redemption schedules, and special voting rights and preferences.

You and the venture capitalist must carefully negotiate the nature and scope of the various rights, preferences and privileges that will be granted to the holders of your company's newly authorized preferred stock. The terms and conditions of the voting rights, dividend rates and preferences, mandatory redemption provisions, conversion features, liquidation preferences and the anti-dilution provisions (sometimes referred to as "ratchet" clauses) are likely to be hotly contested.

CONVERTIBLE DEBENTURE. This is basically a debt instrument (secured or unsecured) that may be converted into equity upon specified terms and conditions. Until converted, it offers investors a fixed rate of return, and provides tax advantages (such as deductibility of interest payments) to the company. Venture capitalists will typically prefer this type of security for high-risk transactions because they'd prefer to be in the position of a creditor until the risk is mitigated or in connection with bridge financing, at which time the venture capitalist would expect to convert the debt to equity. In a volatile financial market, convertible debentures are very attractive to investors who want a downside cushion but also want the ability to participate in the upside if the market rebounds. The advantage to your company is that if the debentures are subordinated, commercial lenders will often treat them as equity on the balance sheet, which would enable your company to obtain institutional debt financing.

Venture capitalists will typically prefer convertible debenture securities for high-risk transactions.

In negotiating the terms of convertible debentures, you and the investors must come to an agreement regarding term, interest rate and payment schedule; conversion rights and rates; extent of subordination; the ability of the company to redeem (or "call") the debentures early; remedies for default; acceleration rights; and underlying security for the instrument.

DEBT SECURITIES WITH WARRANTS. A warrant enables the investor to buy common stock without giving up the preferred position of a creditor, as would be the case if only convertible debt was used in the financing. A venture capitalist will generally prefer debentures or notes in connection with warrants often for the same reasons that convertible debt is used—namely, because of the ability to protect the downside by being a creditor and the ability to protect the upside by including warrants to purchase common stock at favorable prices and terms.

COMMON STOCK. Venture capitalists rarely choose to purchase common stock initially, especially at a company's early stages of development, because straight common stock offers the investor no special rights or preferences, no fixed return on investment, no special ability to exercise control over management, and no liquidity to protect against downside risks. One of the few times that a venture capitalist might select common stock would be to preserve the company's Subchapter S status under the Internal Revenue Code, which would be jeopardized by the authorization of a class of preferred stock. Finally, you should be aware that common-stock investments by venture capitalists could create phantom income, which would have adverse tax consequences for your employees if stock is subsequently issued to them at a cost lower than the price per share paid by the venture-capital company.

Once you and the venture capitalist have agreed upon the type of security you'll use, take steps to ensure that the authorization and issuance of the security is properly carried out under applicable federal and state laws.

Debt Financing for Implementing Business-Growth Plans

N SEEKING CAPITAL TO FUEL YOUR COMPANY'S GROWTH, also consider debt financing for implementing your business-growth strategies. Debt plays an important role in the implementation of the business-growth plan, especially if the growth strategy you've selected for your company involves purchasing assets, inventory, or equipment that can serve as collateral for the loan. The use of debt in the capital structure (commonly known as leverage) will affect both the valuation of your company and its overall cost of capital. The determination of the proper debt-to-equity ratio for your rapidly growing company will depend on a wide variety of factors, which include:

- **the risk of business distress or failure** created by the contractual obligation to meet debt-service payments;
- **the direct and indirect costs to the company** of obtaining the required capital;
- **the need for flexibility in the capital structure** to respond to changing economic or market conditions;
- **the ability of the company to get access** to various sources of financing;
- **the nature and extent of the tangible** (or intangible) assets of the company that are available to serve as collateral to secure the loan;
- **the level of dilution of ownership** and control that the share-

holders (and managers) of the company are willing to tolerate; and

■ **certain tax considerations** (interest payments are a deductible expense, whereas dividends are not).

The maximum debt capacity that your company will ultimately be able to handle involves the balancing of the costs and risks of defaulting on a debt obligation against your desire to maintain control. Many business owners prefer to preserve control over their company in exchange for the higher level of risk that is inherent in taking on additional debt obligations rather than giving up shares in the business through sale of equity; however, before you assume debt, carefully consider the company's ability to meet debt-service payments, based on its financial projections.

If the forecasted projections and analysis reveal that your company's ability to meet debt-service obligations will put a strain on its cash flow (or that the amount of available collateral is not sufficient), then you and your advisers should carefully consider equity alternatives. It's clearly not worth driving your company into voluntary (or involuntary) bankruptcy for the sole purpose of retaining a high level of control. One way to look at this is to recognize that 60% of something is worth a whole lot more than 100% of nothing. The level of debt financing selected by your company should also be compared with key business ratios for your particular industry (such as those published by Dun & Bradstreet). Once you've determined the ideal debt-to-equity ratio, take the time to explore the various debt-financing options available to you as well as the business and legal issues involved in borrowing funds from a commercial lender.

How a Lender Analyzes a Business-Loan Proposal

Although you should give careful consideration to all available alternative sources of debt financing, traditional bank loans from commercial lenders are the most common source of capital for small, growing companies.

Before attempting to understand the types of loans available from commercial banks, you should get to know the perspective of the average commercial bank when it analyzes a company's loan proposal.

Confusion and resentment are not uncommon in the relationship between bankers and founders of emerging-growth businesses. While the entrepreneur often believes that the banker does not understand and appreciate his or her business requirements, the loan officer's perspective may be greatly influenced by past experiences with entrepreneurs who expect to borrow millions of dollars collateralized only by a dream.

It is crucial that you understand the lender's perspective before you ask for money.

Given these inherently conflicting points of view, it is crucial that you understand the lender's perspective before you ask for money. Banks are in the business of selling money, and capital is the principal product in their inventory. Bankers, however, are both statutorily and personally averse to risk. Loan officers are obligated to take all necessary steps to minimize the risk to their institution in each transaction and to obtain the maximum protection in the event of default. Therefore, the types of loans available to growing companies, the terms and conditions of loan agreements and the steps taken by the bank to protect its interest all have a direct relationship to the level of risk that is perceived by the lending officer and the loan committee.

In preparation for the negotiation of the loan documentation, the members of your emerging business's management team who have been assigned to obtain the debt financing from a commercial bank must immediately undertake a risk-mitigation and management program. The lender, whose primary concern is repayment of the debt, will usually look at the following five factors in determining your company' ability to repay the debt:

- **Does your personal investment of savings or personal equity** in your business total at least 25% to 50% of the loan you are requesting? (A lender or investor will not finance 100% of your business.)
- **Do you have a solid credit record** verified by your credit report,

work history, and letters of recommendation?
- **Do you have the experience and training** to operate a successful business?
- **Do your loan proposal and business plan demonstrate your understanding** of and commitment to the success of the business?
- **Will your business have sufficient cash flow** to make the monthly payments?

Preparing for Debt Financing

As you and your financial advisers prepare to obtain the necessary financing for you company, it is crucial that you take every step to manage risk, thereby positioning your company as a suitable borrower in the view of a commercial lender.

The Loan Proposal

The mitigation and management of risk will always have a direct impact on the favorability and affordability of traditional debt financing. For a small and growing company, this will mean a loan-proposal package that demonstrates the presence of a strong management team, an aggressive internal-control and accounts-receivable management program, and financial statements and projections that demonstrate the ability to service the debt. It will also require well-developed relationships with suppliers, distributors and employees, and an understanding of the trends in the marketplace. In addition, many commercial-loan officers will apply the traditional test of the four "C's" of credit worthiness—namely, character (reputation and honesty), capacity (business acumen and experience), capital (ability to meet debt-service payments), and collateral (access to assets that can be liquidated in the event of a default). A loan officer will review all of these elements in determining your company's credit-worthiness and the relative risk to the bank in making the proposed loan.

The exact elements of a loan package will vary depending on the size of the company, its industry and its stage of development; however, most lenders will want answers to the following basic questions:

- **Who is the borrower?**
- **How much capital is needed and when?**
- **How will the capital be allocated** and for what specific purposes?
- **How will the borrower service the debt obligations** (e.g., application and processing fees, interest, principal or balloon payments)? and
- **What collateral can the borrower offer the bank** in the event that the company is unable to meet its obligations?

The answers you provide to each of these questions will assist the banker in assessing the risk factors in the proposed transaction. In addition, your answers will provide the commercial-loan officer with the information he or she will need to persuade the loan committee to approve the transaction. While you and the loan officer may initially have differing perspectives, you should realize that, once the loan officer is convinced of your company's loan-worthiness, he or she will serve as an advocate on your company's behalf in presenting the loan proposal to the bank's loan committee. Therefore, winning over the loan officer is your first step in obtaining the capital you need.

The loan documentation, terms, rates and covenants that the loan committee will specify as a condition to making the loan will be directly related to the ways in which your company is able to demonstrate its ability to mitigate and manage risk, as described in your business plan and formal loan proposal.

The loan proposal should include the following categories of information, many of which you can borrow and modify from your business plan:

SUMMARY OF THE REQUEST. This should provide an overview of your company's history, the amount of capital you need, the proposed repayment terms, the intended use of the capital, and the collateral available to secure the loan.

HISTORY OF THE BORROWER. Give a brief background of your company; its capital structure; its key founders; its stage of development and plans for growth; a list of key customers, suppliers and service providers; management structure and philosophy; plant and facility; the key products and services your company offers; and a description of any intellectual property your company owns or developed.

MARKET DATA. Offer an overview of trends in your industry; the size of the market; your company's market share; an assessment of the direct and indirect competition; proprietary advantages; marketing, public relations and advertising strategies; market-research studies; and future industry prospects.

FINANCIAL INFORMATION. You must provide pro forma financial statements, federal and state tax returns, appraisals of key assets or company valuations, a current balance sheet, credit references, and a two-year income statement. Carefully explain how you intend to use the requested capital in carrying out your growth strategy, an allocation of the loan proceeds, and your company's ability to repay the debt. Finally, you must provide a three-year statement of projected cash flow on a monthly basis to support a discussion of the company's ability to service the debt.

SCHEDULES AND EXHIBITS. Upon request, you must make available to the lender for inspection a schedule of supporting documents, such as agreements with manufacturers or letters of intent for planned operations, insurance policies, key contracts, employment agreements, and leases. Also append résumés of your company's principals, recent articles about the company, a picture of its products or site, and an organizational chart of the management.

Types of Commercial Bank Loans

The term of the loan, the expected use of proceeds, and the amount of money to be borrowed usually categorize loans (one or more types of loans could be tailored to meet your company's requirements). The availability of these various loans will depend on the industry in which you operate and the bank's assessment of your company's credit-worthiness. A variety of loans may be available for implementing your business-growth plan.

Short-term loans are ordinarily used for a specified purpose with the expectation by the lender that the loan will be repaid at the end of the project. For example, a seasonal business may borrow capital to build up its inventory in preparation for the peak season. When the season comes to a close, the lender expects to be repaid immediately. Similarly, a short-term loan could be used to cover a period when a company's customers or clients are in arrears; when the accounts receivable are collected, the loan is be repaid. Short-term loans are usually made in the form of a promissory note (see the discussion of loan documentation, below), payable on demand, and may be secured by the inventory or accounts receivable that the loan is designed to cover, or it may be unsecured. Unless the company is a start-up or operates in a highly volatile industry (thereby increasing the risk in the eyes of the lender), most short-term loans will be unsecured, keeping the loan documentation and the bank's processing time and costs to a minimum. Lenders generally view short-term loans as self-liquidating, in that they can be repaid by foreclosing on the current assets that the loan has financed. Because the bank's transactional costs are low and it perceives the risk on a short-term loan to be low, this type of loan may be somewhat easier for your growing business to obtain. It can also serve as an excellent means for establishing a relationship with a bank and demonstrating your company's credit-worthiness.

> **A short-term loan can serve as an excellent means for establishing a relationship with a bank and demonstrating your company's credit-worthiness.**

Operating lines of credit consist of a specific amount of capital to be made available to the company on an "as needed" basis over a specified period of time. A line of credit may be short-term (60 to 120 days) or intermediate term (one to three years), renewable or nonrenewable, and at a fixed or fluctuating interest rate. With this type of loan, it's important that you negotiate ceilings on interest rates; avoid excessive commitment, processing, application and related up-front fees; and ensure that repayment schedules will not be an undue strain for your company. Also ensure that your obligations to make payments against the line of credit are consistent with your company's anticipated cash-flow projections.

Intermediate-term loans are generally provided over a three- to five-year period for the purposes of acquiring equipment, fixtures, furniture and supplies; expanding existing facilities; acquiring another business; or to provide working capital. The loan is almost always secured, not only by the assets being purchased with the loan proceeds, but also by other company assets, such as your inventory, accounts receivable, equipment and real estate. This type of loan usually calls for a loan agreement, which typically includes restrictive covenants that govern the operation and management of your company during the term of the loan. The restrictive covenants (discussed in greater detail below) are intended to protect the lender and ensure that all payments will be made on a timely basis, before you pay out any dividends, employee bonuses or non-critical expenses.

Long-term loans are generally extended for specific, highly secured transactions, such as the purchase of real estate or a multi-use business facility, in which case a lender will consider extending a long-term loan to a small company for 65% to 80% of the appraised value of the land or building. As a general rule, commercial banks do not provide long-term financing to small businesses. The risk of market fluctuations and business failure over a ten- or 20-year term is simply too high for the commercial lender.

Letters of credit are issued primarily by commercial banks solely in connection with international sales transactions, as a method of expediting the shipping and payment process. Typically, a bank issues a letter of credit when the seller of goods demands that payment be made in the form of a letter of credit. The buyer's bank, often in conjunction with a corresponding bank, will then communicate with the seller of the goods, explaining the documents that it requires (such as a negotiable bill of lading) as a condition to releasing the funds. It is important to understand that, even if there are problems in the performance of the underlying contract between the buyer and the seller, banks issuing the letter of credit may be liable to the seller of the goods for payment if the bill of lading and related documents are properly presented. Any defenses available to the buyer relating to the underlying contract are generally not available to the bank issuing the letter of credit. In recent years, the standby letter of credit has emerged as an indirect debt-financing method that serves as a guaranty of performance. Banks often issue standby letters of credit on behalf of a customer to secure payments to a builder, landlord or key supplier. The operative term of such an instrument is "standby" because if the transaction goes as planned, the instrument will never be drawn upon.

Negotiating the loan demands a delicate balancing between the requirements of the lender and the needs of your company.

Negotiating the Loan

Negotiating the financing documents demands a delicate balancing between the requirements of the lender and the needs of your company. The lender's goal is to have all rights, remedies and protection available to mitigate the risk of loan default. Your company will want to minimize the level of control exercised by the lender (generally through the affirmative and negative covenants of the loan agreement) and achieve a return on its assets that greatly exceeds its debt-service payments.

Before examining each document involved in a typical debt financing (covered later in this chapter), it is important that you have a clear understanding of some general rules of loan negotiation

INTEREST RATES. Rates are generally calculated in accordance with prevailing market rates, the degree of risk inherent in the proposed transaction, the extent of any pre-existing relationship with the lender, and the cost of administering the loan.

COLLATERAL. Assets that have a value equal to or greater than the proceeds of the loan may be pledged. Under such circumstances, you should attempt to keep certain business assets outside of the pledge agreement so that they are available to serve as security in the event that you request additional capital at a later time. Beyond the traditional forms of tangible assets that may be offered to the lender, you should also consider intangibles (such as assignment of lease rights, key-man insurance, intellectual property, and goodwill) as collateral. These assets could be very costly to a firm in the event of default; therefore, consider pledging them only if your ability to repay is certain.

RESTRICTIVE COVENANTS. These are designed to protect the interests of the lender. The typical loan agreement will contain a variety of affirmative and negative covenants.

Affirmative covenants encompass your company's obligations (and those of its subsidiaries, except as otherwise provided) during the period that the loan is outstanding, and may include the following affirmative acts by your company:

■ **furnishing audited financial statements** (income and expenses and balance sheets) at regular intervals (usually quarterly and annually, with the annual statement to be prepared and certified by an independent certified public accountant).

■ **furnishing other information regarding business affairs** and your company's financial condition.

■ **furnishing copies of all financial statements,** reports and returns that are sent to shareholders or to governmental agencies.

■ **providing access to its properties** and to its books of accounts and records.

■ **keeping and maintaining proper books of account.**

■ **complying with all applicable laws,** rules and regulations.

■ **maintaining its corporate existence** (as well as that of any subsidiaries) and all rights and privileges.

■ **maintaining all property in good order** and repair.

■ **maintaining an agreed-upon dollar amount of net worth** (or an agreed-upon ratio of current assets to current liabilities).

- **keeping and maintaining proper and adequate insurance** on all assets.
- **paying and discharging all indebtedness and all taxes** as due (except such as are contested in good faith).
- **purchasing and paying premiums** as due on life insurance on named key personnel (wherein the company is named as beneficiary).
- **maintaining existing management.**

Negative covenants (generally negotiable) encompass certain actions in which your company must obtain the lender's consent. These covenants depend in large part on your company's financial strength and economic and operational requirements. Negative covenants generally require your company to obtain the lender's consent in order to:

- **engage in any business not related** to its present business.
- **create any mortgage, lien, or other security** other than pending security on the property securing the loan.
- **create any mortgage, lien or other encumbrance** (including conditional sales agreements, other title-retention agreements or lease-purchase agreements on any property of the company or its subsidiaries, unless excepted).
- **incur any new indebtedness** except for trade credit or renewals, extensions, or refunding of any current indebtedness. The company's right to incur indebtedness may be conditioned upon compliance with a specified ratio (actual or pro forma) of pre-tax income to interest expense, for a designated period.
- **enter into leases of real or personal property** (as lessee) in excess of a specified aggregate amount. The company's right to make leases may be conditioned upon compliance with a specified ratio (actual or pro forma) of pre-tax income to fixed charges, for a designated period.
- **purchase, redeem or otherwise acquire** or retire for cash any of its capital stock (with stated exceptions), such as from post-tax earnings in excess of a specified amount or for regular sinking-fund requirements on preferred stock.
- **pay any cash dividends** (with stated exceptions), such as from

post-tax earnings earned subsequent to a specified date or in excess of a specified amount.

- **become a guarantor** (except as to negotiable instruments endorsed for collection in ordinary course).
- **make loans or advances to or investments** in any person or entity other than its subsidiaries.
- **merge or consolidate with any other corporation** or sell or lease substantially all or the entirety of its assets. (There may be exceptions where a company is the surviving corporation.)
- **permit net worth or current assets** to fall below a specified level.
- **permit capital expenditure** to exceed a specified amount (which may be on an annual basis, with or without right to cumulate).
- **permit officers' and directors' compensation** to exceed a specified level.
- **sell or dispose all of the stock of a subsidiary** (subject to permitted exceptions) or permit subsidiaries to incur debt (other than trade debt).

Be aware that covenants may be serious impediments to your company's ability to grow and prosper over the long run. Carefully review covenants with your advisers for consistency in relation to other corporate documents, such as your company's bylaws and shareholders agreements. Note, however, that in the rapidly changing area of lender-liability law, some commercial bankers are backing away from the level of control that they have traditionally imposed on a borrower's company.

PREPAYMENT RIGHTS. Negotiate prepayment rights regardless of the actual term of the loan, granting you the right to prepay the principal of the loan without penalty or special prepayment charges. Many commercial lenders seek to attach prepayment charges that have a fixed rate of interest in order to ensure that a minimum rate of return is earned over the projected life of the loan.

HIDDEN COSTS AND FEES. Closing costs, processing fees, filing fees, late charges, attorneys' fees, out-of-pocket expense reimbursement (courier, travel, photocopying, etc.), court costs, and auditing or inspection fees can all be accrued in connection with the debt financing. Try to avoid these and other charges that banks often want to impose in association with certain depository restrictions. For example, you may be charged a fee for not maintaining a certain deposit balance, or you may be required to use the bank as a depository as a condition to closing on the loan.

Understanding the Legal Documents

As you would with any bank loan, you'll be expected to execute several documents in the process of obtaining the loan for your business. Here, in brief, is a rundown of the documents associated with a business loan.

THE LOAN AGREEMENT. This sets forth all of the terms and conditions of the transaction between the lender and your company. The key provisions of this document include the amount, term, repayment schedules and procedures, special fees, insurance requirements, conditions precedent, restrictive covenants, your company's representations and warranties (with respect to status, capacity, ability to repay, title to properties, litigation, etc.), events of default, and remedies of the lender in the event of default. Have an experienced attorney and a knowledgeable accountant review the provisions of the loan agreement and the long-term legal and financial impact of the restrictive covenants. Your company should negotiate to establish a timetable under which certain covenants will be removed or modified as the company demonstrates its ability to repay. Do not rely on any verbal assurances made by the loan officer that a waiver of default on a payment or a covenant will subsequently be available.

THE SECURITY AGREEMENT. The collateral your company will pledge in order to secure the loan is contained in this agreement. This agreement usually references terms of the loan agreement as well as the promissory note (especially with respect to the restrictions on the use of the collateral and the procedures upon default of the debt obligation). The remedies available to the lender in the event of default range from repaying the outstanding balance of the loan by selling the collateral at a public auction to taking possession of the collateral and using it for an income-producing activity.

THE FINANCING STATEMENT. The interests of the lender in the collateral is recorded here and is filed with the state and local corporate and land-records management authorities. It is designed to give notice to other potential creditors of your company that a senior security interest has been granted in the collateral specified in the financing statement. You'll find specific rules regarding this document and the priority of competing creditors in the applicable state's version of the Uniform Commercial Code (U.C.C.).

THE PROMISSORY NOTE. This serves as evidence of the obligation of your company to the lender. Many of its terms are included in the more comprehensive loan agreement. These terms include the interest rate, the length of the term, the repayment schedule, the ability of the company to prepay without penalty, the conditions under which the lender may declare an event of default, and the rights and remedies available to the lender upon such default.

THE GUARANTY. The purpose of this document is to provide further security in order to mitigate the risk of the transaction to the lender. You personally execute this document. Carefully review the terms of the guaranty with your advisers and negotiate its term, scope, rights of the lender in the event of default, and type of guaranty provided. For example, under certain circumstances, the lender can be forced to exhaust all possible remedies against the company before being able to proceed against the guarantor (you) or may be limited to proceed against certain assets of the guarantor. Similarly, you can negotiate the extent of the guaranty so that it is reduced on an annual basis as your company grows stronger and its ability to independently service the debt becomes more evident.

Ongoing Assessment of Banking Relationships

I n recent years, many commercial lenders have begun to compete fiercely for the business of smaller companies. This has resulted in greater access to debt capital for growth companies as well as a broader range of services offered by banks. You should periodically assess your company's banking relationships to ensure that you are receiving the best rates and services currently available to businesses of your size and within your industry. This does not mean that you should discard a long-standing and harmonious banking relationship over a one-percentage-point difference in a interest rate; however, it does mean that you should not remain loyal to a bank that does not offer the full range of services that your company needs.

In periodically assessing your company's banking relationships, consider the following questions:

- **Do you get personal attention** from your designated loan officer? When was the last time you heard from him or her?
- **How did the bank respond to your most recent request** for another term loan or increase in your company's operating line of credit?
- **Does the bank truly understand your industry?**
- **How strict has the bank been** in enforcing loan covenants, restrictions or late charges?
- **Does the bank offer your company** any valuable support services?
- **How do the bank's interest rates and loan terms compare** with those offered by other local commercial lenders?
- **What is the bank's standing in the business community?** What has it done lately to enhance or damage its reputation?
- **Is the bank operating on a solid financial foundation?**
- **Is the bank large enough to grow with the financial needs** of your company as the business expands and additional amounts of capital are required? (This should be considered early on in the company's development so that the relationship is not outgrown just at the time when you need it the most.)
- **How has the bank shown you** that it really appreciates your business?

For a growing company with a steady projected cash flow, debt financing offers an attractive capital-formation alternative. Among its benefits are lower transactional costs, the power of leveraging, tax deductions and an avoidance of dilution of ownership; however, the costs of these benefits are the restrictive covenants and high risk in the event of an inability to meet debt-service obligations. When you seek debt financing for your fast-track growth company, be armed with an experienced management team able to assist in your presentation to the lender, structure a sensible debt-to-equity mix and negotiate an affordable loan.

Capital Formation Through an Initial Public Offering

I N THE MID TO LATE 1990s, MOST FAST-TRACK GROWING companies positioned themselves for an initial public offering (IPO) of their securities as a cornerstone of their quest for rapid growth. Many of these entrepreneurial companies succeeded in offering their securities to the public. In retrospect, however, many of them lacked the management teams, the operating history, the depth of customer commitment, the revenues and the profits to support a public market or their companies' lofty valuations. As a result, the period between March 2000 and June 2001 brought with it a sharp correction as the IPO bubble burst and valuations were adjusted accordingly. Suddenly companies whose shares had traded for hundreds of dollars were now on sale for a few dollars and shareholders lost 70%, 80% and even 95% of their investments.

As a result of these massive losses, there was a rapid return to normalcy. IPOs have been limited to larger companies with more solid track records, loyal customers, strong brands and excellent financial performance (such as insurance companies and the biggest performance surprise of the year 2000, the IPO by Krispy Kreme Doughnuts, which yielded an impressive 200%-plus return). Over the next three to five years, the ability of a fast-track growth company to go public will be limited by these new (which are really just a return to the old) standards.

Understanding the IPO

An initial public offering is the legal process whereby a company initially registers its securities with the Securities and Exchange Commission (SEC) for sale to the general investing public. Many entrepreneurs view the process of "going public" as the epitome of financial success and reward; however, going public can be a critical crossroad for a company following a rapid-growth path. The decision to go public requires considerable strategic planning and analysis from both a legal and business perspective in order to weigh the benefits and costs; understand the process; and understand the obligations of the company, its advisers and shareholders once the company has successfully completed its public offering.

The Benefits of Going Public

For a privately held company on a fast-track growth path, the process of going public offers many benefits, including:

- **greatly increased access** to capital;
- **more liquidity** for the shares;
- **market prestige;**
- **enhancement of the company's public image;**
- **new opportunities for employee ownership and participation;**
- **improved opportunities** for mergers, acquisitions and further rounds of financing; and
- **an immediate increase in the wealth** for the founders and current stockholders.

The Costs of Going Public

Although going public can bring your company many benefits, those must be carefully weighed against the costs of being a public company, which include:

- **a dilution in founders' and existing stockholders' control** of the entity;
- **pressure to meet market and shareholder expectations** for growth and dividends;
- **changes in management styles** and employee expectations;
- **compliance with complex federal and state securities regulations;**

- **stock resale restrictions** for company insiders;
- **vulnerability to stock-market shifts;** and
- **sharing your company's financial success** with hundreds—even hundreds of thousands—of other shareholders.

Legal Expenses Associated With Going Public

In addition to some of the more obvious business costs associated with an IPO, the most expensive aspect of registering the securities is often the hidden costs imposed by federal and state securities laws. The rules and regulations imposed by the SEC make going public a time-consuming and expensive process— one that begins several years before the public offering, and continues (through the SEC periodic reporting process) for as long as the company remains public. In making the decision to go public, you should carefully consider the following legal costs and factors:

PLANNING AND PREPARING YOUR COMPANY FOR THE IPO. From the day that your company is formed there are many legal and structural pitfalls that you must avoid if an IPO is in your company's future. Some of these pitfalls can become a significant impediment to a successful IPO and will be expensive to remedy once the damage has been done. For example, being a public company will require a more formal management style from a legal perspective, which normally entails more regular meetings of the board of directors and close adherence to all formalities imposed by state corporate laws. You're best off operating your company as if it were public right from the start.

DUE DILIGENCE AND HOUSECLEANING. Business owners (and their management teams) who take their companies public frequently complain that they feel as though their business and personal lives are conducted in a fishbowl. Federal and state securities laws dictate that a prospective investor must have access to all material information about a company offering its securities to the public. As a result, well before you are ready to file a registration statement with the SEC, you must go through the due-diligence process (described below). Before you're ready to operate in a fishbowl, you may need to formalize, amend or even terminate the corporate charters, bylaws, shareholder agreements, employment agreements, leases, licenses, accounting methods, and related documents and procedures.

THE REGISTRATION PROCESS. Don't make the mistake of underestimating the time, effort and expense required to prepare the registration statement. Frequently, the six- to twelve-month time frame and the out-of-pocket expenses alone make the cost a prohibitive capital-formation alternative for many growing businesses. While costs do vary depending on a number of factors, if you plan to offer your company's securities to the public you should be prepared to spend anywhere from $200,000 to $500,000 in legal and accounting fees, appraisal costs, printing expenses, consulting and filing fees. And this doesn't include the underwriters and broker commissions that may run as high as 10% or more of the total offering. As discussed later in this chapter, however, the SEC has implemented new regulations for small-business owners that will create cost-savings in legal and accounting fees. Nevertheless, you must remember that few, if any, of your expenses will be contingent on the success of the offering and, therefore, must be paid regardless of whether only a few or a high number of shares are actually sold.

Along with the registration statement, prior to an offering you must file exhibits and attachments that document major business transactions (such as plans of acquisition, reorganization, liquidation, etc.), customer and vendor arrangements, and financial statements. These required disclosures will result in a loss of confidentiality that may be costly in an indirect way, because competitors, creditors, labor unions, suppliers, and others will have access to these documents once they become available to the public.

PERIODIC REPORTING AND ONGOING COMPLIANCE. Most public companies are subject to the ongoing periodic reporting requirements imposed by the SEC. These include quarterly financial reporting (Forms 10-Q and 10-QSB), annual financial reporting (Forms 10-K and 10-KSB), reporting of current material events (Form 8-K), and related reporting requirements such as those for sale of control stock and tender offers. (Reporting requirements are covered in greater detail later in this chapter.) Other ongoing costs of being a public company include: an increased use of attorneys, accountants and other advisers; allocation of staff time to meet with securities analysts and financial press; the implementation of a shareholder- and media-relations program; and the cost of annual reports, shareholder meetings, and solicitations of proxies when shareholder approval is needed for major corporate transactions.

Most public companies are subject to the ongoing periodic reporting requirements imposed by the SEC.

Preparing for the Underwriter's Due Diligence

Prior to the preparation of the registration statement, the proposed underwriter and their financial analysts and attorneys will want to conduct extensive due diligence on your company to ensure the viability of the offering. The due-diligence process means that your growing company's corporate records, personnel, business plans, industry trends, customer data, pricing and business models, products, key agreements, and financial data will be viewed under a microscope. That's why it's important to begin preparing for this process far in advance; otherwise, you might incur significant expenses that could result from being unprepared or encountering embarrassing situations when factual or strategic weaknesses or problems are unexpectedly revealed. The underwriter's legal counsel will be looking for any problems that may be impediments to the offering, including excessive compensation or expenses, a weak management team, nepotism, or problems with your company's underlying intellectual property or business model; therefore, the sooner you address these problems the better. The best way to begin the preparation process is by having your company's lawyers conduct a legal audit (as discussed in Chapter 10).

In a legal audit, a company's management team meets with corporate counsel to discuss strategic plans and objectives and review key documents and records. In the context of preparing for an IPO, they will also analyze and identify current and projected problem areas that may be identified by the underwriter's team so that they can solve them well in advance.

The best way to begin to prepare for the underwriter's due diligence is by having your company's lawyers conduct a legal audit.

Other key concerns of any prospective underwriter or investor analyzing your company will be the three "P's" of due diligence: people, products and profits. In preparing for due diligence, carefully examine your standing in these three areas, and modify your current structure where needed.

PEOPLE. Carefully select your key employees, because their background and role in your company will be closely investigated in the due-diligence process and subsequently disclosed in the prospectus. These employees should be subject to reasonable employment agreements, non-disclosure agreements and incentive programs that ensure their long-term commitment to your company. Carefully examine whether your current management team has the skills and experience to lead a public company. Finally, your professional advisers should have a strong corporate- and securities-law background, and should be able to grow with the company as the services they are required to perform will become more complex.

PRODUCTS. All products and services offered by your company should be protected to the fullest extent possible under patent, trademark and copyright law (see Chapter 18). Negotiate and reduce to a formal written agreement (with the eventual disclosure of these documents kept in mind) any key vendor, licensee, customer or distributor agreement that materially affects the production or distribution of your products and services. Further, the systems used to produce your company's products or services should be sufficient to facilitate future growth, and distribution channels should be in place to bring the products and services to the marketplace.

PROFITS. Your company's capital structure and financial performance will be under the microscope of any potential underwriter. Although the wild market of the late 1990s seemed to have little interest in actual profits (or in the case of some high-tech companies, even revenues), the more conservative financial markets of the early 2000s will require a solid financial track record.

Additional Preparation Tips

As mentioned earlier, you should begin acting as if you already were a publicly traded company long before you consider going public. This is especially true from a management, recordkeeping, shareholder reporting and financial-controls perspective. Immediately implement a more formalized management structure, which will include formal board meetings on a monthly or quarterly basis. In addition to maintaining complete and accurate corporate minutes and resolutions and preparing periodic reports to existing shareholders, begin recruiting an experienced and independent board of directors who will be acceptable to the investing public. (See Chapter 9 for more on selecting a board of directors.) Taking such an approach will not only expedite the process of going public, it will likely enhance your valuation.

Potential Deal Breakers

The following factors will have a negative effect on your company's valuation and the underwriter's willingness to participate in the public offering:

- **inefficient management structure** or major holes in the management team;
- **unprofitable business model** or weak revenue base;
- **overly restrictive shareholder agreements** that affect the company's control;
- **operating in a market** with low barriers to entry;
- **self-dealing among the board of directors** and key stockholders;

- **weaknesses in the company's key intangible assets,** such as brand or operating technology;
- **inadequate corporate records;**
- **capital structure with excessive debt;**
- **series of unaudited and uncertain financial statements;** and
- **poor earnings history.**

Finding the Right Underwriter for Your IPO

In selecting an underwriter, consider a wide variety, ranging from the small local firms who may devote a considerable amount of time and attention to the transaction to the larger firms with a genuine Wall Street presence and reputation. The risk with the latter is that your company's offering may be lost among the bigger transactions or delegated to junior staff members. Devote a significant amount of time to the selection of the lead underwriter, whose skill will be a key ingredient in the success of your IPO.

Interview as many prospective underwriters as possible to ensure that you've made the right choice. Among the key issues you should consider in the selection process are the underwriting firm's reputation, experience, distribution capability, market-making ability, research capabilities, and industry-specific expertise. (see the box on pages 248-249). The size and reputation of the underwriter that your company will be able to attract will depend on (among other things) the strength of your company, the amount of stock being offered, and your company's future business plans.

Underwriting firms typically provide such support services as management consulting, business valuations, development of media/shareholders relations programs, assistance in developing an optimum capital structure or location, and analysis of merger/acquisition candidates (which may or may not be needed when considering a public offering). Carefully review the services offered by firms you are considering to ensure that your company's needs will be fully met.

An Alternative to Traditional IPOs

A stock offering of any type has not traditionally been the first financing strategy for small, growing companies. But changes in federal and state securities regulations, as well as the advent of Internet commerce, have brought a greater range of options to these companies in their efforts to raise capital, with the direct public offering (DPO) being the most popular. But along with the new possibilities, there is also confusion as to what the differences are between direct and initial public offerings.

Direct Public Offerings

A direct public offering is a primary-market stock or debenture sale of securities from the company issuing the shares to the public buying the shares. The issuer usually performs the underwriting, structuring, filing, and selling of its offer without an underwriter and selling syndicate used in an initial public offering. DPOs date back to 1976, but only since 1989, when the SEC simplified registrations for small companies, have they really gained momentum.

The DPO made its debut on the Internet in 1995, when Spring Street Brewing Company displayed its offering prospectus on its Web site, enabling potential investors to learn about the company, download subscription documents and, if they were interested in investing, send a check directly to Spring Street. Later in that same year, when the SEC ruled that "electronic delivery is good delivery," direct public offerings on the Internet became the hottest method of raising capital for small companies.

In 1996, after experiencing the need for "Internet underwriters" first hand, Andy Klein, the CEO of Spring Street Brewing Company created Wit Capital Corp., an online entity that integrated the functions of an investment bank, brokerage firm, and exchange forum. Although Wit Capital subsequently went out of business, many other companies have gotten into the business of displaying offering literature, for both direct and initial public offerings, online.

The rise of DPOs on the Internet stems from two collid-
(continued on page 246)

Finding the Right Underwriter for Your IPO: Key Factors to Consider

Size of Your Company. Many major underwriters will consider only companies that have attained a particular size, level of profitability and that have had a specified minimum period of operations.

Size of the Offering. Some underwriters will not consider offerings below a certain size ($15 million or more is the typical requirement of major national underwriters).

Industry Specialization. Underwriters frequently develop reputations and expertise in particular industries or fields. This knowledge will affect the quality of the underwriter's due diligence as well as the accuracy of its pricing and its ability to sell your company to others during and after the offering.

Research Coverage. It is critical that the underwriter have strong research capabilities and respect in the industry in which you operate. These will be critical in the initial valuation as well as in future trading.

Reputation. The underwriter's image and reputation will have a direct impact on how your company will be viewed.

Quality of Underwriting Group. Some underwriters develop stronger selling syndicates than others.

Distribution Strength. The lead manager must control and influence the channels of distribution. It is important that the underwriters sell out the offering—and do so expeditiously.

Personal Chemistry Between Your Company's Management and the Underwriter's Personnel. You and your management team should begin getting to know underwriters a year or more before the offering. Meet the key people in the organization and get a feeling for their philosophy. Venture-capital investors may try to influence the choice of underwriter, but your company is the one that has to live with the choice. There must be a philosophical fit.

Mix of Retail and Institutional Customers. Some investment bankers sell primarily to institutions and others have large retail-sales organizations. The types of customers to which the underwriter directs its marketing activities may have some impact on its ability to sell your offering in certain markets.

After-Market Support. Underwriters provide a variety of post-offering services, such as performing as a market maker, purchasing shares for its own account, bringing the stock to the attention of analysts and investors and facilitating the bringing of information about your company to the marketplace. Lack of adequate after-market support could have a negative impact on the price of your company's stock.

Quality of Analysts. The underwriter's analysts must be well known in your company's industry. Likewise, they should know the industry well. Additionally, their publications should be widely read in the investment community. Your company should get a research commitment from the managing underwriter. You can check the analysts' reputations by calling some big institutions and inquiring if the *Institutional Investor* or the *Greenwich Survey* recognizes the analysts in the surveys.

Staffing Problems. Make sure that the underwriter will devote sufficient attention to your company's offering and that the offering will not be placed in line behind what the underwriter may consider more exciting opportunities, particularly in times where certain markets are "hot."

Underwriter's References. Check a prospective underwriter's performance by getting a list of the last five or ten offerings in which the underwriter participated, then contacting or visiting the principals of those companies to discuss the underwriter's performance before, during and after the offering. Among inquiries you should make are whether the promised after-market

support was there, the promised research reports were completed and published on time, if the "road show" was well handled, their senior staff attended the meetings or sent junior employees, etc. You can obtain additional references from the institutions to which the underwriting firm sells.

Once selected, your lead underwriter will usually execute a letter of intent, which states the terms and conditions of the proposed distribution of the securities and will typically also set a range for the price of the securities, and hence the valuation of the company. However, the final decision on these issues will be made over the course of the due-diligence process and will finally be determined by the post-effective price amendment (which may adjust the price based on recent events affecting the company or any changes in market conditions). Underwriters have many different methods at arriving at the preliminary valuation and pricing, so be prepared to solicit competing bids to ensure the best valuation for your company. The letter of intent will also govern your relationship with the underwriter throughout the preparation and registration process because the final underwriting agreement is usually not signed until the day the registration statement becomes effective following SEC approval.

ing trends: the rise of Internet commerce and the rise of the online investor. For a small company, the benefits of a DPO include simplified registration procedures, less stringent reporting and auditing standards and maintenance of control. Although a DPO is an excellent vehicle to link small companies with small-company investors, it may not be right for every small business.

The rise of direct public offerings on the Internet stems from two colliding trends: the rise of Internet commerce and the rise of the online investor.

Direct public offerings are also referred to as exempt offerings because they are free of the intense registration restrictions that come with an IPO. In a DPO, a company sells directly to clients, members of the community, vendors, or any other constituency that has a stake in the company and its success. The steps in taking a company public through a DPO may include corporate review, due diligence, registration, and marketing and sales. If a company does not qualify for exemption from registration, there are several registration options that may be considered. Before choosing the one that is right for your company, examine the requirements and limitations of each.

DPO REGISTRATION OPTIONS. If your company chooses a direct public offering as a means of raising growth capital, you can choose either a Regulation A or a SCOR registration.

Regulation A allows an American or Canadian company to raise as much as $5 million over a 12-month period. To be eligible to file a Regulation A offering, your company must not already be a public company, nor an investment, oil or gas, or a blank-check company (that's one that goes public without deciding on its final business-growth plan or focus). There are no restrictions on the types of investors who can participate in a Regulation A offering (that is, they need not be accredited investors). Also, pursuant to Regulation A, you can market the offering by using press releases, cold calling, and doing television and radio commercials.

With a Regulation A offering, technically you will be

exempted from the filing provisions of the Securities Act of 1933 (the Act). That is, you will not have to file a registration statement with the SEC. However, you will need to comply with the antifraud and personal-liability provisions of the Act. And despite the exemption, you will be required to make essentially the same disclosures as if you had filed a registration statement. Regulation A offerings require that you file an offering circular with the SEC at least ten days before the offering is to commence. An offering circular is basically a prospectus, but the financial statements in an offering circular need not be audited, and the offering circular can be in narrative or question-and-answer format. Regulation A does not exempt your company from state securities laws, which vary greatly from state to state. In recent years, the use of Regulation A has lost popularity to Regulation D and registration for small businesses under Forms SB-1 and SB-2.

> **Regulation A does not exempt your company from state securities laws, which vary greatly from state to state.**

SCOR (Rule 4 under Regulation D), which stands for Small Corporate Offering Registration (SCOR)—and is known in some states as Uniform Limited Offering Registration (ULOR)—allows a small company to raise up to $1 million over a 12-month period. The minimum stock price is generally $5 per share. Your company can either issue a SCOR offering directly to the public or use a traditional IPO model, in which an underwriter sells the stock to the public. Although the SCOR program has grown in popularity since its inception in 1985, it is not available in every state.

Your company must have audited financial statements to launch a SCOR. As with a Regulation A offering, a SCOR offering must comply with the antifraud and personal-liability provisions of the Act; however, with a SCOR offering, you are not required to file an offering circular with the SEC. A SCOR is meant to be simpler and less expensive.

RESALE AND LIQUIDITY. For many investors, the test of whether to invest in a company hinges not just on the future success of the enterprise but also on the ability to get their money out of the deal. Exempt public offerings can accommodate this need for liquidity by trading on Nasdaq's Bulletin Board stock market. Because most states have restrictions on the resale of unregistered securities, trading an exempt stock-offering deal on the Bulletin Board isn't always possible. Some states allow for the resale of shares; as a result, some companies sell a small amount to investors in those states, and commence trading on the Bulletin Board. Once trading begins, the company can purchase coverage in journals to gain clearance for investors in nearly 30 states to buy shares that are already trading on the market.

ADVANTAGES AND DISADVANTAGES OF INTERNET DPOs. As with any other method of raising capital for your growing company, a DPO has its advantages and disadvantages.

The advantages are:
- **The due diligence associated with exempt stock offerings** is more compatible with the time constraints of running a business.
- **It's not necessary to hire an investment bank** to sell stocks, which can cost a company 4% to 7% of the capital raised.
- **Small investors who don't generally get a share** of juicy initial public offerings can have a shot at newly minted stocks, which often see immediate run-ups in price.
- **DPOs help companies target long term, small investors** who are interested in the success of the company.

The disadvantages are:
- **Stock sold through a direct offering** can be illiquid or difficult to trade.
- **The absence of a screening process,** along with the wide exposure provided by the Internet, may lead to defrauded investors.

Many companies are eager to raise more than the $5 million maximum that the Regulation A offering allows, but they are not in a position to attract the more prominent underwriters that generally work with large companies. For such a company, conducting a direct public offering on the Internet may be the solution.

The Mechanics of an Initial Public Offering

The process of taking a company public is a lengthy and complex one that involves many steps, from the organizational meeting to post-offering matters. The following pages offer a description of the steps you need to take to complete the offering.

The Organizational Meeting

Once a company has taken all of the necessary preparatory steps to conduct an IPO, it's time to schedule the organizational meeting for all key members of the registration team (lawyers, accountants, lead underwriter, chief executive officer, chief financial officer, etc.). The organizational meeting is conducted to establish a timetable for the preparation of the registration statement and to delegate the initial responsibilities for preparing the first draft.

The Registration Statement

Following the organizational meeting, schedule a series of "drafting sessions" to ensure that all of the data included in the registration statement is accurate, complete and prepared in accordance with SEC Rule 421, the "Plain English" requirement. The goal is to windup with an informative document that will give prospective investors all of the data they will need to make an informed decision regarding the investment. The personal interactions at these drafting sessions can be interesting, as more than a dozen trained professionals and entrepreneurs go over every word of the lengthy document, each from his or her own perspective, and with different agendas, objectives and turf to protect. Ultimately, however, all members of the drafting team work to produce a document they can be proud of and that can be filed with the SEC with a reasonable degree of confidence. An offering typically requires four or five drafting sessions over a 30- to 45-day period, including the final pre-filing drafting session at the financial printer's facilities

(continued on page 254)

Typical Agenda for an Organizational Meeting

The agenda for a typical organizational meeting is as follows:

I. REVIEW AND COMPLETE WORKING-GROUP LIST.

II. DISCUSS STRUCTURE OF OFFERING:
- A. Composition
  1. Size of offering
  2. Primary/secondary components
  3. Over-allotment option (amount and source)
- B. Price range considerations/valuation
- C. Proposed Nasdaq or exchange symbol
- D. Lock-up agreements with principal stockholders
  1. Stockholders covered
  2. Time period
- E. Capitalization
  1. Necessity of recapitalization/stock split
  2. Preferred stock and convertible notes/conversion at a minimum specified price
- F. Distribution objectives
  1. Institutional or retail
  2. Domestic or international
  3. Directed shares (employees, customers, others)
  4. Syndicate structure
- G. Potential existing stockholder issues
  1. Options/warrants; "cheap stock" issue
  2. Registration and piggyback rights
  3. Review market "overhang" (Rule 144)
- H. Offering expense allocation
- I. Use of proceeds

III. REVIEW TIME AND RESPONSIBILITY SCHEDULE:
- A. Review timing objectives
- B. Schedule of due-diligence meetings with management, lawyers, patent counsel, litigation counsel and auditors
- C. Drafting sessions
- D. Timing of filing/offering
  1. Availability of audited financials
  2. Target filing date
  3. Target offering/closing dates
- E. SEC review period
- F. Road-show preparation
- G. Road-show schedule and sites
- H. Other lead-time matters
  1. Schedule for board of directors' meetings
  2. Communications with stock holders

IV. DISCUSS ACCOUNTING AND FINANCIAL ISSUES:
- A. Historical financial information
  1. Annual and quarterly
  2. Audited financial statements
  3. Pro forma financial statements due to acquisitions
- B. Availability of interim

financial statements

C. Historical and projected earnings-per-share calculations
1. Annual and quarterly shares, options and warrants outstanding
2. Weighted average shares outstanding

D. Auditor's comfort letter

E. Auditor's management letters and company responses

F. Options and recent stock sales and related compensation issues

G. Revenue recognition

H. Accounts receivable and inventory

I. Accounts payable

J. Bad debt, returns, reserves

K. Contingencies

L. Tax issues

M. FASB requirements

N. Loan-agreement restrictions

V. REVIEW COMPANY/CORPORATE GOVERNANCE MATTERS:

A. Recent and upcoming senior management team additions or changes

B. Dates of board and stockholder meetings

C. Composition/compensation of board

D. Addition of outside directors, if needed or desired

E. Audit/compensation committees

F. Potential acquisitions

G. Director and officer insurance (amount and scope of coverage)

VI. REVIEW LEGAL MATTERS:

A. Form of registration statement (SB-1 or SB-2)

B. Notice and waiver of registration rights, including indemnification

C. Litigation (actual or threatened)

D. Waivers/restrictions/consents needed to offer the shares

E. Patent and technology matters; patent-counsel opinion

F. Confidential treatment of exhibits

G. Expert opinions (patent, regulatory, etc.)

H. Disclosure issues
1. Certain- and related-party transactions
2. Customer/supplier/ employment agreements
3. Strategic alliances

I. Amendment of certificate of incorporation
1. Preferred stock
2. Increase authorized number of shares of common stock

J. Anti-takeover provisions

K. Selling stockholder indemnification

L. Logistics for the board
1. Preparation of resolutions and appropriate authorizations
2. Formation of pricing committee

(continued on the next page)

Typical Agenda for an Organizational Meeting (continued)

3. Directors' and officers' questionnaires

M. Employee stock plans

1. Amendment of existing plans (to increase shares, etc.)

2. Creation of new plans (e.g., employee stock-purchase plan)

N. Recent and proposed option grants

O. Nasdaq issues

1. Investment banker's compensation

2. Venture-capital restrictions

3. Desire for immediate Exchange Act registration

P. Possible reincorporation in Delaware (if non-Delaware) or other state

D. Pending research reports/ press releases/product announcements and advertising

E. Pending newspaper, magazine articles/media interviews to be published

F. Industry conference presentations/trade shows

G. Other corporate announcements

H. Offering-related press releases

I. Communications with employees

J. Quiet period—gun-jumping memorandum (details how and when the company may speak to the public about its offering)

VII. REVIEW BLUE-SKY ISSUES:

A. Listing criteria for exemption if Nasdaq national market, NYSE or Amex. If not exempt, then go to (b), (c), (d) and (e) below

B. Options/valuation

C. Recent stock sales

D. Where to file (e.g., 50 states, Canada, international)

E. Number of states; cost

VIII. DISCUSS PUBLICITY POLICY:

A. Pre-filing, post-filing/ pre-effective, post-effective

B. Interaction with securities analysts

C. Control of information and releases, inquiries

IX. DISCUSSION OF DUE-DILIGENCE REVIEW:

A. Status of product development

1. New-product introductions

2. Status of product-development agreements

3. New-product development and research agreements

B. Names of principal customers or contracting parties with whom direct contacts may be made by underwriters and counsel

C. Need for immediate contract file and technology review by underwriters and underwriters' lawyers at offices of the company

D. Timing for review of minute books, stock records and all other contracts

E. Discussions with patent and regulatory lawyers, etc.

F. Customers, marketing and communications

1. Overview of distribution channels (sales and profitability of each)
2. Key customers
3. Marketing detail and strategy
4. Pricing strategies
5. Detailed instruction of competition (past, present and future)
6. Market share versus competition
7. Key customer wins and losses
8. Key marketing partners
9. Key distribution partners

G. Operations

1. Overview of manufacturing operations
2. Detail of personnel head count and function
3. Overview of suppliers

H. Financial information

1. Overview of historical quarterly financials for two previous fiscal years
2. Top ten customers in two previous fiscal years and in current year projected by sales volume
3. Quarterly projections for current and next fiscal years; highlights
4. Breakout of head count by functional area
5. Sales forecasts by quarter
6. Financing history; current commercial-bank lines
7. Accounts-receivable aging, days sales outstanding, and historical bad-debt experience
8. Revenue-recognition policy
9. Any deferred revenue/ backlog
10. Policy on capitalized software
11. Discuss related party trans actions, if any

I. Detailed stockholder table with shares, options, prices, etc. by major holders

X. DISCUSS OTHER LOGISTICS:

A. Selection of transfer agent and registrar

B. Form of stock certificates

C. Selection of printer

D. Use and timing of artwork and graphics in prospectus

E. Preliminary and final prospectus quantities

F. Location of volume printing

G. Dress code for future meetings

H. Preparation of exhibits for submission to the SEC's online database, known as "EDGAR"

to edit, check and re-check the final changes prior to the first filing with the SEC.

Other preliminary tasks that you and your IPO team must complete in connection with the preparation of the registration statement include:

- **dealing with the underwriter's due-diligence concerns** and questions;
- **meetings of the board of directors** to authorize the offering;
- **preparation and completion of the confidential questionnaire** for the officers and directors;
- **legal research as to compliance** with applicable state Blue-Sky laws;
- **ensuring compliance** with the National Association of Securities Dealers (NASD) regulations (the NASD is a self-regulatory body that reviews the underwriting and distribution agreements prepared in connection with the public offering to ensure that the terms and conditions are consistent with industry practices); and
- **establishing marketing and distribution strategies,** including the planning and preparation for the road show.

The registration statement consists of two distinct parts: the offering prospectus (which is used to assist underwriters and investors in analyzing the company and the securities being offered) and the exhibits and additional information (which are provided directly to the SEC as part of the disclosure and registration regulations). The registration statement is part of the public record and is available for public inspection.

There are a variety of alternative forms to the registration statement. The form that is right for your company depends on the company's history and size and nature the of the offering. The most common form used is the Form S 1. The S-1 is complicated, with several requirements that must be fulfilled before going public, and requires the description of the company's business, properties, material transactions between the company and its officers, pending legal proceedings, plans for distribution of the securities, and the intended use of the proceeds from the IPO. Forms S-2 and S-3 (subject to certain requirements) are available for companies that are already subject to the reporting requirements of the Securities

Exchange Act of 1934 (the Exchange Act), and Form S-4 is limited to corporate combinations (including mergers, reorganizations and consolidations). All the forms are filed and processed at the SEC's headquarters in Washington, D.C., by the Division of Corporate Finance.

The SEC's Small Business Initiatives

In 1992, the SEC implemented the Small Business Initiatives (SBIs), significantly modifying its special provisions for offerings by small businesses (Regulation S-B) that are not already subject to the reporting requirements of the Exchange Act. The SBIs were designed to streamline the federal registration process in connection with IPOs to encourage investment in small businesses. As defined in Rule 405 of the Exchange Act, a "small-business issuer" is a company meeting all of the following criteria:

- **has revenue of less than $25 million;**
- **is a U.S. or Canadian issuer;**
- **is not an investment company;**
- **if it's a majority-owned subsidiary, the parent corporation is also a small-business issuer.**

Emerging-business issuers can use the Forms SB-1 or SB-2 to register securities to be sold for cash with the SEC. Form SB-1 can be used only to register up to $10 million of securities to be sold for cash (the predecessor, S-18, had a ceiling of $7.5 million). Also, a company must not have registered more than $10 million in any continuous 12-month period (including the transaction being registered). In addition, SB-1 allows for financial statements (which must be audited by an independent party) to be given in accordance with generally accepted accounting principals (commonly referred to as GAAP), and not the detailed requirements of the SEC.

SB-2 allows emerging-business issuers to offer an unlimited dollar amount of securities, therefore allowing companies that meet the SEC's definition of a small business to sell more securities without having to undergo the same extensive disclosure process as larger companies. The relaxed standards of the SB-2 translate into lower transactional costs, reducing the average legal and accounting fees for growing businesses registering to make an IPO from a range of $200,000 to $500,000 to a range of $75,000 to $150,000.

SEC Regulations and the Registration Statement

Regardless of which registration form you and your advisers ultimately select, there are a series of core procedural rules and disclosure items that you must address and prepare in plain English. Failure to disclose material facts in a registration statement can result in civil and criminal prosecution. SEC Regulation S-K (and in the case of small issuers, Regulation S-B) specifies the particular types of information that must be disclosed. In addition to the information expressly required, as an issuer of securities, you must disclose any additional information needed to make the required statements not misleading. The following is a summary of the major items generally required in a registration statement.

COVER PAGE/FOREPART. The SEC has very specific requirements as to the information that must be stated on the cover page and preliminary information of the prospectus. This includes the name of the company, the amount and a brief description of the securities being offered, underwriting discounts and commissions, and risk factors.

INTRODUCTION TO THE COMPANY. Include in this section an overview of your company, its business, employees, financial performance, and principal officers. Also include a brief description of the security your company is offering, proceeds to the company and use of those proceeds.

RISK FACTORS. This section is often viewed as the company's insurance policy. Here you must include a description of the operating and financial risk factors affecting your company's business with particular regard to the offering of the securities (such as a dependency on a single customer, supplier, or group of key personnel; the absence of operating history in the new areas of business that the company wants to pursue; an unproven market for the products and services offered; or a lack of earnings history).

USE OF PROCEEDS. In this section you must provide a discussion of the anticipated use of the proceeds that will be raised by the offering, and include a statement as to whether the proceeds will be used to reduce debt or acquire a new business. If your company does not have a specific plan for a significant portion of the proceeds, this must be disclosed and explained.

CAPITALIZATION. This section includes a description of the capital structure of debt obligations, your company's anticipated dividend policy, and dilution of purchaser's (investor's) equity.

DESCRIPTION OF BUSINESS AND PROPERTY. Here you provide a description of your company's key assets, principal lines of business, human resources, properties, marketing strategies, material contracts, and competitive advantages, as well as those of any of its subsidiaries for the last five years.

MANAGEMENT AND PRINCIPAL SHAREHOLDERS. In this section of the registration statement you must provide details about your key management team and a description of each member's background, education, and role in the company. You must also disclose the compensation paid to the chief executive officer and to the four next most highly compensated executive officers who received compensation in excess of $100,000. Compensation includes annual salary, bonus, and deferred compensation, such as pension-plan contributions, stock options, and stock-appreciation rights. In addition, you must disclose knowledge of any prior violations of the law by management, as well as a table of all shareholders who hold a beneficial interest of 5% or more of any class of shares.

LITIGATION. Describe in this section any material litigation (either past, pending, or anticipated) affecting your company or any other legal proceedings that would adversely affect an investor's analysis of the securities being issued.

MANAGEMENT'S DISCUSSION AND ANALYSIS (MDA). The MDA section of the registration statement may be the first time your company's management team has taken a hard and objective look at its business model, management practices and financial statements and how they got to where they are. There may be some interesting revelations uncovered during the process. In this section, management is afforded the opportunity to discuss its view of your company's financial condition. Such a discussion generally includes the company's capital-expenditure plans and expected sources of capital. Management must analyze the liquidity, capital resources and results of operations of the issuer over the past three years, in narrative and comparative form.

FINANCIAL INFORMATION. Summarize here your company's financial information, such as sales history, net income or losses from operations, long-term debt obligations, dividend patterns, capital structure, founder's equity, and shareholder loans.

SECURITIES OFFERED AND UNDERWRITING ARRANGEMENTS. In this section, present a description of the underwriting arrangements, distribution plan and the key characteristics of the securities your company is offering.

EXPERTS AND OTHER MATTERS. This section must include a brief statement regarding the identity of the lawyers, accountants and other experts you have retained, as well as the availability of additional information from the registration statement filed with the SEC. These might include indemnification policies for the directors and officers, recent sales of unregistered securities, a breakdown of the expenses of the offering, and a wide variety of corporate documents and key agreements.

The Pre-Filing Period

During the pre-filing period (defined as the time period when a company decides to go public, but before a registration statement is filed), your company cannot make either oral or written offers of its issues. Negotiations and agreements between you and your underwriters are exempt from the prohibition against offers and sales. Negotiations or agreements among your underwriters and dealers are not permitted during the pre-filing period, and you and your company's representatives are prohibited from doing or saying anything that has the potential to condition the market to stimulate sales when the securities are ultimately issued. For example, speeches by company officials, press releases, or company advertising can all be considered a potential violation of the federal securities laws, depending on the type of information that is disseminated. During the pre-filing period, instruct your company's officers, directors, and employees not to comment on the proposed offering nor make any press release prior to registration, unless you can show that doing so is consistent with prior practice.

In keeping with prior practice, your company can advertise its products, continue to send out quarterly, annual and other periodic reports to shareholders, continue to make announcements to the press with respect to factual business and financial developments, and continue to hold stockholder meetings as scheduled.

According to the SEC's Rule 135, which is a "safe harbor" provision, certain limited announcements regarding a proposed public offering prior to the filing of a registration statement are permissible. In accordance with the rule, a notice of proposed offering will not be deemed an offer if it is limited to:

- **a statement that the offering will be made** only by prospectus;
- **the name of the issuer,** the title, the amount and basic terms of the securities to be offered;
- **the number of securities to be offered** by selling stockholders;
- **the anticipated timing** of the offering; and
- **a brief statement of the manner and purpose of the filing.** However, the identity of the underwriter cannot be disclosed.

Registration Statement Filing Guidelines

When the initial draft of your registration statement is ready for filing with the SEC, you have two choices: Either file the document with the transmittal letter or schedule a pre-filing conference with an SEC staff member to discuss any anticipated questions or problems regarding the disclosure document or the accompanying financial statements. When you file the registration statement, you will need to submit to the SEC the registration fee, which is a percentage of the maximum aggregate-offering price.

All domestic issuers are required to make all SEC filings electronically via the SEC's Electronic Data Gathering, Analysis and Retrieval system. EDGAR was designed to reduce the burden of making filings and to facilitate providing the public with access to public corporate filings. You can access the EDGAR archives at the SEC's Web site (www.sec.gov). There are two exemptions available from the mandatory electronic filing requirement: the temporary- and continuing-hardship exemptions. You may be granted a temporary-hardship exemption if your company encounters unanticipated technical difficulties that prevent the timely preparation and submission of electronic filings. You must submit a paper filing no later than one day after the required filing date and a subsequent electronic filing within six business days. The SEC may grant a continuing-hardship exemption upon receiving your written application at least ten business days prior to the filing deadline. The SEC staff generally will grant the exemption only if exigent circumstances exist.

When you offer your company's securities to the public,within one day of filing the registration statement with the SEC, you must also file the registration statement, the underwriting agreement and a filing fee with the National Association of Securities Dealers (NASD). The NASD will analyze all elements of the proposed corporate package for the underwriter to determine its fairness and reasonableness. The SEC will not deem a registration statement effective for public offering unless and until the NASD has approved the underwriting arrangements as being fair and reasonable.

SEC Review of the Registration Statement

Once received by the SEC, your registration statement will be assigned to an examining group (which typically includes lawyers, accountants and financial analysts) within a specific industry department of the Division of Corporate Finance. The length of time and depth of the review by the examining group will depend on your company's history and the nature of the securities offered. However, no matter how carefully you have prepared your registration statement, be prepared for a deficiency or comment letter to be sent roughly 30 to 60 days after the filing, suggesting legal and editorial changes to the registration statement and including anywhere from 50 to 200 numbered paragraphs.

As day 30 approaches, have your lawyer contact the SEC to get an idea of when your legal team will receive the SEC's comment letter so it can prepare for a quick response. In addition, schedule another drafting session at the printers within a few days of receiving the SEC's comments.

The modifications of the statement that the SEC staff will request will focus on the quality of the disclosure (such as an adequate discussion of risk factors or the verbiage in management's discussion of the financial performance), not on the quality of the company or the securities being offered. For example, if your company operates in a troubled or turbulent industry and you're publicly offering securities for the first time, you should expect a detailed review by all members of the SEC's examining group. The SEC's concerns regarding a registration statement are generally addressed by filing a material amendment. The review process continues until all concerns raised by the examining group have been addressed.

The final pricing amendment is filed following the pricing meeting of the underwriters and the execution of the final underwriting agreement. After the SEC changes have been incorporated, your underwriters will file an amended registration statement with the SEC. At this point, the underwriting syndicate distributes the preliminary prospectus contained in the amended registration statement.

Waiting Period Restrictions

The time after the registration statement has been filed, but before the SEC declares it effective, is known as the waiting period. The SEC has developed detailed regulations and restrictions on what information may be released to the public or the media during this period, especially with regard to communications that appear to be designed to influence the price of the shares. These regulations are designed to prevent any jumping the gun by you or your representatives. Actual sales of securities are still not permitted during the waiting period, except between the issuer and underwriter. But underwriters may arrange with brokers and dealers for their assistance in selling the issue to retail customers.

Because most investors make their decisions regarding an IPO during the waiting period, the SEC wants to ensure that the information about the offering is distributed to all persons who should have it.

Both underwriters and dealers may solicit offers to purchase so that when the registration statement becomes effective, the securities can be sold very rapidly; however, only certain types of information may be used in making selling arrangements and in conducting this pre-selling. In addition, offers can be made to prospective investors only through the use of oral statements, the preliminary prospectus (also known as the red herring) and tombstone ads, which are short announcements about a proposed offering of registered securities that typically appear in publications such as the *Wall Street Journal*. In accordance with SEC Rule 134, a tombstone ad may include the issuer's name, the type of security being offered, the price at which it will be offered, the identity of the person who will be executing purchase orders, the individual from whom a prospectus may be obtained, the names of the managing underwriters, and the approximate date on which the offering is expected to commence. The tombstone ad must also include a statement that no offer to purchase can actually be accepted during the waiting period and that the ad itself does not constitute a solicitation of an indication of interest from a prospective purchaser.

A Rule 134 communication can be used to solicit offers to purchase if it is preceded or accompanied by a preliminary prospectus. Any other written materials regarding the proposed offering that is transmitted during the waiting period will come within the definition of a prospectus and will violate the federal securities laws.

Because most investors make their investment decisions regarding an IPO during the waiting period, the SEC wants to ensure that the information about the offering is distributed to all persons who should have it. Therefore, the managing underwriter must furnish copies of the preliminary and final prospectus to dealers, and all participating dealers must take reasonable steps to furnish a preliminary prospectus to anyone who asks for one in writing during the waiting period. The SEC ensures that this rule will be adhered to by its ability to control acceleration of the registration statement to influence issuers to cooperate in distributing a preliminary prospectus.

If the issuer has never offered securities before to the public, and thus is not a reporting company, the SEC will not accelerate the offering date unless the underwriters and dealers have sent copies of the preliminary prospectus at least 48 hours prior to mailing a confirmation of sale to all persons who are reasonably expected to become purchasers of the security.

The Road Show

During the comment and review process, your company and your underwriter's representatives are preparing for and then participating in the road show—typically, a whirlwind, two-week campaign through a dozen or more financial markets across the country (and sometimes overseas) that is designed to whet investors' appetites for your IPO. The road show can be a crucial element in setting the value of your offering and building initial demand for your company's shares. If your company's road show goes poorly before key pundits and money managers on Wall Street, demand for your stock issue will wilt. If it goes well, you can expect a robust demand and strong aftermarket in your stock. The goal of this intense schedule of limos, five-star restaurants and fancy hotels is to have preliminary indications of interest at least four times greater than the number of shares to be offered.

Road-show presentations typically run a half-hour and are

accompanied by PowerPoint presentations that must generally be in the format and style that fund managers have become accustomed to expect—that is, crisp and focused, with no more than about 20 slides. Top management may make several presentations in a single day, appearing first at a breakfast meeting with a single investor group, called a one-on-one, then heading off to a standup presentation in a room crowded with groups of investors, mutual-fund managers and other institutional investors. Videotapes are acceptable at the road show if they show nothing more than a person talking. A representative of your company must be present during a videotaped presentation. Slides presentations are also acceptable as long as the slides are not distributed and all materials are 100% consistent with the information contained in the prospectus.

The road show audience will be made up largely of institutional investors and analysts representing mutual funds, pension funds and other investment sources, most of whom have mastered the art of picking winners and know all the right questions to ask. Through experience, they've developed a pretty good nose for how much of a company's presentation is fluff and how much is solid. By the time your company's management team hits the road, they should have been thoroughly coached by your underwriters on questions they are likely to be asked and the most effective way to answer those questions. Some institutional money managers will not let anyone in the room for the presentations but the company's representatives, so they must be prepared to answer questions independently, without relying on the underwriters.

Post-Effective Period

After the SEC declares your company's registration statement effective, you may offer the securities to the public. The registration statement is declared effective 20 days after the final amendment has been filed, unless the effective date is accelerated by the SEC. (Most companies tend to seek an accelerated effective date, which is usually made available if the company has complied with the examining group's suggested modifications.) The next step is for you and your underwriters to agree on a price and execute the underwriting agreement. Prior to executing the underwriting agreement, the underwriters will require a comfort letter, assuring them that there have been no material adverse changes in your company's financial condition and that certain financial information disclosed in the registration statement is from independently audited financial statements.

IPO Valuation and Pricing

Although there is no standard formula in the valuation process, certain factors are always taken into account. The most important determinant,of value will be your company's past and projected operating results and financial condition. Other factors—such as competitive position, management team, industry, growth potential, economic conditions and the state of the stock market—will also play a role in the valuation of your company's stock. Ultimately, however, investor demand (generated as a result of the road show) will determine the final IPO valuation.

The most basic and most effective valuation tool for investment bankers is an analysis of the stock market's current valuation of comparable companies. The bankers will use such comparative analyses to determine and substantiate your company's IPO price. Prices of other successful and similar offerings will also come into play, as will your company's projected earnings and cash flow at the time of the offering. Price/earnings ratios and return on sales of other companies in the industry may be used to extrapolate the price of the stock.

An aggressive valuation may increase investors' expectations and put more pressure on your company's performance in the aftermarket. A higher valuation is also likely to reduce the stock's rate of appreciation. The underwriter will most likely choose a slightly lower price than the estimate, thus guarding against a weak aftermarket and giving buyers an incentive. You'll want a strong aftermarket performance because it generates credibility with investors, creates positive visibility for your company and increases the company's ability to pursue subsequent financing. Consequently, companies should seek the highest *sustainable* valuation rather than the highest *attainable* valuation. Underwriters generally prefer a price range of $10 to $20 a share.

It is likely that you won't know the actual pricing of the offering until the day before it becomes effective and the underwriter's agreement is signed. Until that point, the underwriter is not obligated to conduct the offering at any previously mentioned price or price range. Once you and the underwriter agree on the IPO price, you must file a final prospectus, including the pricing information, with the SEC no later than the second business day after the price has been determined (or after the first use of such prospectus following the effective date). If you and the underwriter are still negotiating or waiting for a better opportunity to enter the market and the final prospectus containing the pricing information is not filed within 15 business days of effectiveness, you will have to file a post-effective amendment with the SEC. The SEC rules regarding the effectiveness of amendments have recently been relaxed. If the post-effective amendment does not contain any material changes, the amendment will become effective immediately after it has been filed.

An aggressive valuation may increase investors' expectations and put more pressure on your company's performance in the aftermarket.

Completion of the Offer of Shares

Once the final underwriting agreement is signed and the final pricing amendment is filed with the SEC, the registration statement will be declared effective and the selling process begins. After a registration statement is declared effective, offers in any form are permitted, as long as they are either accompanied or preceded by a copy of the final prospectus. This privilege is often referred to as the "free writing" privilege.

To facilitate the mechanics of the offering process, consider retaining the services of a registrar and transfer agent who will be responsible for issuing stock certificates, maintaining stockholder ownership records and processing the transfer of shares from one investor to another. Commercial banks and trust companies (which also offer ongoing support services, such as annual-report and proxy mailing, disbursement of dividends and custody of the authorized but unissued stock certificates) usually offer these services.

Once the offer and sale of the shares to the public has been completed, you must schedule a closing. The underwriter's lawyer generally prepares a closing memorandum that will identify the conditions precedent to closing and the documents to be exchanged. These documents include: a legal opinion by your lawyer attesting that the accountant's comfort letter delivered at the time of the pricing still holds true as of the time of the closing; and a certificate from an officer of your company stating that no material adverse changes have affected your business during the period following the date that the registration statement was declared effective.

After a registration statement is declared effective, offers in any form are permitted, as long as they are either accompanied or preceded by a copy of the final prospectus.

In addition to the preceding obligations, you are required to file the SEC's Form SR, which is a report on your company's use of the proceeds raised from the sale of the securities. This information should be substantially similar to what was stated in the prospectus provided to prospective investors. You must file the initial Form SR within 90 days after the registration statement becomes effective and then once every six months until the offering is complete and the proceeds are being applied toward their intended use.

Ongoing Disclosure and Periodic Reporting

The Exchange Act generally governs the ongoing-disclosure and periodic-reporting requirements of publicly traded companies. Section 13 of the Exchange Act grants broad powers to the SEC to develop documents and reports that must be filed. Three primary reports are required.

Form 10-K or KSB (for small business issuers) is the annual report that must be filed within 90 days after the close of your company's fiscal year covered by the report. It must also include a report of all significant activities of your company during its fourth quarter, an analysis and discussion of the company's financial condition, a description of the current officers and directors and principal stockholders, your company's business, management compensation, and a schedule of certain exhibits. The 10-K requires your company's income statements for the prior three years and the balance sheets for the prior two years. There are optional integration provisions contained in the Form 10-K that allow for information from the Annual Report to Stockholders to be integrated with the form 10-K so information does not need to be repeated. The 10-KSB requires the income statement for the prior two years and the balance sheet for the prior year (which can be prepared in accordance with GAAP).

Form 10-Q or 10-QSB (for small business issuers) is the quarterly report that must be filed no later than 45 days after the end of each of the first three fiscal quarters of each fiscal year. This quarterly filing includes copies of quarterly financial statements (accompanied by a discussion and analysis of your company's financial condition by its management) and a report as to any litigation as well as any steps taken by your company that affect shareholder rights or that may require shareholder approval. The 10-Q requires your company's balance sheet from the previous year and a report of the most recent fiscal quarter, while the 10-QSB requires a report on the most recent quarter.

Form 8-K is a periodic report designed to ensure that all material information pertaining to significant events that affect your company is disclosed to the investing public as soon as it is available, but not later than 15 days after the occurrence of the particular event (which triggers the need to file the Form 8-K).

The duty to disclose material information (whether as part of a Form 8-K filing or otherwise) to the public is an obligation that continues for as long as your company's securities are publicly traded. You must establish an ongoing compliance program to ensure that all material corporate information is disclosed as fully and as promptly as possible. A fact is generally considered to be material if there is a substantial likelihood that a reasonable shareholder would consider it important in his or her investment decision. The following are examples of what is typically considered material for disclosure purposes:

- acquisitions and dispositions of other companies or properties;
- public or private sales of debt or equity securities;
- bankruptcy or receivership proceedings affecting the issuer;
- significant contract awards or terminations; or
- changes in the key management team.

Certain publicly traded companies are subject to additional reporting and disclosure requirements. For example, if a company either elects to register its securities under rule 12(g) or it has greater than 500 shareholders and at least $5 million worth of total assets, it will also be subject to the following SEC's rules.

PROXY SOLICITATIONS. Public companies are required by state laws and the rules of the major stock exchanges and markets to hold an annual meeting of stockholders where issues such as the election of directors and the appointment of auditors are voted on by stockholders. Generally, approval can be given only by a majority vote of a quorum. Because of the difficulty of assembling every shareholder of a corporation for matters that require a shareholder vote, voting by proxy is commonly used by most publicly held corporations. When soliciting the proxies of shareholders for voting at annual or special meetings, statutory rules must be carefully followed. A detailed proxy statement that specifies the exact matters to be acted upon and any information that would be required by the shareholder in reaching a decision must accompany the request for the proxy. In addition, a company is required to include in its proxy statement any proposals submitted by stockholders unless the proposal falls into one of the exemptions set forth in Rule 14a-8(c) under the Exchange Act.

REPORTING OF BENEFICIAL OWNERSHIP. Section 16(a) requires that all officers and directors and shareholders who own

10% or more of voting stock file a statement of beneficial ownership of securities, using Form 3. This statement must reflect all holdings, direct and indirect. Section 16(a) also requires that whenever the officers and directors increase or decrease their holdings by purchase, sale, gift or otherwise, they must report the transaction on Form 4 no later than the 10th day of the month following the month in which the transaction occurred.

LIABILITY FOR SHORT-SWING TRANSACTIONS. Section 16(b) requires that officers, directors, employees or other insiders return to the company any profit that they may have realized from any combination of sales and purchases of securities made by them within any six-month period. Any acquisition of securities (regardless of form of payment) is considered to be a purchase. Section 16(b) is intended to discourage the possibility of directors and officers taking advantage of inside information by speculating in a company's stock. Even if the individual involved in the transaction did not actually take advantage of inside information, liability occurs automatically if there is a sale and purchase within six months.

TENDER-OFFER RULES AND REGULATIONS. Sections 13 and 14 generally govern the rules for parties who wish to make a tender offer to purchase the securities of a publicly traded corporation. Any person acquiring (directly or indirectly) beneficial ownership of more than 5% of an equity security registered under Section 12 must report the transaction by filing a Schedule 13D within ten days from the date of acquisition. Schedule 13D requires disclosure of certain material information, such as the identity and background of the purchaser, the purpose of the acquisition, the source and amount of funds used to purchase the securities, and disclosure of the company. If the purchase is in connection with a tender offer, then the provisions of Section 14(d) also apply. These provisions require that the terms of the tender offer be disclosed (as well as the plans of the offeror if it is successful and the terms of any special agreements between the offeror and the target company). Section 14(e) imposes a broad prohibition against the use of false, misleading or incomplete statements in connection with a tender offer.

Rule 10b-5 and Insider Trading

The business and financial press have devoted much attention to the application of the SEC's Rule 10b-5 in the prosecution of insider-trading cases. The text of Rule 10b-5 is:

It shall be unlawful for any person, directly or indirectly, by the use of any means or instrumentality of interstate commerce, or of the mails or of any facility of any national securities exchange to:

- **employ any device, scheme, or artifice to defraud;**
- **make any untrue statement of a material fact** or to omit to state a material fact necessary in order to make the statements made, in light of the circumstances under which they were made, not misleading; or
- **engage in any act, practice, or course of business,** which operates or would operate as a fraud or deceit upon any person, in connection with the purchase or sale of any security.

Although Rule 10b-5 has most often been used in prosecuting insider-trading cases, the rule is also used in a variety of other situations, such as:

- **when a corporation issues misleading information** to the public or keeps silent when it has a duty to disclose;
- **when an insider selectively discloses material,** non-public information to another party, who then trades securities based on the information (generally called "tipping");
- **when a person mismanages a corporation** in ways that are connected with the purchase or sale of securities;
- **when a securities firm or another person** manipulates the market for a security traded in the over-the-counter market; and
- **when a securities firm or securities professional** engages in certain other forms of conduct connected with the purchase or sale of securities.

Therefore, if your company is publicly traded (or may be, at a future stage in its growth), it is imperative that all of your company's officers, directors, employees, and shareholders be made aware of the broad scope of this anti-fraud rule in their transactions that involve the company.

The Internet and Insider-Trading Regulation

There has been speculation that the Internet will significantly change the insider-trading landscape. While the ways in which the Internet will affect insider-trading laws ultimately remain to be seen, it is important that companies are aware of the issues and the possibility of changes. As of now, a hacker could break into a corporation's computer systems and use the information for insider trading without violating the current insider-trading laws in the traditional sense. This is because traditional insider trading deals with information acquired lawfully but used in a breach of duty owed to the source. It would not be difficult to extend the law to add those who steal, not just misappropriate, information.

The essence of insider trading is trading on material, non-public information. Many cases have been determined on whether the information was public or not. With many new means of communication, from e-mail to Web sites, courts will have to reexamine when information loses its "secret" status and becomes public. Information released on the Internet, either through bulletin boards or e-mail, has the potential to reach millions of people. However, much of the investing public does not pro-actively seek out the information, therefore it is difficult to determine whether information released by these means may be considered public.

To protect their prohibited information, some companies may choose to monitor employee e-mail or prohibit employees from using e-mail to contact customers. While it may not be necessary to go to these lengths, you should take the necessary precautions to make certain that prohibited information does not pass over your company's networks and to the public. You should also take steps to ensure that employees are not using new forms of electronic media, such as e-mail, to engage in insider trading or tipping.

Disposing of Restricted Securities

Under the Securities Act, all shares of a public company held by its controlling persons (which typically include its officers, directors and shareholders who hold a 10% or larger share of voting stock) are deemed restricted securities. The sale of restricted securities is generally governed by Rule 144, which requires as a condition of sale that:

- **the company be current in its periodic reports to the SEC;**
- **the restricted securities have been beneficially owned** for at least two years preceding the sale;
- **the amount of securities that may be sold in any three month period** be limited to the greater of 1% of the outstanding class of securities or the average weekly reported volume of trading in the securities on a registered national security exchange (if the securities are listed) for the four weeks prior to the filing of the notice of sale;
- **the securities be sold only in broker's transactions** and the notice of the sale be filed with the SEC concurrently with the placing of the sale order; and
- **if the sale involveS-500 shares or $10,000,** a report of the transaction on Form 144 must be filed.

It is imperative that you and your company's managers understand the planning and registration process prior to pursuing a public offering of your company's securities. Further, you will save a significant amount of time and expense if the process of planning begins early in the development of your company, its methods of operation and the formulation of strategies for the company's growth. As with any method of capital formation, going public has its costs and benefits. Take the time to carefully weigh and understand all of the rules and their implications for your business prior to starting the process of going public.

Classic
Internal-Growth
Strategies

Growth Through Mergers and Acquisitions

ERGERS AND ACQUISITIONS ARE AMONG THE MOST effective ways to expedite the growth of a business. Countless companies in all industries have grown at lightning speed in part due to aggressive merger and acquisition strategies.

The impact of technology and the Internet has increased the pace and size of merger and acquisition deals, particularly as sales and distribution channels are being restructured on an almost daily basis. It has also been technology companies, in search of new ideas, new products, trained knowledge workers, strategic relationships and additional market share, who have been the most acquisitive. Microsoft topped the list with 45 deals worldwide in 1999 worth more than $13 billion. That same year, Intel completed 35 acquisitions deals worldwide, worth more than $5 billion, putting it in second place for total number of acquisitions.

Understanding the Merger and Acquisition Frenzy

At the heart of every merger or acquisition, regardless of the size or industry of the companies involved, are similar strategic objectives: to build long-term shareholder value and take advantage of the synergies that the combined firms will create; however, each industry has its own share of specific objectives.

For example, deals in the pharmaceutical industry—such as Pfizer's battle against American Home Products to acquire Warner-Lambert (a deal valued at more than $71 billion) and the merger of Glaxo-Wellcome with SmithKline Beecham— are driven by the need to create more products and achieve economies of scale by combining research and development efforts.

The objectives of deals in the defense industry include winning private-sector business to compensate for shrinking federal defense budgets, due in large part to large-scale political shifts, such as the end of the Cold War.

Deregulation in the energy and financial-services industries have begun to spawn deals that are driven by the new ability to offer a more diversified range of services, such as the Citicorp-Travelers Group $37.4–billion merger to create CitiGroup or the Deutsche Bank AG's takeover of BankersTrust Corp. for $10.1 billion.

In telecommunications and media, AT&T's $52.2-billion takeover of TCI was driven by the competition to find faster ways into more households with an integrated package of long-distance services, Internet access and cable television.

In the battle for efficiency and synergy, the trends toward consolidation and globalization are likely to continue beyond 2001, and the mega-merger activity is likely to trickle down toward middle-market and smaller companies.

The merger and acquisition frenzy has created intense competition for the same target companies, with a premium placed on the price paid for the business to be acquired and the speed with which the deal can be completed. Deals that used to take months to get done now often close in a matter of days, especially if there are no regulatory approvals to be obtained or shareholder battles to be fought. In this environment, deals are moving so fast and are being bid up so high that the likelihood of problems and errors occurring have increased dramatically. To be an effective player in this marketplace, you need to be armed with as much knowledge and as many tools as possible.

Mergers Versus Acquisition

The terms "merger" and "acquisition" are often confused and used interchangeably by business and financial executives. At the surface level, the difference between a merger and an acquisition may not matter because the net result is often the same: Two companies (or more) that had separate ownership begin operating under the same ownership and management, usually to obtain a strategic or financial objective.

Yet, the strategic, financial, tax and even cultural impact of such deals may be very different depending on whether the transaction is structured as a merger, which typically refers to two companies coming together (usually through the exchange of shares) to become one, or an acquisition, which typically refers to one company (the buyer) purchasing the assets or shares of another (the seller) either with cash, the securities of the buyer or other assets of value to the seller.

In an acquisition that is completed as a stock-purchase transaction, the seller's shares are not necessarily combined with the buyer's existing company; instead, the shares are often kept separate, to become a new subsidiary or operating division.

When the acquisition is conducted as an asset-purchase transaction, the seller's assets become additional assets of the buyer's company. The hope and expectation is that, over time, the value of the assets that have been purchased will exceed the price paid for them, thereby enhancing shareholder value as a result of the strategic or financial benefits of the transaction.

What Is All the M&A Fuss About?

What has driven the merger-mania of recent years? What factors have fueled the current resurgence of merger and acquisition activity? And how are these recent mergers and acquisitions different from those conducted in the M&A frenzy of the 1980s? Although there are no simple answers, common themes and trends exist in M&A transactions:

Recent mergers and acquisitions are clearly more motivated by strategy than their 1980s counterparts. Jobs are often being added, not lost, as a result of these deals. Companies are being built-up, not busted-up.

The financing behind recent M&A deals is more sound and secure than ever before. Buyers are using their stock as currency and sellers are gladly accepting this form of payment in lieu of or in addition to cash, which forces both parties to work together on a post-closing basis to truly enhance shareholder value.

In many cases, mergers and acquisitions are being driven by a key trend within a given industry. Trends most affecting specific industries include:

- **rapidly changing technology** in the computer industry;
- **fierce competition** in the telecommunications and banking industries;
- **changing consumer preferences** in the food and beverage industry;
- **pressure to control costs** in the healthcare industry; and
- **reduction in demand** caused by a shrinking federal defense budget, which is driving the consolidation in the aerospace and defense-contractor industries.

Some deals are motivated by the need to transform corporate identity following a crisis. For example, when ValuJet's reputation became so closely tied to the airline's Florida Everglades crash and the ensuing negative publicity regarding its spotty safety records, the company began looking for a merger partner whose more positive identity ValueJet could assume.

Many deals are fueled by the need to spread the risk and cost of developing new technology (especially in the communications and aerospace industries); of researching new medical discoveries (as is the case in the medical-device and pharmaceutical industries); or of gaining access to new sources of energy (such as in the oil and gas exploration and drilling industries).

Globalization has forced many companies to explore mergers and acquisitions as a means to develop an international presence and expanded market share. This market-penetration strategy is often more cost-effective than trying to build an overseas foothold from scratch.

Many recent mergers and acquisitions have been driven by the need for a complete product or service line to remain competitive or to balance against seasonal or cyclical market trends. Transactions in the retail, hospitality, food and beverage, entertainment and financial-services industries have been in response to consumer demand for "one-stop shopping."

The technology and Internet IPO boom of the late 1990s contributed to the merger and acquisition frenzy. The proceeds from these IPOs created large pools of cash that had been earmarked for acquisitions, and sellers became more willing to take the buyer's stock as currency in the transaction.

The motivation and the underlying goals and objectives for a transaction will often affect the structure of the transaction, pricing and valuation issues, and the ability to obtain necessary third-party or governmental approvals.

The Importance of Synergy

Many well-intentioned entrepreneurs and business executives have entered into mergers and acquisitions that they later came to regret. Such an outcome is often the result of classic mistakes, such as a lack of adequate planning, an overly aggressive timetable to closing, a failure to really look at possible post-closing integration problems or, worst of all, sought-after synergies that are unrealistic and unachievable. The premise of synergy is that the "whole will be greater than the sum of its parts." But the quest for synergy can be very elusive, especially if there is inadequate communication between buyer and seller, which usually leads to a misunderstanding over what the buyer is really buying and the seller is really selling. Everyone says that they want synergy when doing a deal, but few take the time to develop a transactional team and a joint mission statement of the objectives of the deal, or to solve post-closing operating or financial problems on a timely basis in order to achieve it.

Motivators in an Acquisition

Common Seller Motivations	Common Buyer Motivations
■ The desire to retire	■ The desire to grow
■ Lack of successors	■ Opportunity to increase profits
■ Business adversities	■ Desire to diversify
■ Lack of capital to grow	■ Buying up competitors
■ Inadequate distribution system	■ Using excess capital
■ To eliminate personal guaranties or other personal obligations	■ Achieving new distribution channels or efficiencies
■ No ability to diversify	■ Diversify new distribution channels or efficiencies
■ Age and health concerns	■ Particular people, existing business or assets are needed
■ Particular amount of money is needed for estate planning	■ Access to new or emerging technologies
■ Irreconcilable conflict among owners	■ Need to efficiently deploy key people or resources
■ Losing key people	■ Strategic fit between buyer and seller's current operations

What Motivates Buyers and Sellers?

As a leader of an emerging-growth business, it is likely that at least one acquisition will be part of your growth strategy. Therefore, it is important that you not only have a clear understanding of your business objectives as you pursue an acquisition, but that you also have insight into what a seller seeks to achieve through the transaction.

MOTIVATORS IN AN ACQUISITION. As the buyer in an acquisition transaction, your motivators are likely to include one or more of the following:

■ **revenue enhancement;**

■ **cost reduction;**

■ **vertical and/or horizontal operational** and financial synergies;

■ **growth pressures** from investors;

■ **underutilized resources;**

■ **reducing the number of competitors** (increasing market share);

- **gaining a foothold into new domestic and international markets** (especially if current markets are saturated); or
- **diversification** into new products and services.

The seller's motivation in an acquisition transaction can include:
- **the inability to compete** as an independent entity;
- **the desire to obtain cost-savings** and access to the greater resource of the acquiring company; or
- **the need for an exit strategy,** either due to the nearing retirement of the owners or for some other reason.

MOTIVATORS IN A MERGER. As explained earlier, a merger differs from an acquisition. As a result, the motivators for a merger will differ from those for an acquisition, and typically include:
- **the need to improve process engineering** and technology;
- **the desire to increase scale of production** in existing product lines;
- **the desire to acquire capability to produce** subassemblies internally;
- **a need to find additional uses** for existing management talent;
- **a way to redeploy excess capital** into profitable/complementary uses; and
- **a way to obtain tax benefits.**

In a classic merger, there is not a buyer or a seller (though one party may be leading the transaction or may have initiated the contact). Therefore the culture and spirit of the negotiations are different from those of a classic acquisition. In a merger, data gathering and due diligence are mutual, with each party positioning its contribution to the post-merger entity to justify its respective equity share, management and control of the post-merger company.

Planning for an Acquisition

Business strategists often say that it is cheaper to buy than to build a business. This attitude, together with the low interest rates and the large pools of capital that have flowed into large and medium-size companies through initial public offerings both in the United States and abroad, has created an acquisition frenzy that is likely to continue well into this century. The American business market has clearly experienced major industry consolidation in the form of mergers and acquisitions. Notwithstanding all of the excitement, the purchase of an existing business is a complex and challenging task. This section will lead you, the buyer, through the process, with a focus on preparation and preliminary negotiation tips as you begin to understand the seller's perspective.

Assembling the Team

As you seek an acquisition that will support your growth strategy, you will need to have in place an internal acquisition team, which should include representation from your company's finance, marketing, strategic-planning, and operations departments, particularly those individuals who will be vital during the four critical stages for the buyer. You'll also need an experienced set of external advisers, such as lawyers, accountants, investment bankers, valuation experts, and in some cases insurance and employee-benefits experts. The appointed leader of your team must clearly define both responsibilities and authority, including who has the authority to speak on behalf of your company, who may contact prospective sellers, who may negotiate with the selected seller, and so forth.

As you assemble your acquisitions team, also decide whether you will use an intermediary, such as buyer's broker or investment banker, to find and evaluate acquisitions candidates, or whether the flow of transactions will be generated internally, through networking, industry contacts, etc. Although paying a finder's fee to a broker can greatly add to the cost of closing the deal, especially if the seller is in turn using a seller's broker, the buyer's broker can save you the valuable time and expense of chasing after the wrong candidates or trying to figure out which companies have expressed an interest in selling.

There are many different ways to structure your relationship with intermediaries, although most relationships will be driven by the payment of a commission contingent on a suc-

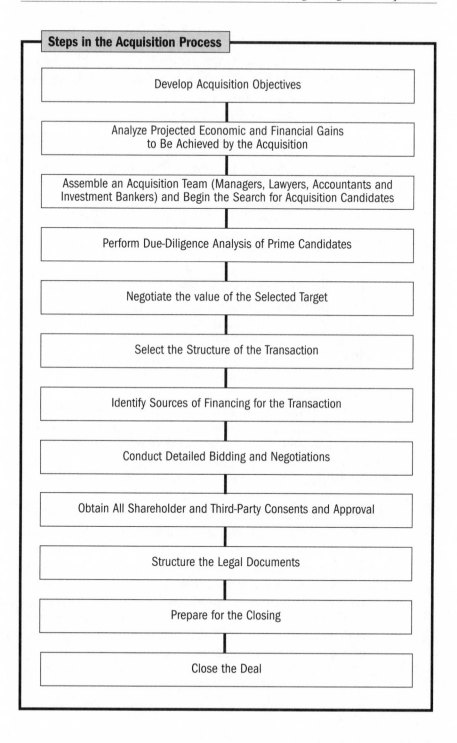

Steps in the Acquisition Process

Develop Acquisition Objectives

Analyze Projected Economic and Financial Gains
to Be Achieved by the Acquisition

Assemble an Acquisition Team (Managers, Lawyers, Accountants and
Investment Bankers) and Begin the Search for Acquisition Candidates

Perform Due-Diligence Analysis of Prime Candidates

Negotiate the value of the Selected Target

Select the Structure of the Transaction

Identify Sources of Financing for the Transaction

Conduct Detailed Bidding and Negotiations

Obtain All Shareholder and Third-Party Consents and Approval

Structure the Legal Documents

Prepare for the Closing

Close the Deal

cessful transaction (generally in the 5% to 12%range, and often paid for by the seller). In addition to the commission, many intermediaries will request a monthly retainer or the ability to bill for certain services (such as assistance in the preparation of the acquisition plan) and certain expenses (such as trips or phone calls with prospective candidates). Negotiate these fees and expenses carefully because they are not usually contingent on a successful transaction (though some brokers will credit the aggregate of the fees paid toward their ultimate commission). If you do retain an intermediary for smaller deals, be sure that you have hired a buyer's broker who has the experience and the orientation to meet your needs.

Developing an Acquisition Plan

You may find that it would be easier to achieve certain corporate goals and objectives by the external acquisition of assets and resources, rather than through internal expansion. As you consider an acquisition as a growth strategy, begin with an acquisition plan that defines your objectives, the relevant trends in your industry, the method for finding candidates, the criteria you will use to evaluate candidates, your budgets and timetables for accomplishing the transaction, the price ranges you will consider, your company's past acquisition track record, the amount of external capital you will need to complete the transaction, and other relevant topics.

IDENTIFYING THE OBJECTIVES. Although the reasons for considering growth through acquisition vary from industry to industry and from company to company, the strategic advantages that motivate you to acquire another company are likely to include:

- **achieving certain operating and financial synergies** and economies of scale with respect to production and manufacturing, research and development, management or marketing and distribution;
- **obtaining rights to develop products and services** owned by the target company. For example, Microsoft acquired WebTV to establish an ownership position in a method of access to the Internet that is likely to grow but that had stumbled without

adequate resources, which Microsoft could bring to the table;

■ **providing growth opportunities** for a surplus of strong managers who would be likely to leave your company unless you acquired other businesses that they could operate and develop. Likewise, the target company may stand to lose a talented management team due to the lack of career-growth potential unless it is acquired by a growing business that can offer higher salaries, increased employee benefits and greater opportunity for advancement;

■ **stabilizing your company's earnings stream** and mitigating its risk of business failure by diversifying its products and services through acquisition rather than internal development. For example, Wendy's International, a major player in the fast-food industry, lacked a presence in the breakfast or baked-goods market, a problem that was mitigated by its acquisition of Tim Horton's, Canada's largest chain of coffee and donut shops;

■ **deploying excess cash** into a tax-efficient project, such as an acquisition, because both distribution of dividends and stock redemptions are generally taxable events to shareholders;

■ **achieving certain production and distribution** economies of scale through "vertical integration," which involves the acquisition of a key supplier or customer;

■ **the ability to use residual assets,** such as intellectual property or franchise rights left by either the death of an owner or key manager or the retirement of key members of the management team at the target company.

■ **strengthening key areas of your business,** such as research and development or marketing (when it's more efficient to fill these gaps through an acquisition than through building the departments internally);

■ **gaining recognition in the marketplace** for your superior products and services that lack customer loyalty and protected trademarks. The acquisition of an older, more established firm can be an efficient method of establishing goodwill;

■ **penetrating new geographic markets** without establishing market diversification from scratch;

■ **taking advantage of a bargain,** which may arise if a target company becomes available at a distressed price as the result of a death or divorce among the company's founders or another business crisis; or

■ **acquiring patents, copyrights, trade secrets** or other intangible assets that will be available to you only by means of an acquisition.

In essence, the statement of the objectives should be a reality check. It should answer the key questions: "Why are we doing this and are we convinced that growth via acquisition makes sense compared with other growth strategies, such as internal expansion, joint ventures, franchising, licensing, or capital formation?" and "Are we really enhancing our shareholder value and competitive position as a result of this deal?"

The Benefits of a Carefully Drafted Acquisition Plan

One of the overriding goals of the acquisition plan is to narrow the field as much as possible. The first step is to choose acquisitions as a growth strategy over alternatives such as franchising or strategic alliances. The decision is narrowed again by selecting the targeted industries, and narrowed further by the development (and enforcement) of specific criteria to screen the possible candidates. This narrowing process in most cases, if carefully followed, will yield a small but viable field of attractive candidates whom you can approach as acquisition targets. Other benefits to having a well-prepared acquisition plan include:

■ **providing a road map** for your company's leadership to follow;
■ **informing shareholders** of key objectives;
■ **reducing professional and advisory fees;**
■ **mitigating the risk of doing a transaction** you'll later regret;
■ **identifying post-closing integration challenges** well in advance; and
■ **informing sellers of your plans for the company** on a post-closing basis. In today's marketplace, with the trend toward roll-ups and consolidation strategies, it is particularly important to the seller to understand, accept and respect your acquisition strategy and growth plans for the consolidated companies on a post-closing basis (especially where the lion's share of

their consideration will be the buyer's stock).

A carefully considered acquisition plan should also identify the value-added efficiencies and cost-savings that will result from the proposed transaction and answer the fundamental question: How will your company's professional management or brand equity enhance the performance or profitability of the seller's company?

Identifying Acquisition Targets

The heart of your acquisition plan should identify the targeted industries and the criteria for evaluating candidates within these targeted industries. The acquisition plan should address the following issues:

- **targeted size** of the candidates;
- **source of acquisition financing** (including logistics for obtaining the capital, where necessary, and the estimated amount and method of payment to the seller);
- **method for finding candidates** (for example, internal search versus use of intermediaries versus responding to unsolicited offers, etc.);
- **desired financial returns and operating synergies** to be achieved as a result of the acquisition;
- **minimum and maximum ranges and rates** of revenues, growth, earnings, net worth, etc. of the seller that would be acceptable to you and your Board of Directors;
- **impact on your company's existing shareholders;**
- **likely competing bidders for qualified candidates;**
- **members of the acquisition team** and their individual roles;
- **nature and types of risks** that you are willing to assume;
- **nature and types of risks** that are unacceptable;
- **desired geographic location** of the target companies;
- **desired demographics and buying habits** of the seller's customers;
- **plans to retain or replace the management team** of the target company (even though this policy may vary on a target-by-target basis, it is useful to include a section addressing your preliminary plans);
- **your willingness to consider turnaround or troubled companies** (you

may want the cost-savings of buying a fixer-upper, or you may prefer a company that is in top-notch shape);

■ **your tax and financial preference** for asset versus stock transactions;

■ **your openness to full versus partial ownership** of the seller's entity or willingness to consider a spin-off sale, such as the purchase of the assets of an operating division or the stock of a subsidiary; and

■ **your interest or willingness to launch** an unfriendly takeover of a publicly held company or buy the debt from the largest creditor of a privately held company.

Narrowing the Field of Acquisition Targets

Once your team has completed the preparation and analysis of the acquisition plan, it should be relatively easy to begin the process of identifying potential candidates and screening them against the criteria that you have established. Although every buyer's criteria will differ depending on the nature and stage of their business growth and the industry in which they operate, some of the more typical buyer's criteria for a potential acquisition include the following:

■ **history of stable financial and growth** performance during different market cycles and conditions;

■ **market leader** in industry niches and geographic regions (recognized brand names with established market share);

■ **products with life cycles** that are not too short or susceptible to obsolescence or rapid technological change;

■ **strong management team** with research and development capability and technological know-how;

■ **stable and economically favorable relationships** with customers, vendors, lenders, and lessors;

■ **room for growth** (or excess) capacity in manufacturing or production;

■ **specified range for current or potential claims** or litigation against the seller (in dollars);

- **specified range for sales** (in dollars), with a minimum for earnings before interest and taxes (EBIT) and a maximum for combined post-closing obligations (such as union contracts or other liabilities;
- **specified range for the purchase price,** including various payment and price considerations (i.e., what percentage of the payment the seller must be willing to accept in buyer's stock, or what percentage of the purchase price will be contingent on the company's post-closing performance;
- **preferred geographical location; and**
- **willingness of the seller's management team** to remain in place for a specified time period.

The specific qualitative and quantitative screening criteria are intended to filter out the wrong deals. When compared with the objectives described in your acquisition plan, they will assist you and your team in selecting the candidates whose strengths and weaknesses best complement your own. Naturally, unless you are very lucky, you're not likely to find all of these criteria in each candidate, and if you do, there will likely be multiple bidders. Therefore, you and your team must be ready to accept some compromise in your criteria, but you must also be careful not to overlook too many warts which could result in a deal that you will later regret.

The Letter of Intent

Once you have narrowed the field of candidates, you must choose two or three finalists. The first step in the process is to gather more detailed information about each of them. This can be done by meeting with each target company's management team or from outside sources such as trade associations, industry publications, chambers of commerce, the target company's suppliers and customers, or private data sources such Standard & Poor's. Your goal is to gather as much intelligence as you can about each of the companies, so that you can choose a single target that best meets your company's growth objectives.

At this stage of the transaction, both you and the finalist you have selected (and your respective advisers) should have developed a strategic plan and taken the time to get to know each other and understand each other's perspective and competing objectives. The next step involves the preparation and negotiation of an interim agreement that will govern the conduct of the parties up until closing.

There are certain valid legal arguments against the execution of any type of interim document, especially because some courts have interpreted them to be binding legal documents (even if one or more of the parties did not initially intend to be bound). However, a letter of intent, which includes a set of binding terms and non-binding terms for the transaction, is a necessary step in virtually all merger and acquisition transactions. Before expending significant resources, most parties involved prefer the organizational framework and psychological comfort that a written document offers. There are many different styles of drafting letters of intent, which vary from law firm to law firm and business lawyer to business lawyer; however, these styles usually fall into one of three categories: binding; non-binding; or hybrids. In general, the type of letter that is right for a particular transaction will depend on the:

- **information to be released publicly** about the transaction;
- **degree to which necessary information** has been gathered and negotiations have been definitive;
- **cost to the buyer and the seller** of proceeding with the transaction prior to the making of binding commitments;
- **rapidity with which the parties** estimate a final agreement could be signed; and
- **degree of confidence in the good faith of each party** and the absence (or presence) of other parties competing for the transaction.

Most often, the hybrid proves to be the most effective format to protect the interests of both parties and to level the playing field from a negotiations perspective.

A letter of intent is often considered an agreement in principle. As a result, you and the seller should be very clear as to whether the letter of intent is a binding preliminary contract or

---

Advantages and Disadvantages of Executing a Letter of Intent

ADVANTAGES

- Tests parties' seriousness
- Morally commits parties to sale
- Sets out in writing areas of agreement, which is important because there may be a long delay before a sales agreement is executed
- Highlights differences and matters needing further negotiation
- Discourages seller from shopping around for a better deal

DISADVANTAGES

- May be considered a binding agreement. It is important to state whether or not a letter of intent is meant to constitute an enforceable agreement.
- Public announcement of prospective sale may have to be made due to federal securities law if either company is publicly held.

---

merely a memorandum from which a more definitive legal document may be drafted once due diligence has been completed. Regardless of the legal implications, however, by executing a letter of intent, you and the seller are making a psychological commitment to the transaction and providing a foundation for more formal negotiations. In addition, a well-drafted letter of intent will provide an overview of matters that require further discussion and consideration, such as the exact purchase price. Although a purchase price cannot realistically be established until due diligence has been completed, the seller may hesitate to proceed without a price commitment. Instead of creating a fixed price, however, the letter of intent should incorporate a price range that is qualified by a clause or provision that sets forth all of the factors that will influence and affect the calculation of a final fixed price. In addition to addressing the price range you are willing to pay and the seller is willing to accept, a letter of intent also includes the following:

PROPOSED TERMS. The first section of the letter of intent typically addresses certain key terms of the deal, such as price and method of payment. These terms are usually non-binding so that the parties have an opportunity to conduct thorough due diligence and have room for further negotiation.

BINDING TERMS. The letter of intent also includes certain binding terms that will not be subject to further negotiation. These are certain issues that at least one side, and usually both sides, will want to ensure are binding and include:

- **Legal ability of seller to consummate the transaction.** Before wasting too much time or money, you will want to know that the seller has the power and authority to close the deal.
- **Protection of confidential information.** Both parties, particularly the seller, will want to ensure that all information provided in the initial presentation as well as during due diligence remains confidential.
- **Access to books and records.** As the buyer, you will want to ensure that the seller and the seller's advisers will fully cooperate in the due-diligence process.
- **Break-up or walk-away fees.** You may want to include a clause making the seller liable for your expenses if the seller tries to walk away from the deal, either due to a change in circumstances or the desire to accept a more attractive offer from a different buyer. The seller may want a reciprocal clause to protect against its own expenses if you walk away or default on a preliminary obligation or condition to closing, such as an inability to raise acquisition capital.
- **No-shop/standstill provisions.** You may want a period of exclusivity where the seller is not entertaining any other offers. The seller will want to place a limit or outside date to this provision to allow it to begin entertaining other offers if you are taking an unreasonable amount of time to conclude the transaction.
- **Good-faith deposit—refundable versus non-refundable.** In some cases the seller will request a deposit or option fee, and the parties must determine to what extent, if at all, this deposit will be refundable and under what conditions. Frequently, there are timing problems with this provision that can be difficult to resolve. For example, you will want the deposit to remain 100% refundable if the seller is being uncooperative, or until you complete the initial round of due diligence to ensure that there are no major problems that will adversely affect the deal. The seller will want to set a limit

on the due-diligence and review period, at which point you will forfeit all or a part of the deposit. The end result is often a progressive downward scale of refundability as the due diligence and the deal overall reach various checkpoints towards closing. To the extent that you forfeit some or all of the deposit, and the deal never closes, you may want to negotiate an eventual full or partial refund if the seller finds an alternative buyer within a certain period of time, such as 180 days.

■ **Impact on employees.** The letter of intent should address plans for employees of the target company, including which staff members (designated by department or level, or in some other way) will be retained and how and when employees will be informed as to the details of the transaction.

■ **Key terms for the definitive documents.** Frequently, the letter of intent will stipulate that it is subject to the specific terms of the "definitive documents," such as the purchase agreement, and that those definitive documents will address certain key matters or include certain key sections, such as covenants, indemnification, representations and warranties, and key conditions for closing.

■ **Conditions to closing.** Both you and the seller will want to articulate a set of conditions or circumstances under which you will not be bound to proceed with the transaction (such as if certain contingencies are not met or if certain events happen subsequent to the execution of the letter of intent). It is important that these conditions are clearly articulated.

■ **Conduct of the business prior to closing.** As the buyer, you should require assurance that what the to-be-acquired business has to offer today will be intact at the time of the closing. Thus, you may want to include terms stating that the seller is obligated to operate the business in the ordinary course. Specifically, this may require that certain assets will be available at the time of the closing, that equipment will be kept in good repair, new customers will be pursued, and that bonuses and other expenses will be paid only in accordance with past practice and no new compensation will be added. These negative covenants help protect you against unpleasant surprises at the time of, or after, closing.

Common Reasons Why Deals Die at an Early Stage

- Seller has not prepared adequate financial statements (e.g. going back at least two years and reflective of the company's current condition).
- Seller and its team uncooperative during the due diligence process.
- Buyer and its team discover a "deal breaker" in the due diligence (e.g. large unknown or hidden actual or contingent liabilities, like an EPA clean-up matter).
- Seller has "seller's remorse," "cold feet" or has not properly thought through its after-tax consideration or compensation.
- Seller becomes defensive when the buyer and its team find flaws in the operations of the business, the valuation, the loyalty of the customers, the quality of the accounts receivable, the skills of the personnel, etc., and then focus on them in the negotiation.
- A strategic shift (or extenuating circumstances) affecting the acquisition strategy or criteria of the buyer (e.g. a change in buyer's management team during the due diligence process).
- Seller is inflexible on price and valuation when buyer and its team discover problems during due diligence.

- **Limitations on publicity and press releases.** You and the seller may want to place certain restrictions on the content and timing of any press releases or public announcements of the transaction, and in some cases may need to follow SEC guidelines. If either or both of the parties to the transaction are publicly traded, then the general rule is that once the essential terms of the transaction are agreed to in principle, such as through the execution a the letter of intent, there must be a public announcement. You and the seller must carefully weigh the timing and content of this announcement and analyze how it will affect the price of the stock. The announcement should not be made too early, or it may be viewed by the Securities and Exchange Commission (SEC) as an attempt to influence the price of the stock.
- **Expenses/brokers.** You and the seller should determine, where applicable, who shall bear responsibility for investment bankers' fees, finder's fees, legal expenses, and other costs pertaining to the transaction.

The Work Schedule

Once you and the seller have signed the letter of intent, one of your lawyer's first responsibilities is to prepare a comprehensive schedule of activities, or work schedule. The primary purpose of the schedule is to outline all the events that must occur and list the documents that must be prepared prior to the closing and beyond and to assign responsibility for their completion. Your lawyer assigns primary areas of responsibility to the various members of the acquisition team as well as to the seller and seller's lawyers. Your lawyer must also ensure that the timetable for closing is met. Once all tasks have been identified and assigned and a realistic timetable established for the completion of those tasks, then a closing time and date can be preliminarily determined.

The legal documents and the specific tasks to be outlined in the work schedule vary from transaction to transaction, usually depending on the specific facts and circumstances of each deal.

Due Diligence

Following the execution of the letter of intent, both you and the seller must begin preparing for the due-diligence process. Due diligence must be a cooperative and patient process between you and the seller and your respective teams. This process involves a legal, financial and strategic review of all of the seller's documents, operating history, contractual relationships, and organizational structure. You and your team must be prepared to ask all of the right questions and to conduct a detailed analysis of the documents the seller has provided. To the extent that the deal is structured as a merger, or the seller is taking your stock as all or part of its compensation, the process of due diligence is likely to be two-way, with each party gathering background information on the other.

Due diligence is usually divided into two parts: financial and strategic, to be conducted by your accountants and management team, and legal due diligence, to be conducted by your lawyers. Both due-diligence teams must compare notes on an ongoing basis on any unresolved issues and potential

---

Common Due-Diligence Investigation Mistakes

■ **Mismatch between the documents provided** by the seller and the skills of the buyer's review team. It may be the case that the seller has particularly complex financial statements or highly technical reports that must be truly understood by the buyer's due-diligence team.

■ **Poor communication and misunderstanding.** The communication should be open and clear between the buyer's and seller's teams.

■ **Lack of planning and focus in the preparation of the due-diligence questionnaires** and in the interviews with the seller's team. The focus must be on asking the *right* questions, not just a lot of questions. Sellers will resent wasteful "fishing expeditions" when the buyer's team is unfocused.

■ **Inadequate time devoted to tax and financial matters.** The buyer's (and seller's) CFO and CPA must play an integral part in the due-diligence process in order to gather data on past financial performance and tax reporting, unusual financial events or disturbing trends or inefficiencies.

■ **Seller becomes defensive** when the buyer and its team find flaws in the operations of the business, the valuation, the loyalty of the customers, the quality of the accounts receivable, the skills of the personnel, etc., and then focus on them in the negotiation.

■ **A strategic shift** (or extenuating circumstances) affecting the acquisition strategy or criteria of the buyer. (e.g. A change in buyer's management team during the due-diligence process)

■ **Seller is inflexible on price** and valuation when buyer and its team discover problems during due diligence

---

risks or problems. The legal due diligence will focus on the potential legal issues and problems that may impede the transaction and determine how the documents should be structured. The business due diligence will focus on the strategic and financial issues surrounding the transaction, including: confirmation of the seller's past financial performance; the integration of the human and financial resources of the two companies; confirmation of the operating, production and distribution synergies and economies of scale to be achieved by the acquisition; and gathering of information necessary for financing the transaction.

Common Due-Diligence Problems and Exposure Areas

There is virtually an infinite number of potential problems and exposure areas for the buyer that may be uncovered in the review and analysis of the seller's documents and operations. The specific issues and problems will vary based on the size of the seller, the nature of its business and the number of years that the seller (or its predecessors) has been in business. Common problems you and your team should be alert to include:

- **"Clouds" in the title** to critical tangible (real estate, equipment, inventory) and intangible (patents, trademarks) assets. Be sure the seller has clear title to these assets and that they are conveyed without claims, liens and encumbrances.

- **Employee matters.** There are a wide variety of employment or labor-law issues or liabilities that may be lurking just below the surface and that will not be uncovered unless the right questions are asked. Questions should be developed to uncover wage and hour law violations, discrimination claims, OSHA compliance, or even liability for unfunded persons under the Multi-Employer Pension Plan Act. If the seller has recently made a substantial workforce reduction (or if you as the buyer are planning post-closing layoffs), then the requirements of the Worker Adjustment and Refraining Notification Act (WARN) must have been met. The requirements of WARN include minimum notice of 60 days prior to wide-scale terminations.

- **The possibility of environmental liability** under CERCLA or related environmental regulations.

- **Unresolved existing or potential litigation.** These cases should be reviewed carefully by counsel.

- **A seller's attempt to "dress-up" the financial statements** prior to sale, often in an attempt to hide inventory problems, research and development expenditures, excessive overhead and administrative costs, uncollected or uncollectible accounts receivable, unnecessary or inappropriate personal expenses, unrecorded liabilities, tax contingencies, etc.

The due-diligence process, when done properly, can be tedious, frustrating, time-consuming and expensive. Yet it is a necessary prerequisite to a well-planned acquisition and can be quite informative and revealing in analyzing the target company and in measuring the costs and risks associated with the transaction. Remember that the key objective of due diligence is not just to confirm that the deal makes sense, but also to determine whether the transaction should proceed at all.

Effective due diligence is both an art and a science. The art is in having the style and experience to know which questions to ask, and how and when to ask them, and the ability to create an atmosphere of both trust and fear in the seller, thereby encouraging full and complete disclosure. In this sense, the due-diligence team is on a search-and-destroy mission, looking for potential problems and liabilities, and finding ways to resolve these problems prior to closing and to ensure that risks are allocated fairly and openly among the parties after closing.

The science is in preparing the specific questions that will be asked of the seller; maintaining a methodical system for organizing and analyzing the documents and data provided by the seller; and quantitatively assessing the risks discovered in the process. One of the key objectives of the due-diligence process is to detect obligations of the seller, particularly those that you will be expected or required to assume after closing, and to identify any defaults or problems in connection with these obligations that will affect you on a post-closing basis.

When done properly, due diligence is performed in multiple stages, continuing until all outstanding questions have been answered, and all relevant data has been gathered and examined and its impact on the transaction has been analyzed.

You and your due-diligence teams should resist the temptation to conduct a hasty once-over (either to save costs or to appease the seller), yet you should also avoid due-diligence overkill, keeping in mind that due diligence is not a perfect process. Information will slip through the cracks, which is precisely why broad representations, warranties, liability holdbacks, and indemnification provisions should be structured into the final purchase agreement. The nature and scope of these provisions are likely to be hotly contested in the negotiations.

Growth Through E-Commerce and Internet-Driven Strategies

I T SEEMS AS THOUGH EVERY TIME YOU PICK UP A BUSI-ness magazine, you can find at least one article on the impact that the Internet and e-commerce have had on the way business is conducted. The Internet has changed the way we communicate, altered our notions of time and space, and created countless opportunities to start new businesses or expand the horizons of existing businesses. The Internet has made the pace and style of growing a business more dynamic, more open and more direct. The increased connectivity gives your company more ways to solidify relationships but also leaves no place to hide if you are complacent or fall behind. Along the way, lawyers and the courts have tried to keep pace with the technology by adapting the law to encompass new types of transactions, new business challenges and new forms of intellectual properties.

The viability of the business models built around an Internet and e-commerce strategy have also evolved. A business model that assumed other companies would spend millions to take banner advertising on your site or that you could build a stand-alone Internet brand that would generate millions in business-to-business revenues are now essentially dead. Many companies have been forced to "morph" into new applications of their technologies in search of real customers and revenue streams.

How and why are owners of rapidly growing companies

using the Internet? Countless business uses have already emerged, including gathering information, collaborating with strategic partners, creating internal efficiencies, controlling inventories, providing customer support and information, researching competitors, providing support and data to key vendors, advertising and marketing, publishing information, selling products and services, and buying products and services. These last two categories, typically referred to as business-to-business (B2B) electronic commerce, will increase dramatically as computer security, consumer-comfort levels and encryption-software capabilities improve over the next five to ten years and the vertical industry marketplaces truly become a reality. In fact, the distinction between the old economy and new economy has already blurred. There is really no difference between e-commerce and other distribution channels other than new legal and strategic issues and challenges, which are addressed later in this chapter. Ultimately, it's all just commerce—growing companies taking advantage of all available technologies to maximize revenue streams and shareholder value.

The Importance of an E-Commerce Strategy

If you believe that your business can achieve growth through new or expanded e-commerce, answer the following questions before you spend money on Web-site designers, electronic-commerce solutions and a Web-hosting company.

WHAT IS YOUR E-COMMERCE STRATEGY? What do you hope to accomplish as a result of establishing—or revamping—a Web site? Will it be an online brochure? An employee-recruitment tool? An electronic catalog? Or will it be a genuine e-commerce platform? Will your site offer links to other sites with which you have established co-branding or revenue-sharing arrangements?

WHAT IMPACT WILL AN ELECTRONIC PRESENCE HAVE ON YOUR EXISTING DISTRIBUTION CHANNELS? Will any points in your current distribution channels become obsolete? Are there any expectations or legal obligations that you have to these channel members before terminating your relationships?

SHOULD YOU HAVE A SEPARATE SUBSIDIARY FOR YOUR E-COMMERCE OPERATIONS? Many fast-track growth companies that launch e-commerce initiatives are spinning them off as separate entities to segregate accounting and cost functions, enjoy certain tax benefits and maintain a distance from a liability perspective. What impact will your decision have on brand awareness as well as all relevant strategic, operational, cultural and taxation issues? Who will be responsible for maintaining and building your e-commerce operations?

WHAT IS YOUR REVENUE MODEL FOR THE SITE? Is the site merely to enhance and support your traditional distribution channels, like an informative electronic brochure? Or is it intended to generate revenues on a standalone basis, more like an electronic catalog? Does your site lend itself to other revenue streams, such as banner advertising? Will you have the traffic to support solid advertising rates?

IF YOU BUILD IT, HOW DO YOU KNOW THAT THEY WILL COME? What is your strategy for attracting traffic to your site? What competitors do you face in cyberspace that you may not be facing in the real world? Do your existing customers need or want you to have an online presence?

WHAT ADDITIONAL CONTENT, IF ANY, WILL BE AVAILABLE TO VISITORS? WHERE WILL THAT CONTENT COME FROM? Will it be internally developed or outsourced? Will there be a charge for the use of this content? Will you develop hot links to other sites? In the competition for sticky eyeballs—that is, visitors to your site who visit often and stay for extended periods of time—what interesting and timely information or content will you use?

Many companies spend a lot of time and money developing an Internet presence without clearly defining an e-commerce strategy or identifying objectives their Web presence

(continued on the page 306)

Determining the Role of the Internet on the Growth of Your Company

From its roots at the Advanced Research Project Agency (ARPA) in the late 1950s and early 1960s as ARPANET (a network of linked computers to share complete research data), to the Department of Defense initiatives to coordinate the activities of business, academic and government research through computer networks in the late 1960s and early 1970s, to the domain-name, server-driven systems in the 1980s, to the explosion of the World Wide Web in the mid 1990s, the Internet has truly emerged as an important strategic tool and electronic distribution channel used by companies of all sizes and in all industries.

In 1980, the ARPANET connected 400 host computers and university, government and military sites. By 1992, the Internet linked more than 17,000 networks in 33 countries, with more than one million hosts. By 2005, it is estimated that there will be more than 50 million host sites on the internet, with uses and applications in the next generation of technology that are difficult to even imagine today. And despite the economic downturn in 2000 and 2001, companies continue to invest in the hardware, software and services they need to build and support their e-business initiatives. Worldwide investment in Internet infra-

structure is expected to reach $1.5 trillion in 2003 and $2.2 trillion in 2004. Information-technology revenues for the U.S. market alone will hit $750 billion in 2001.

Returning to reality and today's business applications of the Internet, there are nine primary categories (and hundreds of hybrids and sub-categories) in which fast-track growth businesses are using Internet technology to build and enhance their performance and productivity. The Internet is proving particularly useful in the areas of customer acquisition and retention, supply-chain management, financial-transaction processing and human resources, communication and training. These categories of e-business applications and enabling technologies, many of which are addressed in more detail later in this chapter and elsewhere in this book, include:

■ **Customer Relationship Management (CRM).** Web-driven CRM applications combine marketing, sales and customer-service data and systems to help companies strengthen their relationships with existing customers and attract new ones. Using data mining, database management and communications software, companies are learning more about how, why and when their customers buy their products and services.

■ **Electronic Marketplaces.** As discussed later in this chapter, the emergence (and subsequent pruning) of B2B (business-to-business) electronic exchanges has created new ways to manage your supply chains and bid for the highest quality and best prices for the products and services your company consumes.

■ **Intranets (Business Employee Data-Sharing, Collaboration and Communication).** The establishment of a secure electronic system that connects all of your employees in all of your locations so that they can communicate and collaborate is key to the growth of your company. The design and function of the intranet needs to be carefully developed, however, to avoid waste and breakdowns.

■ **Wireless Business Applications (M-Commerce, or Mobile Commerce).** The use and applications of the wireless Web as a growth engine for e-commerce is still in its early stages. But this subset of e-commerce is likely to grow as the hardware (cell-phones, PDAs and other mobile devices) get smarter and easier

to use, and as software applications custom-tailored for mobile devices and the speed and cost of connecting improve.

■ **Application Service Providers (ASPs).** The trend toward outsourcing large portions of your data-management, financial and accounting systems and many other functions within your company lead to the creation of the ASP market. This new market offers to host your various general and custom applications (as well as update and maintain them) in exchange for an initial and monthly fee. But as discussed later in this chapter, the risks and alleged cost-savings may not outweigh the need to keep certain key functions on site.

■ **Business-to-Consumer E-Commerce (E-tailing).** Business to consumer e-tailing (B2C) really started to skyrocket in 1998 and 1999 when sites such as Amazon.com and Priceline.com used their proprietary one-click shopping and reverse-auction business models and technologies to capture the loyalty and the mindshare of millions of new electronic customers. In fact, the Super Bowl advertisements in 2000 were dominated by B2C

(continued on the next page)

Determining the Role of the Internet on the Growth of Your Company (continued)

dot.coms, such as Bluenile.com and Pets.com, which are either having difficulty or are now out of business. Wall Street analysts are still waiting for companies that have survived to make a profit, and their patience is waning. Other sites failed because they offered products and services, such as home furniture or certain types of clothing, that did not lend itself to Web-based retailing. Your e-tailing strategy should be a part, not the whole, of your overall sales and marketing strategy. It should be viewed as one distribution channel among many and not as a substitute for a viable business model.

■ **Peer-to-Peer Networks (P2P).** The allure of P2P is the ability of the user to exchange information across a network such as the

Internet at very low cost, high speed and with little administrative burden. The P2P applications and systems allow information to pass directly between two or more users' hardware (as peers) without overtaxing the central server. Although P2P is best known for consumer uses, such as the Napster.com music-sharing site, the business applications of this software and systems are still in their earliest stages.

■ **Distance Learning Programs (E-Learning).** Significant improvements in Webcasting technology and bigger and stronger bandwidths allowed online learning and virtual training to finally come into its own in 2000. In lieu of missing work and incurring heavy travel costs, many fast-track growth companies are using the

---

will achieve. Further, many don't have a clearly defined expectation regarding what visitors will do at the site once they have arrived. The push to "do something" online has resulted in a lot of wasted resources when a strategy is not defined in advance.

Building the Web Site

The proper foundation for adding an e-commerce component to your existing business begins with a well-built and well-designed Web site. Your Web site is the

Internet, private satellite networks, videoconferencing and conference calls as the delivery vehicle for training and education. The ability to post class notes, give lectures via Webcast and establish group and private chat rooms have significantly enhanced the quality of the online educational experience. Several companies, such as VCampus.com, TVWorldwide .com, Blackboard.com, and CampusMBA.com, have developed systems to enable e-learning or which will manage the process of curriculum development and delivery for you on an outsourced basis. And the applications of e-learning are not limited to employee training. They can also be used for customer communications, new-employee orientation and external seminars and meetings.

■ **Custom-Software Applications.**

Many fast-track growth companies cannot afford the standardization of "off the shelf" software. These companies are evolving quickly in a fast-moving marketplace and need custom-tailored software that can be adapted quickly to changing market conditions and customer demands. To keep pace, you can use an ASP (see above) and contract for customization or special support levels, or keep an expensive software development consultant on retainer. Or you can use open-source software (where the source code for the software is legally available for examination, modification and redistribution) and have your own in-house development team put together and maintain the software and systems that you need to manage and grow your business.

consumer's electronic point-of-entry to your company. If the design is unattractive and difficult to navigate, the chances of the targeted industrial or personal consumers ever returning to the site are very low, regardless of whether they came in search of information or goods and services.

Although a comprehensive discussion on how to build a Web site is well beyond the scope of this book, in the unlikely event that you will be establishing a Web presence for the first time, here are a few issues to consider.

CONCEPT DEVELOPMENT. Your presence on the Web is a strategy that requires a game plan, just like any other business-growth strategy. The goals for your site, its functionality, the resources (human and budgetary) that will be assigned to the strategy, your vendors and market partners, your target visitors, etc., need to be identified and reflected in a written concept paper. This document should be developed in draft prior to spending a lot of money on consultants and developers.

CHOOSING A DOMAIN NAME. Your domain name must be a memorable and positive brand image that your targeted online consumers will be attracted to over the long term. Many of the same principles of trademark law will apply (see Chapter 18) to the selection of a Web-site name. Will it be a gimmicky name, such as www.amazon.com—a name that has nothing to do with the products available on the site, but merely suggests a vast place? Or will it be more cut and dried, like many of the electronic B2B marketplaces, such as www.solidwaste.com, where the functionality and purpose of the site are immediately evident? The answer in part depends on your target audience as well as your available marketing budget. An esocentric domain name (such as www.bluenile.com, an online jewelry retailer) will require millions of dollars of advertising to build name recognition. Make sure the domain name you select reflects and is consistent with your overall branding strategy and the purpose and functions of the site. It is also critical that your domain be registered with InterNIC, the agency that registers and maintains a database of domain names. The registration can be accomplished through companies such as NetworkSolutions .com or Register.com, or can be handled by your Internet service provider. If you also intend to use your domain name as a brand identifying your company's products and services, then you will need to register the domain name as a trademark or a service mark with the United States Patent and Trademark Office (USPTO) as described in Chapter 18.

PAYMENT SOLUTIONS. Unless your site is intended to be only informational, you will need to develop a payment-solutions strategy to be fully operational for e-commerce. This process begins with the selection of a payment-software vendor, such as VeriSign, CyberSource or Worldpay. You then need to establish a merchant account, which is a banking relationship that will allow the site to accept credit-card payments and an outsourced credit-card clearing and authorization process. To protect your consumer's credit-card numbers, your payment solution should include a secure server (that is, a system that establishes a secure connection with your customer's Internet browser and encrypts all transmitted information). Your payment solution should also include an accounting system that includes a method for tracking orders—which can be as simple as e-mail notification and electronic receipts or as sophisticated as internal database tracking and online query search capabilities.

CUSTOMER-SERVICE FEATURES. A well-designed Web site should always include a customer relationship management (CRM) system that can organize and support your Web-based commerce and also fit in with your existing systems. These systems help you organize, track and analyze customer data and buying patterns, as well as provide customer-service support via e-mails, call centers and chat-based customer interactions that all must be integrated. The leading vendors in this area include Siebel Systems, PeopleSoft and E.piphany, which offer comprehensive solutions to both rapid-growth businesses and Fortune 1000 companies.

HARDWARE, SOFTWARE, STORAGE AND BACK-END INTEGRATION. Your chief technology officer or your technology consultants will need to make recommendations regarding the right mix and configuration of Web-server hardware, design and database software, HTML (hypertext markup language), basic page-design software and systems, scalable and redundant storage and hardware systems, and systems that allow wireless customers to interface with your site. Leading vendors such as Sun Microsystems, EMC, IBM, Microsoft, and Oracle are good places to start looking for these solutions and systems and often offer working teams that specialize in the needs of small and emerging-growth companies.

SEARCH ENGINE REGISTRATION. Once you have completed all of the preceding steps, how do you make sure that someone visits your site? Beyond traditional advertising and marketing strategies, it is also critical that you submit your domain name to all possible search engines, either through your own efforts or through a third party such as www.submit-it.com, an automatic submission service.

In building your Web site, avoid some of the classic mistakes other business have made, such as:

- **making the site too complex** and almost impossible to navigate;
- **building too much customized** or standalone technology early on when an outsourced or turnkey solution offered by a third-party hosting service may be more efficient;
- **assuming that the buying patterns and desires** of your off-line customers (in terms of demographics, price, information, warranty, selection and support) will be the same as your online customers, when in fact they may be very different; and
- **starting with a system too cheap** or too simple to handle the number of visitors to your site. (As an example of this latter blunder, consider the Victoria's Secret online fashion-show debacle or Encyclopedia Britannica's first Web site attempt. In both cases, the traffic was so much larger than the company had anticipated that the site was logjammed and countless visitors were denied entry.)

Web-Site Development Agreement

In developing your company's Web site, you may choose to work with a Web-site design firm. Before entering into an agreement with the firm, be sure to take the time to know your respective rights and obligations. The Web-site development agreement should clearly address expectations, fees and a timetable and should include the following provisions.

DESCRIPTION OF THE DEVELOPMENT PROCESS. Many disputes arise because the Web-site designer and the business owner fail to communicate a basic understanding between the parties. Start by designating a project manager for both sides who will create a communication method to keep both parties in sync. Devise a schedule with dates for completion of particular pieces of the project. At each interval, review material to date to ensure you are happy with the product and to refocus if necessary. This will allow you to approve layout design, Web-page content and costs on an ongoing basis.

CONTENT. The designer and owner must agree upon the content of a Web site—including any text, pictures, audio and video. The contract should state whether the designer is responsible for the creation of a search feature or any other specialized function. The contract should also describe the source of the content, the developer or the owner, and create an approval process. Be sure to discuss permission to use copyrighted material, and remember that you must take responsibility for obtaining the rights to any material you provide to the developer.

OWNERSHIP OF THE SITE AND ITS PARTS. The Web-site development agreement should clearly state who has rights to the site's content, design and specialty functions. This will ensure that your design does not turn up on someone else's Web site when the outsourced designer takes on its next project. Be sure that the development agreement vests and assigns all rights to your company as the hiring party.

WARRANTIES. At a minimum, an agreement should contain a basic warranty stating that the site will operate as you specified and that copyrightable pieces delivered by the developer do not violate the rights of any other party. You may also wish to warranty the originality of any artwork supplied by the Web-site developer.

Web-Site Hosting Agreements

The majority of owners of growing businesses outsource the hosting of their company's site to a third-party hosting company, which shifts the burden of operating the site away from the company itself. A hosting agreement should include the following provisions.

LIST OF SERVICES. This list should include a detailed description of every service the host will deliver. This will be the basis for calculating all fees, including additional cost for services performed that are not listed in the contract. A host can secure a domain name either with your company's name (for example, www.yourbusiness.com) or through the host (www.host.your-business.com). Be sure to state in the contract any ownership rights over the domain name. Agree on the frequency of updates and the time it will take the host to post new information once you deliver it. Evaluate the need for Web-site security and communicate to the host any needs to restrict access to particular portions of the site. If your site accepts credit cards or personal information, your host must have a strong level of security for processing. The agreement can also include a provision regarding measures to increase traffic to your site, such as registering with search engines or using metatags to lure new viewers to your page. (But be careful to avoid trademark-infringement issues by burying your competition's registered trademarks among your metatags.. To keep track of your site's success, request data on the number of visitors and what activities the visitors engage in while there, as this will help refine and direct changes to your site.

PERFORMANCE STANDARDS. Be clear about what you expect from the host and when you expect it. Define continuous tasks (such as uninterrupted access to the site and proper security) as well as one-time events. Include measures you can take if each performance standard is not met by predetermined criteria.

AGREEMENT TERMINATION. Include an agreement-termination date that can be renewed if desired by both parties. If your company and the host do not come to an understanding or there is a breach in the agreement, as owner of the site you will have to operate it internally or find another provider to host it. You will need access to all information used to develop the site, such as hardware and software (and commercial software licenses, if your company paid for any). Make sure the agreement carefully describes the obligations of the host to relay all information to you upon agreement termination. Be sure to structure the termination clause to allow you as much information as possible.

Linking Agreements

Using Web-site links is the most common way to navigate the Internet, and many businesses took this concept for granted and gave little thought to the legal implications until Ticketmaster successfully sued Microsoft in 1999 for posting a link to its site without Ticketmaster's permission. This spawned a whole new way of viewing links as a revenue stream and created a complex way to direct traffic through sites. Although the concept of a Web-linking agreement arose from a destination site's desire to restrict links to its site, high-traffic sites can negotiate with other sites that want to place links there to increase their own viewership. As a result, Web-linking agreements are beginning to be more common and more complex. The following issues need to be addressed.

FEES. Fees and charges can go either way, depending on who wants the link and why. If you want to place a link on your site it may be necessary to contact the owner of the site and request permission. The owner may not allow linking without consent for a fee. (This is usually a one-time fee for a specified term.)

LINK LOCATION AND VISUAL ASPECTS. The agreement should describe where the link will be placed on the site and where it will connect to, such as the destination's home page or a specific page within the destination site. This will depend on why the original site wants to place the link and where the destination site wants to direct traffic. Include a provision regarding the appearance of the link, such as color, size and the inclusion of a trademark (with permission).

When Is It Time to Update Your Site?

Many Web sites built in the late 1990s are already in serious need of an overhaul. Many growing companies invested hundreds of thousands of dollars—and in some cases, millions—early on to build sites that now have inadequate search tools, poor graphics, inaccessible or incomprehensible content, lack of personalization, easily penetrated security systems, faulty data storage and many other shortcomings.

If your rapidly growing company fails to keep up with available technology, it will be left behind as competitors offer better, faster and more user-friendly access, content and navigational features. Make periodic evaluations of the effectiveness of your company's Web sites, based on the following criteria, an ongoing part of your e-commerce strategy.

CUSTOMER FEEDBACK. At the heart of any effective Web strategy and Web presence is focus on the customer. Ask your e-customers for constant feedback on how your site can be improved from an efficiency, effectiveness, and ease-of-use perspective.

DESIGN. Does your current Web-site design and layout still make sense? Is it reflective of your overall branding strategies, themes, colors and (where applicable) off-line interactions with your customers? In other words, if you have a "brick and click" strategy that combines a traditional bricks-and-mortar presence with an online electronic commerce strategy, is there consistency with the signage and trade dress in the stores and the Web pages? Are your banner advertising and your Web links compatible with your underlying site? Are strategic links seamless or is it obvious to the user that they are now at another company's site? Is your site weighed down with cool-looking graphics or features that distract the visitor from learning more about your company and its products and services? The design should facilitate navigation and use, not interfere with it. Take another look at the overall layout of each page as if you were a prospective customer. Does it meet your needs? Does it help tell the company's story? Is the typography, hierarchy and ordering of pages logical and helpful? What could be done better, made easier or be enhanced with better graphics? The design of the site should be consistent with the company's industry and the expectations of its target customers. For example, a site that offers music, content and merchandise for reggae-music lovers and enthusiasts should be very different in its look and feel than a vertical marketplace Web site offering content and purchasing solutions in the waste management industry.

USER-FRIENDLINESS. If you built your site in 1997 or 1998 and have not updated it since, it is probably in significant need of improvement. Take a hard look at the ease of navigation within the site and to linked sites, the effectiveness of your search capabilities and tools, the relevancy and currency of your content, overall site stickiness (that is, the amount of time that a targeted user spends on your site, typically as a measure of the quality of the site's content, features, user-friendliness and functionality) and customer-service logistics. Your customers may demand onsite customer help, either through interactive voice assistance or at the very least through access to a 24-hour toll-free customer-service phone number. Today's Web surfers demand that tasks they conduct on a Web site—from logging on to responding to requests for data to actual ordering processes—be completed easily and quickly.

TECHNICAL PERFORMANCE. Your site must not only look good and be well organized; it must also be fast and reliable. It must be scalable—ready to handle rapid increases in traffic and usage that will hopefully emerge as your brand becomes well established in cyberspace. Your target customer will leave your site if pages are loading too slowly, tasks seem to take forever to perform and ordering products or services takes longer than the checkout line at the grocery store on the eve of a big snow storm. The user's experience from a speed perspective will be affected by your site's scalability, server design, network traffic and the hardware and Internet connectors used by the visitor to your site. The way to improve the speed and performance of your site is to license a content-delivery network system, such as those developed by Inktomi or Akamai to move your most frequently used content to services that are housed directly in Internet-access facilities.

PRIVACY AND SECURITY CONCERNS. Today's e-commerce customer expects a Web site to offer the latest in security and have a consumer-friendly privacy policy displayed on the home page. User profiles and online shopping carts must be secure, especially if you are asking for credit-card numbers, personal financial information or other information that most consumers would consider private, sensitive or confidential. A failure to provide adequate security, leading to content tampering or consumer fraud by hackers, can be fatal to your company's online presence.

Continuously look at your company's Web strategy and Web site to make sure you are keeping pace with the competition and taking advantage of technology that can enhance your site and keep it ahead of the pack. Common add-ons include: adding a stronger and more precise search engine; enriching the stickiness of your content by adding Web-syndicated news; adding communication tools; building an electronic community at the heart of your site by including e-mail services, calendar/schedule-management features, guest books, polling, bulletin boards and chat rooms; and improving the experience of the user by adding video streaming or even live Webcasting features. Also consider enhancing the profit potential of your site by adding revenue-generation features, such as shared-revenue cross-linking arrangements or a Web-affiliate program. For example, you would place banner ads on your site to sell another company's goods or services. Every time a visitor links to that company's site from yours, you are paid a percentage of any sale made (or sometimes just for the visit). Affiliate networks, such as befree.com and linkshare.com, can track the origin of each click and retain records to ensure you are fairly paid. These affiliate banner-exchange programs can be an excellent way to enhance your site's ability to generate revenues. But they should generally be a fit with the branding and positioning of your site, much in the same way the retail kiosk subtenants within a large department store must be consistent with the department store's overall image and target customer.

Key Legal Issues in Building an Internet Strategy

There are a wide variety of legal and regulatory issues that you must be aware of in connection with establishing and developing your company's electronic presence, as well as in building its e-commerce capabilities.

CENSORSHIP ISSUES AND THE FIRST AMENDMENT. Regulators, courts and interest groups have struggled in recent years to determine how (and if) the content of the Internet should be regulated. On February 8, 1996, President Bill Clinton signed into law a statute called the "Communications Decency Act" (CDA), which was designed to deter online pornography. However, a specially convened federal panel in Philadelphia prohibited the Department of Justice from enforcing the CDA and declared the CDA unconstitutional. This decision, which for the moment extends the reach of the First Amendment over cyberspace, is a battle that is likely to continue for many years. A balance between the regulations applicable to print or broadcast media versus those that will apply to online content in cyberspace will be difficult to achieve, especially as access to cyberspace gets easier and more widespread.

DOMAIN-NAME REGISTRATION AND TRADEMARK RIGHTS. As more and more companies establish a site or home page on the Web, their address or domain name becomes critical. Battles over trademark rights and using another company's name in your domain name have traveled to the courts and are the subject of on-going and heated debate. In *Panavision v. Toeppen,* the 9th Circuit Court upheld summary judgment against one of the Internet's most notorious cybersquatters, ruling that registering a domain name that is also a trademark, with the intention of selling it to the rightful owner of the trademark, violates antidilution laws. There have also been disputes between parties when the same words appear in both parties' trademarks.

In 1999, Congress passed the Anti-Cybersquatting Consumer Protection Act (ACPA) to address the growing problem of cybersquatting. The ACPA makes it illegal for a person to register, traffic in, or use domain names that are identical or confusingly similar to trademarks with the bad-faith intent to profit from that trademark. The ACPA applies to all domain-name registrations. If the court finds a violation of the ACPA, it may award damages and may also order that the domain name be transferred to the owner of the mark or canceled altogether. The courts have not defined "bad-faith intent to profit" and rely on a number of factors to determine whether it is present. Should you decide to register a domain name or discover that someone may be infringing on your trademark, it is very important to seek legal advice.

Also in 1999, the system for domain-name registration was significantly restructured. Network Solutions Inc. had held a government-approved monopoly in domain-name registration since 1993. But with over 20 million Internet domain names already registered, the federal government sought to establish competition and open up the field by signing a deal with the not-for-profit Internet Corp. for Assigned Names and Numbers (ICANN) to create competition in the Internet-address business. Since then, a number of new firms have emerged in the field. They are all linked to InterNIC, the agency that registers and maintains a database of domain names and conducts conflict checks on proposed domain names. InterNIC has established a formal arbitration process for resolving domain-name disputes.

In late 2000, ICANN expanded the universe of suffix domains beyond the well-known dot.com and dot.org and less-known dot.net and dot.tv domains to include the following, known as top-level domains, or TLDs, which went into effect in November 2000:

- **.aero**—Reserved for the air-transport industry. Management of the database for this suffix was awarded to a Belgium-based firm, Societe Internationale de Telecommunications Aeronautiques, which provides network and communication technology to the air-transport community.

- **.biz**—General use, as an alternative to .com for commercial or business use. This database was awarded to JVTeam, NeuLevel (called JVTeam in the application) formed by NeuStar and Melbourne IT.

- **.coop**—Reserved for business cooperatives. Management for this database was awarded to the National Cooperative Business Association, a Washington-based trade group.

- **.info**—This suffix is for general use, and is also an alternative to .com. This was awarded to Afillias, a consortium of 19 Internet-domain-name registrars.

- **.museum**—As the name implies, this suffix is reserved for museums. This suffix was awarded to Museum Domain Management Association, founded by the International Counsel of Museums and the J. Paul Getty Trust.
- **.name**—Reserved for "human domain names," or personal Web sites, this suffix will be managed by Globe Name Registry, a British company formed by Nameplanet.com.
- **.pro**—This is reserved for professionals, such as doctors and lawyers. RegistryPro, a Dublin-based company formed by Register.com and Virtual Internet will manage the database for this suffix.

These new domain names offer an opportunity for fast-track companies who may have missed out on the initial "land rush" to establish a branded Web presence.

METATAG ISSUES. Some Web-site designers place particular words or phrases, called metatags, into the code used to create a site. These words help ensure that your site will appear when someone uses a search engine for a particular search and is called spamdexing. Some Web-site owners have fallen into legal trouble by using trademarks, such as a competitor's or similar product name, as a metatag. Search engines, such as Yahoo! and Excite, sell advertising by selling keywords or search terms to customers so that their banner will appear on the results screen when a searcher uses the term in a search. For example, if a Web surfer uses the word "airline" in a search, a banner for United Airlines might appear, because United purchased the "airline" word from the search engine. Businesses have also been known to buy competitors' trademarks as keywords to try to direct customers to their sites.

Although all these practices may increase traffic to your business's Web site, courts have begun to crack down on uses that involve trademarks. In the Niton case, a competitor, RMD Corp., used metatags such as Niton product names and the phrase "the homepage of Niton Corp." buried in the source code of its Web site. The court found that, combined with material posted on the Web site, RMD was leading users to
(continued on page 322)

Issues to Consider When Establishing a Web Presence

WEB-SITE CREATION

- Where should the Web site be located?
- Where should it be hosted?
- What difference does the location of the server, in one jurisdiction or another, make?
- What contractual arrangements should you have with your site builder or suppliers of content or other elements?
- Do you need international filtering?
- Do you need a transition plan if your current hosting arrangements do not meet your needs?
- If you already have a Web site, do you own all the rights to its content?

DOMAIN NAMES

- What is a domain name and how do you obtain one?
- How do they relate to trademark rights?
- What are the domain-name dispute-resolution procedures?
- How can you tackle domain-name cybersquatters?
- What statutory protections do you have for your trademark rights?

TERMS AND CONDITIONS OF THE WEB SITE

- What terms do you require?
- What difference does it make whether the end user is a business or consumer?
- Can you rely on hypertext links?
- Do you need a "pop up" notice?
- What disclaimers and exclusions of liability can you rely on?
- How do user terms differ from online-trading terms?
- Where should the terms and conditions of the site appear?
- Do you need a privacy policy, and are there countries which require certain statutory compliance?

ONLINE CONTRACTING

- Are "e-mail to e-mail" contracts valid and enforceable?
- What are the best-practice procedures to adopt in relation to Web-site sales?
- Does the site constitute an "offer to the world"?
- What are the differences in the international jurisdictions?
- In which countries do you need to have written confirmation of an online contract?
- Which countries do not recognize invitation to treat ordering procedures?
- How do the E.U. Distance Selling and E-Commerce Directive provisions affect online contracting, and are there similar statutory requirements in other jurisdictions?
- Where does "acceptance" take place in the digital market place?

■ Can you select the governing law and court of jurisdiction?

INTERNATIONAL COMPLICATIONS

■ What are the differing laws that apply to online contracting in the major international markets?

■ Which countries are more problematic than others?

■ Which countries have strict language requirements that impact Web sites?

■ Which countries' consumer laws are problematic?

■ What are the differences between business and consumer contracts and how do they affect your ability to stipulate the governing law or where you can be sued?

■ What are the latest changes to the Brussels Convention and how do they impact where you can be sued?

■ Does the Rome Convention allow freedom of contract for selecting governing law? How does this relate to the e-commerce European Union directive proposals for "home country law control" for Web site operators?

COMPETITION/ANTITRUST LAW

■ What competition/antitrust-law restrictions are there on refusing to supply customers in a certain country?

■ What type of contractual provi-

sions could be a problem?

■ How does market share affect the extent to which you can restrict Web site sales from one distributor to another?

■ How does the Federal Trade Commission and/or the E.U. Commission view online advertising?

TAX

■ What are the key tax considerations that may affect the location for your server and Web site business?

■ What constitutes a "permanent establishment" to determine where you pay tax on your profits?

■ Does it matter if you warehouse in one country and maintain your operational headquarters in another?

■ Who pays the customs duty on goods supplied internationally?

■ What are the VAT or U.S. tax issues regarding online supplies of goods or services and what are the differences from intra-E.U. supplies to those involving countries outside the E.U.?

■ Do your licensing arrangements have unintended tax consequences?

■ Where should title and risk of loss be transferred to minimize state and local taxes?

■ How should relationships between

(continued on next page)

Issues to Consider When Establishing a Web Presence (continued)

affiliates be arranged so as to minimize state and local tax burdens?

■ How should arrangements (general contracts as well as linking arrangements) with third parties—such as suppliers, Web-hosting services and fulfill-ment firms — be structured so as to minimize state and local tax liabilities?

WEB-SITE CONTENT

■ Under what circumstances will you be liable for defamation or infringement of intellectual property rights?

■ Should you be screening for obscene or inflammatory material?

■ What risks are there in hosting a chat room or bulletin board? Are the risks different in the jurisdictions that are important to you?

■ What risks do you run if you do attempt to "edit" third party material that is uploaded to your site's chat room or bulletin board?

■ Under what circumstances can you genuinely claim not to have

been a publisher or an editor?

■ What liability do you have for hypertext links to other Web sites?

■ What liability arises through the use of metatags?

■ Are there any risks in searching and retrieving information from other sites?

■ How does the E.U. E-Commerce Directive affect the liability of intermediary service providers?

DATA PROTECTION AND PRIVACY

■ What are the E.U. Data Protection Directive and 1998 Data Protection Act implications for use of data on the Internet?

■ Do U.S. copyright laws protect databases?

■ What legislation is pending in the U.S. that may protect databases?

■ Do the data protection provisions cover monitoring of site use?

■ What information does a Data Controller have to provide to a data subject in your jurisdiction?

■ What provisions are in place for e-mail "spam" opt-out registers?

■ What data-protection notice do you require?

■ What is the difference between

believe that it was the same company as Niton or affiliated with them. In another case, the Web site of a company that registers domain names included the name of a well-known intellectu-al-property law firm as a metatag. Although the defendants "opt out" and "opt in" privacy arrangements?

- What restrictions are there on transfer of data from the E.U. to other countries?
- Is unsolicited commercial e-mail "spam" legal?

ADVERTISING AND MARKETING

- What governs Internet advertising and marketing?
- Which regulatory codes do you have to comply with?
- Which consumer laws do you have to comply with?
- If allowed in your jurisdiction, what do you have to do in order to legally engage in unsolicited commercial e-mails?
- What are the implications of the E.U. Distance Selling Directive and E-Commerce Directive to on-line advertising and marketing? What is the impact of the Federal Trade Commission?
- How can you guard against being fined or prosecuted in foreign countries?

ENCRYPTION/SECURITY

- What is cryptography?

- What is encryption and how do digital signatures operate?
- What is the relevance to online trading and your online contracting process?
- How does public/private key encryption (PKI) operate?
- Should you consider becoming a certification authority? If no, which one should you use?
- What are the different online payment mechanisms and which are best for which businesses?
- What are the various U.S. proposals and European Directive proposals with respect to PKI?
- What effect will the U.K. Electronic Communications Act have with respect to PKI?
- How does the new U.S. digital-signature legislation affect your online business?

SITE INFRASTRUCTURE/ IT/OUTSOURCING

- What are the key pitfalls to avoid in structuring any kind of Web platform for business?
- What terms are key for any contracts with IT developers and suppliers (e.g., Web hosts) or any other outsourced suppliers?

were not attorneys, they were trying to use the law firm's reputation to redirect Web surfers to their site.

COPYRIGHT COMPLIANCE. Companies should be careful to create a copyright-compliance policy and to implement procedures to aggressively protecting their copyrights by taking action against repeat infringers. The case involving Napster Inc., a small Internet start-up that makes MusicShare software freely available for download by Internet users, demonstrates as much. In 2000, Napster was sued for copyright infringement by various major record labels. The peer-to-peer software that Napster employs to allow users to share data will continue to grow into other applications. This, in turn, will force the owners of the content, such as music or video, not only to create revenues in partnership with these sites, but also to discover new ways to create income. For example, it is no coincidence that rock bands increased their live concert scheduling and promotion of licensed merchandise in 2001 in response to the lost CD and tape sales that Napster music-sharing created.

In addition, when downloading information from another Internet site, you must know and adhere to copyright laws. Copyright compliance can be difficult to enforce, however, when you can't trace who originally reproduced and distributed the material. You should also be aware of other, less apparent laws, such as U.S. export controls, which might apply when certain types of software are downloaded internationally.

DEFAMATION AND INFRINGEMENT IN BULLETIN-BOARD SERVICES AND CHAT ROOMS. As an entrepreneur, you may have explored using electronic bulletin boards and chat rooms for user groups, clubs and others with common interests as a way to reach your target customer. Naturally, such a forum, if not monitored, may lend itself to claims of defamation as well as copyright and trademark infringement, especially where the bulletin-board users are uploading or downloading software, games or other information that may be proprietary or protected by trademark or copyright laws. In some cases where basic content guidelines and rules of conduct were not established, site owners have been found liable for copyright infringement or even defamation.

DISCLOSURE LAWS FOR INTERACTIVE CONTESTS AND PROMOTIONS. There are a wide variety of federal and state consumer-protection laws that you must address before your company offers a contest or sweepstakes via the Internet. Some companies have come under attack for unfair trade practices, fraud and misrepresentation by the Federal Trade Commission and the U.S. Department of Justice for structuring lotteries, promotions and contests in cyberspace that did not meet disclosure laws and other requirements at the federal and state level.

PRIVACY ISSUES. One interesting development on the electronic frontier is the use and publication of one's e-mail address. Mail consumers can choose through the United States Postal Service and the Direct Marketing Association to have their names removed from mailing lists. Telephone consumers can have unlisted telephone numbers. But what rights to privacy do consumers have when it comes to their e-mail addresses and any personal-identity information? The courts have struggled with this issue, and no definitive answer has been determined. At the federal level, the Federal Trade Commission (FTC) has issued a report to Congress asking for the authority to regulate online privacy. After years of promoting a general policy of industry self-regulation with regard to online consumer privacy, the FTC now supports federal legislation. The results of an FTC 2000 survey indicate that while more Web sites are posting privacy policies, only 20% meet the FTC's fair information practices. (For more information visit the Center for Democracy & Technology's Web site, www.cdt.org/previousheads/datatprivacy.shtml.)

As a part of best business practices, your Web site should contain a privacy statement that will inform the viewer of how you collect and use information relayed during the viewer's stay at your site. You may choose a privacy statement that also addresses information gathered from users without their knowledge, such as data passively made available when users merely visit your site. The privacy statement should be posted in a way that makes it easy to locate, read and understand. In addition to including a privacy statement on your Web site, you may choose to adopt formal uniform privacy policies. Such policies assure consumers that their privacy will be protected, helping to build confidence and long-term customer relationships.

As a Web-site owner, it is sound legal and business practice to also inform users that you may disclose personal information when legally compelled to do so. In one recent example, America Online was compelled to disclose otherwise private information in connection with apprehending a criminal suspect who allegedly created a deadly computer virus.

Some Web-site owners have implemented employee training and procedures on ensuring privacy. Others provide mechanisms for customer access, correction and removal of data. Another option you may consider to build consumers' confidence that their privacy will be protected is the Better Business Bureau's Privacy Seal Program, administered by BBBonline (www.bbbonline.org). Once you agree to meet specific privacy standards and to be subject to enforcement measures, you will be entitled to display the program's seal of approval on your Web site.

Another controversial e-commerce marketing practice is the use of mass e-mails of unsolicited offers, also known as spam. The FTC has cracked down on spam, and numerous anti-spam bills have been proposed in Congress. Several states have already adopted anti-spam legislation that allows both Internet-service providers and recipients to recover money damages against the sender. While you may be unable to resist the cheap opportunity to reach hundreds of consumers this way, any business gains you make through this approach could be offset by the cost of litigation.

For most companies, a strict privacy policy, such as the one adopted by America Online, can mean a competitive advantage, because by promoting respect for privacy, these e-commerce companies attract and keep more loyal customers. As a result, many emerging-growth businesses and Fortune 1000 companies are creating a chief privacy officer (CPO), who is responsible for establishing and enforcing the company's online (and off-line) privacy policies. The responsibilities of the CPO should include:

- **setting up a privacy committee;**
- **studying and assessing privacy risks** of all operations involving personal data;

- **developing a company privacy code;**
- **interacting with concerned regulators and consumers,** and providing a contact point for consumers;
- **creating and overseeing employee privacy training;**
- **monitoring privacy laws and regulations** (and the company's compliance); and
- **conducting privacy reviews of all new products** and Internet services.

CHILD PRIVACY ISSUES. Your business must be in compliance with recent laws aimed at regulating the online collection of information from children. If your Web site caters to children under 13 years of age or has actual knowledge that such children are providing information to your Web site, the Children's Online Privacy Protection Act of 1998 (COPPA) requires that you obtain "verifiable parental consent" before collecting or disclosing any information that could be used to identify or contact those child users. This information includes a child's name, telephone number, e-mail and street addresses. If COPPA applies to your Web site, you are required to post a detailed privacy notice, but you may vary your consent methods based on your intended use of the child's information. For more information about COPPA, visit http://www.ftc.gov or e-mail kidsprivacy@ftc.gov..

RIGHTS OF PUBLICITY. The rights of public figures (such as athletes, radio and television personalities, movie actors, etc.) are another Internet-related legal issue, whether in the context of home-page content, advertising or the subject of electronic bulletin-board chatter. For example, the use of a discussion of a celebrity to promote a particular online service or Internet-access provider may raise questions as to whether the celebrity deserves compensation or must grant permission, much in the same way a celebrity would be compensated for an endorsement. Although there is an exception to this right of publicity for incidental use or for newsworthy events or matters of public interest, radio personality Howard Stern challenged Delphi (an Internet-services provider) in 1994 for advertisements with his picture designed to promote a debate on their bulletin board on the merits of his self-declared candidacy for the office of the governor of New York. While the court concluded that Stern's name was used in the context of public debate (and thus protected), it left open protection of the "name and likeness" of celebrities on the Internet, much in the same way their name and likeness are protected in more traditional print and television media.

JURISDICTIONAL PROBLEMS. Many traditional business laws are based on geography. Disputes over which law should govern an online transaction can be more difficult because the Internet does not really "exist" in any one fixed place— it is everywhere. As a result, when disputes arise regarding privacy issues, copyright and trademark infringement, or breach of contract, there are problems determining jurisdiction—the law of which state or even which country should govern the transaction or dispute.

Obtaining jurisdiction over Web-site hosts will depend in large part on the type of site at issue. Courts tend to find a commercial Web site is subject to the jurisdiction of a particular state where that Web site demonstrated some active conduct toward the state. Where a Web site has specifically and actively targeted and solicited business from consumers in a particular state, the court may be likely to find that state to have jurisdiction over the Web site's owner. When that happens, a lawsuit may be brought in the state where the consumer lives. On the other hand, courts may be less likely to find that a state has jurisdiction over a Web site that advertised goods or services only passively. The test for what is active or passive business contact with a state can often be blurry. As a result, some companies specify a jurisdiction and include a choice-of-law provision in their online contracts. Other companies block business from individual states or countries where they would never want to appear in court.

Computer Security Issues

An issue that is indirectly related to the Internet, but is part of the downside of the developments in the information age, is computer security. Many small- and emerging-business owners simply cannot afford expensive software or consulting firms who will design intricate systems to protect against online theft or break-ins, as well as power outages, floods or fires. A well-designed Internet-security architecture will typically include: an authentication system (to determine who will be able to gain access); an authorization system (which decides what each user can do once permitted access); a screening system (which gives users access only to the data, tools or functions that they really need); and a segregation system (which compartmentalizes data to ensure that all of your data and information are sufficiently replicated and decentralized in the event of a disaster or security breach). Here are some steps that you should take to protect the safety and security of your network.

LIMIT ACCESS TO THE OUTSIDE WORLD. Some firms limit the number of computers within the office that have access to the Internet to protect outsiders from having access to key databases or sensitive information. Sometimes referred to as air gapping, this creates a "space" between the outside world and your internal network and internal operating systems. Be sure to create adequate firewalls, password systems and encryption software to protect your confidential or sensitive data.

DEVELOP WRITTEN COMPUTER POLICIES FOR YOUR EMPLOYEES AND CONTRACTORS. Many small and growing companies do not have adequate computer policies in writing to govern computer use by their employees, contractors or others who have access to their system. You should establish policies regarding ownership of intellectual property, downloading data to diskettes, use of computer data or transport of diskettes, security, privacy, backup policies, electronic-mail monitoring (giving rise to privacy issues), and when or how employees may be permitted to log into the system from home or another remote site.

UNDERSTAND YOUR RIGHTS AND OBLIGATIONS UNDER THE ECPA. The Electronic Communications Privacy Act (ECPA) is a federal law passed in 1996 that prevents the unauthorized access to electronic communications, including e-mail, via the Internet. It is illegal under the ECPA to intercept e-mail during transmission or to wrongfully access e-mail while it is stored in a computer system. However, the ECPA does not protect the privacy of messages sent on internal company electronic-mail systems, treating these types of communications as ordinary interoffice memorandums that may be read by authorized employees or supervisors without violating the ECPA. A fast-growing company should use the ECPA to protect the security of its electronic communications and should understand that the law does not prevent the monitoring and enforcement of internal e-mail communications.

The Digital Signature Act

The Electronic Signatures in Global and National Commerce Act, also known as the E-Sign Act, was signed into law in mid 2000, and its major provisions went into effect later that year. What impact will this new law have on the growth and facilitation of e-commerce and on your business? The E-Sign Act represents the federal government's attempt to provide a common legal framework that will govern e-commerce in the future. The law was designed to facilitate the growth of e-commerce by protecting the legal status of electronic signatures, contracts, and records.

The E-Sign Act's provisions apply to transactions that take place in interstate commerce and in foreign commerce. The law's basic mandate is that no electronic signature, contract, or record may be denied legal effect simply because it is in electronic, and not written, form. The law also contains provisions permitting the retention of records in electronic form where applicable law requires that records be retained, allows for electronic notarizations and acknowledgments under certain conditions, and recognizes that contracts created or delivered by "electronic agents" cannot be denied legal effect. The E-Sign Act carves out certain exceptions, however. Contracts already governed by trust and estate laws, divorce, adoption, or other family laws, and some provisions of the Uniform Commercial Code, are not subject to the E-Sign Act's more liberal provisions.

Despite the E-Sign Act's intent to expand the reach of e-commerce in our economy, the law was also carefully designed to protect the interests of consumers. For example, if provided in electronic form, records that are required by law to be provided to consumers must be capable of review, retention, and printing by consumers. The law also requires consumers to affirmatively consent before receiving an electronic record and mandates that businesses disclose the rights a consumer has to receive documents in a non-electronic format. Under the law, consumers may also withdraw their consent to receive electronic documents at any time. The E-Sign Act does not favor any type of electronic signature technology over another. Under the law, electronic-signatures may take the form of secure passwords, smart cards, biometric technologies, digital certificates, or future

The E-Sign Act's stamp of approval on e-commerce contracts will likely result in lower costs to businesses and customers.

technologies that are now only in the development stage. The law ensures that the marketplace and its participants, rather than a government agency, will determine how best to facilitate safe and efficient electronic business transactions.

The E-Sign Act's stamp of approval on e-commerce contracts will likely result in lower costs to businesses and customers. As the need for contracting parties to travel to distant cities for face-to-face meetings is reduced, companies will expend fewer resources on staff travel and lodging. Businesses will be required to spend less on document storage and retention, as electronically stored records become more commonplace. These lower operating costs for businesses will likely translate into lower prices for consumers, who will in turn demand a greater quantity of products and services from e-businesses. Law-enforcement officials also support the E-Sign Act, which they believe will provide incentives for technology companies to develop more sophisticated electronic-signature security devices that are less vulnerable to attack by cyber-criminals. Law-enforcement officials believe that these improved security devices will slow the growth of high-tech fraud, which has resulted in the loss of billions of dollars to the U.S. economy.

Despite the law's favorable implications for e-commerce, you should be wary of changing your business model simply because of the E-Sign Act. Before you make the full leap into e-commerce, be aware of when reliable e-signature technology will be available and determine the cost of implementing this technology. At present, several companies are developing electronic-signature applications, but no application has yet developed broad acceptance in the marketplace. You must decide whether it is time to begin investing in a new technology, or whether it makes sense to wait for a potential breakthrough that may be months or perhaps years away. It might be worth monitoring consumer-demand patterns and reviewing various forecasts of e-commerce growth in the coming years, particularly in your own sector of the economy. Using these forecasts, you can more accurately assess the risk of going forward with a new investment in electronic signature or related technology. Although the rewards from investing in new electronic-signature technology may seem automatic upon first glance, they will not materialize for every business.

When You Should Consider an Application-Service Provider (ASP)

Like many small and fast-growth companies have done to preserve cash and control their administrative expenses, you may find that it makes sense for your company to outsource key software and database-driven functions to an application-service provider (ASP). The ASP would take over responsibility for hosting, troubleshooting, monitoring and updating your company's software and allow your company to have access to more sophisticated and up-to-date software programs and technological solutions than you could afford if the programs were installed at your own site. Using an ASP also saves time and money that would otherwise be allocated to costly training programs and delays in efficiency that are caused by employees getting up to speed on new programs. The use of an ASP can also eliminate overspending for unnecessary hardware and software when the growth of your company or the demand for its products and services may still be unclear. Further, instead of paying for the installation of software and all of those seat-license fees, under most ASP pricing schedules, you pay only for the time that your company uses the ASP's programs. The downside risks of using an ASP to run key applications of your business are loss of control, potential delays in access, the availability of applications and reliability issues. For example, not all software programs have been re-written or lend themselves to e-delivery or third-party hosting, so the menu of applications offered by the ASP may be limited. An even tougher problem is when the ASP is having technical problems (or worse, financial challenges) that prevent you from getting rapid access to your mission-critical information. Financial-market conditions have led to some consolidation and difficulties in the ASP industry that may pose a real risk to rapid-growth companies who need access to their data on a 24/7 basis. A worst-case example involves Red Gorilla, a San Francisco–based ASP that provided online billing and administrative services to small companies and law firms. In October 2000, the company abruptly went out of business without any notice to its customers.

> **Instead of paying for the installation of software and all of those seat-license fees, under most ASP pricing schedules, you pay only for the time that your company uses the ASP's programs.**

ASP companies offer software and solutions to cover a wide range of business functions—including billing and expense-report accounting, e-mail and calendar tools, payroll, accounts-receivable collections, and customer-relationship management (CRM) programs. ASPs come in a variety of shapes and sizes, including those with the following business models:

- **Co-location.** The client—be it an ASP, a software vendor, or an individual corporation—owns the server and the applications but houses them at a facility owned by a co-location provider, who collects a monthly fee based on square footage and bandwidth. The client manages both the server and the applications, which are appropriate for both external Web sites and internal business purposes.
- **Application hosting.** This is co-location with the application-management function turned over to the application-hosting

provider. The client, however, is responsible for enterprise-specific content. Note that this is not e-commerce hosting.

■ **Web hosting.** Application hosting for e-commerce services.

■ **Application-service provider.** Application hosting taken one step further. The classic ASP manages all aspects of the applications, including maintenance and upgrades, providing functionality and associated services to multiple customers using a pay as you go model. There is limited customization, and clients access the applications via the Internet.

■ **Applications-management outsourcing.** The AMO maintains, manages, converts, enhances, and supports an applications portfolio housed at the client site or at the outsourcing vendor's facilities.

■ **Data-center outsourcing:** This is application hosting with some significant differences, such as a high level of customization or no application upgrades.

■ **Full-service outsourcing:** This includes all of the above, customized and carefully defined contractually.

Developing an Electronic-Exchange Strategy

As the owner of a fast-track growth company, you should also develop a strategy for participating in one or more electronic exchanges (also known as B2B marketplaces). These vertical markets have been established for a wide variety of purposes—including developing e-commerce, disseminating industry news, organizing special events, enabling collaboration among vendors and customers, enabling networking for jobs or customers, and establishing chat rooms for executives to compare notes and engage in brainstorming. Determine how these electronic exchanges fit into your overall e-business strategy. That may range from participation as organizer, manager and owner or co-owner of the marketplace to being a vendor of your products and services to using one or more electronic marketplaces as a source of procurement for raw materials, supplies, services and other resources that your

Revenue/Pricing Models in Electronic Exchanges

It is critical to do your homework on how you will pay or get paid when participating in an electronic exchange. The modes include:

Real-time dynamic pricing—This neutral system of pricing (neither favors the buyer nor the seller) allows companies to engage in real-time bidding for commodities such as oil or semiconductors. The model is a Bid-Ask exchange system, similar to the Nasdaq stock exchange and as a result is more reflective of the perceived value of the product at the time of the sale.

Reverse auctions—This approach is most commonly used when a buyer wants a specific item (based on type, quality or delivery schedule). The buyer submits a request for quote (RFQ), asking sellers to respond. Reverse auctions favor the buyer.

Forward auctions—This method, which works best for unique items like art or antiques, lets a seller put a product up for auction and then sell to the highest bidder. Because pricing trends upward, the process usually favors the seller.

company regularly consumes. You must also ensure that you have an adequate infrastructure and technology platform that allows you to participate in these various capacities.

As a potential participant in these exchanges, either as a buyer or a seller, take a look at your costs and the revenue model for the exchange. Membership fees, transactional fees, finders fees, event-participation fees, advertising fees or sponsorship fees all may be part of the marketplace operator's revenue model, and you should know your obligations and expected commitments in advance of your participation. Successful exchanges have driven down costs in the supply chain by removing unnecessary channel intermediaries and share data to create marketplace efficiencies. There must be a baseline level of trust by and among channel/marketplace participants and a commitment to using common operating systems and cost-accounting structures. When well operated, these exchanges help companies manage inventories (to avoid excesses and shortages), improve customer service and force each link in the supply chain to truly add value or perish. On the procurement side, participants use tools such as reverse-auctions (see the box above) to secure the latest prices from their vendors and professional/services providers and to identify new market partners and outsourcing opportunities. These same systems can be used on the sales and marketing side in order to identify new customer opportunities and new revenue streams to build the business.

Many industries—from specialty chemicals to agricultural seeds and supplies to electricity and gas—have begun using electronic exchanges to automate the buying, selling and distribution process to create highly efficient channels, which are particularly effective when organized around a set of commodity products. However, more specialized industries may not lend themselves to electronic exchanges. Further, not every customer (nor every vendor) will be inclined or motivated to participate in an electronic exchange, particularly for highly specialized or very personalized services. As a result, don't entirely abandon conventional distribution channels; instead, view your participation in an electronic exchange as a supplemental channel. Before joining an exchange, do careful research to determine which exchange to join. The Internet boom of the late 1990s created as many as a dozen or more competing exchanges within the same industry—clearly too many, and consolidation and failures in the B2B marketplace sector are likely. To remain competitive, these exchanges are developing new features and services, such as providing industry-trend reports by recognized experts, billing and payment services, transportation and logistics services and even private negotiating "rooms," where online buyers and sellers can go to nail down the final details of a transaction on a confidential basis.

Finally, these exchanges all use different pricing models and systems, from real-time dynamic pricing to forward auctions to reverse auctions.

Conclusion

Notwithstanding all of the dot.bombs, hype and turmoil, few can argue that the technological developments in the late 1990s—which include the growth of the Internet—have permanently changed the ways that companies of all sizes operate, communicate with their customers, employees and strategic partners and market their goods and services.

Yard sales and classified advertising may never be the same with eBay.com chugging along, and wireless business services and applications will take communications, productivity and efficiency to new heights. But whether there is a burning need for custom-designed breakfast cereal (such as that offered by General Mills' mycereal.com) remains to be seen. Thousands of ill-advised electronic storefronts have shut down, high-end Web consulting firms have folded and Web-business incubators have gone cold. But as our domestic and overseas economies work through this downturn, and as the over-enthusiasm wanes, I am confident that those businesses that view technology and the Internet as just another essential element of building a successful company will do very well over the course of this decade. A well-crafted e-commerce strategy, when coupled with a competitive advantage, a compelling online value proposition, and durable revenue, cost and profit models, will go a long way in helping ensure your success.

Growth Through International Expansion

ANY FAST-TRACK GROWING COMPANIES HAVE decided to go global as a critical component of their overall expansion strategy. Companies of all sizes and in different industries have ventured abroad as pioneers of doing business in the global village, and have often discovered receptive and lucrative new markets. Many countries, even developing ones, view the expansion of U.S. companies into global markets through partnering, alliances, franchising, licensing, distribution and other methods not only as a way to import U.S. products and services, but also as a readily acceptable source of technological development and system support that introduces know-how to their fledgling business community in a cost-effective manner.

The globalization of the U.S. economy is now a fact of life. Technological developments, the globalization of companies and their brands, international megamergers that create large multinational companies, the economic interdependence created by a truly integrated international financial system and the advent of strong regional associations such as the European Union, NAFTA and ASEAN have all contributed to the need for companies of all sizes and in virtually every type of industry to be thinking globally.

Your next customer may be located outside the U.S.—but

so may be your fiercest competitor. Your best solution for outsourcing may be an overseas company—but so may be your next legal battle. Your next round of capital may be from a foreign investor and your next hire may be a citizen of another country, triggering immigration challenges and costs. Geography no longer stands in the way of an emerging company's aspirations, but it also no longer serves as a barrier to protect local market share. Business-growth strategies need to be built around a global vision—where quality, pricing, service and distribution are globally competitive but are also custom-tailored to meet local requirements and market conditions.

Stages of International Expansion

As the leader of an emerging-growth company, you cannot just wake up one morning and declare your business to be global. You must first develop a strategy for how you will globalize your business. You may choose to enter overseas markets primarily through opening offices abroad or by partnering with other companies. Or you might decide to begin by accepting orders from abroad through your Web site. Or you might decide the best strategy would be to acquire a series of overseas businesses as part of a global merger-and acquisitions-program. The progression toward being a truly global company usually develops in the following stages.

DOMESTIC EXPORTER. The company operates primarily in its home country but exports its products and services abroad via e-commerce or other channels.

INTERNATIONAL COMPANY. The company conducts marketing and production functions in both its home country and abroad, but all key management decisions are centralized in the home-country headquarters.

MULTINATIONAL ENTERPRISE. The company conducts all key business functions in multiple countries, management is decentralized and divisions are operated and managed as truly local entities.

GLOBAL COMPANY. The company operates in many different countries (and often several different lines of business) and is governed and structured as an integrated global entity In his book, *Global Literacies* (Simon & Schuster, 1999), Dr. Robert Rosen discusses four key characteristics that a company's leadership must have to be successful in the adoption of a global business-expansion strategy. These include:

■ **personal literacy, to understand and respect** the challenges of doing business abroad;

■ **social literacy, to engage and challenge** others to collaborate on a global basis;

■ **business literacy, to focus and mobilize** the resources of the organization toward global business objectives; and

■ **cultural literacy, to include to value and leverage** the cultural differences that a global organization will face among its various business operations.

Global Literacies and other books on this topic are an excellent starting point for understanding more about the leadership challenges that a growing company will face in doing business abroad, the details of which are beyond the scope of this chapter.

Key Factors to Consider Before Doing Business Abroad

If you are considering embarking on an international expansion program—especially if you are thinking about expanding abroad via franchising, licensing, joint ventures or technology transfer—take these factors into account.

LANGUAGE BARRIERS. Although it may seem simple enough at the outset to translate your core marketing and operational materials into the local language, marketing the system and the product may present unforeseen difficulties if the concept itself does not "translate" well. A classic example is the Chevy Nova, which translates in Spanish-speaking countries as "doesn't move"—not an ideal name for a vehicle.

MARKETING BARRIERS. Such barriers most frequently go to the deepest cultural levels. For example, although many overseas markets have developed a taste for "fast food" burgers and hot dogs, the speed aspect is less important in some cultures than in others. Many European cultures demand the leisure of relaxing on the premises after eating a meal rather than taking the meal to go. In France, cultural differences even forced McDonald's to allow for beer and wine sales. In addition to different cultural norms, non-cultural factors may need to be considered. In Singapore and Japan, for example, the high cost and limited availability of retail space would pose a major hurdle for a company trying to open a retail outlet. Other concepts may rely on a large regional mall, which is readily available in North America but not common in the Middle East.

LEGAL BARRIERS. A country's laws may not be conducive to the establishment of certain types of distributorship arrangements. Tax laws, customs laws, import restrictions, corporate organization and agency/liability laws may all prove to be significant factors that influence how you can do business in a foreign market. For example, technology-transfer laws and foreign-investment laws may "force" a business you intended as a master franchise or licensing arrangement to be essentially a joint venture instead.

ACCESS TO RAW MATERIALS AND HUMAN RESOURCES. In some countries, raw material and skilled labor critical to your operations may be unavailable. These resources may need to be brought in from other regions, or the business venture may have to be established elsewhere.

GOVERNMENT BARRIERS. The government of your target nation may not be receptive to foreign investment in general or to certain types of distribution relationships. A given country's past history of expropriation, government restrictions, high tariffs, or limitations on currency repatriation may also prove to be decisive factors in determining whether the cost of market penetration is worth the potential benefits. Find out which tax treaties are in place between your country and the targeted nation and, if necessary, consider seeking governmental intervention. (The U.S. Trade Representative or the Department of Commerce's International Trade Administration may be of assistance.) Also, have your corporate lawyers (provided that they are experienced in international matters) review the laws of the targeted nation and establish a liaison with local counsel abroad.

Know Your Targeted Market

In considering a global-expansion strategy, take the time to fully understand the intricacies of each of the targeted markets you are considering. By knowing your target market, you can avoid costly disputes. Conduct a variety of market studies and research to measure market demand and competition for your company's products and services. Be sure to gather data on:

- economic trends
- political stability
- currency exchange rates
- foreign investment and approval procedures
- restrictions on termination and non-renewal (where applicable)
- regulatory requirements
- access to resources and raw materials
- availability of transportation and communication channels
- labor and employment laws
- technology-transfer regulations
- language and cultural differences
- access to affordable capital
- and suitable sites for the development of units
- governmental assistance programs
- customs, laws and import restrictions
- tax laws and applicable treaties
- repatriation and immigration laws
- trademark registration requirements, availability and protection policies
- the costs and methods for dispute resolution
- agency laws and availability of appropriate media for marketing efforts

Basic Guidelines for International Expansion

These potential stumbling blocks do not always mean that overseas expansion is ill-advised. On the contrary, after you have made a thorough review of the relevant market you might conclude that such expansion holds great potential for your company. However, before you begin a program of international expansion, carefully examine a broad range of legal and strategic issues, including the following represent some of the basic elements necessary for a successful international expansion.

STRONG DOMESTIC FOUNDATION. Make sure that adequate capital, resources, personnel, support systems and training programs are in place to assist your business abroad. For example, if your business will require multi-language skills, you should have multi-lingual staff members available before venturing into your targeted market.

STRATEGIC PARTNERS. Finding the right partner in your targeted market is of paramount importance. Regardless of the specific legal structure you select for international expansion into a particular market, the master developer in the local market should always be philosophically and strategically viewed as your "partner." And, just as there should always be a dating period before a marriage or a due-diligence period before an acquisition, such is also the case in selecting an international partner. There is no substitute for face-to-face negotiations between parties.

The most promising candidates to be your international partner will often be those with proven financial resources who have already established a successful business in the host country. In your search for the right strategic partner, consider the following critical questions:

- **What systems do you have in place** for recruiting and selecting the right candidate?
- **What procedures will you employ** for reviewing their qualifications?
- **What fall-back plan do you have in place** if you wind up selecting the wrong person or company?

Upon narrowing your field of potential partners, only careful negotiating and contract preparation will provide any degree of protection for a business risking entry into a new market.

REALISTIC VALUATION. Many growing businesses entering overseas markets have grandiose ideas about the initial prices that an overseas partner will pay for the right to distribute their goods and services, license their technology, or serve as the subfranchisor in their market. Realism and patience should guide your expectations. If you overprice, you'll scare away qualified candidates or leave your partner with insufficient capital to develop the market. If you underprice, you'll be lacking the resources and incentive to provide quality training and ongoing support. The fee structure should fairly and realistically reflect the division of responsibility between you and your partner. Other factors influencing the structure will be currency exchange and tax issues, pricing strategies, market trends, the availability of resources and personnel to provide on-site support, and which party will bear responsibility for translation of the manuals and marketing materials as well as adaptation of the system, products, and services to meet local demand and cultural differences.

Be patient regarding expectations of return on investment and profits from overseas expansion. In addition to normal economic cycles and break-even analysis, certain countries dictate legal structures that are essentially "forced joint ventures," placing restrictions on a growing business's ability to "quickly" pull out capital from the targeted country. In structuring the actual agreement, carefully consider the structure of the relationship, the term of the agreement and the scope and length of non-disclosure and non-compete clauses. These provisions and their enforceability will take on increased importance when distance and differences in legal systems complicate them. Also, give careful thought to structuring the financial provisions of the agreement. Although it may be tempting to try to mitigate potential downstream losses by seeking a higher initial fee, consider a more balanced approach to fees and ongoing royalties.

TRADEMARK PROTECTION. As a general matter, trademark laws and rights are based on actual use (or a bona fide intent to use) in a given country. Unlike international copyright laws, your properly registered domestic trademark does not automatically confer any trademark rights in other countries. Be sure to take steps to ensure the availability and registration of your trademarks in all of your targeted markets. Also, be sure that your trademark translates effectively in the targeted country and native language. Many growing businesses have had to modify their names, designs or slogans because of pirating problems or an inability to translate the name effectively for a foreign market. For example, many U.S. automotive-services franchisors, particularly those in oil-change and tune-up services, had to retool their trademarks and brand identities that over-emphasized speed and efficiency. Although these are good selling points for the busy U.S. consumer, in many overseas cultures, automobile owners prefer quality over speed, and speed means compromising quality.

ADAPTATION OF PRODUCTS AND SERVICES. The format of your proprietary products or services that have been successful in America or even Canada may or may not be successful in another country. Be sensitive to different tastes, cultures, norms, traditions, trends and habits within a country before you make final decisions on prices, sizes or other characteristics of your products or services. Conversely, be careful not to make drastic changes to your product or service at the cost of quality, integrity, uniformity or consistency. There are many comical (yet expensive) lessons and stories involving North American businesses that learned the hard way that what works well at home may not be successful abroad. For example, many U.S. restaurant businesses have had to modify their serving sizes to accommodate the different eating habits of other cultures. As it turned out, not every culture will appreciate the SuperMax Big Gulp or the Triple-Size Super Sundae. On the contrary, some overseas markets prefer consuming a more reasonable portion at a competitive price and will not patronize an establishment where there are likely to be leftovers, which are perceived as wasteful.

RATIONALE. Growing businesses have widely varying reasons for selecting a targeted country or market. Sometimes they are "pulled" into a market by an interested prospect familiar with their concept. This can be dangerous if you rely only on the assurances of the interested candidate that there is an actual demand for products and services. Sound reasoning must guide your decision to expand into a particular foreign market.

Compliance Programs

M any U.S. and foreign laws regulate the international business activities of U.S. companies. If your company does or plans to do business overseas, make sure that you have an updated compliance program to address the legal issues pertaining to such activities. The adverse consequences arising from an unlawful transaction can be substantial, including revocation or suspension of export or import privileges, debarment from government contracts, negative publicity, and the expense and disruption of responding to a government investigation.

There are two categories of laws that govern the international business activities of U.S. companies. The first consists of laws that can also be applied in the domestic context, such as antitrust, employment, and economic-espionage laws; the second consists of laws that are targeted more specifically to companies that engage in international business. One example of the latter is the U.S. Foreign Corrupt Practices Act (FCPA), which prohibits bribery of foreign government officials and officials of public international organizations. The scope of the FCPA can extend liability to a U.S. company based on the activities of its consultants, joint-venture partners, or a recently acquired subsidiary. The U.S. government has also imposed various export and import controls as sanctions against some countries. Likewise, the U.S. government regulates imports and exports according to customs laws and regulations. Be aware of these laws and restrictions as they relate to your business to make sure that your company's practices are in compliance.

There are a number of ways that you can establish and communicate standards relating to your company's international business activities. One way is to establish a code of conduct that sets forth general policy statements regarding the company's values and objectives. Distribute this code to all company employees, agents, and business partners. You may also choose to supplement your code of conduct with a pamphlet or an employee handbook that provides more details and identifies instances when employees should seek further guidance from company lawyers, compliance officials, or supervisory personnel. It is important that your company's compliance materials be carefully written to take into account the company's specific operations, practices, personnel, corporate culture, and history.

Furthermore, establish an environment in which employees and agents recognize that your company is serious about compliance. Accomplish this initially by hiring competent and honest personnel and then be willing and able to conduct an internal investigation if any violations are suspected.

Advantages and Disadvantages of Various Overseas-Business Forms

Once you have made the decision to do business overseas, your business objectives, available resources, and other tax and legal considerations will generally determine the business form. Keep in mind, however, that no single form may satisfy all of your company's needs. To select the business form that will best achieve your objectives, you should be familiar with the advantages and disadvantages of the principal forms of doing business overseas and the major legal issues arising from each one.

Direct Exporting

ADVANTAGES

- **lower costs** (few new resources are required)
- **you retain complete control** of operations
- **allows for a trial period**

- **less exposure** to liability (except for product liability)
- **generally not subject** to foreign tax, unless it is a permanent establishment

DISADVANTAGES

- **distance from the market** and less ability to respond to customers' needs
- **less-timely service** because no one from your company is on the scene
- **less-visible commitment** to the market and no local warehouse from which to meet customer emergencies

Cooperative Relationship

ADVANTAGES

- **local presence** helps you learn the market and avoid mistakes due to ignorance of culture
- **lower investment costs** than forming a company

DISADVANTAGES

- **less control** over the business as well as technology
- **other party** may have a different agenda
- **does not allow** the opportunity to establish a long-term presence
- **profits** must be shared with another party

Distributor/Sales Representative

ADVANTAGES

- **greater presence** in the market
- **local party** has a greater stake in the success of the business, will therefore be more committed to it
- **availability** of local inventory from which to ship goods
- **less cost and delay** than for a foreign company establishing a distribution network for the first time

DISADVANTAGES

- **must share profits** with another party
- **higher exposure** to liability claims
- **less control** of product distribution

Branch Office

ADVANTAGES

- **local presence** with people loyal to your company
- **more control** over distribution network
- **better commitment** and faster access to market developments

DISADVANTAGES

- **higher costs** of establishing a new office and hiring necessary personnel
- **more exposure** to liability due to actions of employees
- **your company** is more susceptible to foreign jurisdiction in lawsuits

Joint Venture

ADVANTAGES

- **shared risks,** costs and financing
- **opportunity to work** with a knowledgeable local partner and a more established presence in the market
- **local partner** may have complementary strengths
- **allows for the establishment** of a business culture with an exchange of ideas

DISADVANTAGES

- **must share profit,** control, and know-how
- **your effort and image** may be hurt due to a weak local partner.

Wholly Owned Corporation

ADVANTAGES

- **complete control of profits,** operations, and management
- **can unilaterally withdraw** if business does not succeed

DISADVANTAGES

- **no local partner** to advise on customs and culture
- **greater costs** and liability than if acting through an agent or with a partner
- **potential start-up delays** from establishing an operation in a new market

The Fundamentals of Exporting as a First Step into Overseas Markets

Direct exporting (or importing) is often the first step in an international-expansion strategy. Federal and state government agencies, universities, and private firms have developed a range of programs, products and services aimed at encouraging and assisting early-stage and minority-owned firms to "go global." While these programs and approaches differ in some ways, there are many key questions and issues you must address regardless of the approach you choose.

WHETHER TO EXPORT. Conduct an export-readiness assessment to address the following questions:

- **Should your company consider exporting?**
- **Is your firm ready to export?**
- **What are the rules?**
- **Is your firm ready and able to comply** with all laws and regulations? The Bureau of Export Administration is probably a good starting point for finding out.
- **Do you have the arrangements in place** to help you become a global player? Service providers from both the public and private sectors have devised a number of "tests of export readiness."
- **Must you comply with ISO 9000** and other standards? ISO 9000 standards for quality manufacturing and service and the related certification and monitoring systems are adhered to by at least 100 countries. Certification, while lengthy and expensive, is becoming an important competitiveness factor, especially for sales in the European Union. Service providers from the public and private sectors assist exporters in various ways, from referring them to technical authorities to providing consulting services that help firms meet certification requirements. In addition to the ISO 9000 family of standards, you may also be required to comply with ISO 14000 standards for environmental practices. To reach compliance, you will have to be certified by an auditor with appropriate credentials. The International Standards Organization is the parent body for these stan-

dards, while the American National Standards Institute is the United States affiliate.

WHEN TO EXPORT. Consider the following when determining your company's readiness and timing:
- **Is your company at the right stage of development** to consider exporting?
- **Are your firm's products appropriate for,** or can they be modified for, the global market?
- **Will your products be competitive in cost** and quality?
- **How adaptable are your firm,** staff, and facilities for exporting? Export planning to answer these questions typically involves four major assessments: management's commitment to exporting; the firm's capacity to meet export demands; the organizational infrastructure to support exporting; and the skills of the staff involved in the exporting process.

HOW TO EXPORT. The many issues you need to consider in determining how to export your goods or services include:
- **Trade financing.** This is an entire field of finance that can be far more complex than domestic-business financing. Trade financing refers to borrowing or lending based on specific export (or import) transactions, backed by various documents that provide evidence that the pertinent transactions are either in process or have been executed. Such documents may include warehouse receipts, accounts receivable, transport documents, bills of lading or drafts. Export financing, on the other hand, is typically based on letters of credit and not necessarily on specific-transaction documents. Trade financing is the enabler for many small companies who need the financing to facilitate the transaction.
- **Methods of operation.** In exporting your company's products or services, you have a number of modes to choose from, including merchandise exports (tangible goods sent out of the country), service exports (international earnings other than those derived from the exporting of tangible goods), and investments (ownership of property in exchange for financial return). Two forms of investment are direct investment, which gives you a controlling interest in a foreign

company, and venture investment, which gives a non-controlling interest in a company or ownership of a loan to a foreign company to give your company a minority interest in international operations.

■ **Exporting through domestic intermediaries.** You may choose to conduct your company's export operations through export intermediaries, referred to as silent exporters, such as an export-management company (EMC) or an export-trading company (ETC). An EMC is compensated on a commission basis or may take legal title to the merchandise it sells. Although ETCs are similar to EMCs, they conduct business on a transaction-by-transaction basis, with less responsibility to the buyer and the seller. Assistance typically focuses on referring exporters to lists of EMCs and ETCs.

> **Because differences in culture can have a substantial impact on how business is conducted, service providers have targeted this as an important technical-assistance issue.**

■ **Market research.** Information collection and analysis are necessary to determine which foreign markets have the best potential for your company's products. Key considerations include identifying the largest markets; the fastest growing markets; market trends; market practices; and competitive firms, products, and business practices.

■ **Export-product preparation.** Key product-preparation factors you must consider include product adaptation, engineering and redesign, branding, labeling and packaging, installation, warranties and servicing.

■ **Country customs and culture.** Because differences in culture can have a substantial impact on how business is conducted, service providers have targeted this as an important technical-assistance issue.

■ **Training programs.** Training for exporting may be a viable resource for your company as you prepare for exporting. Typically such programs will help you address the following issues: how to organize for exporting, export marketing and strategy, export operations, export procedures, export financing, export research, and how to use assistance resources.

WHERE TO EXPORT. Where are the best prospective markets and strategic-alliance partners for your company's exporting initiative? You can find answers to these and related questions from resources such as the following:

- **Trade missions and shows.** Thousands of trade missions and trade shows are offered throughout the world. They aim to help locate buyers and provide a first-hand account of how a product will fare in international markets. They can also provide you an opportunity for assessing the competition and meeting potential partners.

- **Catalogue shows.** The aim of catalogue shows is the same as trade missions and trade shows; however, they can save you the substantial expense of traveling abroad. Services typically include compiling the information for the catalogue and disseminating the catalogue to buyers overseas.

- **Partner identification and facilitation.** Export partners come in many different forms, such as agents, distributors and foreign representatives. There are also many different contractual arrangements—such as joint ventures partnerships, licensing arrangements, and franchising—that can be used for entering into a relationship with different partners. Assistance services aim to provide advice about on to identify and screen partners and on contractual issues.

HOW TO KEEP ABREAST OF CURRENT DEVELOPMENTS. To develop and maintain a successful export program, it's important that you stay informed of the latest developments and trends, including:

- **Trade policies, regulations, laws and standards.** The institutions that support and facilitate trade do so through a complex maze of licensing, policies, regulations and standards. Keep abreast of changes in these regimes to become an effective competitor—and to stay out of trouble. Key issues to consider include changes in U.S. law, changes in the laws and regulations of countries where you export, and tax considerations. There are many service providers in the public and private sectors that provide information about the latest developments in these and related areas as well as other export issues.

Advantages and Disadvantages of Export as a Growth Strategy

L ike most business-growth strategies, adopting an aggressive exporting strategy can offer your company many
opportunities, but carries with it a number of risks and
challenges. Some of the competitive advantages and disadvantages and challenges that you may encounter as you move into
the export market are listed below.

ADVANTAGES
- enhanced domestic competitiveness
- increased sales and profits
- increased global market share
- reduced dependence on existing markets
- opportunity to exploit corporate technology and know-how
- increased sales potential of existing products
- stabilization of seasonal market fluctuations
- enhanced potential for corporate expansion
- market for excess production capacity
- access to information about foreign competition

DISADVANTAGES AND CHALLENGES
- the cost of development of new promotional material
- the possibility of needing to wait longer for payments
- the need to modify your product or packaging
- the need to apply for additional financing
- the need to obtain special export licenses

Developing an International Business-Expansion Plan

A s part of the development of your company's overall
growth strategies and plans, you should develop an
international business-expansion plan, which is an
essential tool for properly evaluating all the factors that would
affect your company's ability to expand on an international

basis. Creating an international business-expansion plan is important for defining your company's present status, internal goals and commitment, and will help you anticipate future goals, assemble facts, identify constraints and create an action statement. It should also set forth specific objectives, an implementation timetable and milestones to gauge success. Such a plan is also required if you intend to seek export-financing assistance. Preparing the plan in advance of making export-loan requests from your bank can save time and money. The document should define your company's:

- commitment to international trade;
- export-pricing strategy;
- reason for exporting;
- potential export markets and customers;
- methods of foreign-market entry;

Conducting Market Assessments

For each target market, the management team of your fast-track growth company should analyze the region using the following key market factors:

Demographic/Physical Environment
- Population size, growth, density
- Urban and rural distribution
- Climate and weather conditions
- Shipping distance
- Product-significant demographics
- Physical distribution and communication networks
- Natural resources

Political Environment
- System of government
- Political stability and continuity
- Ideological orientation
- Government involvement in business
- Attitudes toward foreign business (trade restrictions, tariffs, non-tariff barriers, bilateral trade agreements)
- National economic and developmental priorities

Economic Environment
- Overall level of development
- Economic growth (GNP, industrial sector)
- Role of currency (inflation rate, viability, controls, stability of exchange rate)
- Balance of payments
- Per capita income and distribution
- Disposable income and expenditure patterns
- Foreign trade in economy

- **exporting costs and projected revenues;**
- **export-financing alternatives;**
- **legal requirements;**
- **transportation methods; and**
- **overseas partnership and foreign-investment capabilities.**

The Globalization of Your Web Site

If your primary foray into global business is going to be via your Web site, then you need to complete an assessment of your site and its readiness and user-friendliness for global business.

A first step would be to conduct market research to determine which target customers in which countries may be most receptive to the products and services offered on your site.

Social/Cultural Environment

- Literacy rate, educational level
- Existence of middle class
- Similarities and differences in relation to home market
- Language and other cultural considerations

Market Access

- Limitations on trade (high tariff levels, quotas)
- Documentation and import regulations
- Local standards, practices, and other non-tariff barriers
- Patents and trademark protection
- Preferential treaties
- Legal considerations for investment, taxation, repatriation, employments

Product Potential

- Customer needs and desires
- Local production, imports, consumption
- Exposure to and acceptance of product
- Availability of linking products
- Industry-specific key indicators of demand
- Attitudes toward products of foreign origin
- Competitive offerings

Local Distribution and Production

- Availability of intermediaries
- Regional and local transportation facilities
- Availability of manpower
- Conditions for local manufacture

Common Mistakes in Developing an International Business Strategy

Entrepreneurs and growing companies often make strategic and operational mistakes when first expanding abroad. Among the more common are:

■ **Failure to obtain qualified advice.** To be successful, a growing company must first clearly define goals, objectives, and potential problems that may be encountered. Unless your company has resources on staff with considerable global business expertise, it is advisable to bring on consultants to help with this process.

■ **Insufficient commitment by top management to international business.** It may take more time and effort to establish a presence in an overseas market than in a domestic one. Although the early delays and costs involved in going abroad may seem difficult to justify when compared to established domestic trade, you should take a long-range view of this process and carefully monitor international-marketing efforts through these early difficulties.

■ **Insufficient care in selecting overseas distributors.** The selec-

tion of each foreign distributor is crucial. The complications involved in overseas communications and transportation require international distributors to act with greater independence than their domestic counterparts. Also, because your company's history, trademarks, and reputation are usually unknown in the foreign market, foreign customers may buy on the strength of a distributor's reputation. You should therefore conduct a thorough evaluation of the personnel handling its account, the distributor's facilities, and the management methods employed.

■ **Chasing orders from around the world instead of establishing a basis for profitable operations and orderly growth.** If you initially expect the partners or distributors you appoint overseas to actively promote your products and services, then these partners and

Identifying these targeted markets in advance will help your company formulate a more focused local advertising and marketing campaign to drive traffic to your site. It may also dictate what site-design changes will be necessary, such as page layout, graphics, site-navigation tools and the need to offer multilingual options on the site.

Take a look at the Web sites of competitors who are already getting a significant portion of overseas traffic. Some distributors must be trained and assisted, and their performance must be continually monitored. This requires a commitment by you to allocate staff to actively monitor and support the partners and distributors in their geographical region.

■ **Neglecting export business when the U.S. market booms.** Too many entrepreneurs and growing companies turn to exporting when business falls off in the United States. When domestic business starts to boom again, they neglect their export trade or relegate it to second place. Taking such an approach can seriously harm the business and motivation of your overseas representatives, strangle your company's export trade and leave your company without recourse when domestic business falls off again.

■ **Assuming that a given market technique and product will automatically be successful in all countries.** What works in one market may not work in others. Each market has to be treated separately to ensure maximum success. Often, growing companies carry out institutional advertising campaigns, special discount offers, sales-incentive programs, specific credit-term programs, warranty offers, etc., in the U.S. market but fail to make similar assistance available to their international partners and distributors.

■ **Unwillingness to modify products to meet regulations or cultural preferences of other countries.** Foreign distributors and market partners cannot ignore local safety and security codes or import restrictions. If necessary modifications are not made at the factory, the market partner or distributor must do them— usually at greater cost and, perhaps, not as well. The resulting smaller profit margin makes the account less attractive.

may have translated every page of their site into multiple languages, and others may have only "localized" their shopping cart or product-ordering pages.

It was predicted that in 2001 the number of non–English speaking Internet users (167 million) would surpass the number of Internet users who speak English as a primary language (160 million). This shift will continue, therefore you must bear in mind that you may be leaving large links of potential customers behind if your site is available only in English.

Be sensitive to cultural and social differences relating to certain colors, designs, symbols, slang terms and Internet-usage patterns in the different countries that you are targeting. However, also make sure that your brand and proprietary Web-design features are used consistently to protect this intellectual property on a worldwide basis. So that your new overseas target customer base knows how and where to find you on the Web, register your site with popular local search engines, and develop a localized marketing or partnering strategy.

It is also critical to understand the legal issues that may govern the offer and sale of your products and services via the Internet in other countries. A comprehensive discussion of the international regulation of e-commerce is beyond the scope of this chapter (and is evolving almost daily). But the U.S., through the Federal Trade Commission (FTC), along with 28 other countries as members of the Organization for Economic Cooperation and Development (OECD) have agreed to a set of guidelines for domestic and international electronic commerce. The FTC/OECD's guidelines are designed to:

- **set out principles for voluntary "codes of conduct"** for businesses involved in electronic commerce;
- **offer guidance to governments** in evaluating their consumer-protection laws regarding electronic commerce; and
- **give consumers advice** about what to expect and what to look for when shopping online.

The goal of the guidelines is to build consumer confidence in the global electronic marketplace by working to ensure that consumers are just as safe when they are shopping online as when they are shopping offline—no matter where they live or where the company they do business with is based. You must follow the recommendations listed below for your fast-track growth company to comply with the guidelines. The box on pages 362-363 offers a checklist to help you be sure your company complies with the guidelines.

USE FAIR BUSINESS, ADVERTISING AND MARKETING PRACTICES. Provide truthful, accurate and complete information to consumers, and avoid deceptive, misleading or unfair claims, omissions or practices. Be able to back up all representations and claims, such as about how well a product works or how quickly a product will arrive. Also make sure that advertising and marketing material is identifiable as such and, when appropriate, identify its sponsor.

PROVIDE ACCURATE, CLEAR AND EASILY ACCESSIBLE INFORMATION ABOUT YOUR COMPANY AND THE GOODS OR SERVICES IT OFFERS. Disclose the information that consumers need to understand with whom they're dealing and what they're buying. Post your company's name, its physical address (including the country) and an e-mail address or telephone number consumers can use if they have questions. Also, provide a clear, complete description of the product or service being offered.

DISCLOSE FULL INFORMATION ABOUT THE TERMS, CONDITIONS AND COSTS OF THE TRANSACTION. Provide consumers a full, itemized list of costs involved in the transaction, designating the currency involved, as well as terms of delivery or performance, and terms, conditions and methods of payment. If applicable and appropriate to a transaction, you must also include information about restrictions, limitations or conditions of the purchase; instructions for proper use of the product and any safety or health care warnings; warranties and guarantees; cancellation or refund policies; and whether after-sale service is available.

ENSURE THAT CONSUMERS KNOW THEY ARE MAKING A COMMITMENT TO BUY BEFORE CLOSING THE DEAL. Take steps to protect consumers who are merely "surfing the Net" from unknowingly entering into a sales contract when interacting with your site. Your site must give the consumer a chance to change the order before committing to the purchase or to cancel it altogether.

PROVIDE AN EASY-TO-USE AND SECURE METHOD FOR ONLINE PAYMENTS. Adopt security measures appropriate to the transactions to make sure that personal information is less vulnerable to hackers.

Checklist to Make Sure Your Site Complies With FTC/OECD Guidelines

The following information should be available on your Web site:

About You
- What kind of business you operate
- Your physical business address, including the country, and an e-mail address or a telephone number consumers can use to contact you easily

About the Sale
- What you are selling, with enough details that consumers can make an informed buying decision
- A list of total costs you'll collect from the customer, and the currency used
- The existence of other routine costs
- Any restrictions or limitations on the sale
- Any warranties or guarantees

associated with the sale
- An estimate of when the buyer should receive the order
- Details about the availability of convenient and safe payment options

About Your Consumer Protections
- Your return policy, including an explanation of how a consumer can return an item, get a refund or credit or make an exchange
- Where the consumer should call, write or e-mail with complaints or problems
- The opportunity for consumers to keep a record of the transaction
- Your policies on sending unsolicited e-mail solicitations

PROTECT CONSUMER PRIVACY DURING ELECTRONIC-COMMERCE TRANS-ACTIONS. Disclose your privacy policies or information-practice statement prominently on your Web sites and offer consumers choices about how their personal information is used. Your site should offer a feature that gives consumers the opportunity to refuse having their personal information shared with others or used for promotional purposes.

ADDRESS CONSUMER COMPLAINTS AND DIFFICULTIES. You must have policies and procedures to address consumer problems quickly and fairly, and without excessive cost or inconvenience to the consumer.

to consumers, including an opportunity for consumers to decline these offers

■ Information about easy-to-use and affordable dispute resolution programs you participate in

About Your Use of Fair Information Practices

■ Notice to consumers about your information-collection practices, such as what personally identifiable information you collect, how you use it, and whether and with whom you share it

■ Choices about how personally identifiable information is used and whether it is shared with others

■ Procedures to ensure accuracy, including (for example) allowing consumers reasonable access to their information

■ Security measures appropriate to the transactions on your web site?

In Addition, Consider the Following Questions

■ Do you provide truthful, accurate and clear information on your Web site?

■ Can you back up the claims you make about your goods and services?

■ Are your advertising and marketing materials identifiable to consumers as such?

■ Do you disclose who's sponsoring an ad if it's not otherwise clear to consumers?

■ Do you respect consumers' choices not to receive e-mail solicitations?

■ Do you take special care when advertising to children?

ADOPT FAIR, EFFECTIVE AND EASY TO UNDERSTAND SELF-REGULATORY POLICIES AND PROCEDURES. Your site should extend to electronic commerce the same basic level of protections applicable to your other distribution channels. The FTC/OECD policies encourage businesses to work with consumer representatives to develop policies and procedures that give consumers the tools they need to make informed decisions and to resolve complaints.

The FTC/OECD guidelines also encourage participating governments to take steps to boost consumer confidence in the electronic marketplace. The guidelines encourage governments to evaluate their consumer-protection laws to make sure they extend to online shopping, and to ensure that consumers have recourse if they are dissatisfied.

The guidelines also recommend that governments work together to combat cross-border fraud and help establish a climate for electronic commerce that balances the needs and interests of businesses and consumers. The countries that have agreed to adopt and follow the guidelines include:

Australia	Hungary	Norway
Austria	Iceland	
Belgium		Poland
	Ireland	Portugal
Canada	Italy	Spain
Czech Republic	Japan	
Denmark		Sweden
	Korea	Switzerland
Finland	Luxembourg	Turkey
France	Mexico	
Germany		United Kingdom
	The Netherlands	United States
Greece	New Zealand	

External-Growth
Strategies

Protecting, Leveraging and Auditing Your Company's Intellectual Capital

ITH THE SHIFT IN OUR ECONOMY FROM THE Industrial Age to the Information Age, companies of all sizes in virtually all industries are facing the challenge of how to adapt to the knowledge era to enhance their performance and productivity. Countless articles in business publications remind us daily that "Intellectual Capital" represents the most important asset of most companies and represents a rapidly increasing portion of a growth company's overall valuation and balance sheet. Today's fast-track growth-company leaders need to be very focused on the creation, protection and extraction of value from the company's intellectual-property assets.

In this new economy, the speed of access to data and the quality of the information often determines the competitiveness of a business and ultimately its success or failure. Small and growing companies that are able to extract reliable information, transform it into knowledge and efficiently meet customer needs will grow and prosper, while others will be left at the entrance ramp. Major changes in organizational structure and culture are affecting how and where we work, how and where we offer our products and services, and the types of legal issues that entrepreneurs and growing companies are going to face in this new economy.

What Is Intellectual Capital?

Intellectual capital is a difficult concept to grasp because, unlike a physical inventory it encompasses intangible items used to measure a company's success and wealth. Most fast-track growing companies are discovering that intellectual capital may be hard to quantify, but that it is essential for survival. Intellectual capital typically falls into three categories.

HUMAN CAPITAL. Everything in this category exists within the skills, experience and ability of your employees. Creativity, innovation and cutting-edge thinking drive a company forward and allow it to compete in an environment that is constantly becoming more complex and idea-dependent. Human capital is hard to quantify, but it is usually measured in terms such as turnover and employee satisfaction.

ORGANIZATIONAL CAPITAL. This category includes only things owned by the company, such as patents, trademarks, copyrights, formulas and databases. Converting human capital into organizational capital is difficult and means collecting and retaining employee ability so it belongs to the company.

RELATIONSHIP CAPITAL. Many companies now recognize the relationship between customer loyalty and increased profits. This same concept can be applied to the preservation and growth of any strategic relationships with outside parties that help to create value for the fast-track growth company. Some organizations have been developing systems for better monitoring and maintenance of key relationships as these assets grow in importance.

Intellectual capital has become the inventory of the new economy, and it is critical that you recognize and fully utilize your organization's intellectual assets. Without knowing your inventory levels of intellectual capital, you cannot accurately allocate the proper amount of resources to develop your business in the most profitable direction. Taking the time to study all of your growing company's assets may enable you to discover new ways to use your company's intangible assets. As Peter Schwartz wrote in the September 2000 issue of *Red Herring*:

A Changing look at Company Assets

OLD ECONOMY ASSETS	NEW ECONOMY ASSETS
■ Real estate	■ Brands/Goodwill
■ Equipment	■ Relationships (customers, strategic partners)
■ Inventory	
■ Monopolies	■ Knowledge workers (Full-time versus free agents, etc.)
■ Cash	
■ Mineral rights	■ Software and systems
■ Government-awarded franchises (cable TV rights, etc.)	■ Regulatory approvals (FDA, FCC, etc.)
	■ Content/customer lists

"In the organization of today's economy, it is knowledge that counts more than anything, Knowledge has value, but so does knowledge about knowledge. It is a world where the Internet spreads knowledge instantaneously around the world, and we get dramatic network effects. The more people that get on the Web, the greater its value. The rules of the new economy are shaped not by physics, but by information. Creating value is about creating new knowledge and capturing its value. The most important property is intellectual property, not physical property. And it is the hearts and minds of people, rather than their hands, that are essential to growth and prosperity of a company. Committed employees creating new ideas, delivering value, and innovating to create growth are the key assets of the new economy. Singapore is the new national paradigm: It is a tiny nation that has created remarkable growth built entirely on human capital."

Protecting and Leveraging Your Intangible Assets

The focus of this chapter is protecting assets in the new digital economy by using the intellectual-property laws as your weapon of choice. The primary assets of technology-driven, services and data-oriented, netcentric businesses are intangible, especially at the early stage of a company. Because these assets cannot be touched or felt, they are not protected in the same way and by the same laws that protect tangible assets. Today's entrepreneur must rely on the tools and sometimes weapons offered by the various branches of intellectual-property law to protect a company's intellectual property. The key is to match the intangible asset you are trying to protect and leverage with the most effective legal and strategic tools available. This requires a basic understanding of the laws that protect intellectual property as well as the strategies that are most effective for leveraging intellectual property.

Before turning to the specific branches of intellectual-property law, it is also important that you be aware that many of these laws are being developed and fine-tuned on an almost daily basis. Rapidly changing areas of the law include:

- **the rights of independent contractors** to ownership of works created for hire in the absence of a contract;
- **the impact of shop rights** on free agents, contract workers and telecommuters;
- **the ability of copyright law** to keep pace with the dissemination powers of the Internet;
- **the application of patent laws** to proprietary business models, plans and systems;
- **the establishment of a new branch** of intellectual-property law known as trade dress and its application to cyberspace in the past few years;
- **the protection of brands** and personal likenesses in the context of URL address registration under applicable cybersquatting laws; and
- **the application of unfair competition,** corporate advertising and passing-off laws to metatags and other methods of directing traffic to your Web site.

Your Adviser's Role

For companies that have grown through the leveraging of their intellectual property, the legal counsel's role is to serve as legal and strategic adviser by:

- **working with clients** to find their intellectual property and hidden intangible assets (through intellectual-property protection and leveraging audits, covered later in the chapter;
- **protecting the intellectual property** (through registration strategies, confidential agreements, etc.);
- **developing strategies** to leverage the intellectual property (through joint ventures, alliances, licensing, etc.); and
- **looking at these strategies** in comparison with other growth strategies as alternatives.

Your adviser's strategic analysis may include questions such as:

- **What protectable competitive advantages** has the company developed?
- **What intellectual-property-law strategies** can be used to protect ownership and use?
- **How can this intellectual property** be leveraged into revenue and profit streams?
- **How can we use intellectual property** to create substantial competitive advantages with durable revenue streams?

The Importance of Developing and Leveraging Intangible Assets

As an entrepreneur, your ability to grow a business and achieve success depends on the abilities that you and your team demonstrate in key areas. These include inventing and exploiting new products and services; opening up new distribution channels; fostering new production and training techniques; implementing new promotional and marketing campaigns; establishing new pricing methods; and adapting to changes in competition, consumer preferences or demographic trends. Your ability to identify, develop and protect intellectual-property rights is critical. Doing so can help your company:

- **improve the overall value** and rate of growth by increasing intangible assets;
- **create competitive advantages** and barriers for competitors to enter the marketplace;

Using Intellectual Property for Business Growth

Your company's management of its intangible assets should include the following three broad areas:

CREATION	PROTECTION	LEVERAGING
■ Generating intellectual assets, such as technology (through research, development, engineering)	■ Protecting your intellectual property from the competition	■ Licensing your company's technology or other intellectual assets
■ Screening and valuing intellectual assets	■ Protecting the corporation from unintentional infringement of someone else's intellectual property	■ Selling intellectual assets such as customer lists, technology, etc.
■ Capturing and documenting assets		■ Blocking use of proprietary assets such as technology systems, or formulas by competitors
		■ Creating new products/services/ competencies

- **understand the intellectual-property rights** of other firms;
- **create licensing opportunities** and additional revenue sources;
- **build consumer goodwill** and brand loyalty; and
- **provide maximum control** over the development and ownership of the ideas and inventions of employees.

Patents

A patent grants an inventor the right to exclude others from making, using, selling or offering to sell an invention throughout the United States, or from importing the invention into the United States for a limited period of time. To obtain a patent, the inventor submits an application to the United States Patent and Trademark Office (USPTO). The application must be submitted within one year of public use or publication of the invention. The three categories of patents are:

■ **Utility patents.** These are the most common and are issued to protect new, useful, non-obvious and adequately specified articles of manufacture, machine processes, compositions of matter (or any improvements thereto) for a period of 20 years from the filing date of the application.

■ **Design patents.** These are issued to protect new, original, ornamental and non-obvious designs for articles of manufacture for a period of 14 years from the date the patent is granted.

■ **Plant patents.** The least used; these are issued to protect certain new varieties of plants that have been asexually reproduced for a term of 20 years from the filing date of the application.

The patent-application and patent-registration process can last from two to five years and can be very costly. Because of this, before attempting to obtain a patent, conduct a cost-benefit analysis to determine if the benefits of being able to exclude others from making, using or selling the invention outweigh the significant costs of prosecuting and protecting the patent. As part of this analysis, consider:

■ **the projected commercial value** of the invention;

■ **out-of-pocket expenses** to obtain the patent, including legal fees, advertising, marketing and retooling costs;

■ **the invention's proximity** to existing patented and nonpatented technology (from a patent-infringement and a commercial-development perspective);

■ **the ability to exploit the invention** during the time frame of exclusivity granted by a patent;

■ **the market value of the invention** two to five years down the road, after completion of the patent-application process; and

■ **the availability of adequate alternatives** for protecting the invention, such as state trade-secret laws.

If you decide to pursue a patent, before retaining a patent attorney, make sure that you compile and maintain careful records relating to the research and testing of the invention.

The records should contain key dates, including the date the invention was conceived and the date it was reduced to practice (meaning that the invention is well beyond the conceptual stage, and has either actually been developed and tested, or is so clearly described in the application that a third party skilled in the particular art could understand and actually develop the technology.) The records should also demonstrate your diligence in developing and testing the invention. Make sure the records contain the corroboration of independent witnesses who are capable of understanding the nature and scope of the invention and who will verify the dates when the invention was conceived and when it was reduced to practice.

The next step is to conduct a search at the USPTO to reveal whether any patents in your field have already been issued. You can hire a patent attorney or patent-search agent to conduct the search at the USPTO's public search room, located in Virginia, just outside of Washington, DC. The USPTO also offers a wealth of information and services on its Web site (www.USPTO.gov). You can conduct an initial patent search and file a patent application online and monitor your application's status electronically. You will also find information on trademarks, Official Gazette and Federal Register notices and a list of registered patent attorneys and agents. Thoroughly discuss with your adviser the ramifications of any previously issued patents; their existence may factor into your decision to apply for a patent.

The Application Process

The patent application process is complicated. First, the actual application must be compiled, including the following distinct parts:

- **a clear and concise declaration** that you are the original and sole inventor of the subject matter of the application;
- **drawings of the invention** (where necessary);
- **one or more "claims of exclusivity"** (these claims define the actual boundaries of the exclusive rights you hope to be granted —if drafted too narrowly, imitators and competitors may be able to develop similar technologies and processes without

fear of infringement; if drafted too broadly, you run the risk of rejection by the USPTO examiner or a subsequent challenge to the patent's validity by a competitor); and

■ **the appropriate filing fees.**

Once your application is filed, a patent examiner at the USPTO will review the application to determine whether your invention can be patented. As part of this review, the examiner will determine whether or not you have met the following statutory requirements:

■ **The invention consists of patentable subject matter** (such as a process, machine, composition of matter or article of manufacture, or new and useful improvements to one of these);

■ **You are the original inventor** or discoverer of the subject matter described in the patent application;

■ **The subject matter is new or novel** (i.e., it is not already known or used by others, has not been previously described by someone else in a printed publication and is not merely a new use of an existing product);

■ **The subject matter is useful** and not merely of scientific or philosophical interest; and

■ **The subject matter is non-obvious to others** in that particular trade or industry (i.e., the differences between the subject matter of the application and the current body of knowledge of those skilled in that area are more than marginal), as determined in the broad discretion of the USPTO examiner.

Protecting Your Patent

Once you obtain your patent, it is imperative that you institute an aggressive patent-protection program to preserve your rights and continue to protect your interests. While the costs of such a program may be high, especially if you undertake any patent litigation, the rewards will be worthwhile. Should you successfully pursue an infringer, you may be entitled to an award of damages (which may be tripled by the court in extraordinary cases), as well as equitable relief, such as an injunction or accounting for profits. Your patent-protection program should include:

■ **the use of proper notices** of the existence of the patent on all labeling and marketing of the invention;

■ **ongoing monitoring** of new industry developments;

■ **policing (and limiting) the activities** of employees, licensees and others who come into contact with the subject matter of the patent;

■ **exploiting and saturating the market** created by the patented product; and

■ **pursuing known** or suspected infringers of the patent.

Business-Model Patents

The United States Circuit Court for the Ninth Circuit deemed novel methods of business patentable in the late 1990s. Ruling in the landmark case of *State Street Bank v. Signature Financial Group, Inc.*, the court found that Signature's patent for its "hub and spoke" mutual-fund management process was valid. With the increased popularity of the Internet, many ways of doing business in cyberspace are being viewed as novel and patentable. Perhaps the best-known Internet-related business-model patents are for Priceline.com's reverse-auction method and Amazon.com's "1-Click" purchase feature. Both of these patent owners are aggressively trying to enforce their patents, Priceline by challenging a similar service offered by Microsoft and Amazon by challenging Barnesandnoble.com's "Express Checkout" online-purchasing feature. With the onslaught of these business-model patents, if your business model is dependent on e-commerce, consider the benefits of patent protection; however, the window may be closing on the number of business-model patents that the USPTO is willing to grant, given the current backlog of filings.

Trademarks and Service Marks

Brands have become increasingly important in the information and services economies, and the best way for a growing company to protect its brands is under the federal trademark laws. These laws define a trademark or service mark as a word, name, symbol or device used to indicate the origin and ownership of a product or service. Trademark status may also be granted to distinctive and unique packaging, color combinations, building designs, product styles and overall presentations. Trademarks and service marks are afforded the same legal protections, but trademarks are used to identify and distinguish products, while service marks identify and distinguish services. These terms are used interchangeably throughout this chapter.

Trademark rights generally arise out of use of the mark in connection with specific products or services. Once the mark is established, its owner has the right to use it in connection with the product it was intended to identify, to the exclusion of all subsequent users. In the United States, these rights may be protected by state statutory or common law, as well as by federal law (under the Lanham Act of 1996). Registering the mark with the USPTO can enhance protection.

A properly selected, registered and protected mark can be of great importance to your business in establishing, maintaining and expanding its market share. There is perhaps no better way to build and maintain a strong position in the marketplace than to build goodwill and consumer recognition in the identity (or brand) of your products or services. The mark is the consumer's first impression of the nature and quality of the product or service you offer. As a result, many companies select a mark that is easily understood by the public. While this allows the mark to serve as compressed advertising, it may be difficult to register and protect the mark if it is too descriptive in nature. For example, a trademark like Innovative Design Services clearly describes the underlying focus of the company, but is not likely to be viewed as sufficiently distinctive to warrant registration. When selecting a mark, consider the following factors:

- **the nature of the product or service** the mark will identify;
- **the purchasing habits** of the targeted consumer;
- **the ease of recognition and pronunciation** (keep it short and sweet, when possible);
- **marks currently used or registered by competitors** and others in the industry;
- **the availability of promotional dollars;** and
- **the adaptability of the mark to various applications** and media.

Types of Marks

When you select a mark, be sure that you will be able to protect it. Not all words or phrases are entitled to trademark protection. As a preliminary matter, the mark must identify the product or service as coming from a particular source. The mark may not, however, be generic in nature or merely describe the product or service it identifies. For example, a chain of auto-body shops under the name "Auto Body Repair Shop" would not get a service mark because its name is too generic, but "MAACO" is a nationally known name for such a service. Your mark's type will determine how easily you can protect it. Here are the major types of marks.

COINED, FANCIFUL OR ARBITRARY MARKS. This is the strongest category of mark that can be protected. This type of trademark is either a coined word, like Xerox, or a word in common usage that has no meaning when applied to the goods or services in questions, such as PUFFS (for facial tissues), Yoo-Hoo (for chocolate drinks) or Wonder (for bread). These marks are inherently distinctive for legal and registration purposes; however, because of the obscurity of the mark, the burden is on the owner to establish recognition and goodwill.

SUGGESTIVE MARKS. This category is the next strongest and most practical form of trademark protection and requires the consumer to use some degree of imagination to determine the products or services identified by the marks. These marks suggest to the consumer the underlying product or service without directly describing them. Examples of suggestive marks include Sun Maid (for raisins), Chips Ahoy (for cookies) and Champs (for retail sporting-good stores).

DESCRIPTIVE MARKS. Trademarks that are merely descriptive of the products they identify cannot be protected unless the owner can establish distinctiveness, dubbed "secondary meaning." This means that the owner must demonstrate that the public associates the particular mark with the goods of the specific producer. This category includes names like Holiday Inn (for motels), Reddi wip (for whipped topping) and Quaker oats (for oat cereal), all of which are descriptive, but registered because of their acquired distinctiveness.

There are several categories of marks that may not be protected under federal law unless the applicant can show secondary meaning, similar to that required for descriptive marks. These include:

- **immoral, deceptive** or scandalous marks;
- **marks that may disparage** or falsely suggest a connection with persons, institutions, beliefs or national symbols, or may bring them into contempt or disrepute;
- **marks that contain the flag,** coat of arms or similar insignia of the United States, or of a state, municipality or foreign nation;
- **marks that are the name,** portrait or signature of a living individual, unless that person gives written consent;
- **marks that are the name,** portrait or signature of a deceased President of the United States during the life of his widow, unless she gives her written consent;
- **any mark that so resembles a mark** already registered with the USPTO as to be likely, when applied to the applicant's goods, to cause confusion or a mistake or to deceive;
- **marks that are primarily geographically descriptive** or deceptively misdescriptive of the applicant's goods; or
- **marks that are primarily a surname.**

Federal Registration

One of the most important benefits to be gained from federal registration of your mark is that it serves as constructive notice to the rest of the country that the trademark belongs to you. This is of utmost importance because state common law and statutory protection usually extends only to the geographic area in which you are offering or selling your products or services. Without a federally registered mark, if a company in another geographic location decides to sell competing products under a similar mark, you may be barred from entering that local market if doing so would create consumer confusion. As long as your registration pre-dates another's use of the mark, you will have the right to demand that the other user stop using the mark—even in markets you have yet to enter. However, because common-law rights are grounded in actual and prior use, even federal registration will not give you the right to stop others who used the same mark in their local market prior to your registration. Consequently, it is important to apply for registration as early as is practicable.

You may apply for registration of a mark based on either "actual use" or a bona fide intention to use the mark in interstate commerce. This allows you to conduct some market research and further investigation, without the need to actually put the mark into commerce.

As long as your registration pre-dates another's use of the mark, you will have the right to demand that the other user stop using the mark—even in markets you have yet to enter.

Regardless of whether you file under the actual use or intent to use provision, you must prepare and file the application in the classification appropriate for the goods and services offered. A trademark examiner will then review your application to determine if it meets the statutory requirements and whether similar trademarks have already been registered in the same or similar lines of business. You or your attorney must respond to any concerns of the examiner. This process continues until the application is either refused or recommended by the examiner for publication in the Official Gazette (which serves as notice to the general public).

Once the notice is published, anyone who believes that he or she would be injured by registration of the mark may file a Notice of Opposition within 30 days of the publication date. If an Opposition is filed and the parties fail to resolve their differences, there will be a hearing before the Trademark Trial and Appeal Board (TTAB). The TTAB has the authority to determine only who has the right to register the mark—not who has the right to use the mark. Objections regarding rights to use a mark in a given geographic area must be raised in a court of law. TTAB is also the appropriate body to appeal a final refusal of an application for registration. If no Opposition is filed (or if an opposition is resolved in your favor), an application based on actual use will proceed to registration and a certificate of registration will be issued in a few months.

If the application is based on an intent to use the mark, once it is published and successfully makes it through the publication process, you will be issued a notice of allowance. You will then have six months to file a statement of use, with actual examples of use (commonly referred to as specimens), such as marketing materials, receipts, invoices, newspaper clippings, etc., attached. After satisfactory review of the statement of use and specimens, the mark will be registered. You may request up to four successive six-month extensions of time for filing the statement of use. Failure to file by the deadline will result in an abandonment of the application and forfeiture of all fees paid.

Federal trademark registrations are effective for ten years, and may be renewed for additional ten-year periods.

Federal trademark registrations are effective for ten years, and may be renewed for additional ten-year periods. Registrations may, however, be canceled after six years unless you file an affidavit of continued use with the USPTO, demonstrating that you are still using the mark in commerce and have not abandoned it. A similar affidavit of use must accompany any application to renew the registration.

Supplemental Registration

Although most marks are registered on the Principal Register of the USPTO, a mark that is actually in use in commerce, but that does not qualify for registration on the Principal Register, may qualify for registration on the Supplemental Register. Descriptive marks are often registered on the Supplemental Register. Registration on the Supplemental Register does not provide the same level of protection afforded by registration on the Principal Register, but it does give you:

- **the right to bring suit** in federal court and obtain certain statutory remedies for infringement;
- **a possible right** to apply for registration in those foreign jurisdictions requiring home-country registrations;
- **protection against federal registration** by another user of the same or a confusingly similar mark; and

■ **the right to use the encircled "R"** (®) symbol to claim rights to the mark.

The Application for Registration

The application to register a mark on the Principal Register consists of:

■ **a written application;**

■ **a drawing of the mark** (which must be a black and white, or typed, rendition of the mark; this is used to print the mark in the Official Gazette and on the registration certificate);

■ **the required filing fee** (which, effective January 10, 2000, is $325) for each class of goods or services covered in the application; and

■ **three examples (specimens)** showing actual use of the mark in connection with the goods or services (unless the application is based on an intent to use the mark). Specimens showing use of a trademark could include labels, product packaging or pictures of the product showing the mark on the actual goods. Specimens showing use of a service mark could include advertising or marketing materials describing the services. Intent-to-use applications must submit examples of use with the Statement of Use filed after the Notice of Allowance is issued (or they may amend their applications to include a statement of use prior to the publication of their marks).

Benefits of Registering Your Trademark

Registration can be a complex and lengthy process (taking anywhere from 12 to 18 months for applications with few problems), but the commercial rewards may be substantial if the registered mark is properly used. These rewards include:

■ **the right to protect** against others using your mark in the future;

■ **the right to bring legal action** in federal court for trademark infringement;

■ **the right to seek recovery** of profits, damages and costs in an infringement action (and, possibly, to seek triple damages and attorney fees in egregious cases);

- **the right to deposit** the registration with the United States Customs Service to stop the importation of goods bearing an infringing mark; and
- **the right to file** trademark applications in foreign countries.

Trademark Protection

Once your mark is registered, you must develop an active trademark-protection program designed to educate company staff, consultants, distributors, suppliers, and anyone else who may come in contact with your company's marks as to proper usage and protection of the marks. As with trade-secret laws, the courts will usually help only those who have attempted to help themselves. Therefore, if your company tolerates misuse of its marks by the public or fails to enforce quality-control standards in any licensing of a mark, it may lose its trademark rights—one of its most valuable weapons in the war for market share.

Begin developing a well-managed trademark-protection program with a formal compliance manual drafted with the assistance of a trademark lawyer and your company's advertising agency. Include detailed guidelines for proper trademark usage, quality and grammar. For example, a trademark is correctly used only as a proper adjective, and therefore it should always be capitalized and always modify a noun. A commonly misused trademark in this context is Xerox, which is often used improperly as a noun (to refer to the end product instead of the source of the process), or even as a verb (to refer to the process itself). Always use the trademark in conjunction with the generic name of the class of products to which it belongs (for example, Band-Aid (bandages or ChapStick lip balm. Once a trademark has been registered, develop compliance guidelines that address the following:

- **proper display of the marks** (use of the ®, ™ or ℠ symbol);
- **all documents, correspondence** and other materials on which the trademark must be displayed; and
- **all authorized and unauthorized uses of the marks** and prohibited uses (for example, may not be used as part of a licensee's corporate name).

In addition to a creating a compliance manual, you must implement strategies to monitor competitors and other third parties from improper usage or potential infringement of your mark. Designate a staff member to search the Internet, read trade publications, business press, marketing materials of competitors, and in-house production, labeling, and correspondence to ensure that your mark is properly used and not stolen by competitors. If an infringing use is discovered, aggressively protect your mark. This will require working closely with a trademark lawyer to ensure that all potential infringers receive letters demanding that such practices be immediately discontinued and the infringing materials destroyed. Make sure that your staff and lawyers gather as much evidence as possible and keep accurate files on each potential infringer in the event that trademark-infringement litigation becomes necessary. However, before taking your trademark battle to court, carefully weigh the cost of litigation and the likely results of a suit against the potential loss of goodwill and market share. You may discover that allocating funds toward advertising instead of legal fees makes better business sense, especially if the likelihood of winning is remote.

Infringement and Dilution

Under the Lanham Act, infringement is a demonstration by the owner of a registered mark that a third party is using a reproduction or imitation of the registered mark to market of goods and services in such a way as to be likely to cause confusion, mistake or deception on the part of the ordinary purchaser.

In defining the "likelihood of confusion," the focus has always been on whether the ordinary purchaser of the product in question is likely to be confused as to the source of origin or sponsorship; nevertheless, coming up with an exact definition for this standard has caused much debate. There are a wide variety of factors that the courts have listed as criteria for determining whether a likelihood of confusion exists, such as:

■ **the degree of similarity and resemblance** of the infringer's marks to your registered marks (in visual appearance, pronunciation, interpretation, etc.);

- **the strength of your registered mark** in the relevant industry or territory;
- **the intent** of the infringer;
- **the degree of similarity of the goods or services** offered by the infringer to those offered by you under the registered mark;
- **the overlap (if any) in the distribution and marketing** channels of the infringer and you; and
- **the extent to which you can show** that consumers were actually confused (usually demonstrated by consumer surveys and affidavits).

In addition to a federal cause of action for trademark infringement, the Federal Trademark Dilution Act and many state trademark statutes provide owners of certain marks with an anti-dilution remedy. This remedy is available when a third party is using a mark in a manner that has the effect of diluting the distinctive quality of a mark that has been registered under the state statute or used under common law. In such cases, the owner of the registered mark and the diluting party need not be in competition; nor must a likelihood of confusion be demonstrated. However, to make a claim for dilution, the trademark must have a "distinctive quality," which means that it must enjoy very strong consumer loyalty, recognition and goodwill. Under the federal law this anti-dilution protection is available only to "famous marks," such as Coca Cola, Chevrolet or Palmolive.

The goodwill and consumer recognition that trademarks and service marks represent have tremendous economic value, and are often a growing company's most valuable asset. Therefore it is usually worth the effort and expense to register and protect them properly. This will require a commitment by your management to implement and support a strict trademark-compliance program that includes usage guidelines for all departments inside the company, as well as for suppliers, licensees, service providers, and distributors. Online monitoring services, clipping services, semi-annual trademark searches, media-awareness programs, designation of in-house compliance officers, warning letters to infringers and diluters, and even litigation are all essential to maintaining an effective trademark-protection program.

Copyrights

A copyright is a form of protection available to the author of original "literary, dramatic, musical, artistic, graphical, sculptural, architectural, and certain other intellectual works which are fixed in any tangible medium of expression." The owner of a copyright generally has the exclusive right to do or authorize others to do the following: reproduce the copyrighted work; prepare derivative works; distribute and transmit copies of the work; and perform or display the copyrighted work.

Congress has struggled to keep up with the many modes of authorship that were not contemplated when the original copyright laws were written in 1790. Computers, photography, television, sound recordings, motion pictures, video, the Internet, and advanced telecommunications have presented new challenges to legislators as to how to protect the rights of innovators and pioneers. Copyright law has been the workhorse that has been forced to evolve and adapt to these new challenges. The most recent major revision of copyright laws was the 1976 Copyright Act. Under the revised laws, a copyright is recognized and can be protected as soon as a literary or artistic work is created in any tangible medium of expression. This gives the copyright owner control over access to and publication of the work from the start. Copyright protection is typically available only to the person whose labor created the work; however, it is also available for certain types of compilations (the assembly of preexisting materials) and derivative works (translations, recreations, etc.). The Sonny Bono Copyright Term Extension Act of 1998 added 20 years to the copyright term. The term of protection is now 95 years from publication date or 120 years from creation date, whichever expires first.

COPYRIGHT PROTECTION OF WORK-FOR-HIRE. As defined by the Copyright Act, a "work-for-hire" is a work prepared by an employee within the scope of his or her employment, or a work specially ordered or commissioned if the parties expressly agree in a signed written instrument that the work will be owned, as a work-for-hire, by the commissioning party, not the creator. Under the work-for-hire doctrine, works developed by an employee are considered to be works owned by the employer. But in a more recent Supreme Court case, this presumption does not necessarily apply to freelance workers or independent contractors unless there is a written agreement stating that it is the clear intent of the parties that the copyright to the work will belong to the "commissioning party" and not the "creating party."

NOTICE OF COPYRIGHT. Any works protectable by copyright should include a "notice of copyright" to put the world on notice that the author claims the work as a copyright. The prescribed notice consists of: use of the symbol © or the word "copyright"; the year of first publication of the work; and the name of the copyright owner. However, the lack of copyright notice does not necessarily mean that the author does not intend to protect his or her rights to the work (see the box on page 388).

COPYRIGHT REGISTRATION. Pursuant to the Copyright Act, copyright protection arises as soon as the work is created and fixed in a tangible medium of expression. The work need not be registered prior to its publication; however, registration is essential to taking advantage of the many benefits and protections offered under the Copyright Act, which include the right to sue for infringement and the ability to obtain damages and stop others from using the work. Materials are protected without registration, provided they contain the required statutory notice of copyright. Any materials filed for copyright registration become public record; therefore, before registering a work, consider whether registration would compromise the confidentiality of any trade secrets that may be contained in the work. For example, the contents of your company's new marketing brochure are a natural candidate for copyright registration; however, the contents of your confidential operations manual should not be registered due to its proprietary contents.

COPYRIGHT INFRINGEMENT. To be able to enforce rights in court for copyright infringement, the author must register and deposit

The Ever-Changing World of Copyright Law

Copyright protection can extend to computer programs, as a set of statements or instructions to be provided to a computer in order to achieve a specific result.

To be protectable, the work must be fixed in a tangible medium of expression. Copyright protects the expression of ideas, but not ideas, procedures, facts, or principles on a stand-alone basis.

Copyright-law issues permeate the legal issues surrounding the Internet. Don't put on the Web what you don't intend others to use without adequate notice. Some courts have interpreted the ability of a "Web surfer" to view or browse your "work" as an "implied license" to use your work. Make sure you use the appropriate copyright notices.

The purchase of copyrighted work does not necessarily mean you own the underlying copyright. The object of the copyright can be separated under the law from the intangible copyright interest. The actual copyright interest can only be transferred by a signed agreement or by operation of law. For example, if you buy a sculpture, you have the right to display it in your home or office. But, without the actual agreement of the copyright owner, you do not have the right to sell pictures of it; nor may you create a mold to reproduce the sculpture for distribution.

Independent contractors and freelance workers normally own the copyright in what they create—not the company who pays for it, unless a written agreement specifies otherwise.

The absence of a formal copyright notice does not mean that the given work may be duplicated without the permission of the creator. It is not safe to assume that something is in the public domain merely because it lacks a formal copyright notice.

As recently as late June 2001, the Supreme Court continued to struggle with the impact on copyright law and policy. In *Tasini v. NY Times,* the Court upheld the rights of freelance workers to be paid when their original works are included or revised on electronic data-bases or Web sites. The repurposing of this content into an electronic format constitutes a separate act of publication and not a mere "revision"—the position taken by several major publishers.

copies of the work in the Library of Congress depositary. The Copyright Office then examines the application for accuracy and determines whether the work submitted is copyrightable. Unlike the Patent and Trademark Office, the Copyright Office will not compare the works with those already registered, and does not conduct interference or opposition proceedings. The copyright laws do provide remedies for private civil actions. Remedies for copyright infringement include injunctions against unauthorized use, attorneys' fees, damages for lost profits, and certain statutory damages However, these enforcement rights and remedies must be weighed against the fact that once a written work is registered, it becomes public and may be viewed by competitors. Thus, it may make more sense to protect proprietary materials as trade secrets, rather than expose them to the public through the Library of Congress.

Typically, copyright infringement involves the unauthorized use or copying of the work. However, because it is usually difficult to prove copying, the copyright holder must provide proof of access to the work and substantial similarity from the viewpoint of a reasonable person. This shifts to the alleged infringer the burden of proving that the work has been independently created. Before claiming copyright infringement, be aware that there are several limitations on the exclusive rights of a copyright owner. In addition, there are several acts ways that copyrighted work can be used without triggering an actionable remedy for infringement. These include use of the basic idea expressed in the work; the independent creation of an identical work without copying and "fair use" of the work for purposes of criticism, comment, news reporting, teaching, scholarship or research.

Federal copyright laws make willful copyright infringement for commercial profit a crime. The court is required to order a fine of not more than $10,000, or imprisonment not exceeding one year, or both, as well as seizure, forfeiture and destruction or other disposition of all infringing reproductions and all equipment used in their manufacture. Under federal law, civil remedies available to the holder of any exclusive rights in the copyrighted work include:

- **an injunction** against future infringement;
- **actual damages** suffered by the copyright owner;
- **any additional profits** of the infringer; and
- **full costs incurred** to enforce the copyright, including reasonable attorneys' fees.

Trade Secrets

A trade secret may consist of any type of information, including a formula, pattern, compilation, program, device, method, technique, or process that derives independent economic value from not being generally known to other persons who can obtain economic value from its disclosure or use. The information does not need to be unique or even invented by its owner to be protected, as long as the data is kept confidential and provides value to the company. A company uses its trade secrets to gain an advantage over competitors, and therefore its secrets must be treated as confidential and proprietary. Unlike other forms of intellectual-property protection, there are no federal civil statutes that provide for the registration of trade secrets. State law typically protects trade secrets. The scope of protection available for trade secrets may be defined by a particular contract or fiduciary relationship as well as by state statutes and court decisions.

Many emerging-growth companies owe their success in part to the competitive advantage provided by some confidential formula, method, design or other type of proprietary know-how. Such companies generally understand the importance of protecting their trade secrets against unauthorized disclosure or use by a current or former employee, licensee, supplier or competitor. For a small company, especially where trade secrets may be the company's single most valuable asset, disclosure can cause severe and irreparable damage.

Courts have generally set forth three requirements for information to qualify for trade secret protection:

- **the information must have some commercial value;**
- **the information must not be generally known** or readily ascertainable by others; and
- **the owner of the information must take all reasonable steps** under the circumstances to maintain its confidentiality and secrecy. Examples of trade secrets include business and strategic plans, research and testing data, customer lists, manufacturing processes, pricing methods, and marketing and distribution techniques

In addition to the three major requirements for trade-secret protection, the courts have considered many other factors in deciding the extent to which protection should be afforded for trade secrets. Among those factors most often cited are:

- **the extent to which the information is known by others** outside the company (including the efforts by the company to keep the information guarded from disclosure);
- **the value of the information, including the resources** expended to develop the information and whether the information truly provides a competitive advantage;
- **the amount of effort that would be required by others** to duplicate the effort or reverse-engineer the technology; and
- **the nature of the relationship** between the alleged infringer and the owner of the trade secret.

For many small companies, the cost of complicated security systems to protect their trade secrets is beyond their means. Combined with the mobile nature of today's work force, turnover caused by promotion within, and the chaotic nature of most growing businesses, it becomes practically impossible to prevent a determined employee from gaining access to the company's proprietary information. Therefore, it is often easier to simply ignore the problem and do nothing at all about it. However, there are some fundamental, affordable and practical measures that a growing company can readily adopt to protect the data that is at the core of its competitive advantage.

Implementing a Trade-Secret Protection Program

If an emerging-growth business tries to protect every aspect of its operation by rubber-stamping everything as a "TRADE SECRET," it is likely that virtually nothing will be afforded protection if put to the test. Genuine trade secrets may be diluted if the owners (and their managers) try to protect too much.

If you want to establish a trade-secret protection and compliance program, start with a trade-secret audit to identify genuinely confidential and proprietary information. Although each type of business will have its own priorities, most companies, consider financial, technical, structural, marketing, engineering, and distribution documents to be candidates for protection. Classify these documents, and implement security measures to protect them. Draft an office manual (separate from the employee handbook) for employees, and write it in basic terms to inform them of trade-secret protection procedures. Reinforce the importance of following procedures with timely interoffice memoranda, employee seminars and incentive programs. Impress the importance of protecting the company's trade secrets on employees from the moment they join the company—at new employee orientation programs—to the time of their departure from the company—at which time they should be fully briefed on their continuing duty and legal obligation to protect the secrets of their former employer. Periodically consult with the technical and creative staffs to identify new and existing trade secrets, and reiterate the duty of nondisclosure. In addition to these measures, the central components of a compliance program are as follows:

- **Conduct appropriate background checks on employees** with access to critical or confidential information.
- **Ensure that you have adequate building security,** such as restricted access to highly sensitive areas, fences or gates to protect the premises, visitor control and log-in procedures, alarm systems, and locked desks, files and vaults for proprietary documents. Post signs and notices in all appropriate places.
- **Stamp confidentiality notices on documents** that are trade secrets to give users notice of the documents' proprietary status, and restrict the photocopying of these documents to limited circumstances.
- **Designate a trade-secret compliance officer** to oversee all aspects relating to the proper care and monitoring of trade secrets.
- **Restrict employee access to trade secrets** to a "need to know" basis. In other words, unless employees really need the information to do the job properly, they shouldn't have access to the information.
- **Review all advertising and promotional materials** and press releases to protect trade secrets. Restrict access for interviews by reporters and other members of the media. This will help

you avoid horror stories like the one of the company that was so proud of its new product that it inadvertently disclosed the proprietary features of the discovery in its promotional materials.

- **Ensure that all key employees,** marketing representatives, service providers, licensees, prospective investors or joint venturers, customers, suppliers, or anyone else who has access to your company's trade secrets has signed a carefully prepared confidentiality and non-disclosure agreement.
- **Police the activities of former employees,** suppliers and licensees. Include post-term obligations in agreements that impose a requirement on the employee to keep you aware of his or her whereabouts.
- **Use passwords and data encryption** to restrict access to terminals and telephone access through modems if trade secrets are contained on computers.
- **Establish controlled routing procedures** for the distribution and circulation of certain documents.
- **Use a paper shredder** as appropriate.
- **Restrict photocopying of documents.** Use legends and maintain logbooks on the whereabouts of originals.
- **Monitor the trade press and business journals** for any news indicating a possible compromise or exploitation of your trade secrets by others.
- **Provide employees with guidelines** on the care and use of confidential documents. Alert them never to leave such data unattended in the office, cars, airplanes, hotel rooms, trade shows, conventions, meetings, or conferences.
- **Conduct exit interviews with all employees** who have had access to the company's trade secrets. Remind them of their obligations not to use or disclose confidential and proprietary data owned by the company, and of the costs and penalties for doing so. Notify the future employer in writing of these obligations, especially if it is directly or indirectly competitive. Conversely, avoid litigation as a defendant by reminding new employees of the company's trade-secret policies and that they are being hired for their skills and expertise, not for their knowledge of a former employer's trade secrets.

Trade-Secret Misappropriation

All states have long upheld the protection of trade secrets as a matter of common law. At least 43 states also have adopted some version of the Uniform Trade Secrets Act, which affords civil remedies for trade-secret piracy. Many states also have penal codes making trade-secret theft a crime. Congress enacted the Economic Espionage Act in 1996, creating broad federal criminal remedies to deter misappropriation, and a number of international treaties and agreements also now address trade-secret piracy. In spite of all these legal measures, corporate espionage costs U.S. businesses an estimated $100 billion annually.

Trade-secret misappropriation—often referred to as corporate espionage or trade-secret piracy—occurs when a trade secret is obtained by another party's breach of a confidential relationship or through other improper means. To be able to bring an action for misappropriation, you must either establish a legal duty owed by those who come in contact with the information not to disclose or use the information or prove that the information came into the hands of the misappropriator through a wrongful act.

The simplest way to create this duty is by agreement. The owner of a small or growing business should have a written employment agreement with each employee who may have access to the employer's trade secrets. As discussed in Chapter 7, the employment agreement should contain provisions regarding the non-disclosure of proprietary information as well as covenants of non-exploitation and non-competition applicable both during and after the term of employment. These covenants will be upheld and enforced by a court if they are reasonable, consistent with industry norms and not overly restrictive. In the event of any subsequent litigation, such an agreement will go a long way toward proving to a court that you intended to take (and, in fact, took) reasonable steps to protect your company's trade secrets. However, the agreement should be only the beginning of an ongoing program to make employees mindful of their continuing duty to protect the trade secrets of the employer.

The duty of nondisclosure might also arise when you submit proposals or business plans to prospective investors, lenders, licensees, franchisees, joint-venturer interests, lawyers, accountants, or other consultants. Take steps to ensure confidentiality at the commencement of any such relationship where trade secrets may be disclosed in presentations, meetings and documents.

PROTECTING TRADE SECRETS. To bring a lawsuit against another party for trade-secret misappropriation, you (the plaintiff) must demonstrate:

- **existence of a trade secret;**
- **communication to the defendant;**
- **the defendant was in a position of trust or confidence** (or otherwise had some duty not to disclose); and
- **information constituting the trade secrets** was used by the defendant to the injury of the plaintiff.

In analyzing whether these essential elements are present, the court will consider the following:

- **Was there any relationship of trust and confidence,** either by express agreement or implied, that was breached?
- **How much time, value, money and labor** has been expended in developing the trade secret?
- **Has the trade secret** reached the public domain? Through what channels?
- **Has the company maintained a conscious** and continuing effort to maintain secrecy (agreements of non-disclosure, security measures, etc.)?
- **What were the mitigating circumstances** surrounding the alleged breach or misappropriation?
- **What is the value of the secret** to the company?

REMEDIES FOR MISAPPROPRIATION. The most important and most immediate remedy available in any trade-secret misappropriation case is the temporary restraining order and preliminary injunction, which immediately restrains the unauthorized user from continuing to use or practice the trade secret, pending a hearing on the owner's charge of misappropriation. Prompt action is necessary to protect the trade secret from further unauthorized disclosure. If the case ever makes it to trial, the court's decision will address the terms of the injunction and may award damages and profits resulting from the wrongful misappropriation of the trade secret. However, be aware that—as with the protection of other forms of intellectual property—there are certain risks you should evaluate before instituting a trade-secret suit. The most serious risk to consider is that the trade secret at issue, or collateral trade secrets, may be disclosed during the course of the litigation. Certain federal and state rules of civil procedure and laws of evidence will protect against this risk to a limited extent. Also bear in mind that trade-secret law is very unsettled and often turns on the facts of each case, and that establishing the paper trail needed to prove your claim may prove to be an elusive goal. Because successfully litigating a misappropriation claim can be costly (perhaps even beyond your company's means), prevention is a much more effective alternative.

Protective Measures for Departing Employees

There is a fine line between what knowledge belongs to the employee and what belongs to the former employer. Courts have attempted, relatively unsuccessfully, to develop some objective standard for what an employee in that position would have learned, regardless of where he might have been employed. However, a few states, such as Pennsylvania, have determined that a former employee may use trade secrets that were created by that employee while working for the former employer. At least another dozen states, including California, severely limit or even prohibit the nature and scope of non-competition agreements.

In analyzing a claim against a departed employee, consider the following factors:

■ **what information** the employee was exposed to that truly constituted a trade secret;

■ **the terms of any employment** or non-competition agreements to which the employee was a party;

■ **steps taken by your company** to protect the secret;

■ **the extent to which this secret** could have been discovered through "reverse engineering";

- **the extent to which the employee used** any company assets or resources to form his own business;
- **the extent to which the employee acquired** this knowledge independent of the company;
- **the extent to which the employee contracted** current vendors or customers of the company during or after his or her employment with the company;
- **the similarity of the product** or service to be offered; and
- **the proximity of the new business** to the former employer.

Overall, the law does not mandate nor will it enforce an agreement requiring employees to "clean their mental slate" on departure. Further, the courts are hesitant to stifle competition and the entrepreneurial spirit of the employee, absent some express agreement or foul play. In spite of such obstacles to successful litigation of misappropriation of your company's trade secrets, seek a legal remedy for a clear breach of an agreement, a breach of a non-competition clause, or misappropriation of a customer list or proprietary data.

Protecting Trade Secrets Against Netspionage

In the age of the Internet, it is increasingly difficult to secure trade secrets and other intangibles. Even the most cutting-edge information-technology (IT) security might not be enough to protect these assets. This is especially true for companies with a significant Internet presence, which tend to be targets of so-called corporate "netspionage." More than 59% of companies with a significant Internet presence suffered computer break-ins during 1998. To mitigate against the risk of netspionage, your IT team should take the following measures:

- **Periodically test** firewalls and other security systems.
- **Monitor** the intranet, extranet and Internet for indications of theft.
- **Deploy** strategic cryptographic systems.
- **Implement** intrusion-detection technology.
- **Establish** electronic evidence-recovery capability.
- **Respond to** incidents and investigate anomalies.

Trade Dress

Trade dress is a relatively new branch of intellectual-property law that refers to a combination or arrangement of elements that comprises the interior or exterior design of a business, usually in the context of a retail or restaurant business. Trade dress can include symbols, designs, product packaging, labels and wrappers, exterior building features, interior designs, menu design, uniforms, etc., used to build brand awareness and customer loyalty. Trade dress is protected by federal and state trademark laws if it distinguishes the goods or services of one company from those of its competitors. Protectable trade dress consists of three elements:

■ **a combination of features** (used in the presentation, packaging or "dress" of goods or services);

■ **these features are nonfunctional;** and

■ **their distinctiveness reveals to consumers** the source of goods or services.

For example, in *Taco Cabana International, Inc. v. Two Pesos,* the jury found the following combination of restaurant decor features to be protectable:

■ **interior and patio dining areas** decorated with artifacts, bright colors, paintings, and murals;

■ **overhead garage doors** sealing off the interior from patio areas;

■ **festive exterior paintings** having a color scheme using top-border paint and neon stripes;

■ **bright awnings and umbrellas;**

■ **a food-ordering counter** set at an oblique angle to the exterior wall and communicating electronically with the food-preparation and pickup areas;

■ **an exposed food-preparation area** accented by cooking and preparation equipment visible to the consumer; and

■ **a condiment stand** in the interior dining area proximate to the food-pickup stand.

To enhance the strength of your company's trade dress, consider the following suggestions:

■ **Adopt** a combination of several features.

■ **Ensure** that several of the features are unique.

- **Avoid** using features that are arguably functional.
- **Use** the features consistently and continuously.
- **Include** as many of the features as possible in advertising.
- **Refer to** trade-dress features in advertising and promotional literature.
- **Advertise** as extensively as your company's budget permits.
- **Apply** the "theme" of the trade dress throughout the entire business.
- **Keep** competitors from adopting similar combinations of features and from using features that are unique to your trade dress.
- **Where possible,** federally register the trade dress or its various components.
- **Do not advertise** utilitarian advantages of any trade dress you wish to protect.
- **Keep** detailed records of instances of possible consumer confusion between your trade dress and a competitor's subsequently adopted trade dress.

It is also crucial for your business to avoid being on the defending end of a dress-infringement claim. To prevent such claims, avoid copying competitors' trade dress, investigate competitors' potential trade-dress rights, and consult a skilled trademark lawyer. Also, it may also be advisable to use disclaimers and to be more cautious when there is a potentially aggressive opponent.

Show-How and Know-How

Certain types of intellectual property are treated as such primarily because some third party is willing to buy or license it from a company or individual that possesses a particular expertise. In such cases, show-how consists of training, technical support and related educational services, whereas know-how usually takes the form of information that has been reduced to written rather than spoken form. Know-how and show-how usually arise in the context of a licensing agreement where the licensee is requesting support services in addition to the tangible technology or patent that is the central subject matter of the agreement. To the extent that the know-how or show-how is confidential and proprietary, the law of trade secrets will generally govern it, unless otherwise covered by a patent. To the extent that the know-how or show-how is non-proprietary and constitutes common knowledge, it will be governed by the term and conditions of the agreement between the parties.

Ideas and Concepts

As a rule, a mere idea or concept does not qualify for patent, copyright, trade-secret, or trademark protection. The right to the exclusive use of an idea is lost by voluntary disclosure unless the following three elements are present:

■ **the idea is in a concrete form;**

■ **the idea is original and useful; and**

■ **the idea is disclosed in a situation where compensation for its use is contemplated.**

If this test is satisfied, the idea may qualify as a "property right" and may be protected under theories of implied contract, unjust enrichment, misappropriation, breach of a fiduciary relationship, or "passing off." Recovery under these circumstances usually will depend on the relationship between the idea submitter and the idea receiver, as well as the facts surrounding the disclosure.

The law of intellectual property generally seeks to protect and reward the creative firm, innovator, or entrepreneur for their efforts by prohibiting misappropriation or infringement by competitors. It is therefore crucial that you incorporate the legal considerations to protect these "crown jewels" into your strategic-marketing plan. If proper steps are not taken to protect these new products, services, and operational techniques, then it will be extremely difficult to maintain and expand your company's share of the market because others will be free to copy these ideas as if they were their own.

The proper protection and, where possible, registration of

intellectual property is essential to building and sustaining your company's growth. The procedures and expenses necessary to protect these valuable intangible assets are crucial to the continued well being of your company and its ability to continue to survive in a competitive marketplace.

The Importance of Periodic Intellectual-Property Audits

Despite the critical importance of the role of intellectual property and intangible assets as key components of the net worth and overall shareholder value of many fast-track growing and established businesses, many companies fail to appreciate and take inventory of the assets they have developed and grossly under-leverage these assets. Terms such as "intellectual-asset management" and "innovation and invention-capture management" are just now creeping their way into the nation's corporate boardrooms. Most companies severely lack any dedicated resources, systems or strategies for managing and leveraging their intellectual capital, which up until recently has been simply ignored or misunderstood. From a legal perspective, companies of all sizes are just starting to realize the importance of intellectual-property infringement-avoidance programs from both an offensive perspective (actively pursuing those who are infringing on your assets) and a defensive one (making sure that your research, development and promotional efforts don't step on the toes of others). In these instances, ignorance is anything *but* bliss—it may cost your company's shareholders a lot of money in terms of lost business opportunities or costly legal disputes.

At a time when all companies are under pressure to make more out of what they already have developed and to create incremental revenue streams and new opportunities, businesses of all sizes need to conduct periodic intellectual-property protection and leveraging analysis (IPPLA). An IPPLA will give you a realistic and creative assessment regarding what intellectual-property assets your company has, the strength of these assets and the opportunities for leveraging them into new markets or revenue streams as well as for improving existing distribution channels. In conducting an IPPLA, the questions you and your team should discuss with your legal and strategic advisers include:

- **Which of our technologies** have non-competing applications that could be licensed to others?
- **Which of our brands** offer value in a brand-extension licensing or co-branding relationship?
- **What distribution channels** or partnering opportunities can be strengthened if we had greater control?
- **What growth and expansion strategies** are competitors using? Why? How are their circumstances different from ours, if at all?
- **Where are the strategic and financial holes** in our current licensing and alliance relationships?
- **What is the company's** online and e-commerce strategy? How could it be strengthened or improved?

Often, the impetus for the IPPLA may be the senior management of your company or its chief patent lawyer. The impetus could also come from board members or outside shareholders (or venture capitalists in earlier-stage venture-backed companies) who are pressuring the company to produce new revenue streams before another infusion of capital can or will be committed. However, going through a strategic-planning process such as the IPPLA is a particularly important growth step that should be undertaken on an ongoing and regularly scheduled basis, especially in a weaker economy, because:

- **Fast-track growth companies like yours** must protect and use their intangible assets to penetrate new domestic markets or to fuel international expansion.
- **Capital-efficient growth** is the mandate of many CEOs and CFOs during turbulent financial markets. The IPPLA process may help uncover ways to generate new revenue streams from assets that have already been created, saving money and shifting the costs of additional research and development to third parties.

Overview of IPPLA Procedures

1. PREPARE THE IPPLA PLAN

■ Define areas of inquiry
■ Identify legal and strategic working team
■ Establish time schedules
■ Outline responsibilities
■ Define preliminary documents to review and company personnel to interview
■ Identify documents to review prior to onsite IPPLA

2. GATHER INFORMATION

■ Assign a coordinator of document requests
■ Collect and review information concerning the nature of the property and transaction to be investigated
■ Identify issues regarding the laws of particular states or countries

3. WRITE A REPORT OF RESULTS OF IPPLA

■ Memorialize results in a report
■ Consider whether report should be privileged communication and not discoverable

Report should include:

■ List of intellectual-property assets

■ Development history
■ Status of trademarks, copyrights, patents and other intellectual property
■ Intellectual-property defects and remedial actions needed

4. TAKE ANY NEEDED REMEDIAL ACTION

■ Undertake any necessary federal, state and international filings/recordations
■ Execute ownership documents (i.e., assignments)
■ Pursue infringers, correct infringements
■ Define prospective legal, marketing and research strategies
■ Clarify employee/consultant ownership rights
■ Require all employees and consultants to sign, before commencing any work, written agreements transferring ownership of all works of authorship produced by them
■ Include in such agreements clauses obligating the signatory to execute confirmatory assignment documents with respect to specific works

---

■ **Companies of all sizes and in all industries** are under pressure to create new opportunities and new distribution channels from existing assets (technologies, systems, brand, relationships, know-how, etc.). The IPPLA may identify a need or an opportunity to restructure your company around the IP portfolio or create subsidiaries or spinout companies based on IP leveraging opportunities.

■ **As a fast-track growth business,** you need to periodically re-evaluate whether current distribution channels and market-partners are really working effectively to generate the highest and best shareholder value and income streams and profits. Ask questions such as: Is this the highest and best strategy available to meet our objectives? What is the origin of these relationships? What politics or red tape will we face if these agreements and relationships are re-evaluated? Should we restructure around a real or perceived imbalance in the economics of any existing relationships?

■ **The strategic-planning review** can give your company the opportunity to identify and then repair channels and relationships that are broken, ineffective, or that require greater controls to yield better results.

■ **With high levels of employee turnover** and competition for a qualified work force, it is more important than ever that your employees are educated on their obligations to protect your company's IP on an in-term and post-term basis.

■ **Your company may be sitting on a portfolio of patents,** technologies and brands that can be licensed in non-competing ways to augment existing initiatives and your core businesses. Brand-extension licensing and co-branding opportunities may offer ways to strengthen customer loyalty and overall brand recognition, such as Caterpillar's decision to expand its brand into footwear and other accessories.

■ **You may also want to consider licensing technology** from third parties, since your fast-track growth company may not have the resources to conduct research and development at the same levels and may need or want to explore access to technologies and brands that are already established or readily available on an off-the-shelf basis. Your company may also find such licensing-in opportunities that, when paired with the company's current technology portfolio, can create new products, services and market opportunities.

■ **Technology licensing,** brand-extension licensing, joint ventures and strategic alliances, business-format franchising, and outsourcing are all intellectual-property leveraging strategies that should be discussed regularly and adopted inside your boardroom. Such ventures need to be coupled with an effective IP portfolio analysis to be effective.

■ **Intellectual-property leveraging strategies** can serve as precursors to capital-formation transactions, such as venture investments and acquisitions, especially in David/Goliath transactions as well as peer-to-peer transactions, and a careful IP portfolio analysis can aid your company in leveraging its intellectual properties.

In today's merger and acquisition frenzy, the IPPLA may be an excellent way for your company to prepare for a buyer or a merger partner's due-diligence process to ensure that you fill gaps to establish proof of ownership of these assets. The results of the IPPLA may also be necessary to support your company's proposed valuation if and when it is a target in an M&A transaction.

In an environment of constantly changing and evolving market relationships, the IPPLA will help you identify any assets in your company's IP portfolio that are subject to the rights of third parties. Such rights may exist by virtue of coauthorship, coinvestorship, joint venture, teaming, co-branding, license or statutory or contractual rights of termination or reversion.

Your fast-track growth company may simply not have the time, resources or expertise to identify, develop, and implement new strategies for leveraging its IP portfolio without the help of a catalyst. Or your company might simply need to take a fresh look or gain a new perspective as to how your IP can be leveraged (classic "too close to the trees to see the forest" syndrome). An intellectual-property audit can identify opportunities a company has been overlooking.

In addition to helping your company identify its intangible assets and develop opportunities to leverage those assets, the IPPLA also serves important legal objectives, including:

■ **to determine the origin of your company's intangible assets** and the extent of management's interest in licensing technology and related intellectual properties;

- **to determine the scope of rights** that third parties may have, by license, ownership, or otherwise, in your company's intangible assets;
- **to detect problems in ownership** of the existing intellectual-property assets and institute systematic procedures for protecting your company's intellectual-property rights;
- **to detect instances in which early measures may be needed** to avoid some of the more common defenses available by misappropriators and infringers; and
- **to avoid liability for third-party claims** of infringement resulting from the development of new products.

As part of the auditing process, your fast-track growth company's IPPLA team should conduct the following analyses:

- **Review contracts** with employees, consultants, vendors and customers to determine whether such contracts adequately protect and perfect your company's intellectual-property rights, including non-compete agreements, technology-licensing agreements, and other third-party contracts.
- **Research and analyze** your company's trademarks, trade dress, and service marks (nationally and internationally) to determine whether you have established adequate protection and whether the company has preserved the trademark rights of others as part of joint ventures and co-branding arrangements.
- **Research and analyze** your company's patents (nationally and internationally) to assess the validity of patent applications and risks for infringement, as well as to determine which patents are core (that is, central to the company's core businesses and objectives) and which are non-core, which may be perfect candidates for licensing or sale.
- **Identify** any unique technologies or business methods that may be appropriate for further patent protection or brands, sub-brands or slogans that may be eligible for trademark protection.
- **Assess** your company's policies and practices regarding handling of confidential information, customer lists and trade secrets.
- **Interview** key managers and technical personnel to measure

awareness of intellectual-property issues and compliance with company policies (including a review of these policies).

■ **Based on the results of this research,** have your legal-review team prepare a comprehensive IPPLA report. This should include an inventory of your fast-track growth company's intellectual-property assets, a prioritized plan of action for correcting deficiencies and reducing risk, and recommendations on implementation and training for key personnel.

Preparing for the IP audit

In preparing for the IPPLA, have your company's legal and strategic review and analysis team prepare an audit plan outlining:

■ **the specific areas of inquiry** (e.g., divisions, lines of business, affiliated or non-affiliated agency operations);
■ **the scope of inquiry** (e.g., only registered assets or a broader scope);
■ **the schedule of the IPPLA;**
■ **the parties responsible for each part of the IPPLA; and**
■ **the form of the final report to be produced.**

As part of their initial information gathering, the legal and strategic audit team will identify those intellectual-property rights, such as patents, copyrights and trademarks, that have already been registered or are in the process of being registered. The team must then obtain copies of all affiliate agreements. These include administrative services and cost allocation; employment and consulting agreements (including Web-site design agreements); license and maintenance agreements; joint-venture agreements; distribution agreements; security documents and UCC filings; confidentiality agreements; litigation files (including outside counsel responses to auditor's letters); source-code escrow agreements (in connection with software); database licenses; and relevant corporate policy statements, including document-retention policies.

After the relevant documentation has been identified and organized, the legal and strategic audit team should then prepare an electronic index of the materials, noting with

---

Overview of the IPPLA Strategic Process

PRE–IPPLA:

- Understand the company, its markets, products and key objectives
- Understand the company's key challenges and key trends affecting growth plans
- Analyze the portfolio of IP assets to ensure the best and most effective IP protection strategies have been adopted
- Analyze the company's IP–leveraging track record, philosophy and experiences
- Know what has worked, what hasn't and why
- Conduct strategic planning and brainstorming to identify new IP–leveraging strategies

and opportunities

- Determine which strategies should be pursued and with whom

POST–IPPLA

- Develop recruitment procedures and section criteria for attracting prospective licensees and market partners
- Develop documents and business plans to implement various IP-leveraging strategies
- Monitor, support and refine IP–leveraging strategies
- Outsource fully or partially the IP–leveraging process
- Restructure existing channels and relationships

---

respect to each intellectual-property asset:

- **the nature of your company's ownership interests** (for example, sole or joint ownership, exclusive or non-exclusive license, the royalty or other costs associated with the license and the estimated legal duration and period of technological use-fulness of the asset) and whether the nature of the interest is in doubt;
- **any restrictions on the use of the asset** (for example, product or agency-related restrictions, territorial restrictions, assignment or transfer restrictions, time restrictions, non-compete clauses);
- **relevance of the asset to your company** (for example, whether the asset is a critical or a replaceable asset) and its connection with other assets;
- **whether the asset has been pledged;** and
- **potential for a third-party claim of infringement** or damages due to the company's use of the asset.

In the course of analyzing the assets, the legal and strategic audit team may find it necessary to directly interview your company personnel who have been responsible for the development, acquisition or use of individual assets.

The length of your company's IPPLA, its budget, the team deployed, etc,. may vary based on the depth and breadth of your company's IP portfolio, its IP-leveraging track record, its IP-leveraging objectives, and other factors. The typical IPPLA is made up of two parts: Part A, the IP-protection review and evaluation; and Part B, the IP-leveraging strategy formulation. Once you have completed the IPPLA, your company's lawyer's role may include business- and strategic-planning; assistance in the preparation of the series of licensing memoranda; legal work on the protection and registration of intellectual properties that have not been properly protected; regulation or restructuring of channels and relationships that are broken; and the legal and compliance work in connection with the implementation of one or more IP-leveraging strategies.

Growth Via Business-Format Franchising

O VER THE PAST THREE DECADES, FRANCHISING HAS emerged as a popular expansion strategy for a variety of product and service companies. Recent International Franchise Association (IFA) statistics demonstrate that retail sales from franchised outlets comprise nearly 50% of all retail sales in the United States, estimated at more than $900 billion and employing some nine million people in 2000. Notwithstanding these impressive figures and the favorable media attention that franchising has received over the past few years, it is not a suitable growth strategy for every type of business. Numerous legal and business prerequisites must be satisfied before any company can seriously consider franchising as an alternative for rapid expansion.

What has made franchising so popular in the U.S. and around the world? From the perspective of the franchisor, franchising represents an efficient method of rapid market penetration and product distribution, without the typical capital costs associated with internal expansion. From the perspective of the franchisee, franchising offers a method of owning a business, but with a mitigated chance of failure due to the initial and ongoing training and support services offered by the franchisor. From the perspective of the consumer, franchised outlets offer a wide range of products and services at a consistent level of quality and at affordable prices.

The Changing Franchising Landscape

Franchising is viewed by many companies as a way to leverage their brands, systems, proprietary products and expertise to create new revenue streams and open new markets without significant capital expenditures. However, a number of business trends and legal changes will affect the growth of franchising:

- **The typical franchisee and multi-unit developer** is smarter and wealthier than ever before, thereby leveling the playing field in both negotiation and enforcement issues.

- **With the broad availability of franchise opportunities,** franchising has become more competitive than ever before. Estimates put the number of franchisors in the United States at more than 5,000. A prospective franchisee may have 20 or more different franchisors to choose from in a given industry niche, and more sophisticated companies have looked at franchising as a growth-and-branding strategy.

- **The Federal Trade Commission** (FTC) has become more active in enforcement actions. It brought twice as many actions against non-complying franchisors in 2000 as it did in all the years since the FTC passed its Trade Regulation Rule 436 in 1979.

- **Franchising is not just about fast food and auto services anymore.** A series of non-traditional sectors, such as energy services, health care, financial services, and other regulated industries, are adopting franchising as a growth strategy, raising a host of new legal issues and challenges.

- **A focus on alternative distribution channels,** such as carts, kiosks, satellite units, seasonal units, in-store units, etc., has raised a host of structural issues and triggered territorial-encroachment issues as franchisors fight for market share.

- **Two new franchisee associations** have formed in recent years, giving franchisees a powerful lobby in Washington.

- **Franchising has truly become a global business-growth opportunity** as more U.S.-based franchisors than ever launch franchising programs overseas and foreign franchisors penetrate the elusive and competitive U.S. market.

- **To more closely monitor franchising activities** within their borders, many states (including Florida, Kentucky, Nebraska, and

Utah) have passed amendments to existing business-opportunity laws.
- **Increases in the number of initial public offerings,** private placements and mergers and acquisitions by and among domestic and international franchisors have opened up the capital markets for the franchising community.
- **In recent years, there has been a new emphasis on the role of the franchisee** in the franchisor's decision-making and planning processes through advisory councils, board seats and better use of telecommunications and computer technologies.
- **More Fortune 500 and multinational conglomerate firms** have made entries into franchising, changing the franchising landscape for businesses of all sizes.

Reasons for Franchising

There are a wide variety of reasons cited by successful franchisors as to why they selected franchising as a method of growth and distribution. Among the reasons cited were the ability to:
- **obtain operating efficiencies** and economies of scale;
- **increase market share** and build brand equity;
- **use the power of franchising** as a system to get and keep more and more customers, thereby building customer loyalty;
- **achieve more rapid market penetration** at a lower capital cost;
- **reach the targeted consumer more effectively** through cooperative advertising and promotion;
- **sell products and services** to a dedicated distributor network;
- **replace the need for internal personnel** with motivated owner/ operators; and
- **shift the primary responsibility** for site selection, employee training and personnel management, local advertising, and other administrative concerns to the franchisee, licensee, or joint-venture partner with the guidance or assistance of the franchisor.

Many companies prematurely select franchising as a growth alternative then haphazardly assemble and launch a program.

Types of Franchisees

RESOURCES NEEDED/BUSINESS ACUMEN REQUIRED

Lowest -▶ Highest

| Buying a job (home-based; low investment) | Sales & distributorships (product driver) and routes | Retail store (business format emphasis) | Management-driven (multiunit) larger territory or region who manage or lead a team of managers on a permit or district basis as well as satellite carts, kiosks, etc. | Financial investment (large-scale projects such as hotels) |

Other companies are urged to franchise by unqualified consultants or advisers who may be more interested in professional fees than in the long-term success of the franchising program. This will cause financial distress and failure for both the franchisor and franchisee and usually results in litigation.

Building a Strong Foundation for Franchising

To grow your business through franchising, you must build a secure foundation from which your company's franchising program will be launched. Responsible franchising is the only way to avoid failure and to ensure a harmonious relationship with your franchisees. Among the key components of a responsible franchising strategy are:

■ **A proven prototype location** (or chain of stores) that will serve as a basis for your franchising program. The store or stores must have been tested, refined, and operated successfully and be consistently profitable. The success of the prototype should not be too dependent on the physical presence or specific expertise of the founders of the system.

- **A strong management team** made up of internal officers and directors (as well as qualified consultants) who understand both the particular industry in which your company operates and the legal and business aspects of franchising as a method of expansion.
- **Sufficient capitalization** to launch and sustain the franchising program to ensure that you will have the capital to provide both initial as well as ongoing support and assistance to franchisees. (The lack of a well-written business plan and adequate capital structure is often the principal cause of demise of many franchisors.)
- **A distinctive and protected trade identity** that includes federal- and state-registered trademarks as well as a uniform trade appearance, signage, slogans, trade dress, and overall image.
- **Proprietary and proven methods of operation and management** that can be reduced to a comprehensive operations manual, cannot be too easily duplicated by competitors, maintain their value to the franchisees over an extended period of time, and that can be enforced through clearly drafted and objective quality-control standards.
- **Comprehensive training programs for franchisees** at the outset of the relationship and on an ongoing basis that integrate all of the latest education and training technologies, and that take place both at your company's headquarters and onsite at the franchisee's proposed location.
- **Field support staff who are skilled trainers and communicators** and who are available to visit and periodically assist franchisees, as well as monitor quality-control standards at your franchisees' locations.
- **A set of comprehensive legal documents** that reflects your company's business strategies and operating policies. You must prepare offering documents in accordance with applicable federal- and state-disclosure laws, and your franchise agreements should strike a delicate balance between your rights and obligations and those of your franchisees.
- **A demonstrated market demand for your company's products and services** that will be distributed through the franchisees. Your

products and services should meet certain minimum quality standards, not be subject to rapid shifts in consumer preferences (fads), and be proprietary in nature. Your market research and analysis should be sensitive to trends in the economy as well as your specific industry, the plans of your direct and indirect competitors, and shifts in consumer preferences. It is also important to understand what business you are really in. For example, many of the major oil-company franchisors thought they were in the gasoline business, but eventually realized that they were in the convenience business and quickly added mini-marts, fast-food outlets and quick-service restaurants to their gas stations—either directly or through co-branding.

- **A set of carefully developed, uniform site-selection criteria** and architectural standards that can be readily and affordably secured in today's competitive real estate market.

- **A genuine understanding of the competition** (both direct and indirect) that your company will face in marketing and selling franchises to prospective franchisees, as well as the competition franchisees will face when marketing products and services.

- **Relationships with suppliers, lenders, real estate developers,** and related key resources that are part of the operations manual and system.

- **A franchisee profile and screening system** to identify the minimum financial qualifications, business acumen, and understanding of the industry that you will require of prospective franchisee.

- **An effective system of reporting and record-keeping** to maintain the performance of your franchisees and ensure that they accurately report royalties and pay them promptly.

- **Research and development capabilities** for the ongoing introduction of new products and services offered to consumers through the franchised network.

- **A communication system** that facilitates a continuing and open dialogue with your franchisees, and as a result reduces the chances for conflict and litigation within your franchise network.

- **National, regional, and local advertising, marketing,** and public-relations programs designed to recruit prospective franchisees as well as consumers to your franchise sites.

Responsible franchising starts with an understanding of the strategic essence of the franchising structure. There are three critical components of the franchise system:

■ **The brand, which creates the demand,** allowing the franchisee to initially obtain customers. The brand includes your company's trademarks and service marks, its trade dress and decor and all of the intangible factors that create customer loyalty and build brand equity.

■ **The operating system, which essentially "delivers the promise,"** thereby allowing the franchisee to maintain customer relationships and build loyalty.

■ **The ongoing support and training that you provide,** supplying the franchisee with the tools and tips to expand its customer base and build its market share.

The responsibly built franchise system is one that provides value to its franchisees by teaching them how to get and keep as many customers as possible who consume as many products and services as possible, as often as possible. The focus must always be on the customer, where the franchisor essentially licenses and delegates the task of local brand building and market expansion to the franchisee in its local territory.

Most litigation in franchising revolves around the gap between the actual needs of the franchisees to remain competitive in the marketplace and the reality of what support the franchisor is capable of providing. A commitment to quality, fairness, and effective communication with your franchisees will go a long way in reducing disputes. To be a successful franchisor, you must be committed to supporting and servicing the franchises you grant and maintaining a focus on quality of franchisees and training. Franchisors who develop strategic plans that primarily focus on quantity of franchisees and expansion are surely headed for disaster.

To focus on quality, as the franchisor you need to build a model profile of the type of franchisee that you need to attract, then stay disciplined to the application of those criteria in the recruitment and selection process. The success or failure of every franchise system is dependent on the quality and commitment of the franchisees you select. They must understand your company's mission, core values and vision and be ready to serve as a strategic partner in the expansion of your business-growth plan.

Strategic Prerequisites to Launching a Franchising Program

The operation and management of a successful prototype is the most important strategic prerequisite for the success of any business-format franchise system. This prototype location is where you will resolve virtually all operating problems, test recipes and new products or services, make equipment and design decisions, test management and marketing techniques, establish a trade identity and goodwill, and prove financial viability. You must sell a tried and tested package to a franchisee, and the contents of that package must be clearly identified prior to sale. It is irresponsible and potentially in violation of the law to ask someone to part with his or her life savings to invest in a business model that is not ready for replication.

At the heart of a successful franchising program is the concept of a system or prescribed business format that is operated according to a uniform and consistent trade identity and image. Therefore, to successfully franchise your business you must be able to reduce all aspects of running the business to an operations and training manual franchisees can use in the day-to-day operation of their business. You must adequately and clearly communicate your operation methods to franchisees at the outset of your relationship and in an ongoing training program. If your company offers services that are highly personalized or a product that is difficult to reproduce, then franchising may not be the most viable growth alternative for your company because of the difficulty of communicating specific guidelines in the operator's manual or in the training program. Similarly, if all the "kinks" in your system have not yet been worked out, it is probably premature to consider franchising.

There are a number of other important business and strategic factors that you must consider before franchising. First, franchising should not be viewed as a solution to under-capitalization or as a "get rich quick" scheme. While it is true that franchising is less capital-intensive than construction of additional company-owned sites, the initial start-up costs for legal, accounting and consulting fees can be extensive. Second, you must view franchising as the establishment of a series of long-term relationships and be aware that the ongoing success of your company as a franchisor will depend on the harmony of these relationships. Make your support staff available to franchisees, to provide ongoing services as well as to maintain quality control and uniformity throughout the system. You must contin-

> **The ongoing success of your company as a franchisor will depend on the harmony of many long-term relationships.**

ue to develop new products and services so that franchisees can continue to compete with others in their local markets. You should also continually develop innovative sales and marketing strategies to attract new customers and retain existing patrons of the franchised outlet. If you expect franchisees to continue to remit to you your share of the royalty payments on gross sales each week or month, then you should strive to provide them with an array of valuable support services on an ongoing basis to meet their changing needs.

Franchising as a Strategic Relationship

When you consider franchising as a growth strategy for your business, always bear in mind that first and foremost, franchising is about the establishment and continuation of strategic relationships. You and your franchisee knowingly and voluntarily enter into a long-term relationship, each of you depending on the other for success. You're not simply "selling" a product or a program or a thing to a franchisee; rather, you and the franchisee are making a voluntary and bilateral decision to create a mutually beneficial relationship. The focus of that relationship should be, "How can we work together for each other's benefit?" You must build a relationship where the enemy is not each other, but rather the competition. The franchisor-franchisee relationship has been compared to the relationship between parent and child, between a football coach and his team, between a conductor and his orchestra, and between a landlord and his tenants. The award of the franchise has been compared to the granting of a driver's license: One may use and renew the privilege of driving subject to following the rules of the road and paying ongoing fees. In other words, the franchisee may enjoy the freedom to operate the franchise, but must adhere to certain rules and requirements as a condition of doing so.

The franchisee may enjoy the freedom to operate the franchise, but must adhere to certain rules and requirements as a condition of doing so.

Like the most sacred of relationships, marriage, if the parties are to stay committed to each other for the long-term, then both franchisor and franchisee must respect one another, stay loyal to one another and each day search for ways to strengthen their bond. A recent survey seems to indicate that this new focus on the strategic aspects of the relationship seems to be working. While over one-half of our nation's marriages wind-up in divorce, nearly 92% of the nation's franchisees said they would get married to their franchisor again.

Given the high satisfaction ratings, it is not surprising that nearly two-thirds (65%) of the franchise owners said they would purchase the same franchise again if given the opportunity. Of those who wouldn't buy the same franchise again, nearly half (43%) said they would consider buying a different one. In 2000, on average, franchise owners reported annual gross incomes of $91,630, with 24% earning $100,000 or more. Most of the franchisees (64%) said they would be less successful if they had tried to open the same type of business on their own and not as part of a franchise system.

If you want your franchise system and franchisee satisfaction ratings to meet or exceed these levels of success, you must build a culture of honesty, trust, passion and genuine commitment to long-term success. This often begins in the recruitment process by carefully screening and educating qualified candidates to ensure that your long-term objectives are truly shared and best interests truly aligned. Of course, some degree of franchisee failure will be inevitable due to circumstances that are beyond your control, such as changes in local market conditions or changes in the franchisee's personal life.

Understanding the Franchisee of the New Millennium

To develop a successful relationship with your franchisees, you need to understand the profile of today's prospective franchisee. As a general rule, franchisees are getting smarter, are better educated, and better capitalized than their "mom and pop" predecessors of the 1970s and 1980s. These new, sophisticated franchisees are better trained to ask all the right questions and hire the right advisers in the investigation and franchise-agreement negotiation process. And as franchising has matured, prospective franchisees have more resources (seminars, media articles, trade shows, International Franchise Association programs, etc.) than ever to turn to for information and due diligence. Today's franchisees are also more likely to organize themselves into associations and take action if they are not receiving the required levels of support and assistance. To work with this new generation of franchisees, you need to mold your franchising operations to meet their needs or risk heading down the road to disaster and litigation.

The Importance of Quality Control

Many owners of growing companies fear that the decision to franchise will result in the loss of quality control over the operations and management of their business. In reality, as a franchisor you have a variety of vehicles for maintaining the level of quality that you and your consumers have come to expect. A well-planned franchising or licensing program will include a wide variety of system standards, training methods and operational manuals to establish quality-control guidelines, as well as a carefully assembled field-support staff to educate franchisees and enforce the your quality-control guidelines.

To succeed, a franchise system demands quality control. Thus, if your franchise system does not maintain and enforce an effective quality-control strategy, it is not likely to survive in the competitive marketplace. Under federal trademark laws, the licensor of a trademark has an obligation to control the quality of the products and services offered in connection with the trademark. Thus, by establishing and enforcing quality-control standards, you not only assure uniformity of quality but also satisfy a legal obligation imposed upon the owner of a trademark. Failure to monitor and control the operations of a franchisee could result in a "statutory abandonment" of your rights in the trademark, because it may no longer distinguish a particular product or service from those offered by others in the market. Therefore, the trademark laws provide a justification and basis for the implementation of reasonable controls over franchisees in all aspects of the business format.

Developing System Standards

The glue holding the typical franchise system together consists of the uniform policies, procedures and specifications that must be followed by all franchisees. These rules and regulations, typically found in your franchising-operations manual, must be:

- **carefully planned and developed** by the franchisor;
- **clearly articulated by the franchisor** to the franchisees, both initially and on an ongoing basis;
- **accepted by the network of franchisees** as being understood and reasonable;
- **consistently applied;** and
- **rigidly enforced,** typically through your field-support staff.

Obviously, the development of uniform standards is of little value unless there are systems in place for monitoring and enforcing these standards, as well as penalties for noncompliance with the standards, which are typically found in the franchise agreement.

Compliance with quality-control standards requires mutual respect by and among the parties involved. You must be reasonable and resist the temptation to go hog wild in the development and enforcement of system standards; the franchisee, in turn, must understand that reasonable standards are in the best interests of all franchisees in the network. Franchisees typically have a love-hate relationship with system standards. On the one hand, they love reasonable standards that result in happy consumers and weed out non-complying franchisees; on the other hand, they detest standards that are unattainable, vaguely communicated, and arbitrarily or too rigidly enforced.

Your franchising-system standards, which are prescribed in your operations manual and other written and electronic communications you make with franchisees, are deemed to be part of the franchise agreement under the contract-law doctrine of incorporation by reference. System standards dictate, among other things:

- **the required and authorized products and services** to be offered and sold;
- **the manner in which the franchisee may offer and sell** these products and services (including product preparation, storage, and handling and packaging procedures);
- **the required image and appearance of facilities,** vehicles and employees;
- **designated and approved suppliers** and supplier-approval procedures and criteria;
- **types, models and brands of required operating assets** (including equipment, signs, furnishings, furniture and vehicles) and supplies (including food ingredients, packaging and the like);
- **use and display of the trade and service marks;**
- **sales, marketing, advertising and promotional programs** and the materials and media used in these programs;
- **terms and conditions of the sale and delivery** of items that the franchisee acquires from your company and its affiliates;
- **staffing levels and training;**
- **days and hours of operation;**
- **participating in market research** and testing, and product and service development programs;

- payment, point-of-sale and computer systems;
- reporting requirements;
- insurance requirements; and
- other operational rules.

These standards, which you implement at the beginning and during the course of the franchise relationship, and your

You must build a certain degree of flexibility into your franchise agreements to allow the peaceful implementation of system changes.

willingness and ability to enforce those standards system-wide, will usually determine the success of your franchise system. It is essential that you communicate system standards to franchisees in well-organized and understandable formats. The obvious dilemma is that many of these system standards are moving targets. They can and will change as technology and market conditions change. You must be able to modify the system standards without seeking an addendum to the franchise agreement every time a modification is necessary. To accomplish this, build a culture where change is inevitable, expected and warmly embraced by franchisees, and where franchisees trust your judgment, so that they will view changes to the system as a positive evolution of the business format, not as a burden. In addition, you must build a certain degree of flexibility into your franchise agreements to allow the peaceful implementation of system changes.

Enforcing System Standards

As a franchisor, you have an obligation to develop system standards and procedures that are reasonable and attainable, and you must clearly communicate and uniformly enforce the standards. In enforcing the standards, you must strike a balance to ensure that your demands are neither too loose nor too rigid. If the penalties for noncompliance are too loose, you will be viewed as a toothless lion who neither intends nor has the power to insist on compliance. If the enforcement is too rigid, franchisees will resent and even disregard the standards, resulting in litigation and poor franchisee morale throughout your network.

The enforcement strategy you adopt should depend in part on your company's stage of growth as a franchisor. For example, in the early stages, a gentle rap on the knuckles (in lieu of an actual termination) of a non-compliant franchisee may be more prudent because of the impact of a dispute on your company at this stage. Before taking any action, carefully consider the costs of litigation, the perception of actual and prospective franchisees, and the nature of the infraction. However, if early in the development of your franchise you adopt a "quasi-acquiescence" policy of enforcement, the issue of an expressed or implied waiver, or an equitable defense against enforcement known as "laches," may affect your ability to enforce standards in the future. As your franchise system grows and matures, it will become easier to rigidly enforce system standards and apply significant penalties for noncompliance. As your ability to withstand the impact of a dispute increases and the perception of your franchises is enhanced, the threat of termination will be a more powerful deterrent to franchisees.

Factors you should consider in determining how to proceed against a franchisee in non-compliance with system standards include the following:

- **whether the franchisee in question** has a "high profile" within the system;
- **the exact nature of the franchisee's infraction(s)**;
- **the current condition** and stability of your industry;
- **the availability of a replacement franchisee** for this specific site;
- **the quality of the training program** and operations manual in the area where the infractions have incurred;
- **the existence of any potential counterclaims** by the franchisee;
- **the quality of the evidence** gathered by the field-support personnel to prove the incidents of noncompliance;
- **the reaction of the other franchisees** within the system to the enforcement action; and
- **the geographic location** of the franchisee in question.

The penalties that you may apply to the non-complying franchisee include a formal warning, a written notice of default, a threat of termination, actual termination, damages

40 Common Reasons Why Franchising Programs Fails

- Lack of adequate control
- Difficulty attracting qualified franchisees
- Choice of the wrong consultants
- Lack of proper disclosure documents
- Failure to provide adequate support
- An unproven and unprofitable prototype
- Lack of franchise communications systems
- Premature launch into international markets
- Complex and inadequate operations manuals
- Inadequate site-selection criteria

- Inability to compete against larger franchisors
- Lack of proper screening system for prospective franchisees
- Disregard for franchise registration and disclosure laws
- Lack of business and strategic planning
- Not joining the International Franchise Association (IFA)
- Entering oversaturated markets
- Lack of quality control
- Inexperienced lawyers and accountants
- Breakaway franchisees
- Unreasonable pressure to sell franchises

or fines, a forced sale or transfer, or a denial of a benefit, such as eligibility for participation in a new program. If support for those penalties is not found in your franchise agreement, it must be separately negotiated.

A Commitment to Creativity and Competitiveness

Market conditions and technologies that affect franchising are changing constantly and the successful franchisor must keep pace. The ability to adapt your franchising system to allow for growth and market penetration into alternative and non-traditional venues is critical. For example, the more creative and aggressive franchisors in the retail and hospitality industries are always searching for new locations where captive consumers may be present, such as airports, hotels, hospitals, highway roadside-travel plazas, universities, sports arenas or military bases. TCBY, a successful franchisor based in Little Rock, Ark., has nearly 50% of its 3,000 frozen-yogurt stores worldwide in these alternative venues. In other cases,

- Unworkable economic relationship with franchisees
- Lack of effective compliance systems
- Royalty underpayments/ nonpayments by franchisees
- Operational systems that can be easily duplicated
- Lack of effective financial controls
- Lack of experienced management
- Unprotected trademarks
- Excessive litigation with franchisees
- Inadequate training program
- Decentralized advertising
- Lack of ongoing research and development
- Unbridled geographic expansion
- Choice of the wrong subfranchisors
- Unprofitable and unhappy franchisees
- Inadequate public relations
- Unwillingness to enforce franchise agreement
- Weak relationships with key vendors
- Improper earnings claims
- Premature termination of franchisees
- Lack of market research

franchisors have pursued co-branding strategies to penetrate these new markets. A notable example of this is the trend of combining convenience stores or fast-food outlets with gas stations to provide consumers with an enhanced experience and offer them an integrated solution to their needs. And again, a trend toward co-branding and the ability to share costs, positioning toward differentiation, and penetrate new market segments at a relatively low cost has opened up many doors for the creative and aggressive franchisor who is committed to capturing more market share and serving more and more customers.

Common Reasons for Franchisor Failure

Each year since the early 1990s, between seventy-five to one hundred franchisors went out of business. This figure represents 3% to 5% of all franchisors operating during those years. The box above features a list of the 40 most common factors contributing to franchisor failure. Read the list carefully to mitigate the risk of your fast-track growing company meeting the same fate in launching and building its franchising program.

Federal Rules and Regulations

The offer and sale of a franchise is regulated at both the federal and state level. At the federal level, FTC Rule 436 (the FTC Rule), adopted in 1979, specifies the minimum amount of disclosure that must be made to a prospective franchisee in any of the fifty states. The FTC Rule regulates two types of offerings.

PACKAGE-AND-PRODUCT FRANCHISES. This type of offering has the following characteristics:
- **the franchisee sells goods or services** that meet the franchisor's quality standards (in cases where the franchisee operates under the franchisor's trademark, service mark, trade name, advertising, or other commercial symbols designating the franchisor that are identified by the franchisor's Mark);
- **the franchisor exercises significant assistance** in the franchisee's method of operation; and
- **the franchisee is required to make payment of $500 or more** to the franchisor or a person affiliated with the franchisor at any time before to within six months after the business opens.

BUSINESS-OPPORTUNITY VENTURES. The characteristics of this type of offering are:
- **the franchisee sells goods or services** that are supplied by the franchisor or a person affiliated with the franchisor;
- **the franchisor assists the franchisee** in securing accounts for the franchisee, or securing locations or sites for vending machines or rack displays, or providing the services of a person able to do either; and
- **the franchisee is required to make payment of $500 or more** to the franchisor or a person affiliated with the franchisor within six months after the business opens.

The components of these offerings are defined as follows:

Franchisor's mark. This element is satisfied when the franchisee is given the right to distribute goods or services under the franchisor's trademark or service mark.

Significant control and assistance. The key to this element is that the control or assistance must be "significant." According to the *Final Guides to the Franchising and Business Opportunities Ventures Trade Regulation Rule*, published by the Federal Trade Commission. The term "significant" "relates to the degree to which the franchisee is dependent upon the franchisor's superior business expertise." The *Final Guides* states that the dependence on the business expertise of the franchisor may be conveyed by the franchisor's controls over the franchisee's methods of operation or by the franchisor furnishing assistance to the franchisee in areas related to methods of operations.

Required payment. This element is met if a franchisee is required to pay the franchisor at least $500 as a condition of obtaining the franchise or of commencing operations. Payments made at any time prior to, or within six months after commencing operations will be aggregated to determine if the $500 threshold is met. The payments may be required by the franchise agreement, an ancillary agreement between the parties or by practical necessity (such as required supplies that are only available from the franchisor).

Relationships covered by the FTC Rule include those within the definition of a "franchise" and those represented as being within the definition when the relationship is entered into, regardless of whether, in fact, they are within the definition. The FTC Rule exempts fractional franchises, leased-department arrangements, and purely verbal agreements. The FTC Rule excludes relationships between employer/employees and among general business partners, membership in retailer-owned cooperatives, certification and testing services, and single-trademark licenses.

Among other things, the FTC Rule requires that every

franchisor offering franchises in the United States deliver an offering circular, or a disclosure document (containing certain specified disclosure items), to all prospective franchisees (within certain specified time requirements). The information in the disclosure document must be current as of the completion of the franchisor's most recent fiscal year. In addition, a revision to the document must be promptly prepared whenever there has been a material change in the information contained in it. The FTC Rule requires that the disclosure document must be given to a prospective franchisee at the earlier of either the prospective franchisee's first personal meeting with the franchisor, or ten business days prior to the execution of a contract, or ten business days before the payment of money relating to the franchise relationship. In addition to the disclosure document, the franchisee must receive a copy of all agreements that it will be asked to sign at least five business days prior to the execution of the agreements.

The FTC has adopted and enforced its Rule pursuant to its power and authority to regulate unfair and deceptive trade practices. The FTC Rule sets forth the minimum level of protection that must be afforded to prospective franchisees. To the extent that a state offers its citizens a greater level of protection, the FTC Rule will not preempt state law. There is no private right of action under the FTC Rule, however, the FTC itself may bring an enforcement action against a franchisor that does not meet its requirements. Penalties for noncompliance have included asset impoundments, cease-and-desist orders, injunctions, consent orders, mandated rescission or restitution for injured franchisees and civil fines of up to $10,000 per violation.

State Rules and Regulations

In addition to the FTC Rule, more than a dozen states have adopted their own rules and regulations for the offer and sale of franchises within their borders. These states, known as the regulation states, generally follow a more detailed disclosure format, known as the Uniform Franchise Offering Circular (UFOC), than the FTC Rule requires. Each state franchise-disclosure statute has its own definition of a "franchise," which is similar to, but not the same as, the definition set forth in the FTC Rule. If the proposed business relationship meets the FTC's statute or that of the state in which it is offering franchises, then the franchisor must comply with the applicable registration and disclosure laws.

There are three major types of state definitions of a franchise or business opportunity.

MAJORITY-STATE DEFINITION. In the states of California, Illinois, Indiana, Maryland, Michigan, North Dakota, Oregon, Rhode Island and Wisconsin, a franchise is defined as having three essential elements:
- **A franchisee is granted the right** to engage in the business of offering, selling, or distributing goods or services under a marketing plan or system prescribed in substantial part by a franchisor.
- **The operation of the franchisee's business** is substantially associated with the franchisor's trademark or other commercial symbol designating the franchisor or its affiliate.
- **The franchisee is required to pay a fee.**

MINORITY-STATE DEFINITION. The states of Hawaii, Minnesota, South Dakota and Washington have adopted a somewhat broader definition of franchise. In these states, a franchise is defined as having the following three essential elements:
- **A franchisee is granted the right** to engage in the business of offering or distributing goods or services using the franchisor's trade name or other commercial symbol or related characteristics.
- **The franchisor and franchisee** have a common interest in the marketing of goods or services.
- **The franchisee pays a fee.**

NEW YORK DEFINITION. The state of New York has a unique definition. Under its law a franchisee is defined by these guidelines:
- **The franchisor is paid a fee** by the franchisee.
- **Either the business is essentially associated with the franchisor's trademark** or the franchisee operates under a marketing plan

or system prescribed in substantial part by the franchisor.

VIRGINIA DEFINITION. The Commonwealth of Virginia also has its own definition of a franchise, which stipulates that:

- **A franchisee is granted the right** to engage in the business of offering or distributing goods or services at retail under a marketing plan or system prescribed in substantial part by a franchisor.
- **The franchisee's business** is substantially associated with the franchisor's trademark.

Virginia and New York have definitions that are broad in certain respects. Virginia does not have a fee element to its definition. New York requires a fee, but specifies either association with franchisor's trademark or a marketing plan prescribed by the franchisor. Therefore, in New York, no trademark license is required for a franchise relationship to exist. However, the regulations in New York exclude from the definition of a franchise any relationship in which a franchisor does not provide significant assistance to or exert significant controls over a franchisee.

The requirements of the registration states differ. Those that require a full registration of a franchise offering prior to the offering or selling of a franchise are California, Illinois, Indiana, Maryland, Minnesota, New York, North Dakota, Rhode Island, South Dakota, Virginia, and Washington. Hawaii requires filing of an offering circular with the state authorities and delivery of an offering circular to prospective franchisees; Michigan and Wisconsin require filing a "Notice of Intent to Offer and Sell Franchises"; Oregon requires only that pre-sale disclosure be delivered to prospective investors; and Texas requires the filing of a notice of exemption with the appropriate state authorities under the Texas Business Opportunity Act.

The Mechanics of the State Registration Process

Each of the registration states has slightly different procedures and requirements for the approval of a franchisor prior to offers and sales being authorized. In all cases, however, you must assemble a disclosure package consisting of an offering circular, franchise agreement, supplemental agreements, financial statements, franchise roster, mandated cover pages, acknowledgment of receipt, and the special forms that are required by each state, such as corporation-verification statements, salesperson-disclosure forms, and consent to service of process documents. With the assistance of your lawyer, carefully check the specific requirements of each state. Initial filing fees range from $250 to $750, with renewal filings usually ranging between $100 to $250.

The first step in the registration process is for your lawyer to custom-tailor the UFOC format to meet the special requirements or additional disclosures required under the particular state regulations. Once the documents are ready and all signatures have been obtained, you must file the package with the state franchise administrator, and a specific franchise examiner (usually a lawyer) is assigned to you. The level of scrutiny applied by the examiner in reviewing the offering materials will vary from state to state and from franchisor to franchisor. Your company's sales history, financial strength, litigation record, reputation of legal counsel, time pressures and workload of the examiner, geographic desirability of the state, and its general reputation will have an impact on the level of review and the timetable for approval. You should expect to see at least one comment letter from the examiner requesting certain changes or additional information as a condition of approval and registration. The procedure can take as little time as six weeks or as long as six months, depending on the concerns of the examiner and the skills and experience of your lawyer.

The initial and ongoing reporting and disclosure requirements vary from state to state. For example, the filing of an amendment to the offering circular is required in the event of a "material change"; however, each state has different regulations as to the definition of a material change. Similarly, although all registration states require the annual filing of a renewal application or annual report, only Maryland requires that quarterly reports be filed. If you develop advertising materials for use in attracting franchisees, they must be approved in advance in all registration states except Virginia and Hawaii. All franchise registration states except Virginia require the filing of salesperson-disclosure forms. California,

New York, Illinois and Washington require their own special forms. It is critical that your legal-compliance officer stay abreast of all of these special filing requirements.

Preparing the Disclosure Document Under UFOC Guidelines

The UFOC format of franchise disclosure consists of 23 categories of information that you must provide to the prospective franchisee at least ten business days prior to the execution of the franchise agreement. Because this format has been adopted by many states as a matter of law, you may not change the order in which you present this information, nor are you allowed to omit any of the disclosure items in the document. In addition, many sections of the UFOC must be a mirror-image of the actual franchise agreement (and related documents) that you will present to the franchisee to sign. There should be no factual or legal in consistencies between the UFOC and the franchise agreement. A description of the information required by each disclosure item of the UFOC begins on page 440.

Subfranchising, Area-Development Agreements and Related Documents

Most franchises are granted to individual owners who will be responsible for managing a single site in accordance with the franchisor's business format and quality-control standards. A recent trend in franchising, however, has been to award "multiple-unit franchises" to more aggressive entrepreneurs who will be responsible for the development of an entire geographic region. The two primary types of multiple-unit franchises are:

■ **subfranchisors,** who act as independent selling organizations that are responsible for the recruitment and ongoing support of franchisees within their given region; and

■ **area developers,** who have no resale rights but rather are themselves responsible for meeting a mandatory development schedule for their given region.

There are a number of variations on these two principal types of multiple-unit franchises. For example, franchisors have experimented with co-development rights among adjacent franchisees of a nearby territory, franchises coupled with management agreements (under those circumstances where the franchisee deserves to be more passive), equity participation by franchisors with franchisees (and vice-versa), employee ownership of franchisor-operated units and co-development rights between the franchisor and franchisee. Another common franchise relationship is one in which franchisees that start out as single-unit owners wind up as multiple-unit owners through the use of option agreements or rights of first refusal.

As a rule, the inclusion of multiple-unit franchises in your franchising-development strategy allows for even more rapid market penetration and fewer administrative burdens. Often franchisees demand the right to develop and operate multiple units. However, there is a wide range of legal and strategic issues that you must address when multiple-unit franchises are included in your overall franchising program.

Structuring Area-Development Agreements

The key issues in structuring an area-development agreement usually revolve around the size of the territory, fees, the mandatory timetable for development and ownership of the units. You should reserve certain rights and remedies in case the franchisee defaults on its development obligations. The area developer must usually pay your company an umbrella development fee for the region, over and above the individual initial fee that is to be payable as each unit becomes operational within the territory. The amount of the fee varies, depending on factors such as the strength of your company's trademarks and market share, the size of the territory and the term and renewal of the agreement. This development fee is essentially a payment to you that prevents you from offering any other franchises within that region, unless there is a default.

Structuring Subfranchising Agreements

An agreement you enter with a subfranchisor is typically referred to as a regional development agreement, which grants the subfranchisor certain rights to develop a particular region. The regional development agreement is not in itself a franchise agreement to operate any individual franchise units; rather, it grants the subfranchisor the right to sell franchises to individuals using your company's system and proprietary marks solely for the purpose of recruitment, management, supervision and support of individual franchisees. To the extent that the subfranchisor itself develops units, then an individual franchise agreement for each such unit must be executed.

The relationship between franchisor and subfranchisor is unique and somewhat complicated. If the appropriate individual is chosen for this role, the relationship can be mutually beneficial, providing your company with benefits that include rapid market penetration, the delegation of obligations you would otherwise be required to fulfill to each franchisee in your network, and the ability to collect a percentage of the initial franchise fee and royalty fees from each franchisee, generally without the same level of effort that would be required in a single-unit relationship.

Subfranchise agreements present myriad issues that are not raised in the sale of a single-unit franchise or an area-development agreement. This is primarily because the rewards and responsibilities of the subfranchisor are much different than the area developer or single-unit operator. In most subfranchising relationships, you must share a portion of the initial franchise fee and ongoing royalty with the subfranchisor, in exchange for the subfranchisor assuming responsibilities within the given region. The proportion of shared fees is directly related to the exact responsibilities of the subfranchisor. In addition, you must provide the subfranchisor with a comprehensive regional operations manual that covers sales and promotions, training and field support over and above the information contained in the operations manuals provided to individual franchisees. Some of the key issues that you must address in a subfranchise relationship include:

- **How will the initial and ongoing franchise fees be divided** between you and the subfranchisor? Who will be responsible for the collection and processing of franchise fees?
- **Will the subfranchisor be a party** of the individual franchise agreements? Or will "direct privity" be limited to you and individual franchisee?
- **What is the exact nature of the subfranchisor's responsibility** to the individual franchisees within its region, in terms of recruitment, site selection, training and ongoing support?
- **Who will be responsible for the preparation** and filing of franchise offering documents in states where the subfranchisor must file separately?
- **What mandatory development schedules** and related performance quotas will be imposed on the subfranchisor?
- **Will the subfranchisor be granted the right to operate** individual units within the territory? If yes, how will these units be priced?
- **What will the subfranchisor be obligated to pay** your company initially for the exclusive right to develop the territory?
- **What rights of approval will you retain** with respect to the sale of individual franchises (e.g., background of the candidate, any negotiated changes in the agreement, decision to terminate, etc.)?
- **What rights do you reserve** to modify the size of the territory or repurchase it from the subfranchisor?

Creative Regulatory Alternatives to Franchising

Every year, I am asked by representatives of a few fast-track growth companies to advise them on how to structure a relationship that avoids the definition of a "franchise" under federal or state laws. The first question I ask is "Why?" to ensure that they seek to avoid compliance with these registration and disclosure laws for the appropriate legal or strategic reasons. Among the common reasons given for avoiding a franchise relationship are:

- **an overseas franchisor** who is uncomfortable with concept of disclosure, which may not be required in their country of origin;
- **a midsize or large company** feels that (as a pioneer) industry is not ready for or will react adversely to the kinds of controls that a franchise relationship typically implies;
- **a company or individual officer** who prefers not to disclose (raising other legal problems);
- **a small company concerned with the perceived costs** of preparing and maintaining the legal documents;
- **the real or perceived belief** that, by becoming a franchisor, the company somehow increases its chances of being sued (a myth I usually try to debunk); or
- **some other specific circumstance** or myth or fear that predisposes the company's management team to avoid franchising.

I usually try to solve such problems with creative thinking and structural alternatives. For example, a foreign franchisor may want to set up a new subsidiary in lieu of disclosing the parent company's (usually privately held) financial statements. If the subsidiary is properly capitalized and certain other specific conditions are met, the confidentiality of the parent company's data may be preserved. To satisfy the second example's needs, I have often created the "non-franchise franchisor," which is a company that has essentially agreed to prepare and provide a UFOC even though the details of their relationships are in a regulatory grey area. This way the franchisor appeases the regulators but also placates the industry participants who may be more comfortable with a "strategic partner" or "licensee" designation than a franchisor-franchise relationship.

If the company still insists on avoiding compliance with these laws, then we go through an exercise of determining from a cost-benefit analysis which leg of the "three-legged stool" they will agree to sacrifice. In today's brand-driven environment, the willingness to license the system without the brand (to avoid the trademark-license leg) has not been very popular. Similarly, in an economy where "cash flow is king," most of these clients have not been willing to waive the initial franchise fee or wait over six months for their financial rewards. And the age-old trick of "hiding" the franchise fee in a training program or initial inventory package was figured out by the regulators a long time ago. So it is often the third leg of the stool, the one that is most difficult to interpret—support and assistance to the franchisee—where the creative structuring must take place.

The courts and the federal and state regulators have not provided much clear guidance as to the degrees of support or the degrees of assistance that will meet the definition and those which will not. The mandatory use of an operating system or marketing plan will meet the third element of the test, but what if the use of the system is optional? What if the plan or system is not very detailed and provides lots of room for discretion by the franchisee without penalty for adopting the plan or system to meet local market conditions? And if you choose this path, does allowing this degree of discretion and flexibility sacrifice your ability to maintain quality control? In addition, a competitive environment where most growing companies are trying to provide more and more support and assistance (as well as exercise more control) to their partners in the distribution channel, would providing less than the norm just to avoid the definition of a "franchise" really make sense? These legal and strategic decisions should not be made hastily without properly analyzing the long-term implications.

Guidelines for the Uniform Franchise Offering Circular

COVER PAGE:

The franchisor must disclose certain risk factors here that a franchisee might encounter. For example, the franchisor must use prescribed language to disclose as a risk that its franchise agreement includes an out-of-state form and/or choice of law provision.

ITEM 1:

The Franchisor, Its Predecessors and Affiliates. In this section, you must include an overview of your current and past business operations. You must identify your company by using "we," initials or two words of reference. "Franchisor" and "Franchisee" are not to be used. The addition, you must disclose, in general terms, "any regulations specific to the industry in which the franchise business operates."

ITEM 2:

Business Experience. This section requires disclosure of the identity of each of your company's directors, trustees, general partners (where applicable) and officers or managers who will have significant responsibility in connection with the operation of your business or in the support services to be provided to franchisees. You must disclose the principal occupation for the past five years of each person listed in Item 2, including dates of employment, nature of the posi-

tion, and the identity of the employer. The identity and background of each franchise broker (if any) authorized to represent you must also be disclosed in this Item.

ITEM 3:

Litigation. A full and frank discussion of any litigation, arbitration, or administrative hearings affecting your company, its officers, directors, or sales representatives over the past ten years, along with the formal case name, location of the dispute, nature of the claim, and the current status of each action should be included in this section. Item 3 does not require disclosure of all types of litigation but rather focuses on specific allegations and proceedings that would be of particular concern to the prospective franchisee. "Ordinary routine litigation incidental to the business" is not to be considered material. Litigation is deemed "ordinary routine" if it "ordinarily results from the business and does not depart from the normal kind of actions in the business."

ITEM 4:

Bankruptcy. This section requires that you disclose whether your company or any of its predecessors, officers, or general partners, have during the past ten years been adjudged bankrupt or reorganized due to insolvency. The court in which the bankruptcy or reorganization proceeding occurred, the formal case title, and any material facts and circumstances surrounding the proceeding must be disclosed.

ITEM 5:

Initial Franchise Fee. In this section you must disclose the initial franchise fee and related payments you will receive prior to opening the franchise, as well as the manner in which the payments are to be made, your use of the proceeds, and whether or not the fee is refundable in whole or in part. If the initial franchise fee is not uniform, you must disclose the formula for or range of initial fees you received in the most recent fiscal year prior to the application date.

ITEM 6:

Other Fees. You must disclose in tabular form any other initial or recurring fees payable by the franchisee to your company or any affiliate. The nature of each fee must be fully discussed, including but not limited to royalty payments, training fees, audit fees, public-offering review fees, advertising contributions, mandatory insurance requirements, transfer fees, renewal fees, lease-negotiation fees, and any consulting fees you or an affiliate charge for special services. You should disclose the amount and time of the payment, and the refundability of each type of payment. You may use a "remarks" column or footnotes to elaborate on the information about the fees disclosed in the table. In addition, if fees are paid to a franchisee cooperative, you must disclose the voting power of its outlets in the cooperative. Further, the range of any fees imposed by that cooperative must be disclosed if your outlets have controlling voting power.

ITEM 7:

Initial Investment. Here you must estimate, in a prescribed tabular form, each component of the franchisee's initial investment that the franchise is required to expend in order to open the franchised business, regardless of whether such payments are made directly to your company. Real estate, equipment, fixtures, security deposits, inventory, construction costs, working capital, accounting and legal fees, license and permit fees, and any other costs and expenditures should be disclosed. The disclosure should include to whom such payments are made, under what general terms and conditions, and what portion, if any, is refundable. Any payment that is required to be paid during the "initial phase" of the business must be disclosed. The guidelines instruct that "a reasonable time for the initial phase of the business is at least three months or a reasonable period for

(continued on the next page)

Guidelines for the Uniform Franchise Offering Circular (continued)

the industry." The guidelines also require disclosure of additional funds you require during the initial phase and the factors, basis and experience upon which you base your calculation.

ITEM 8:

Restrictions on Purchase of Products and Services. Any obligation of the franchisee to purchase goods, services, supplies, fixtures, equipment, or inventory that relates to the establishment or operation of the franchised business from a source designated by your company should be disclosed, along with the terms of the purchase or lease as well as any minimum-volume purchasing requirements. If you will or may derive direct or indirect income based on these purchases from required sources, then the nature and amount of such income must be fully disclosed. Remember that such obligations must be able to withstand the scrutiny of the antitrust laws. In addition to disclosing whether your company or its affiliates will or may derive revenue or material consideration as a result of franchisees' required purchases or leases, you must also disclose the estimated proportion of these required purchases and leases to all purchases and leases by the franchisee of goods and services necessary to establish and operate the franchise. You

must disclose whether there are any purchasing or distribution cooperatives serving its system. Based on your company's financial statements from the year immediately preceding, you must disclose your 1) total revenues, 2) revenues derived from required purchases and leases of products and services, and 3) the percentage of total revenues from such required purchases and leases. If your company's affiliates also sell or lease products or services to franchisees, you must also disclose the percentage of the affiliates' revenues derived from these sales or leases. You must also disclose any fees you require for approval of a new supplier. In addition, you must disclose whether you offer franchisees inducements, such as renewal or additional franchises, for purchasing goods or products from designated or approved sources.

ITEM 9:

Franchisee's Obligations. You must set forth the franchisee's obligations in a prescribed tabular form with regard to 24 specific categories. The table must cite the relevant sections of both the franchise agreement and the offering circular.

ITEM 10:

Financing. In this section, you must disclose the terms and conditions of any financing arrangements offered to franchisees either by your company or any of its affiliates. You must also disclose the exact terms of any direct or indirect debt financing, equipment or real estate leasing programs, operating lines of credit, or inventory financing. If any of these financing programs is offered by an affiliate, then you must disclose the exact relationship between your company and the affiliate. In this section of the UFOC you must disclose terms that may be detrimental to the franchisee upon default, such as a confession of judgment, waiver of defenses, or acceleration clauses. You must also disclose the terms and conditions of "indirect offers of financing" made to franchisees. An "indirect offer of financing" includes 1) a written arrangement between your company, or its affiliate, and a lender for the lender to offer financing to franchisees, 2) an arrangement in which your company or its affiliate receives benefits from a lender for franchisee financing, and 3) your company's guarantee of a note, lease or obligation of the franchisee. You are permitted, but not required, to make disclosure in tabular form. You must disclose the annual percentage rate of interest (APR) you charge for financing, computed in accordance with Sections 106-107 of the Consumer Protection Credit Act, 15 U.S.C. (sections) 106-107. If the APR varies depending on

when the financing is issued, you must disclose the APR as of a disclosed recent date. You must disclose to the franchisee the consequences of any default of its obligations, including operation of any cross-default provisions, acceleration of amounts due, and payment of court costs and attorneys' fees. In addition, you must include in the offering circular specimen copies of any financing documents.

ITEM 11:
Franchisor's Obligations. This section is one of the most important to the prospective franchisee because it discusses the initial and ongoing support and services you will provide. Here you must disclose only those pre-opening obligations that you are contractually required to provide to franchisees. Pre-opening assistance that you intend to provide, but which you are not contractually bound to provide, may not be included. Accordingly, this disclosure must begin with the following sentence: "Except as listed below, (franchisor) need not provide any assistance to you." You must make comprehensive disclosures regarding advertising, including 1) the type of media in which the advertising may be distributed, 2) whether the media coverage is local, regional or national in scope, 3) the source of the advertising (e.g., in-house or advertising

(continued on the next page)

Guidelines for the Uniform Franchise Offering Circular (continued)

agency), 4) the conditions under which franchisees are permitted to use their own advertising, and 5) if applicable, the manner in which the franchisee advertising council operates and advises your company. You must make specific disclosures regarding local or regional advertising cooperatives, including 1) how the area and/or membership of the cooperative is defined, 2) how franchisees' contributions to the cooperative are calculated, 3) who is responsible for administration of the cooperative, 4) whether cooperatives must operate from written governing documents and whether the documents are available for review by franchisees, 5) whether cooperatives must prepare annual or periodic financial statements and whether such statements are available for review by franchisees, and 6) whether you have the power to form, change, dissolve or merge cooperatives. You must disclose information about advertising funds you administer, including 1) the basis upon which outlets owned by your company contribute to the fund, 2) whether franchisees contribute at a uniform rate, and 3) the percentages of the fund spent on production, media placement, administrative and other expenses. You must also disclose whether franchisees are obligated to advertise in the area in which the franchise is to be located and the per-

centage of funds used for advertising that is principally a solicitation for the sale of franchises. You are required to disclose whether franchisees must buy or use an electronic cash register or computer system. If there is such a requirement, you must describe in nontechnical language 1) the hardware components, 2) the software program, and 3) whether such hardware and software are proprietary property of your company, an affiliate or a third party. If the hardware or software are not proprietary, you must disclose 1) whether the franchisee has any contractual obligation to upgrade or update the equipment, and if so, any limitations on the frequency and cost of such obligation, 2) how it will be used in the franchise, and 3) whether you have any independent access to information or data in the system. The new guidelines expand disclosure regarding site-selection procedures to include the factors you considered in site selection or approval. In addition, you must include a copy of the table of contents of the franchise operating manual in the offering circular unless the prospective franchisee will view the manual before purchasing the franchise.

ITEM 12:

Territory. The exact territory or exclusive area, if any, you will grant to the franchisee should be disclosed, as well as the right to adjust the size of this territory in the event that certain contractual conditions are not met, such as the failure to achieve certain performance quotas. You must disclose your right to establish company-owned units or to grant franchises to others within the territory, and must include a detailed description and/or map of the franchisee's territory as an exhibit to the franchise agreement. In addition to disclosing whether you have established or may establish additional franchised or company-owned outlets that compete with franchisees' outlets, you must disclose whether you have established or may establish "other channels of distribution" under your company's mark. You must disclose the conditions under which your company will approve the relocation of a franchise or the establishment of additional franchises. In addition, you must disclose whether your company or an affiliate operates or has plans to operate another chain or channel of distribution under a different trademark to sell goods or services that are similar to those offered by the franchise. If your company operates competing systems, you must also disclose the methods you will use to resolve conflicts between them regarding territory, customers and support you will provide. If the principal business

address of the competing system is the same as your company's, you must also disclose whether you maintain separate offices and training facilities for the competing system.

ITEM 13:
Trademarks. You need only disclose the principal trademarks, rather than all trademarks, to be licensed to the franchisee. If a principal trademark is not federally registered, you must include a statement that "by not having a Principal Register federal registration for (trademark), (franchisor) does not have certain presumptive legal rights granted by a registration."

ITEM 14:
Patents, Copyrights and Proprietary Information. If your company claims proprietary rights in confidential information or trade secrets, you must disclose the general subject matter of the proprietary rights and the terms and conditions under which they may be used by the franchisee.

ITEM 15:
Obligation to Participate in the Actual Operation of the Franchised Business. You are required to disclose obligations arising from your company practices, personal guarantees, and confidentiality or non-competition agreements.

(continued on the next page)

Guidelines for the Uniform Franchise Offering Circular (continued)

ITEM 16:

Restrictions on What the Franchisee May Sell. In this section you must disclose any special contractual provisions or other circumstances that limit either the types of products and services the franchisee may offer or the types or location of the customers to whom the products and services may be offered.

ITEM 17:

Renewal, Termination, Transfer and Dispute Resolution. These disclosures must be presented in a prescribed tabular form. The table must contain abbreviated summaries regarding 23 specific categories with references to relevant sections of the franchise agreement. Preceding the table, the offering circular must state: "This table lists important provisions of the franchise and related agreements. You should read these provisions in the agreements attached to this offering circular."

ITEM 18:

Public Figures. You must disclose any compensation or benefit given to a public figure in return for an endorsement of the franchise and/or products and services offered by the franchisee, along with the extent to which the public figure owns or is involved in the management of the franchise. The disclosure is only required if a pub-

lic figure endorses or recommends an investment in the franchise to prospective franchisees. Consequently, you need not disclose franchisees' rights to use the names of public figures who are featured in consumer advertising or other promotional efforts.

ITEM 19:

Earnings Claims. If you are willing to provide the prospective franchisee with sample earnings claims or projections, they must be discussed in Item 19.

ITEM 20:

List of Franchise Outlets. You must provide a full summary of the number of franchises sold, number of operational units, and number of company-owned units, including an estimate of franchise sales for the upcoming fiscal year that are broken down by state. You must include the names, addresses, and telephone numbers of franchisees. With the exception of the list of franchise names, addresses, and telephone numbers, you must disclose all information required by this Item in tabular form. You must disclose the number of franchised and company-owned outlets sold, opened and closed in its system as of the close of each of its last three fiscal years. You must list operational outlets separately from those not opened, and provide disclosure on a state-by-state basis.

You may limit disclosure of the franchisees' names, addresses and telephone numbers to those franchised outlets in the state in which the franchise offering is made if there are 100 outlets in that state. If there are fewer than 100 in the state, you must disclose the names, addresses and telephone numbers of franchised outlets from contiguous states and, if necessary, the next closest states until at least 100 are listed. For the three-year period immediately before the close of the most recent fiscal year, you must disclose the number of franchised outlets that have 1) had a change in "controlling ownership interest," 2) been canceled or terminated, 3) not been renewed, 4) been re-acquired by your company or 5) otherwise ceased to do business in the system. You must disclose the last known home address of every franchisee who has had an outlet terminated, canceled, not renewed, or who otherwise voluntarily or involuntarily ceased to do business under the franchise agreement during the most recently completed fiscal year, or who has not communicated with you within ten weeks of the application date. In addition, you must disclose information about company-owned outlets that are substantially similar to the company's franchised outlets. The same table may be used for both franchised and company-owned outlets as long as the data regarding each is set out in a distinct manner.

ITEM 21:

Financial Statements. You must include your company's balance sheet for the past two fiscal years. Disclosures of statements of operations, stockholders equity, and cash flow are required for the company's past three fiscal years. If the most recent balance sheet and statement of operations are as of a date more than 90 days before the application date, you must also include an unaudited balance sheet and statement of operations for a period falling within 90 days of the application. If you do not have audited financial statements for the past three fiscal years, you have two options: You may provide an audited financial statement for the past fiscal year and, if the audit is not within 90 days of the application date, an unaudited balance sheet and income statement for a period falling within 90 days of application. Or you can provide an unaudited balance sheet as of the date within 90 days of the application and an audited income statement from the start of your company's fiscal year through the date of the audited balance sheet.

ITEM 22:

Contracts. You must attach as an exhibit a copy of the franchise

(continued on the next page)

Guidelines for the Uniform Franchise Offering Circular (continued)

agreement as well as any other related documents to be signed by the franchisee in connection with the ownership and operation of the franchised business.

ITEM 23:

Receipt. You are required to provide two copies of the receipt in the offering circular, one to be kept by the prospective franchisee and the other to be returned to you.

You must disclose the name, principal business address and telephone number of any subfranchisor or franchise broker offering the franchise in the state. The receipt must contain an itemized listing of all exhibits to the offering circular. If not previously disclosed in Item 1, you must disclose the name(s) and address(es) of your agent(s) authorized to receive service of process.

Growth Through Technology, Merchandise and Character Licensing

AST-TRACK GROWTH COMPANIES SHOULD CONSIDER various types of technology and brand licensing as the centerpiece of their intellectual-property leveraging and external-growth strategies. Licensing is a contractual method of developing and exploiting intellectual property by transferring rights of use to third parties without the transfer of ownership. Virtually any proprietary product or service may be the subject of a license agreement, ranging from the licensing of the Mickey Mouse character by Walt Disney Studios in the 1930s to modern-day licensing of computer software and systems, biotechnology and optical networking. From a legal perspective, licensing involves complex issues of contract, tax, antitrust, international, tort, and intellectual-property law. From a business perspective, licensing involves weighing its value against that of alternative types of vertical-distribution systems.

In this era when companies of all types and sizes are under pressure to create additional revenue streams, licensing has emerged as a very popular and effective strategy. After over ten years of limiting the use of its intellectual property for internal purposes only, Procter & Gamble announced in May 2001 that it would begin licensing its manufacturing processes and systems to certain third parties. Even nonprofit organizations are jumping in with both feet to replace lost charitable contributions, with Sierra Club and National Geographic both announcing in June 2001 their plans to license branded lines of shoes, clothing, backpacks, swimwear and hiking gear.

The benefits that licensing offers your growing company are similar to those offered by franchising, namely:

- **spreading the risk and cost** of development and distribution;
- **achieving more rapid** market penetration;
- **earning initial license fees** and ongoing royalty income;
- **enhancing consumer loyalty** and goodwill;
- **preserving capital** that would otherwise be required for internal growth and expansion;
- **testing new applications** for existing and proven technology; and
- **avoiding or settling litigation** regarding a dispute over ownership of the technology.

The risks of licensing are also similar to those inherent in franchising, and include:

- **a somewhat diminished ability to enforce** quality-control standards and specifications;
- **a greater risk of another party infringing upon** your intellectual property;
- **a dependence on the skills, abilities, and resources** of the licensee as a source of revenue;
- **difficulty in recruiting, motivating, and retaining** qualified and competent licensees;
- **the possibility that your entire reputation** and goodwill may be damaged or destroyed by the act or omission of a single licensee; and
- **the administrative burden of monitoring** and supporting the operations of the network of licensees.

Failure to consider all of the costs and benefits of licensing could easily result in a strategic decision you will later regret, or a license agreement that proves unprofitable, due either to an underestimation of the licensee's need for technical assistance and support or to an overestimation of the market demand for your products and services. To avoid such problems, conduct a certain amount of due diligence prior to engaging in any serious negotiations with a prospective licensee. This preliminary investigation should include market research, legal steps to fully protect intellectual property, and an internal financial analysis of the technology with respect to pricing, profit margins, and costs of production and distribution. It should also include a more specific analysis of the prospective licensee's financial strength, research and manufacturing capabilities, and reputation in the industry.

There are two principal types of licensing: technology licensing, where the strategy is to find a licensee for exploitation of industrial and technological developments; and merchandise and character licensing, where the strategy is to license a recognized trademark or copyright to a manufacturer of consumer goods in markets not currently served by the licensor.

Technology Licensing

The principal purpose behind technology-transfer and licensing agreements is to join the technology proprietor, as licensor, and the organization that possesses the resources to develop and market the technology properly, as licensee. This marriage is made between companies and inventors of all shapes and sizes. It occurs often between an entrepreneur, as licensor, who has the technology but not the resources to penetrate the marketplace adequately, and a larger company, as licensee, that has sufficient research and development, production, human resources, and marketing capability to make the best use of the technology. The industrial and technological revolution has witnessed a long line of very successful entrepreneurs who have relied on the resources of larger organizations to bring their products to market, such as Chester Carlson (xerography), Edwin Land (instant cameras), Robert Goddard (rockets), and Willis Carrier (airconditioner). As the base for technological development becomes broader, large companies look not only to entrepreneurs and small businesses for new ideas and technologies, but also to each other, foreign countries, universities, and federal and state governments to serve as licensors of technology.

Why Growing Companies Develop Technology-Licensing Programs

- **To match promising technology** with the resources necessary to bring it to the marketplace
- **To raise capital and earn royalty income.** (Many entrepreneurs who have had doors slammed in their face by commercial banks and venture capitalists have ultimately obtained growth capital and cash flow from licensees.)
- **As a defensive strategy,** which can occur from one of two perspectives: The licensor may want to have its competitors as licensees, thereby keeping them from developing their own competitive technology and turning them into allies instead; or the licensee may want to preempt a competitor or, gain access to its confidential information by approaching the competitor to obtain a license. (Beware: Some competitors will acquire an exclusive license to technology merely to sit on it so that the technology never enters the marketplace. Be prepared to negotiate certain performance standards or limits to exclusivity in the agreement in order to avoid such a trap.)
- **To shift (or share) the product liability risk** inherent in the production or marketing of hazardous or dangerous products with the licensee
- **To reach new geographic markets** unfamiliar to the technology proprietor, such as overseas, where the technology may need to be adapted or otherwise modified to meet local market conditions
- **To make the widest possible use of the technology** by licensing other applications or by-products of the technology that may be outside the licensor's expertise or targeted markets
- **To avoid or settle actual or pending litigation.** (Many litigants in intellectual-property infringement or misappropriation cases wind up settling cases using some form of a cross-license in lieu of costly attorney's fees and litigation expenses.)

In the typical licensing arrangement, the proprietor of intellectual-property rights (patents, trade secrets, trademarks, and know-how) permits a third party to make use of these rights according to a set of specified conditions and circumstances set forth in a license agreement. Licensing agreements can be limited to a very narrow component of the proprietor's intellectual-property rights, such as one specific application of a single patent. Or agreements can be much broader in context, such as in a classic technology transfer agreement, where an entire bundle of intellectual-property rights are transferred to the licensee, typically in exchange for initial fees and royalties. The classic technology-transfer arrangement is actually more akin to a sale of the intellectual-property rights, with a right by the licensor to get the intellectual property back if the licensee fails to meet its obligations under the agreement.

Tips for the Prospective Technology Licensor

FIND THE RIGHT DANCE PARTNER. Approach your quest for the appropriate licensee with the same zeal and diligence that you would adopt in the search for a marriage partner. Leave no stone unturned, either in narrowing the field of prospective licensees or in the due-diligence process applied to a particular proposed licensee. Before the commencement of the negotiation of the license agreement, carefully examine a potential licensee's goals and objectives, financial strength, and past licensing practices, as well as the qualifications of the licensee's jurisdiction (other states, other countries) and the skills of the licensee's sales and marketing team. Until these criteria have been examined and meet your satisfaction, severely restrict access to your intellectual property.

AVOID THE INFERIORITY COMPLEX. As an entrepreneur looking to license your technology to a larger business, you may face an uphill battle; however, this is not sufficient reason to merely roll over in the licensing negotiations. Too many entrepreneurs who were impressed and intimidated by the larger company's resources and lawyers "sold their souls" at far below the current or eventual market value of the technology. Know the real value of your licensing offer and don't let the bigger, more powerful licensee bully you into a deal you will later regret.

DON'T SHOW YOUR HAND TOO SOON. Many prospective licensors make the mistake of telling too little or saying too much in the initial meetings and negotiations with the prospective licensee. Although finding the right balance of disclosure to

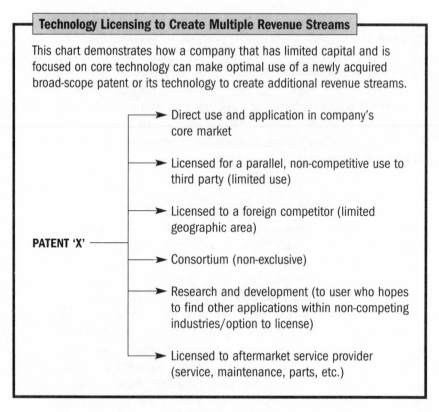

Technology Licensing to Create Multiple Revenue Streams

This chart demonstrates how a company that has limited capital and is focused on core technology can make optimal use of a newly acquired broad-scope patent or its technology to create additional revenue streams.

PATENT 'X'

→ Direct use and application in company's core market

→ Licensed for a parallel, non-competitive use to third party (limited use)

→ Licensed to a foreign competitor (limited geographic area)

→ Consortium (non-exclusive)

→ Research and development (to user who hopes to find other applications within non-competing industries/option to license)

→ Licensed to aftermarket service provider (service, maintenance, parts, etc.)

pique the interest of the licensee without revealing too much is never easy, there is a commonly accepted solution: the licensing memorandum (see the box on pages 456-457). By using this document in tandem with confidentiality agreements, you can provide the prospective licensee with the information it needs to conduct the preliminary analysis without jeopardizing your own rights. The memorandum should contain a discussion of the technology you are offering for license and the portfolio of intellectual-property rights that protect the technology. In addition, include background information on your company, the projected markets and applications of the technology, the proposed terms and financial issues between you and the licensee, and a discussion of existing competitive technology and technological trends that could affect the future value of the license.

BE PREPARED, BECAUSE THINGS CAN AND WILL CHANGE. Like marriages, most licensing agreements are intended to continue over a long period of time. As a result, it is difficult to predict technological, social, economic and political trends that will affect your rights and obligations as well as those of the licensee during the term of the agreement. Licensing agreements, like all legal documents, require a certain degree of precision to be enforceable and workable for the parties; however, they should also include a degree of flexibility and be based on an element of trust to allow for the inevitability of change. Technologies become obsolete, governments get overthrown, rock stars lose popularity, movie sequels flop, and a corporation's personnel may be restructured. Obviously, not every such change in the external environment can be anticipated, nor can every detail be addressed. Therefore, the licensing agreement must be flexible enough to handle unforeseen changes.

Merchandise and Character Licensing

The use of commonly recognized trademarks, brand names, sports teams, athletes, universities, television and film characters, musicians, and designers to foster the sale of specific products and services is at the heart of today's merchandise and character licensing environment. Manufacturers and distributors of products and services license these words, images and symbols for products that range from clothing and housewares to toys and posters. Certain brand names and characters have withstood the test of time, while others have fallen prey to fads, consumer shifts, and stiff competition.

Trademark and copyright owners are motivated to license for a variety of reasons. Aside from the obvious desire to earn royalty fees and profits, many manufacturers view this licensing strategy as a form of merchandising to promote the underlying product or service. The licensing of a trademark for application on a line of clothing helps to establish and reinforce brand awareness at the consumer level. For example, when heavy-equipment manufacturer Caterpiller licensed a shoe and boot manufacturer to produce a line of footwear, the

Outline of a Licensing Memorandum

In most cases, an eight- to ten-page licensing memorandum should accompany the offer letter (or be distributed at, or after, regional informational seminars) and include the following sections:

Introduction or executive summary. This should present a brief overview of the licensor's portfolio of patents and licensing strategy.

Description and brief history of the licensor. The credentials of the licensor and the technology available for licensing should be explained. Because licensing transactions usually involve ongoing and inter-active relationships, an effort should be made here to persuade each prospective licensee that the licensor is interested in a long-term working relationship.

Summary of technology. This should be a short non-technical description that emphasizes the operating and business advantages to the potential licensee, without ignoring possible weaknesses, problems, or further developmental work that may be required before the technology can be expected to generate profits. Technical analyses and illustrations can be provided in annexes to the memorandum. If it is feasible, provide photos or actual samples of the licensed products. In recent years, licensors have also prepared an audio or visual presentation for prospective licensees.

Reference to intellectual-property portfolio. The existence (if any) of patents or pending patent applications in all or part of the proposed licensed territory should be summarized in this section. Copies of any issued patents proposed to be licensed can be annexed to the memorandum for prompt analysis by the patent department of the prospective licensee, thus helping to shorten the time of deliberation. The licensing memorandum should include a professional opinion letter from your patent lawyer regarding the presumed breadth or enforceability of the patents concerned.

It can be expected, however, that any serious prospective licensee will have the key patents evaluated independently, though the focus of the licensors must be on keeping the protectable scope of patents intact. If the possibility exists for a dialogue between the patent advisers, this can help

hope was to build brand awareness, expand its sales base, maintain consumer awareness, and enjoy the royalty income from the sale of the footwear. Manufacturers who use licensing to revive a mature brand or failing product have adopted similar strategies. In certain instances, such as the licensing of reduce the chance of misunderstandings, and perhaps accelerate the discussions between the parties.

Descriptions of the types of know-how possessed by the licensor, as well as the means of making this available to the licensees, should be explained here. The availability of trouble-shooting and consulting services, including the extent to which this can be offered without special charges, should also be discussed.

If trademark licensing is expected to be part of the deal, the condi-tions desired by the licensor should be discussed here. If the mark already possesses goodwill, or is particularly apt or attractive, that should be emphasized, with illustrations provided.

Profits expected from licensed technology. Include a brief cash-flow and profitability analysis of the anticipated business. This might even be hypothecated in three tracks—optimistic, pessimistic, and realistic. These figures will provide a basis for the proposal by the licensor concerning requested payments by the licensee.

Suggested transaction. This is the bottom line of the licensing memorandum. It should constitute a proposed business framework for the transaction, including the already-approved form of the license agreement. The licensor should also indicate terms under which it is prepared to sell to the licensee certain ingredients, components, subassemblies, or models, particularly since this can constitute sources or remuneration to the licensor from the overall relationship, in addition to royalties.

The key points and assumptions underlying the form of the current license agreement and economic terms should also be discussed and analyzed in this section. The licensor should give the impression that it has carefully thought through the structure and that it is not merely "highballing" as a first offer. The degree of the licensor's willingness to consider counter-proposals and alternate ideas should also be addressed.

Formulation of anticipatory licensee concerns with form of current license agreement, and development of negotiating and fallback positions on each key point.

Harley-Davidson merchandise, the spin-off product that has been licensed was almost as financially successful as the underlying product it was intended to promote.

Brand-name owners, celebrities, academic institutions and anyone else who owns a marketable property must be very careful not to grant too many licenses too quickly. Although the financial rewards of a flow of royalty income from hundreds of different manufacturers can be quite seductive, they must be weighed against the possible loss of quality control and dilution of the licensed name, logo, or character. Further, granting too many licenses in closely competing products may create the perception among licensees and retailers that quality control has suffered or that the popularity of the licensed character, celebrity, or image will be short-lived. This may result in smaller orders and an overall unwillingness to carry inventory. This is especially true in the toy industry, where purchasing decisions are being made—or at least influenced—by the whims of children who may strongly identify with a character image one week, then turn to a totally different character image the next week. To convince retailers of the longevity of a product line, manufacturers and licensees must develop advertising and media campaigns to hold the consumer's attention for an extended period of time. To ensure this, the licensing agreement must balance the risks and rewards between licensor and licensee in the areas of compensation to the licensor, advertising expenditures by the licensee, scope of the exclusivity, and quality-control standards and specifications.

In merchandise licensing, the name, logo, symbol or character is typically referred to as the "property," and the specific product or product line (for example, T-shirts, mugs and posters) is referred to as the "licensed product." This area of licensing offers opportunities and benefits to both the owners of the properties and the manufacturers of the licensed products. As the owner of the property, you can strengthen and expand brand recognition, goodwill, and royalty income. For the manufacturer of the licensed products, there is an opportunity to leverage the goodwill of the property to improve sales of the licensed products. The manufacturer has an opportunity to hit the ground running in the sale of merchandise by gaining access to and use of an already established brand name or character image.

Naturally, each party should conduct due diligence on the other. The manufacturer of the licensed product should demonstrate to you an ability to meet and maintain quality-control standards, financial stability, and an aggressive and well-planned marketing and promotional strategy. To the manufacturer of the licensed property, you should display a certain level of integrity and commitment to quality, disclose your future plans for the promotion of the property, and be willing to participate and assist in the overall marketing of the licensed products. For example, say a star basketball player seeks to license his name in connection with a line of basketball shoes. If he is unwilling to appear for promotional events designed to sell the shoes, this would present a major problem and would likely lead to a premature termination of the licensing relationship.

Key Elements of a Licensing Agreement

Once you make the decision to enter into formal licensing negotiations, you and the licensee should have clear communications regarding the terms and conditions of the license agreement (see the sample license agreement that begins on page 465). Naturally these provisions vary, depending on whether the license is for merchandising an entertainment property, exploiting a given technology, or distributing a particular product to an original equipment manufacturer (OEM) or value-added reseller (VAR). As a general rule, any well-drafted license agreement should address the these topics.

DEFINED TERMS. What many entrepreneurs may initially view as "legal boilerplate" is often the most hotly contested component of the license agreement. This initial section of the license agreement is intended to define some of the key aspects of the relationship with respect to the specific field of the technology or merchandise you are licensing. This includes the territory to be covered, the milestones and objectives that the licensee must meet, the specific patents or trademarks that will be included within the scope of the license, and the nature of the compensation you are to receive.

SCOPE OF THE GRANT. The exact scope and subject matter of the license must be initially addressed and clearly defined in the license agreement. Any restrictions on the geographic scope, rights of use, permissible channels of trade, sublicensing, assignability, or improvements to the technology (or expansion of the character line) covered by the agreement should be clearly set forth in this section.

EXCLUSIVITY OF THE LICENSE GRANTED. The term "exclusive" in the context of a license agreement is often misunderstood. Exclusivity could apply to a territory, an application of the technology, or a method of production of the products that result from the technology. Exclusivity may or may not include you and may or may not permit the granting of sublicenses or cross-licenses to future third parties who are not bound by the original license agreement. Exclusivity may or may not be conditioned on the licensee meeting certain predetermined performance standards. Exclusivity may be conditional for a limited time period on the continued employment of certain key technical staff of the licensee. You must discuss all of these issues in the negotiations and ultimately address them in the license agreement.

TERM AND RENEWAL. Include in this section the commencement date, duration, renewals and extensions, conditions to renewal, procedures for providing notice of intent to renew, grounds for termination, obligations upon termination, and your reversionary rights in the technology.

PERFORMANCE STANDARDS AND QUOTAS. To the extent that your consideration will depend on royalty income that will be calculated from the licensee's gross or net revenues, you may want to impose certain minimum levels of performance in terms of sales, advertising, and promotional expenditures and human resources to be devoted to the exploitation of the technology. The licensee will probably argue for a "best efforts" provision that is free from performance standards and quotas. In such cases, you may want to insist on a minimum royalty level that you will receive regardless of the licensee's actual performance.

PAYMENTS TO THE LICENSOR. Virtually every type of license agreement includes some form of initial payment and ongoing royalty to the licensor. Royalty formulas vary widely, however. They may be based on gross sales, net sales, net profits, fixed sum per product sold, or a minimum payment to be made to the licensor over a given period of time. They may also include a sliding scale to provide some incentive to the licensee as a reward for performance.

QUALITY-CONTROL ASSURANCE AND PROTECTION. You must set forth quality-control standards and specifications for the production, marketing, and distribution of the products and services covered by the license. In addition, include in the agreement procedures that allow you an opportunity to enforce these standards and specifications. This might include having the right to inspect the licensee's premises; the right to review, approve, or reject samples produced by the licensee; and the right to review and approve any packaging, labeling, or advertising materials to be used in connection with the exploitation of the products and services that are within the scope of the license.

INSURANCE AND INDEMNIFICATION. Take all necessary and reasonable steps to ensure that the licensee has an obligation to protect and indemnify you against any claims or liabilities resulting from the licensee's exploitation of the products and services covered by the license.

ACCOUNTING, REPORTS, AND AUDITS. You must impose certain reporting and record-keeping procedures on the licensee to ensure an accurate accounting for periodic royalty payments. In a technology-licensing agreement, additional reports should be prepared monthly or quarterly that disclose the licensee's actual use of the technology. The report should also list research studies or market tests that have directly or indirectly used the technology; the marketing, advertising, or public relations strategies planned or implemented that involve the technology; progress reports and timetables regarding the meeting of established performance objectives;

and reports of any threatened or actual infringement or misappropriation of your technology. The report should also disclose any requests for sublicenses or cross-licenses that have been made by third parties to the licensee. Further, reserve the right to audit the records of the licensor in the event of a dispute or discrepancy, and include provisions as to who will be responsible for the cost of the audit in the event of an understatement.

DUTIES TO PRESERVE AND PROTECT INTELLECTUAL PROPERTY. Carefully define the obligations of the licensee, its agents and employees to preserve and protect the confidential nature and acknowledge the ownership of the intellectual property being disclosed in connection with the license agreement. In this section, also describe any required notices or legends that must be included on products or materials distributed in connection with the license agreement (such as the status of the relationship between licensee and licensor or identification of the actual owner of the intellectual property).

TECHNICAL ASSISTANCE, TRAINING, AND SUPPORT. In this section of the agreement include any obligation you have to assist the licensee in the development or exploitation of the subject matter being licensed. Your assistance may take the form of technical and consulting services or access to documents and records. Draft provisions to deal with scheduling conflicts, the payment of travel expenses, the impact of your disability or death, the availability of written or videotaped data in lieu of your physical attendance, the regularity and length of periodic technical support meetings, and the protection of confidential information. Also outline any fees over and above the initial license and ongoing royalty fees you are to be paid for support services you provide.

WARRANTIES OF THE LICENSOR. A prospective licensee may demand that you provide certain representations and warranties in the license agreement. These may include warranties regarding the ownership of the intellectual property, such as absence of any known infringements of the intellectual property or restrictions on the ability to license the intellectual property. The warranties could also include pledging that the technology has the features, capabilities, and characteristics previously represented in the recruitment and initial negotiations.

INFRINGEMENTS. The license agreement should contain procedures under which the licensee must notify you of any known or suspected direct or indirect infringements of the subject matter being licensed. The responsibilities for the cost of protecting and defending the technology should also be specified in this section.

Special Issues Related to Merchandise- and Character-Licensing Agreements

With regard to merchandise and character licensing, the definition of the scope of permitted use is usually accomplished with the use of schedules, illustrations, and exhibits. For example, suppose that as a manufacturer of children's sportswear, you wanted to license the likeness of basketball star Michael Jordan for a new line of clothing. There are a number of issues the agreement can address, such as: Will the property consist of unlimited use of the name and likeness of Mr. Jordan, or will it be only for a specific drawing or caricature of his face? Similarly, will the licensed products be defined as virtually any style or size of children's sportswear or will they be limited to "children's short-sleeved T-shirts up to size 20 and matching children's short pants?" Naturally, there is room for much variation and negotiation in these defined terms. To avoid claims and litigation over unauthorized use of the property, you and the licensee should clearly communicate your intent to your lawyers before preparing the merchandise-licensing agreement.

The key economic issue in the merchandise-licensing agreement is the section dealing with royalty payments that must be paid to you by the licensee in exchange for the use of your property over a period of time. The royalty obligation is usually stated as a fixed percentage of the licensee's sales of the licensed products or as a lump sum per unit of the licensed product. Royalty rates are based purely on market forces and your and your lawyer's negotiation skills as well as those of the licensee and its team. This section must also address the basis for the calculation of the royalty payment (the definition of gross revenues, net sales, etc.). It should also specify any minimum royalty payments that must be paid quarterly or annually by the licensee to the licensor, and any adjustments to the royalty rate that are tied to performance, inflation, a change in market conditions, etc. This section should also deal with royalties on non-cash sales, and the licensee's obligation to prepare reports and statements to support the calculation of the royalty payment.

Sample License Agreement

THIS LICENSE AND DISTRIBUTION AGREEMENT (the "Agreement") is made this _____ day of _____, by and between _____ (the "Licensor"), whose address is _____, and _____ (the "Licensee"), whose address is _____.

WITNESSETH:

WHEREAS, Licensor has developed and currently manufactures, markets and sells food vacuum sealers and related accessories which are primarily marketed to preparers (the "Products") and, in connection therewith, is the owner of U.S. Patent Nos. _____ and _____, patent applications, if any (the "Licensed Patents"), and certain valuable technical information, know-how and data relating to the Products (collectively with the Licensed Patents, the "Product Technology");

WHEREAS, Licensor uses the [unregistered] trademark and such related mark or other marks in marketing the Products, [a portion/all] of which are shown on Exhibit A, attached hereto and incorporated herein by reference (the "Licensed Marks");

WHEREAS, Licensee desires to obtain the exclusive right to use the Product Technology and Licensed Marks in connection with the manufacturing, marketing and selling of food vacuum sealers or any product to which any application of Product Technology may be made by Licensee, which products may be sold for _____ Dollars or less at retail, and related accessories (the "Accessories") primarily for home use (collectively, the "Home Products");

WHEREAS, Licensor desires to license the Product Technology and Licensed Marks to Licensee and allow Licensee to manufacture, market and sell Home Products pursuant to the terms hereof; and

WHEREAS, Licensee desires to license the Product Technology and Licensed Marks from Licensor and manufacture, market and sell Home Products pursuant to the terms hereof.

NOW THEREFORE, in consideration of the foregoing and the mutual covenants and agreements contained herein, the parties hereto agree as follows:

1. GRANT AND ACCEPTANCE OF LICENSE. Subject to the terms and conditions in this Agreement, Licensor hereby grants to Licensee, and Licensee hereby accepts, the exclusive worldwide right and license to use the Product Technology to enable Licensee to

(continued on the next page)

Sample License Agreement (continued)

manufacture, market and sell Home Products in the Licensed Territory during the Term (defined in Section 10 below). Licensor agrees that he shall not use the Product Technology in the manufacture, marketing and sale of Home Products or any competitive product line within the Licensed Territory during the Term, nor shall he grant to any other person or entity a license or other right to so use the Product Technology. Nothing herein shall be construed to limit or prohibit Licensor from manufacturing, marketing and selling Products in the Licensed Territory during the Term. The "Licensed Territory" shall mean the entire world for purposes of this Agreement.

2. TERM OF LICENSE. Unless sooner terminated by the terms of Section 10 hereof, the license granted herein shall continue until the expiration of the Term.

3. TRADEMARK LICENSE. Subject to the terms and conditions of this Agreement, and for so long as Licensee shall have the exclusive right and license to use the Product Technology (as provided in Section 1), Licensor licenses and grants to Licensee the exclusive right and license to use any or all of the Licensed Marks in connection with the marketing of Home Products in the Licensed

Territory; provided, that Licensor retains the right to use the Licensed Marks in connection with the sale of Products (including promotional materials used to promote the Products). Licensee shall have the right to use any trade names or trademarks it deems appropriate in marketing the Home Products and may register in the name of Licensee such trademarks (other than the Licensed Marks) with the U.S. Patent and Trademark Office or any state agency without the approval of Licensor.

4. DISTRIBUTION ARRANGEMENTS. Licensor hereby grants to Licensee the exclusive right to manufacture, market and sell Home Products in the Licensed Territory. In connection therewith, Licensee shall have the right to use the Product Technology and Licensed Marks in accordance with the terms of this Agreement. Licensee agrees to use its reasonable efforts to establish a designated manufacturing facility to manufacture Home Products in commercial quantities, and to promote the sale of the Home Products within the Licensed Territory. In that regard, Licensee shall at its expense and within a reasonable time after the date hereof, begin to develop and carry out a marketing and sales program (which includes the use of direct mail, catalogs, promotional material and television commercials/infomercials) designed to promote sales of Home Products, and exert its reasonable efforts to create, supply and service in the Licensed Territory as many Home Products as is commercially practical; provided, however, nothing contained in this Agreement shall effect or limit Licensee's right to develop, manufacture, distribute, advertise, market and sell any other products and/or services. Licensee shall be solely responsible with regard to establishing a designated manufacturing facility and marketing and sales program and Licensor shall have such responsibility financial or otherwise. Subject to the quality-control standards set forth in Section 6 hereof, Licensee shall have complete control with respect to the manufacturing, marketing and selling of Home Products in the Licensed Territory, including without limitation, the wholesale and retail prices at which Home Products are sold. Licensor agrees to name Licensee as an "Additional Insured" on all policies of insurance having coverage for product liability.

5. ROYALTY PAYMENTS. Licensee agrees to pay Licensor an annual royalty equal to _____ percent (_____ %) [PARTIES TO DISCUSS] of Net Sales generated from the sale of the Home Products exclusive of Accessories. Licensee agrees to pay Licensor an annual royalty payment equal to _____ percent (_____ %) [PARTIES TO DISCUSS] of Net Sales generated from the sale of Accessories. Such royalty shall be paid within sixty (60) days after the end of each calendar year. During the Term of this Agreement, royalty payments shall accrue on a monthly basis. For purposes of this Agreement, Net Sales shall be defined as _____ [PARTIES TO DISCUSS].

6. QUALITY CONTROL.
(a) Standards. Licensee shall insure that all Home Products it distributes (by sale, transfer or otherwise) are manufactured consistent with the reasonable and necessary quality-control standards, if any, established and delivered in writing to Licensee by Licensor.
(b) Inspection. From time to time and upon reasonable prior notice by Licensor, Licensor may request Licensee to submit samples of Home Products manufactured by Licensee or its designee for Licensor's approval, which approval shall not be unreasonably withheld. Unless otherwise approved by Licensor, the quality of all Home Products manufactured, marketed and sold by Licensee pursuant to this Agreement shall be of a quality at least equal to such samples. Licensee agrees to provide Licensor with requested samples

(continued on the next page)

Sample License Agreement (continued)

of Home Products within thirty (30) days after Licensor requests such samples.

7. TECHNICAL ASSISTANCE.

Licensor shall, at his sole expense and at the request of Licensee, provide technical assistance to Licensee or any of its designees during the Term of the Agreement in connection with the use of Product Technology (including, but not by way of limitation, technical assistance relating the manufacture, design and promotion of Home Products). Licensor further agrees to fully assist and cooperate with Licensee in procuring acceptance and listing of Home Products by Underwriters Laboratories Inc. and the Canadian Standards Association. Licensor hereby agrees to provide such technical assistance initially for a minimum of four (4) hours per day until such time as Home Products can be manufactured by Licensee or its designee in commercially reasonable quantities, as determined by Licensee in its sole discretion. Once Home Products are being manufactured in commercially reasonable quantities, Licensor agrees to provide technical assistance as requested by Licensee, including that which is necessary to manufacture, market and sell new products and accessories, and implement developments and improvements relating to the

Products, as provided in Section 8(a) below.

8. NEW TECHNOLOGY.

(a) Licensor's New Products, Accessories, etc. Licensor shall promptly provide and make available to Licensee any information about new products, accessories, developments or improvements relating to the Products. Licensee shall have the right to review and research such information on a confidential basis to determine whether it is reasonably adaptable for use with or application on Home Products for such time as it deems appropriate. Further, Licensee shall have the first right of refusal to license such information from Licensor. Any such information licensed by Licensee shall, for purposes hereof, be included within the meaning of "Product Technology" and thereby subject to the terms of this Agreement.

(b) Licensee's New Products, Accessories, etc. Any new products, accessories, developments or improvements relating to the Home Products that are developed by Licensee or any party with whom Licensee has entered in a contract, agreement or other similar arrangement during the term of this Agreement (the "New Technology") shall remain the property of Licensee. Licensee may determine whether and to what extent it desires to seek trademarks or patents or take other necessary legal steps to protect the New Technology without any interference by Licensor. In the event Licensee shall not seek trademarks or patents or take other necessary legal steps to protect any or all elements of the New Technology, Licensor shall have the right, in his discretion and at his expense, to seek trademarks or patents, or take other legal steps to protect any and all elements of the New Technology. Licensee shall reasonably assist Licensor in seeking such trademarks or patents, or such protection if requested, including securing and execution of trademark or patent applications and other appropriate documents and papers; and Licensor shall pay or reimburse Licensee for all expenses incurred by Licensee in connection with providing such assistance.

9. CLAIMS; INFRINGEMENT.

Licensor represents and warrants that he has full power and authority to grant the license to Licensee as provided herein; the Product Technology and Licensed Marks are free and clear of all liens, claims and encumbrances of any nature whatsoever; and there are no governmental or regulatory proceedings, investigations or other actions pending or concluded that adversely affect the Product Technology or Licensed Marks. Licensor represents and warrants to Licensee that there are no patent, trademark or copyright infringements with respect to the Product Technology or the Licensed Marks, nor are there any threatened, pending or contemplated actions, suits or proceedings against Licensor, or otherwise with respect to the same. No such infringement actions, suits or proceedings would result by reason of the transactions contemplated by this Agreement. Licensor shall promptly notify Licenseer of any allegation or claim that the use of the Product Technology or the Licensed Marks infringes upon the rights of any other person or entity. Licensor agrees to defend Licensee and its directors and officers against any infringement, unfair competition or other claim respecting Licensee's use of the Product Technology or the Licensed Marks. Further, Licensor hereby agrees to indemnify, defend and hold harmless, Licensee and its directors and officers from and against any and all claims or actions, suits, proceedings, damages, liabilities, costs and expenses (including, without limitation, reasonable attorneys' fees) arising out of:

(a) any patent, trademark or copyright infringement by Licensor;

(b) Licensor's unfair competition, misappropriation of confidential information, technology, know-how or trade secrets, and resulting from Licensor's use of the Product

(continued on the next page)

469

Sample License Agreement (continued)

Technology or Licensed Marks; or **(c) otherwise arising by reason** of Licensee's legitimate use of the foregoing in compliance with this Agreement.

10. TERMINATION OF AGREEMENT.

(a) Duration. Unless sooner terminated as otherwise herein provided, the term of this Agreement shall commence upon the date hereof and shall expire on the [_____ (_____)] anniversary of that date (the "Initial Term"). Licensee shall have the right and option to renew this Agreement for term commencing on the day following the Initial Term and expiring on the [_____ (_____)] anniversary of the day following the Initial Term by giving Licensor notice of the exercise of such option at least ten (10) days prior to the end of the Initial Term. The Initial Term, along with such renewal term, if any, shall be referred to herein as the "Term."

(b) Termination by Licensor. In addition to any other right of Licensor contained herein to terminate this Agreement, Licensor shall have the right to terminate this Agreement by written notice to Licensee upon the occurrence of any one or more of the following events:

(i) failure of Licensee to make any payment required pursuant to this Agreement when due; or

(ii) intentional, persistent and material failure of Licensee to comply in any material respect with the quality-control standards required pursuant to Section 6.

(c) Termination by Licensee.

(i) In addition to any other right of Licensee contained herein to terminate this Agreement, Licensee shall have the right to terminate this Agreement by written notice to Licensor upon the occurrence of any one or more of the following events:

(A) the insolvency of Licensor;

(B) the institution of any proceeding by Licensor, voluntarily or involuntarily, under any bankruptcy, insolvency or moratorium law;

(C) any assignment by Licensor of substantially all of his assets for the benefit of creditors;

(D) placement of Licensor's assets in the hands of a trustee or receiver unless the receivership or trust is dissolved within thirty (30) days thereafter; or

(E) any breach by Licensor of any representation, warranty or covenant contained in this Agreement that, if curable, is not cured by Licensor within thirty (30) days after its receipt of written notice thereof from Licensee. If such breach is not cured within such thirty (30) days period, or is not curable, then termination shall be deemed effective on the date of such notice.

(ii) If at any time following the first ____(____) months of the Term,

Licensee determines in good faith that its continued use of Licensor's Product Technology in the manufacture, marketing and sale of Home Products is commercially impracticable by reason of:

(A) a continued failure (after Licensee has exerted its best efforts to overcome such failure) in the performance of Home Products; or

(B) Licensee's inability, after exerting its best efforts, to produce Home Products at its designated manufacturing facility, Licensee may, at its option, terminate this Agreement without further obligation to Licensor (other than payment for accrued royalties, if any) upon thirty (30) days prior written notice to Licensor.

(d) Exercise. Licensor or Licensee, as the case may be, may exercise the right of termination granted hereunder by giving the other party ten (10) days prior written notice of that party's election to terminate and the reason(s) for such termination. After the expiration of such period, this Agreement shall automatically terminate unless the other party has previously cured the breach or condition permitting termination, in which case this Agreement shall not terminate. Such notice and termination shall not prejudice either party's rights to any sums due hereunder and shall not prejudice any cause of action or claim of such party accrued or to accrue on account of any breach or default by the other party.

(e) Failure to Enforce. The failure of either party at any time, or for any period of time, to enforce any of the provisions of this Agreement shall not be construed as a waiver of such provision or of the right of such party thereafter to enforce each and every such provision.

(f) Effect of Termination. Subject to the terms of Section 8 hereof, in the event this Agreement is terminated for any reason whatsoever:

(i) Licensee shall return any plans, drawings, papers, notes, writings and other documents, samples and models pertaining to the Product Technology, retaining no copies, and shall refrain from using or publishing any portion of the Product Technology; and

(ii) Licensor shall return any plans, drawings, papers, notes, writings and other documents, samples and models, retaining no copies, pertaining to New Technology. Upon termination of this Agreement, Licensee shall cease manufacturing, processing, producing, using, selling or distributing Home Products and shall retain no right of any kind to use anywhere in the world the Product Technology or the Licensed Marks; provided, however, that Licensee may continue to sell in the ordinary course of business for a period of one-hundred-eighty (180) days

(continued on the next page)

Sample License Agreement (continued)

after the date of termination reasonable quantities of Home Products which are fully manufactured and in Licensee's normal inventory at the date of termination and Licensee may fulfill all outstanding purchase orders received by Licensee through the date of termination (irrespective of the one-hundred-eighty (180) day period) if all monetary obligations of Licensee to Licensor have been satisfied.

11. INDEPENDENT CONTRACTOR. Licensee's relationship to Licensor hereunder shall be that of a licensee and licensor only. Licensee shall not be the agent of Licensor and shall have no authority to act for or on behalf of Licensor in any matter. Persons retained by Licensee as employees or agents shall not by reason thereof be deemed to be employees or agents of Licensor.

12. COMPLIANCE. Licensee agrees that it will comply in all material respects with all material laws and regulations relating to its manufacture, marketing, selling or distributing of Home Products and its use of Product Technology and the Licensed Marks. Licensor agrees that it will comply in all respects with all federal, state and local laws and regulations relating to the manufacture and distribution of Products and its use of Product

Technology and the Licensed Marks. Licensor will not at any time take any action which would cause Licensee or Licensor to be in violation of any such applicable laws and regulations. Licensor represents and warrants that the Products comply and shall continue to comply with the requirements necessary for acceptance and listing by Underwriters Laboratories Inc. and the Canadian Standards Association.

13. DEFINITIONS. The following terms, whenever used in this Agreement, shall have the respective meanings set forth below.

(a) "Accessories" means accessory products related to the Home Products including, without limitation, bags, canisters, trays, valves and containers.

(b) "Products" means food vacuum sealers and related accessories currently manufactured, marketed and sold by Licensor which are marketed primarily to gourmet-food preparers.

(c) "Home Products" means food vacuum sealers or any product to which, any application of Product Technology may be made by Licensee, which sealers or products may each be sold for _____ Dollars or less at retail, and the Accessories.

(d) "Licensed Patents" means U.S. Patent Nos. _____ and _____, and patent applications related to the Products, if any, owned by Licensor.

(e) "Licensed Marks" means the [unregistered] trademark and such related mark or other marks used by Licensor in marketing the Products, [a portion/all] of which are shown on Exhibit A, attached hereto and incorporated herein by reference.

(f) "Product Technology" means, subject to Section 8(a) hereof, the Licensed Patents and certain valuable technical information, know-how and data of Licensor relating to the Products.

14. GENERAL AND MISCELLANEOUS.

(a) Governing Law. This Agreement and all amendments, modifications, alterations, or supplements hereto, and the rights of the parties hereunder, shall be construed under and governed by the laws of the State of New York and the United States of America.

(b) Interpretation. The parties are equally responsible for the preparation of this Agreement and in any judicial proceeding the terms hereof shall not be more strictly construed against one party than the other.

(c) Place of Execution. This Agreement and any subsequent modifications or amendments hereto shall be deemed to have been executed in the State of New York.

(d) Notices. Any notice herein required or permitted to be given, or waiver of any provision hereof, shall be effective only if given or made in writing. Notices shall be deemed to have been given on the date of delivery if delivered by hand, or upon the expiration of five (5) days after deposit in the United States mail, registered or certified, postage prepaid, and addressed to the respective parties at the addresses specified in the preamble of this Agreement. Any party hereto may change the address to which notices to such party are to be sent by giving notice to the other party at the address and in the manner provided above. Any notice herein required or permitted to be given may be given, in addition to the manner set forth above, by telecopier, telex, TWX, or cable, provided that the party giving such notice obtains acknowledgement by telecopier, telex, TWX or cable that such notice has been received by the party to be notified. Notice made in this manner shall be deemed to have been given when such acknowledgement has been transmitted.

(e) Assignments. Licensor shall not grant, transfer, convey, sublicense, or otherwise assign any of his rights or delegate any of his obligations under this Agreement without the prior written consent of Licensor. Licensee shall have the right to freely grant, transfer,

(continued on the next page)

Sample License Agreement (continued)

convey, sublicense, or otherwise assign any of its rights or delegate any of its obligations under this Agreement.

(f) Entire Agreement. This Agreement constitutes the entire agreement between Licensor and Licensee with respect to the subject matter hereof and shall not be modified, amended or terminated except as herein provided or except by another agreement in writing executed by the parties hereto.

(g) Headings. The Section headings are for convenience only and are not a part of this Agreement.

(h) Severability. All rights and restrictions contained herein may be exercised and shall be applicable and binding only to the extent that they do not violate any applicable laws and are intended to be limited to the extent necessary so that they will not render this Agreement illegal, invalid or unenforceable. If any provision or portion of any provision of this Agreement not essential to the commercial purpose of this Agreement shall be held to be illegal, invalid or unenforceable by a court of competent jurisdiction, it is the intention of the parties that the remaining provisions or portions thereof shall constitute their agreement with respect to the subject matter hereof, and all such remaining provisions or portions thereof shall remain in full force and effect.

(i) Survival of Representations and Warranties. The parties hereto agree that all representations and warranties of Licensor contained herein shall survive the expiration or termination of this Agreement, and shall continue to be binding on the parties without limitation.

(j) Attorneys' Fees, etc. In the event either party brings any action, suit or proceeding against the other party to enforce any right or entitlement which it may have under this Agreement, either party shall, to the extent it is successful in pursuing or defending the action, and in addition to all other rights or remedies available to it in law or in equity, be entitled to recover its reasonable attorneys' fees and court costs incurred in such action.

IN WITNESS WHEREOF, the parties hereto have executed this License and Distribution Agreement as of the day and year set forth above.

Witness:

_____

"Licensor"

_____

"Licensee"

_____

Exhibit A
Licensed Marks

Growth Through Joint Ventures and Strategic Alliances

P ARTNERING RELATIONSHIPS WHEREBY TWO OR MORE companies work together to achieve a specific purpose or toward the attainment of common business objectives can be a successful growth strategy for fast-track growth companies. Joint ventures and strategic partnerships are frequently designed to obtain one or more of the following:

■ **direct capital infusion in exchange** for equity and/or intellectual property or distribution rights;

■ **a "capital substitute,"** by which the resources that would otherwise be obtained with the capital are obtained through joint venturing;

■ **a shift of the burden and cost** of new-product development (through licensing) in exchange for a potentially more limited upside;

■ **an entry strategy** into new domestic or overseas markets through partnering or joint ventures;

■ **distribution and commercialization** (particularly between defense and government contractors looking for new applications and markets for products initially developed for the military and government sectors); and

■ **financial savings** through sharing the risks and the costs of commercialization, marketing, distribution, and other expenses.

The participants to these partnering agreements could be at various points in the value chain or distribution channel. For example, agreements can be made by and among direct or potential competitors. This would allow them to cooperate rather than compete, either as a precursor to a merger or to join forces to fend off an even larger competitor. Or parallel producers might join forces to widen or integrate product lines. Parties linked at different points in the vertical-distribution channel might form an alliance (perhaps to achieve distribution efficiencies).

When structuring these relationships, it is important to consider the respective position of each party. Typically, a relationship can fit into one of the following categories:

- **In Goliath/Goliath partnering transactions,** two very large companies get together to co-market or cross-promote each other's brands, either to capture more customers or to achieve certain efficiencies. An example would be two major airlines serving different primary geographic routes honoring each other's frequent flier programs, or McDonald's promoting a new Disney film by offering licensed toys with the purchase of a kid's meal. Such arrangements are negotiated with parallel leverage and are not the focus of this book.

- **In David/David partnering relationships,** two small companies, both with limited resources, come together to create synergies from each other's strengths on a peer-to-peer basis, to achieve a defined business purpose or set of objectives. An example might be two small government contractors with complementary skills entering into a team agreement to jointly bid on a new government Request for Proposal (RFP) that neither could qualify for on a standalone basis. The key to peer-to-peer partnering relationships is for both parties to avoid greed and structure the agreement so that both parties' objectives will be met and their respective rewards will be parallel to their efforts and assumption of risk.

- **In David/Goliath partnering relationships,** a small company partners with a much larger strategic ally, which may be a large domestic corporation, a foreign conglomerate or even a university or government agency looking to commercialize a given technology. In recent years, the mindset of the typical entrepreneur has shifted dramatically. Where at one time entrepreneurs feared partnering with larger companies because of concern about giving up control, now entrepreneurs actively seek alliances with bigger, more powerful companies because of the credibility boost, technology leveraging and access to markets that a larger player is likely to bring to the table. An alliance with a Goliath may also be a powerful boost to employee morale as well as a help for recruiting new employees and attracting new investors. However, in your search for a strategic alliance, avoid merely "running around and collecting cool logos to include in your PowerPoint presentation," as Michael Provance of ASAP Ventures puts it. In other words, such strategic relationships must entail more than just piggy-backing on a more established brand and reputation; they must eventually lead to new technologies, new customers, increases in market share, revenues and profits and increases in shareholder value, measurable against clearly established benchmarks. Otherwise, such relationships are excess strategic baggage that should be unloaded as soon as possible, especially if they are not working and especially if they are standing in the way of your ability to establish more productive ones.

Strategic relationships must entail more than just piggy-backing on a more established brand and reputation.

■ **In value webs/federations there are multiple participants** to the joint venture or strategic alliance, each maintaining its operational and ownership autonomy, but all coming together to share resources, distribution channels or costs in some way to increase revenues or reduce expenses. The alignment of shared interests may be very broad in scope (such as in the airlines or telecommunications industries) or very narrow (such as joint teaming for a specific project, cooperative advertising or a shared Web site). In emerging-technology industries, value webs may be created by five or six companies who each bring a technical component or solution to the table to meet a customer's (or series of customers) real or perceived needs.

Understanding Joint Ventures and Strategic Alliances

With technology developing rapidly, competition becoming more intense, business operations becoming more global in nature and industry convergence taking place on a number of different fronts, the number and the pace of deal-making between companies of all sizes is likely to increase over the next few years. Thus, combining and sharing core competencies and resources within a structure where autonomy can be preserved must be a key component in any fast-growing company's business strategy.

Although joint ventures and strategic alliances may seem to be different names for the same type of business arrangement, there are differences.

- **Joint ventures are typically structured as a partnership** or as a newly formed and co-owned corporation where two or more parties come together to achieve a series of strategic and financial objectives on either a medium-term or a long-term basis. The scale and scope of these relationships is usually more complex and larger in nature, such as to join forces in a global economy to create international barriers to entry by others. When considering a joint venture as a growth strategy, give careful thought to the type of partner you are looking for and what resources you and the partner will be contributing to the newly formed entity. Just as in raising a child, each parent will be making their respective contribution of skills, abilities and resources.

- **Strategic alliances include any number of collaborative working relationships** where no formal joint venture entity is formed but where two independent companies become interdependent by entering into a formal or informal agreement built on a platform of mutual objectives, strategies, risks and rewards. These relationships are commonly referred to as teaming, design-collaboration agreements, joint research and development agreements, strategic partnering, alliances, Web-linking agreements, joint marketing and promotional agreements, cross-licensing, outsourcing, and co-branding. They are typically more focused on market efficiencies, joint efforts to acquire or develop customer relationships or remain competitive in an intense marketplace.

Regardless of the specific structure, the underlying industry or even the actual purpose of the strategic relationship, all successful joint venture and strategic-alliance relationships share a common set of essential success factors, including:

- **a complementary unified force** or purpose that bonds the companies together;
- **a management team** committed to the success of the venture;
- **a genuine synergy,** in which the "sum of the whole truly exceeds its individual parts";
- **a cooperative culture and spirit** between the strategic partners that leads to trust, resource-sharing and a friendly chemistry between the parties;
- **a degree of flexibility** in the objectives of the joint venture to allow for changes in the marketplace and an evolution of technology;
- **an alignment of management styles** and operational methods, at least to the extent that they affect the underlying project; and
- **focus and leadership** from all key parties necessary to the success of the new venture or business enterprise.

The benefits of strategic alliances and joint ventures are many, and can include:

- **developing new markets** (domestic/international);
- **developing new products** (research and development);
- **developing and sharing technology;**
- **combining complementary technology;**
- **pooling resources** to develop a production/distribution facility;
- **acquiring capital;**
- **executing government contracts;** and
- **access to new distribution channels** or networks or sales and marketing capability.

Finding the Right Partner
In reviewing possible candidates for a strategic alliance or joint venture, conduct a thorough review of all candidates you are

Tips for Structuring Strategic Relationships

- **Include middle-level management** and technical personnel, who will ultimately be responsible for the success or failure of the relationship, in the goal-making process.
- **Consider the impact of the deal** on other potential alliance partners. Don't get yourself into an overly oppressive exclusive relationship unless you are prepared for that level of fidelity. Keep your eyes and ears open for other opportunities.
- **Start the planning process** before signing the definitive documents.
- **Understand the impact of the deal** on customers and vendors. How will customers and vendors perceive this alliance or joint venture? Will they be forced to shift relationships? Will they be willing to do so? What is in it for them?
- **Take steps to establish mutual trust** and respect and balance the sharing of risks and rewards.
- **Be sensitive to your partner's needs** and attitudes.
- **Avoid overly aggressive timetable** that only lead to frustration and disappointment.
- **Be sure to understand** how your employees and shareholders will view the alliance. Will it have a positive impact on morale? Shareholder value?
- **Clearly address the responsibilities** and contributions of each party and identify systems and procedures to create account-

considering and extensive due diligence on final candidates. Develop a list of key objectives and goals to be achieved by the relationship, and compare this list with those of your final candidates. Take the time to understand the corporate culture and decision-making process within each company, and consider the following issues:

- **What are your specific expectations for this relationship?** Does the party with whom you are negotiating have the authority to make the commitment of resources to meet these expectations? Or do you need to go higher up?
- **How does this fit with your own processes?**
- **What is each prospective partner's previous experience** and track record in other joint-venture relationships?
- **Why did these previous relationships succeed or fail?**
- **What level of fidelity will be expected of you?** Will you have the

ability and consequences for failure to meet responsibilities.

■ **Develop an agreement** that includes provisions for resolving conflicts. The agreement should also include enough flexibility to allow the relationship to evolve and adapt to new challenges and shifts in market conditions.

■ **Avoid ambiguous goals** that could result in uncoordinated activities and confusion among employees who are on the front line trying to make the venture succeed.

■ **Commit to making the relationship work.** Adjust your management style if necessary for the success of the venture, and expect the same from your venture partner.

■ **Select a legal structure** that clearly fits with the operational objectives of the partnering arrangement.

■ **If the relationship is no longer working,** don't be afraid to bring it to a prompt end.

■ **Make alliances** and partnering relationships a core part of your business-growth strategy, not just random events. Do them often. Do them right. The more experience a fast-track growing company can gather by seeking out partnering relationships, the greater the chances of success.

■ **Strive for a true sense** of partnership, rather than a sense of superiority, in order to learn and profit from what each partner has to offer.

ability to partner with other companies? Under what terms and conditions?

Frequently, a small company (David) looking for a joint-venture partner selects a much larger company (Goliath) that offers ready capital, research-and-development capabilities, personnel, distribution channels and general contacts that the small company desperately needs. For the larger company, the motivation in such a relationship lies in getting access and distribution rights to new technologies, products and services. But before committing to any relationship, consider all the factors at play and all their implications. Be sensitive to the politics, red tape and management practices that may be in place at a large company that may be foreign to your smaller firm. Try to distinguish between what the big

Joint Ventures Versus Strategic Alliances

	JOINT VENTURES	STRATEGIC ALLIANCES
Term	Usually medium- to long- term	Short term
Strategic Objective	Often serves as a precursor to a merger	More flexible and non-committal
Legal Agreements and Structure	Actual legal entity formed	Contractually driven
Extent of Commitment	Shared equity	Shared objectives
Capital Resources	Each party makes a capital contribution of cash or intangible assets	No specific capital contributions (may be shared budgeting or even cross-investment)
Tax Ramifications	Risk of double taxation unless pass-through entities utilized	No direct tax ramifications

company is promising and what it will actually deliver. If your primary motivation is capital, then consider whether alternative (and perhaps less costly) sources of money may be a better solution for your company's needs. If your primary motivation is access to technical personnel, consider whether it might be more prudent to purchase these resources separately rather than enter into a partnership in which you may have to sacrifice a certain measure of control. Also, consider whether strategic relationships or extended-payment terms with vendors and consultants can be arranged in lieu of the joint venture.

Drafting a Memorandum of Understanding for Joint Ventures and Strategic Alliances

When you believe you have found the right partner, it is very beneficial to both parties to draft a memorandum of understanding before you draft the definitive joint-venture or alliance agreement. The memorandum of understanding should state all critical points of the relationship and provide both parties' legal advisers with a starting point for the preparation of the formal agreements. The memorandum of understanding should address the following topics.

SPIRIT AND PURPOSE OF THE AGREEMENT. This section should outline the reasons why the partnering arrangement is being considered and what its perceived mission and objectives are. It should also describe the strategic and financial desires of the participants and provide "operating principles" that will engender communication and trust.

SCOPE OF ACTIVITY. This section should identify the products, services, buildings, or other specific projects that will be included and excluded from the venture; target markets (i.e. regions, user groups, etc.) for the venture; and any markets to be excluded or to remain the domain of one of the partners. If the venture has purchase and supply provisions, state that the newly formed entity or arrangement will purchase or supply specific products, services, or resources from or to the owners.

KEY OBJECTIVES AND RESPONSIBILITIES. In this section, clarify and specify objectives and targets to be achieved by the relationship; when these objectives are expected to be achieved; any major obstacles that are anticipated; and the point at which the alliance will be self-supporting, be bought out, or terminated. Each participant should designate a project manager who will be responsible for its company's day-to-day involvement in the alliance. If a separate detached organization will be created, designate the key persons to be assigned to the venture. Outline responsibili-

---

An Exception to the Rule . . . With an Unhappy Ending

Although most strategic alliances are short- to medium-term in length, the nearly 100-year strategic alliance between Ford Motor Company and Bridgestone/Firestone came to an end with some very public and high profile finger-pointing over liability issues in SUVs.

The strategic alliance can be traced back to the friendship of Henry Ford and Harvey Firestone and was bolstered over the years by the intermarriage of their descendents.

Many lessons can be learned from this breakup, including the risks of associating two products so closely in the minds of consumers, which can make a subsequent divorce very confusing to the customer and damaging to the goodwill of both partners. It also makes things difficult when the cross-marketed products and services create injury—as with the Ford Explorers equipped with Firestone tires that lead to an abrupt end to the long-standing relationship.

Similar challenges to long-standing strategic relationships include the Dow Chemical and Corning Glass Works joint venture that was launched in 1943 and is now in bankruptcy due to the breast-implant litigation that crippled the jointly owned company in the mid '90s. But Corning's commitment to alliances remains strong—they have entered into more than 40 different significant joint ventures and alliances, creating high-profile and long-standing companies such as Owens Corning, Samsung Corning and Pittsburgh-Corning.

Another more recent but very strong alliance that seems likely to last is the relationship between Intel and Microsoft that cross-markets each other's products and closely collaborates on product compatibility.

---

ties to make it clear to all partners who will be doing what.

METHOD FOR DECISION-MAKING. Each partnering relationship will have its own unique decision-making process. This section of the memorandum should describe who is expected to have the authority to make what types of decisions in what circumstances, who reports to whom, etc. Clearly designate if one company will have operating control.

RESOURCE COMMITMENTS. Most partnering relationships involve the commitment of specific financial resources (such as cash, equity, staged payments or loan guarantees) for the achievement of the ultimate goals. Other "soft" resources may be in the form of licenses, knowledge, R&D, a sales force, contracts, production, facilities, inventory, raw materials, engineering drawings, management staff, access to capital, the devotion of specific personnel for a certain percentage of their time, etc. If possible, these "soft" resources should be quantified with a financial figure so that a monetary value can be affixed and valued along with the cash commitments to this internal commitment. In some circumstances, the purchase of buildings, materials, consultants, advertising, and so forth will require capital. Itemize these external costs and allocate them between the partners using an ageed-upon formula. Note if any borrowing, entry into equity markets (public offerings, private placements, etc.) or purchase of stock in one of the partners is anticipated. In anticipation of additional equity infusions, the partners should agree about their own ability to fund the overruns, or enable the venture to seek other outside sources. Address the manner of handling cost overruns. If applicable, mention pricing and costing procedures.

ASSUMPTION OF RISKS AND DIVISION OF REWARDS. This section should answer questions such as: What are the perceived risks? How will they be handled and who will be responsible for problem-solving and risk assumption? What are the expected rewards (new product, new market, cash flow, technology, etc.)? How will the profits be divided?

RIGHTS AND EXCLUSIONS. Issues to be addressed here include: Who has rights to products and inventions? Who has rights to distribute the products, services, technologies, etc.? Who gets the licensing rights? If the confidentiality and non-competition agreements have not yet been drafted in final form, address them in basic form here. Otherwise, if the other agreements have been signed, simply make reference to them.

ANTICIPATED STRUCTURE. This section of the memorandum of understanding should describe the intended structure (written contract, corporation, partnership, or equity investment).

Regardless of the legal form, if possible, spell out the terms, percentages or formulas for exchange of stock. Address, at least at a preliminary level, default provisions and procedures.

Structuring the Joint Venture

Unlike franchising, distributorships and licensing, which are almost always vertical in nature, joint ventures and strategic alliances are structured at either horizontal or vertical levels of distribution. While there is no way to structure a strategic alliance, which is governed only by an agreement, joint ventures are, in fact, a legal entity. At the horizontal level, the joint venture is often the first step or precursor to a merger. Two companies that operate at the same level in the distribution channel join together (either by means of a partnership-type agreement or by joint ownership of a specially created corporation) to achieve certain synergies or operating efficiencies. Consider the following key strategic issues before and during joint-venture negotiations:

- **Exactly what types of tangible and intangible assets** will each party contribute to the joint venture? Who will have ownership rights in the property contributed during the term of the joint venture and thereafter? Who will own property developed as a result of joint development efforts?

- **What covenants of nondisclosure or non-competition** will be expected of each party during the term of the agreement and thereafter?

- **What timetables or performance quotas** for completion of the projects contemplated by the joint venture will be included in the agreement? What are each party's rights and remedies if these performance standards are not met?

- **How will management and control issues be addressed** in the agreement? What will be the respective voting rights of each party? What are the procedures in the event of a major disagreement or deadlock? What is the fallback plan?

Once you and your prospective partner have clearly resolved these issues, you can proceed with the preparation of a formal joint-venture agreement or corporate shareholders agreement with the assistance of counsel

Structuring the Agreement

The precise terms of the agreement necessary for your joint venture will depend on the nature and the structure of the arrangement. At a minimum, however, address the following topics in as much detail as possible.

NATURE, PURPOSE, AND TRADE NAME FOR THE JOINT VENTURE. Set forth the legal nature of the relationship between the parties, along with a clear statement of purpose to prevent future disputes as to the scope of the arrangement. If a new trade name is established for the venture, make provisions regarding the use of the name and any other trade or service marks registered by the venture on termination of the entity or project.

STATUS OF THE RESPECTIVE JOINT VENTURERS. Clearly indicate in the agreement whether each party is a partner, shareholder, agent, independent contractor, or any combination thereof. Agent status, whether actual or imputed, can greatly affect liability between the venturers and with regard to third parties.

REPRESENTATIONS AND WARRANTIES OF EACH JOINT VENTURER. Standard representations and warranties will include obligations of due care and due diligence as well as mutual covenants governing confidentiality and anti-competition restrictions.

CAPITAL AND PROPERTY CONTRIBUTIONS OF EACH JOINT VENTURER. Establish a clear schedule of all contributions, whether in the form of cash, shares, real estate, or intellectual property. Detailed descriptions are particularly important if the distribution of profits and losses is to be based upon overall contribution. Also, clearly define the specifics of allocation and distribution of profits and losses among the venturers.

MANAGEMENT, CONTROL, AND VOTING RIGHTS OF EACH JOINT VENTURER. If the proposed venture envisions joint management, it is necessary to specifically address the keeping of books, records, and bank accounts; the nature and frequency of inspections and audits; insurance and cross indemnification obligations; and responsibility for administrative and overhead expenses.

RIGHTS IN JOINT-VENTURE PROPERTY. Growing companies should be especially mindful of intellectual-property rights and should clearly address the issues of ownership, use and licensing entitlements, not only for the venturers' presently existing property rights, but also for future use of rights (or products or services) developed in the name of the venture itself.

RESTRICTIONS ON TRANSFERABILITY OF OWNERSHIP INTEREST IN THE JOINT VENTURE. Place stringent conditions on the ability of the venturers to transfer interests in the venture to third parties.

DEFAULT, DISSOLUTION, AND TERMINATION OF THE JOINT VENTURE. Clearly define the obligations of the venturers and the distribution assets, along with procedures in the event of bankruptcy and grounds for default. It is critical to plan for the separation—even before you get married!

DISPUTE-RESOLUTION PROCEDURES. The parties may wish to consider arbitration as an alternative mechanism for dispute resolution.

MISCELLANEOUS. Make provisions indicating the governing law, remedies under force majeure situations, procedures for notice and consent, and the ability to modify or waive certain provisions.

Co-Branding and Cross-Licensing as Types of Strategic Alliances

Co-branding has emerged as a very popular type of strategic alliance. At the heart of the relationship, two or more established brands are paired and positioned in the marketplace to bring added value, economies of scale and synergistic customer recognition and loyalty to increase sales for both partners and create differentiation from the competition. Co-branding has appeared in many different forms.

FINANCIAL-SERVICES CO-BRANDING. In the early 1990s, credit-card companies pioneered co-branding with airlines and telecommunications companies for shared rewards.

CONSUMER-PRODUCT INGREDIENT CO-BRANDING. In this type of arrangement, one brand appears as an ingredient in another brand as a way of enhancing the second brand's image and increasing sales and consumer loyalty for both brands. Familiar examples of this include Post using Sun-Maid raisins in its Raisin Bran cereal, Archway using Kellogg's All-Bran in its cookies, Ben & Jerry's Heath Bar Crunch ice cream, and Pop-Tarts with Smucker's fruit fillings.

IMPLIED-ENDORSEMENT CO-BRANDING. Unlike consumer-product ingredient co-branding, here the co-branded name or logo is used to build consumer recognition, even if there is no actual ingredient used in the product. Examples include the use of the John Deere logo on the back of a Florsheim boot and the Pizza Hut logo on the Doritos Pizza Craver tortilla chips.

ACTUAL COMPOSITE CO-BRANDING. In this case, the co-branded product actually uses a branded pairing of popular manufacturing techniques or processes, as is the case with Timberland boots made with Gore-Tex fabric, furniture with Scotchgard protectants, and Dell or Gateway computers with Intel inside.

DESIGNER-DRIVEN CO-BRANDED PRODUCTS. Certain manufacturers have co-branded with well known designers to increase consumer loyalty and brand awareness. The Eddie Bauer edition of the Ford Explorer is an example of this co-branding approach.

RETAIL-BUSINESS FORMAT CO-BRANDING. This type of co-brand-

Advantages and Disadvantages of Co-Branding and Cross-Licensing

ADVANTAGES

- **Alliances may allow for cost-sharing,** for such things as marketing and packaging or (if in the same location) rent and utilities.
- **Opportunity may exist to expand** into international markets.
- **Brand recognition can be established in foreign markets;** opportunity exists to offer value to a foreign company by co-branding with your American product.
- **For retail establishments,** added conveniences for customers can increase traffic and revenues for both companies.

DISADVANTAGES

- **It can be difficult to build consensus** between partners.
- **Marketing has to be agreed upon by both parties,** resulting in loss of timeliness in marketing and loss of flexibility.
- **Bad publicity for one company** can affect the other.
- **If one brand fails to live up to its promises,** the co-branding or cross-licensing relationship can dissolve.
- **If the co-branding** or cross-licensing attempts are a failure, consumers may become confused about new products, resulting in diminished perceived value for both companies' products.

ing is growing rapidly within the retailing, hospitality and franchising communities. Companies come together for the purpose of attracting additional customers and creating complementary product lines to appeal to different consumer tastes or consuming patterns and to sell additional products or services to a "captured customer." The pairing up of Baskin-Robbins and Dunkin' Donuts and the combination of fast-food restaurants and gas stations are examples of this type of co-branding.

Campaigns and strategies to build brand recognition, brand loyalty and brand equity have been launched by thousands of companies that recognize that a well-established brand can be the single most-valuable asset on the balance sheet. Companies with strong quality-oriented brands (as well as professional sports teams, athletes and celebrities) have sought to create new sources of revenue and leverage their largest intangible asset—their reputation—to add to the strength of their income statements. This new focus on brand value has set the stage for a wide variety of co-branding and brand-extension licensing transactions. Some of these transactions have proved to be natural extensions of the brand. For example, the licensing of the Starbucks name for a limited line of ice creams, Sunkist for orange soda or Hershey's for chocolate milk were brand-extension licensing projects that have all been very successful and allowed the owners of the trademarks to enjoy instant entry into a new industry with minimal capital investment or market research.

The brand on a standalone basis must represent an attitude or a feeling or a cachet that is not weakened when it is applied to another product.

The ability to penetrate new markets, generate new income streams, build the value of the company's brand name, and increase overall brand awareness has made co-branding a very viable and profitable strategy for companies. However, the temptation to extend the equity and value of your brand into other areas poses certain risks. There are quality-control issues, the risk of over-branding or misbranding from a consumer perspective and product-liability issues. The key to successful brand extension is that the brand itself must stand for something greater than the original product and that the consumer's perception of the extended brand is a natural one.

The brand on a standalone basis must represent an attitude or a feeling or cachet that is not weakened when it is applied to another product. It worked well when the Gap extended its brand by licensing perfume and when Calvin Klein licensed its brand for eye wear, but backfired for Harley-Davidson when it extended its brand by awarding a license for a line of cigarettes. Although the extension seemed natural, consumers were not convinced that the motorcycle manufacturers had a brand that would lend quality and value to a pack of smokes, no more than you would show loyalty to a Hershey's chocolate brand of cosmetics.

Even non-licensed extensions of brand that would seem to be a home run have failed due to inadequate market research. For example, when American consumers started eating more chicken than beef, A.1. steak sauce launched a poultry sauce that did very poorly, notwithstanding a multimillion-dollar advertising budget. Researchers missed the fact that in consumers' minds the A.1. brand had been associated with steak and not necessarily with sauce in general. Yet other brand-extension licensing deals have succeeded in spite of seemingly flawed logic. One might think that the last thing anyone wants to smell like is a sweaty basketball player, yet the Michael Jordan line of men's cologne has sold reasonably well. This superstar's cachet has transcended what would otherwise be an unattractive licensing feature.

In developing an effective brand-extension licensing program, make the following essential components a key part of your strategy.

- **Discipline.** Avoid the temptation to overbrand. A key part of brand management is determining your "zone of appropriateness" and figuring out what your brand does not represent. This can be even more important than understanding what it *does* represent.
- **Market research.** It is critical to really understand your customers and their reasons for being loyal to your brand. A clear understanding of the source of that loyalty will lead to natural zones of expansion into other products and services.
- **Due diligence.** It is equally critical to select brand-extension licensees who have a strong reputation in their underlying industry and the resources to execute a well-written market-development plan.
- **Quality control.** You must take a proactive role in maintaining and enforcing quality-control standards in the manufacturing and distribution of your branded products or services. This includes not only direct quality issues but also indirect issues, such as the distribution channels selected by your branding partner and the nature of its advertising and marketing campaigns, etc.

If you understand why consumers have an affinity toward your brand and if consumers' trust is not violated or misinterpreted, you can build brand awareness and brand equity through an effectively managed brand-extension program.

Other Growth Strategies

Traditional joint-venture deals, strategic alliances and co-branding deals are not the only ways for a business to get on the fast track. These business arrangements also have direct as well as distant cousins; one or more may be worth using to grow your business.

Distributorships and Dealerships

Many growing product-oriented companies choose to bring their wares to the marketplace through independent third-party distributors and dealerships. Manufacturers of electronic and stereo equipment, computer hardware and software, sporting goods, medical equipment, and automobile parts and accessories commonly use this type of arrangement.

In a distributorship arrangement, a distributor typically buys the product from your company, at wholesale prices, with title passing to the distributor when payment is received. The distributor does not have to pay a fee for the grant of the distributorship and is typically permitted to carry competitive products. The distributor is expected to maintain some retail location or showroom where your products are displayed. The distributor must also maintain its own inventory storage and warehousing capabilities and provide in-store and local promotion, adequate inventory controls, financial stability, preferred display and stocking, prompt payment, and qualified sales personnel. You are typically obligated to provide technical support; advertising contributions; supportive repair, maintenance, and service policies; new-product training; volume discounts; favorable payment and return policies; and brand-name recognition. Although the distributorship network offers a viable alternative to franchising, it is not a panacea. The management and control of distributors may be even more difficult than that involved in franchising (especially without the benefit of a comprehensive franchise agreement) and many state anti-termination statutes regulate the termination of these relationships.

In developing distributor and dealership agreements, be careful to avoid inclusion within the broad definition of a franchise under FTC Rule 436, which would require the preparation of a disclosure document. To avoid such a classification, impose minimal controls over the dealer in your agreement,; the sale of products must be at bona fide wholesale prices, and your assistance in the marketing or management of the dealer's business must be minimal. A well-drafted distributorship agreement should address the following key issues:

- **What is the scope of the agreement?** Which products is the dealer authorized to distribute and under what conditions? What is the scope, if any, of the exclusive territory to be granted to the distributor? To what extent will product, vendor, customer, or geographic restrictions be applicable?
- **What activities will the distributor be expected to perform** in terms of manufacturing, sales, marketing, display, billing, market research, maintenance of books and records, storage, training, installation, support, and servicing?
- **What obligations will the distributor have to preserve** and protect your intellectual property?
- **What right, if any, will the distributor have to modify** or enhance your warranties, terms of sale, credit policies, or refund procedures?
- **What advertising literature, technical** and marketing support, training seminars, or special promotions will you provide to enhance the performance of the distributor?
- **What sales or performance quotas** will you impose on the dealer as a condition to its right to continue to distribute your products or services? What are your rights and remedies if the dealer fails to meet these performance standards?
- **What is the term of the agreement** and under what conditions can it be terminated? How will post-termination transactions be handled?

Cooperatives

A cooperative (co-op) is an association of member companies in the same or similar industries. It is essentially a business owned and controlled by the people who use its services and who finance and operate the business for their mutual benefit. By working together, they can reach an objective unattainable by acting alone. These mutually beneficial services can include obtaining production supplies, processing and marketing member products, or providing functions related to purchasing, marketing or providing a service. The co-op may be the vehicle to obtain services otherwise unavailable or that are more beneficial to members. The underlying function of the co-op is to increase member income or in other ways enhance members' way of living. A co-op may or may not be incorporated and may or may not have its own staff or operate independently from its constituent members. There is typically a common trade identity that each independent member may use in its advertising and promotion; however, ownership of the actual trademarks rests with the cooperative itself. The following are the four most basic operating characteristics of a co-op.

SERVICE AT-COST. The purpose of a co-op is to provide a service to its user-owners at the lowest possible cost, rather than generate a profit for investors. However, the co-op must generate income sufficient to cover all administrative costs and meet continuing capital needs. Because many costs cannot be absolutely determined before year-end, it is important for a co-op to charge competitive market prices, or fees for services, and then determine its at-cost basis at year-end.

FINANCIAL OBLIGATION AND BENEFITS PROPORTIONAL TO USE. Financial obligations and benefits are tied to use rather than to the amount of investment. Most co-ops' bylaws provide a system of returning capital contributions to maintain proportionality on a current basis. The bylaws should also include a provision that establishes the co-op's obligation to return net margins (total income from all sources, minus expenses) to patrons. When the net margin is returned to members based on their use of the co-op, it is called a patronage refund.

DEMOCRATIC CONTROL. Control is vested with the voting membership, either on an equal basis or according to use, rather than based on the amount of stock each member holds. Democratic control is usually expressed as one member, one vote. A few cooperatives have limited proportional voting based on use.

LIMITED RETURN ON EQUITY CAPITAL. This feature means that payments for use of members' equity capital (primarily in the form of stock dividends) are limited. It does not mean that benefits realized from the co-op, monetary or otherwise, are limited. The overriding value of the co-op to its owners is in the range of services or economies of scale that it provides. Limiting the return on equity capital is a mechanism to support distribution of benefits according to use. It helps to keep management decisions focused on providing services attuned to members' needs. Both federal and state laws recognize limiting the payment for the use of equity capital. Some state laws require that co-ops either limit the dividends on stock or member capital to 8% per year or follow one-member, one-vote control.

Co-ops usually perform any one or a combination of four kinds of service functions, but with varying strategic emphasis:

- **Purchasing co-ops provide members with consumer goods,** products for resale through their members or equipment and supplies for their business operation. Individual co-ops may form federations of cooperatives to obtain further benefits of group purchasing.
- **Marketing co-ops market the products their members produce.** Marketing includes assembling, processing and selling products or services in a variety of channels, much in the way that Sunkist aggregates and markets the production of Florida orange growers.
- **Service co-ops provide services related to the production of a product or service** for business or the home. These services may include credit, electricity, telephones, insurance, research, telecommunications, common management, or other shared services.
- **Production co-ops pool production and distribution resources** in large-scale industries, such as agricultural products or electrical utilities.
- **Retail co-ops are often confused with franchise systems.** With a retail co-op, each location is independently owned and operated, without outside control and oversight (as with a franchise). The brand is used more for the purpose of cooperative advertising than for prescribing a business system, as it would

under a franchise. ACE Hardware and NAPA Auto Parts are two well-known businesses that operate as retail co-ops.

■ **Co-ops have been especially effective in certain inventory-intense industries,** such as hardware, automobile parts and accessories, pharmacies, and grocery stores. Retail co-ops, if properly structured, are exempt from FTC Rule 436 and from some state franchise laws. The guidelines for exempting other co-ops from franchise laws are much more stringent; in fact, no state has exempted buyers co-ops to date. Have your lawyer periodically review the organization and ongoing operation of any co-op you join to ensure that certain federal and state antitrust and unfair-competition laws are not violated.

Multilevel-Marketing Plans

Multilevel marketing (MLM) is a method of direct selling of products or services through distributors or sales representatives outside of a retail-store context and often in a one-to-one setting. In some cases, distributors purchase the manufacturer's products at wholesale prices and profit by selling the product to the consumer at retail price. In other instances, distributors sponsor other sales representatives or distributors and receive commissions on the sales made by the sponsored representative or any further representative sponsored in a continuous "down-line sales organization." Leading merchandisers who use this form of marketing include Shaklee Corp., Amway Corp., and Mary Kay Cosmetics.

Numerous overlapping laws that vary from state to state regulate MLM companies. MLM programs are affected by a combination of pyramid statutes, business-opportunity statutes, multilevel-distribution laws, franchise and securities laws, various state lottery laws, referral-sales laws, the federal postal laws, and Section 5 of the Federal Trade Commission Act. Many MLM plans have been targeted for prosecution and litigation based on these laws. To date, enforcement of statutes and regulations has been selective and arbitrary, and many regulatory officials have developed negative attitudes toward the legality of any one MLM program. Therefore, from a legal standpoint, MLM is an uncertain and speculative activity, and there is no assurance that even the most legitimate MLM program will be immune from regulatory inquiry.

Georgia, Louisiana, Maryland, Massachusetts, New Mexico, and Wyoming have laws specifically regulating companies that adopt multilevel-marketing programs. An MLM company operating in any of these states typically must file an annual registration statement giving notice of its operations in that state and must appoint that state's secretary of state as its agent for service of process.

A multilevel-marketing company is typically defined by these states as an entity that "sells, distributes, or supplies, for valuable consideration, goods or services, through independent agents or distributors at different levels and in which participants may recruit other participants in which commissions or bonuses are paid as a result of the sale of the goods or services or the recruitment of additional participants."

In addition to imposing the annual registration requirement, several states have placed additional regulations governing the activities of the MLM companies, such as:

- **requiring that MLM companies** allow their independent representatives or distributors to cancel their agreements with the company, and upon such cancellation the company must repurchase unsold products at a price not less than 90% of the distributor's original net cost;
- **prohibiting MLM companies** from representing that distributors have or will earn stated dollar amounts;
- **prohibiting MLM companies** from requiring distributors to purchase certain minimum initial inventories (except in reasonable quantities); and
- **prohibiting that compensation** be paid solely for recruiting other participants.

BUSINESS OPPORTUNITY LAWS AND MLM. A "business opportunity" is typically defined as the sale or lease of products or services to a purchaser for the purpose of enabling the purchaser to start a business and in which the seller represents that:

- **the seller will provide locations** or assist the purchaser in finding locations for the use of vending machines;
- **the seller will purchase products** made by the purchaser using

the supplies or services sold to the purchaser;

■ **the seller guarantees the purchaser** will derive income from the business opportunity which exceeds the price paid for the business opportunity, or that the seller will refund all or part of the price paid for the business opportunity if the purchaser is unsatisfied with the business opportunity; and

■ **upon the payment by the purchaser** of a certain sum of money (usually between $25 and $500), the seller will provide a sales program or marketing program that will enable the purchaser to derive income from the business opportunity that exceeds the price paid for the business opportunity.

This definition (or some variation thereof) can be found in more than twenty state statutes. While the first two elements do not apply to MLM companies, the third and fourth elements would in all probability relate to MLM companies that offer to repurchase sales kits and unsold inventory if a distributor discontinues selling and its sales kits exceed the amounts specified in the various state statutes. Business-opportunity offerers are required to file a registration statement with the appropriate state agency (usually the Securities Division or Consumer Protection Agency) and a disclosure statement (similar to that required of franchisors) that would then be provided to each prospective offeree. MLM companies are, however, often exempt from the coverage of the business-opportunity laws by virtue of sales-kit exemptions in the statutes. This type of exemption excludes from the calculation required payment monies paid for sales demonstration equipment or materials sold to the purchaser at the company's cost. MLMs are also exempt from the business-opportunity laws for the sale of an ongoing business. This allows the sale of a distributorship or business opportunity to another without triggering the business-opportunity laws. The following states have adopted business opportunity statutes:

California	Kentucky	Nebraska	Texas
Connecticut	Louisiana	New Hampshire	Utah
Florida	Maine	North Carolina	Virginia
Georgia	Maryland	Ohio	Washington
Iowa	Minnesota	South Carolina	

Consumers often confuse legitimate mult-level marketing programs, which are generally valid methods for distributing products and services to the public, with pyramid schemes, which are generally unlawful schemes that are subject to criminal prosecution in many states. Numerous laws and regulations have been enacted to prohibit pyramid schemes. Some of the state laws enacted declare unlawful "pyramid sales schemes," "chain distributions," "referral selling," "endless chains," and the like. Pyramid-distribution plans have also been declared unlawful as lotteries, unregistered securities, violations of mail-fraud laws, or violations of the Federal Trade Commission Act.

Pyramid schemes generally consist of several distribution levels through which the products or services are resold until they reach the ultimate consumer.

Broadly speaking, a pyramid-distribution plan is a means of distributing a company's products or services to consumers. Pyramid schemes generally consist of several distribution levels through which the products or services are resold until they reach the ultimate consumer. A pyramid differs from a valid multilevel-marketing company in that in its elemental form it is merely a variation on a chain letter and almost always involves large numbers of people at the lowest level who pay money to a few people at the utmost level. New participants pay a sum of money merely for the chance to join the program and advance to the top level, where they will profit from the initial payments made by later participants.

One of the most common elements of pyramid schemes is an intensive campaign, often using high-pressure sales tactics, to attract new participants who serve to fund the program by providing the payoff to earlier participants. A pyramid scheme always involves a certain degree of failure by its participants. A pyramid plan can work only if there are unlimited numbers of participants. At some point the pyramid scheme will fail to attract new participants, and those individuals who joined later will not receive any money because there will be no new bottom level of participants to support the plan.

To avoid prosecution, the promoters of pyramid schemes often attempt to make their plans resemble multilevel-marketing companies. Pyramid schemes, therefore, often claim to be in the business of selling products or services to consumers. The products or services, however, are often of little or no value, and there is no true effort to sell them because emphasis remains almost solely on signing up new participants who are needed to "feed the machine."

There are several methods of distinguishing a legitimate multilevel-marketing program from an unlawful pyramid scheme.

INITIAL PAYMENT. Typically, the initial payment required of a distributor of products and services of a multilevel-marketing program is minimal; often the distributor is required to buy only a sales kit that may be purchased at cost. Because pyramid schemes are supported by the payments made by the new recruits, participants in a pyramid scheme are often required to pay substantial sums of money just to participate in the scheme.

INVENTORY LOADING. Pyramid schemes typically require participants to purchase large amounts of nonrefundable inventory to participate in the program. Legitimate multilevel-marketing companies usually repurchase any such inventory if the distributor decides to leave the business. Many state laws require the company to repurchase any resalable goods for at least 90% of the original cost.

HEAD-HUNTING. Pyramid schemes generally make more money by recruiting new prospects ("head-hunting") than by actually selling products. Multilevel-marketing programs, on the other hand, make money by the sale of legitimate and bona fide products to consumers.

More than twenty five states have laws prohibiting pyramid schemes, whether as "endless chains," "chain distribution schemes," or "pyramids." Programs with the following three elements are prohibited:

- **an entry fee or investment** that must be paid by the participant in order to join;
- **ongoing recruitment** of new prospects; and
- **the payment of bonuses, commissions,** or some other valuable consideration to participants who recruit new participants.

Generally, the purchase by a participant of a sales kit (at cost) is not deemed to be an entry fee or investment.

Managing the
Challenges of Growth

Managing Disputes: Litigation and Alternative Strategies

A S A FAST-TRACK GROWTH COMPANY EXPANDS RAPIDLY, the number of vendors, customers, employees, consultants, investors, and competitors with whom it comes into contact will also increase. The more outside relationships that a company has, the greater the chances that business conflicts and problems will arise. The management and disposition of these conflicts is a time-consuming and expensive process that can be a significant impediment to the continued success of a growing company.

Horror stories of the "litigation that broke the company's back" (because of the drain on company resources) provide insight into the basic rule of thumb that in litigation "there are really no winners, only successful or unsuccessful litigants." As railroad titan Cornelius Vanderbilt once said to a business rival, "I will not sue you, for the law is too slow. I will ruin you."

Like Vanderbilt, most owners would prefer to engage in battle in the marketplace or in the boardroom rather than in the courtroom. Nonetheless, there will be situations where the parties cannot resolve their differences quickly and must resort to a courtroom battle. In the event that you are faced with such a situation, you must understand the basic rules of litigation and alternative dispute resolution (ADR).

Avoiding Litigation

Most disputes and conflicts among companies are the result of misunderstandings over the rights and obligations of the parties to particular agreements or situations. Circumstances that are likely to lead to litigation include failure to: provide acceptable products or services; pay the bills on a timely basis; meet the expectations of an investor; comply with the covenants imposed by a lender; adequately compensate an employee or consultant; complete a proposed transaction or investment; or consider the antitrust laws in dealing with competitors. An understanding of the financial, legal and strategic issues discussed throughout this book, a good working relationship with your lawyer and a well-managed legal-compliance program will help you reduce the risk of litigation. Other methods that your company may adopt to stay out of the courtroom include the following.

MANAGEMENT, MANAGEMENT, MANAGEMENT. If your growing company is well-managed, you are far less likely to get entangled in a legal dispute with an employee, investor, creditor or competitor than a company that is managed haphazardly. This is generally because the well-managed company is far more inclined to:

■ **meet its contractual obligations** on a timely basis;

■ **deal fairly with its employees,** shareholders and competitors;

■ **apply quality-control standards** to the production of goods and services; and

■ **regularly communicate** with its lawyer to identify and solve risks and problems well before they mature into a formal dispute.

AVOIDING UNDERCAPITALIZATION. If your fast-track growing company is undercapitalized, it is much more likely to experience financial problems that will lead to litigation. Your company's lack of capital translates into:

■ **a reduction in the quality** of its products and services;

■ **paying bills late;**

■ **not preparing legal documents** and not following legal procedures in connection with the issuance of securities or the hiring and termination of employees; and

■ **breaking covenants** with lenders and investors.

Undercapitalization will lead to these and other acts of desperation that will only lead to conflicts and problems and increase your risk of facing litigation.

GETTING IT IN WRITING AND GETTING IT RIGHT. Many business disputes that result in litigation arise because of the lack of a written agreement or because of a poorly prepared written agreement that fails to anticipate contentious situations or in which the rights and obligations of the parties are unclear or ambiguous. Therefore, as the owner of a growing company, take steps to ensure that an agreement or series of agreements covers each significant transaction. Further, these documents, taken as a whole, should clearly reflect both the spirit and intent of the transactions and the respective rights and obligations of each party. In addition, be certain that an arbitration or mediation clause is included in any contract. Such alternatives can be much less expensive than litigation. Arbitration is usually binding, while mediation is not, so you should decide which type of ADR best suits your contract. Also, include a clause that states that the losing party pays the other party's legal fees, thus forcing someone to think before they breach a contract or commence litigation. It is also important to include a "loser pays" provision if you anticipate arbitration, because in many states an arbitrator cannot award legal fees to the prevailing party if the contract does not specifically provide for such an award.

SEEING THE "BIG PICTURE." When you're negotiating a contract, hiring an employee or dealing with a competitor, it is very easy to get too caught up in the narrow objective of the given transaction and fail to see the big picture. Analyze every transaction in which your company is engaged with its legal implications and potential risks in mind. Think about the short-term and long-term risks and problems associated with each transaction, and discuss them with your lawyer before executing any documents.

BEING A SKEPTIC. As your company grows, you will take a wide variety of risks and seize a broad range of opportunities, each with its respective share of costs and benefits. The financial intermediary that you may have hired to raise an unlimited amount of capital within 30 days, or the sales representative who promises to deliver more customers than your company can handle, are both a dime a dozen. Be skeptical at the outset, rather than trying to build your company on shallow representations and then spending valuable time and money in court trying to enforce such worthless promises. Either force the party with whom you wish to do business to document his or her claims and promises, or forego the transaction.

ESTABLISHING A LEGAL-COMPLIANCE PROGRAM. Take steps to ensure that employees at all levels within your growing company are made aware of the legal risks of their actions. It is important to develop legal-compliance programs with the assistance of your lawyer. These programs should include:

- **periodic legal audits;**
- **legal-compliance manuals,** postings and employee seminars;
- **form letters and checklists** for routine transactions; and
- **established procedures and policies** for record-keeping and file management.

Misunderstanding and miscommunication are at the core of virtually every commercial lawsuit. Talking openly and creatively with the opposing party is often the most effective way of resolving a dispute before it develops into full-blown legal action.

Problem-Resolution Strategies

Although a comprehensive discussion of problem-solving techniques is beyond the scope of this chapter and this book, I have found over the years in representing rapid-growth companies that many disputes leading to litigation or arbitration stem from an inability of the company's leadership to develop basic problem-resolution skills. Whether the disputes are the result of competing egos, a lack of understanding or a lack of time, many of these costly conflicts could be avoided. To do so, all parties involved must take the time to calmly and methodically understand each other's side of the story, then seek a reasonable compromise between their differing positions.

The immediate tendency of the leadership of many fast-track growth companies is to ignore a problem in hopes it will eventually go away, either by solving itself or becoming irrelevant. Because many entrepreneurs do not relish head-on conflicts or are too busy to deal with them, an attitude that "ignorance is bliss" and that somebody else will take care of problems may begin to set in. Such an approach to dealing with potential legal problems can present many short-term or long-term issues and will send a message throughout your organization that the denial of a real problem is acceptable and will not be penalized. Often, a company's leadership admits that a problem exists only at the latter stage of a conflict, but even then fails to assume responsibility for the problem or for the solution. The problem-solving process can begin only after the growing company's leadership has accepted the existence of the problem and the responsibility for finding a solution. Otherwise, the first step in the problem-solving process—discussion—will be tainted with politics, bruised egos and finger pointing, all of which will stand in the way of working toward an acceptable solution.

> **Because many entrepreneurs do not relish head-on conflicts or are too busy to deal with them, an attitude that "ignorance is bliss" and that somebody else will take care of problems may begin to set in.**

Litigation Planning and Strategy

If you face a problem or conflict that cannot be resolved, and you determine that litigation is the most sensible and efficient way to resolve the business dispute (or if a suit is brought against your growing company), then you must take the following steps:

■ **Identify your goals and objectives** and communicate them to your lawyer. Well before initiating any litigation, you must make your lawyer aware of any specific business objectives,

Deciding When to Litigate: Questions to Ask . . .

. . . when deciding to litigate

- What are the legal fees and costs of the litigation?
- What are the costs in hidden downtime?
- What are the costs associated with public-relations issues?
- What are the capital costs (disclosure of pending litigation)?
- What are the costs of alternatives to litigation?
- What are the costs of not litigating?
- What public-relations issues are involved in the litigation?
- What aspects of the litigation might interest the media?
- What aspects of the litigation might produce strong emotions in a jury?
- How might shareholders, competitors and customers react to the litigation?
- What legal precedents are relevant to this litigation?
- What factors affect the possibility of settlement?
- Who is the opposing attorney?
- What kind of suit is this?
- How complex are the legal issues?
- What effect will this suit have on our public relations or "public image?
- Are there other simultaneous proceedings?
- What are the weaknesses of our position?
- What are the weaknesses of our opponent's position?
- What company policies are relevant to this litigation?
- What are the chances of getting help from other members of the trade in this litigation?

. . . to determine the total legal costs of proposed litigation

- What is the hourly rate for the lawyer or lawyers involved?
- How much assistance will the lawyer or lawyers need, and

budgetary limitations or time constraints that affect your company;

- **Gather all documents relevant to the dispute** and organize them in advance of the time that the opponent serves the first discovery request (one of the first events in any litigation);
- **Explore alternative methods of dispute resolution.** Keep in mind that if your contract mandates that disputes be resolved through arbitration, you may be compelled to "demand" arbitration in lieu of pursuing a lawsuit in court;
- **Discuss with your lawyer the risks, costs and benefits** of entering

what are the hourly rates for those who will be assisting?

■ What types of expert witnesses will be needed, and how much will it cost to have them prepare and testify?

■ What types of fees will be involved? (For example, filing fees, fees for the reproduction of documents, depositions and trial transcripts, and costs of travel involved in discovery)

... about proposed contract litigation

■ What amount of money is at issue in this dispute?

■ What is the financial condition of the debtor?

■ Where is the debtor located? Is the debtor in our state or in another state? (If the debtor is in a different state, costs of collecting the debt are likely to rise considerably.)

■ What reputation as creditors do

we wish to maintain?

... about proposed regulatory litigation

■ What publicity is this action likely to attract? What is the public's perception of the issues likely to be?

■ Would a consent decree be in our best interest in this case?

■ What is our ongoing relationship with this regulator? What relationship do we wish to have? How will this action affect that relationship?

■ Does this action involve a new regulation? Is the agency likely to be using it as a test case?

■ Are other companies involved or likely to be involved in this action? If so, might they help us in the suit?

■ What is the nature of the regulatory environment involved in this action? How is the current environment likely to affect our case?

into litigation and your parameters for settlement;

■ **Review with your lawyer the terms for payment** of legal fees and costs (as well as payments of any experts needed);

■ **Review the terms of insurance policies with your risk management team** to determine whether there is insurance coverage for defense costs or for any judgment rendered against the company;

■ **Develop a litigation-management system** for monitoring and controlling costs; and

■ **Appoint a responsible individual to serve as a liaison** with your lawyer, and maintain clear lines of communication with your legal team throughout all phases of the litigation.

Regardless of the subject matter, there are certain factors that you must consider before you decide to litigate. The box on the preceding page provides a checklist for helping you decide when you should litigate.

The decision to resolve a dispute through litigation must be based on a genuine understanding of the specific legal rights, remedies and defenses available in a particular case. Also bear in mind that in formal litigation the parties lose control over the timing of the resolution of the dispute. You will be subject to the whims and scheduling challenges of the local judge and court system. These types of delays tend to favor a defendant, who may have an incentive to drag things out.

For example, suppose that a supplier is shipping goods that are inferior to those you originally anticipated. When you review the contract, you find the quality-control specifications seem to be clear; however, a material difference of opinion has developed. Before you file a complaint for breach of contract, carefully review:

- **alternative methods** for resolving the dispute;
- **the legal elements** of a breach-of-contract claim in the jurisdiction that governs the agreement;
- **the various defenses** that may be available to the supplier;
- **the direct and indirect costs** of litigation; and
- **the range of damages** that you may recover if a breach is successfully established.

Pursue formal action only after you are satisfied that the answers to these questions indicate that litigation is a prudent and viable alternative. Similarly, if a creditor or landlord sues your company, attempt to resolve the dispute before responding with a formal answer. Keep in mind, however, that answers to most complaints are due within 20 days after a suit is filed, so dispute-resolution efforts should begin immediately. If the other side agrees to delay the filing of your answer while settlement discussions are ongoing, have your lawyer confirm this understanding in writing at the time that such an agreement is reached, and be sure that the court's rules permit such an extension.

An Overview of the Mechanics of Litigation

The first step in civil litigation is preparing and filing a complaint, which must adequately state your legal claim or claims against the other party. Set forth each allegation in a separate paragraph that is written in a clear and concise manner, with any necessary exhibits attached to the end of the complaint. Each allegation should relate to a claim on which you are entitled to relief and to make a demand for judgment. Complaints generally begin with separate paragraphs identifying each party and the legal reasons that the court selected is empowered to hear the particular case. The drafter then highlights the important facts of the case before moving on to the legal claims. If the complaint meets all statutory and procedural requirements, including the payment of a filing fee, the clerk of the court will then prepare a summons. The sheriff or a process server delivers the summons and complaint to the other party, who becomes the defendant. The summons directs the defendant to serve an answer to the complaint upon your lawyer, usually within twenty days after service of process is made.

In lieu of answering your specific allegations, the defendant may submit certain preliminary motions. These motions—which are essentially specific requests for the court to act—include procedural motions to dismiss (due to a lack of personal jurisdiction, improper service of process, improper venue, etc.); motions to dismiss due to failure to state a claim on which relief can be granted; motions to strike; or motions for a more definite statement. Certain of these claims—such as allegations that the court lacks personal jurisdiction over the defendant—must be raised immediately or they will be considered waived. However, the issue of whether the court is empowered to decide the case can never be waived. Once the answer is filed, it will contain three principal components:

- **admission of the allegations** contained in the Complaint that are true;
- **denial of those allegations** that in the opinion of the defendant are not true (he defendant may also state that he is without sufficient information to admit or deny a particular allegation); and
- **a listing of any affirmative defenses** to the causes of action asserted by the plaintiff, or to the procedures employed by the plaintiff in filing and serving the complaint.

The defendant must also file any counterclaims that he or she may have against you that arise from the same transaction or occurrence that gave rise to the original complaint. Failure to bring such "compulsory" counterclaims at the outset will normally prevent the defendant from raising them later on. The complaint and answer-and any counterclaims and answers to counterclaims-are usually collectively referred to as the pleadings.

Once all of the pleadings and preliminary motions are filed, the parties are then permitted to begin the process of discovery, a pretrial procedure for obtaining information that will be necessary to the disposition of the case. Discovery serves a number of important purposes, including:

- **narrowing the issues of dispute;**
- **preventing surprises** by allowing each party to learn the nature and scope of the testimony and other evidence that is available concerning each issue in dispute;
- **preserving information** that may not be available at the actual trial, such as the statement of a very ill witness; and
- **encouraging resolution** of the dispute prior to trial.

Despite its many benefits, discovery is also the process that tends to significantly increase legal fees and expenses. The greatest amount of time in any litigation is usually allotted to the discovery period, because this phase of litigation often involves travel and the review of voluminous documents by both attorneys and witnesses. Indeed, in the federal courts, discovery cannot begin until the parties have exchanged certain categories of documents and information specified by the court's rules. (The Eastern District of Virginia—known as the "Rocket Docket"—has done away with this procedure, presumably because it impedes the court's efforts to maintain its well-deserved reputation as that rare forum in which lawsuits are disposed of quickly and efficiently.)

One of the key issues to consider is the permissible scope of the discovery. The general rule is that virtually any information is discoverable, provided that it is relevant and not subject to any category of evidentiary privilege. Such privilege is usually limited to information exchanged between a doctor and patient, attorney and client, priest and penitent, husband and wife, or parties to a joint defense effort (even if different attorneys represent them). The five principal discovery devices available to litigants are.

DEPOSITIONS. A deposition generally involves the pre-trial examination and cross-examination of a live witness—under oath—by legal counsel in the presence of a court reporter. The person being deposed is almost always accompanied by a lawyer, who is permitted to object to the questions asked. Any person who has information relevant to the case, whether or not that person is a party to the action, may be subject to a deposition, although a non-party may only be called to testify via a subpoena issued under the authority of the court. The written record of the deposition may be admitted at trial as substantive evidence and may be used to impeach a witness whose trial testimony is inconsistent with the testimony given during the deposition.

WRITTEN INTERROGATORIES. An interrogatory is a written question that one party may pose to another party. It must be answered in writing, under oath, within thirty or forty-five days, depending upon the rules of the particular jurisdiction where the action was brought. Unlike depositions, interrogatories may be served only upon parties to the litigation. Most courts will limit the number of interrogatories that may be filed and the scope of the questions so that they are not overly burdensome or interposed simply as part of a fishing expedition. If a party objects to a specific interrogatory, it must specify its grounds for refusing to answer, at which time the burden shifts to the proponent of the question to convince the court why an answer is necessary. An answer to an interrogatory may also include a reference to a particular business document or set of records, provided that the other party is given an opportunity to inspect the documents, and the burden of obtaining the answer from the records is substantially the same for each party.

REQUESTS FOR PRODUCTION OF DOCUMENTS OR INSPECTION OF LAND. A party may request that another party produce and permit inspection, copying, testing or photographing of business documents, tangible assets, financial books and records or anything else that may be relevant to the litigation. Similarly, a party may seek entry to the business premises of another party for the purpose of inspecting, photographing or surveying it, or for any other relevant reason, provided that the inspection does not violate any evidentiary privilege. Discovery requests are limited to parties to the litigation, with the exception of requests made pursuant to a "subpoena duces tecum," which is a written demand that a non-party produce certain documents and records in connection with the deposition of that non-party. Fortunately for non-parties, the production of subpoenaed documents often eliminates the litigants' need to expend the time and effort necessary to depose them, and the deposition itself will not actually be held.

PHYSICAL AND MENTAL EXAMINATIONS. A party may request that another party submit to a mental or physical examination by a physician or psychiatrist. The mental or physical condition of the party, however, must be relevant to the issues that are in dispute. The court will grant such a request only if good cause is shown, and it will usually limit the scope of the examination to the actual issues in controversy. So, even if you firmly believe that your opponent is unbalanced, unless he is bringing a claim against your company for personal injury or emotional distress, your ability to explore his mental condition will be very limited. Of course, if you feel that an opponent's weaknesses are not fully revealed through the printed transcript of his testimony, your lawyer can attempt to arrange for the deposition to be videotaped. A poor showing on a "video depo" sometimes convinces a litigant to settle a case earlier than he had planned because he—or more likely his lawyer—fears that his trial testimony will not prove persuasive to a judge or jury.

REQUESTS FOR ADMISSIONS. A party may serve a request for admission on another party to authenticate specific documents, to obtain the admission or denial of a specific matter, or to confirm the application of certain law to a given set of facts. For example, you may wish to use this procedure to designate certain facts as undisputed to save the time and expense of having to prove them later. (An undisputed fact might be the date that the contract was signed or the date that an accident took place.)

Failure to respond to such a request will be deemed an admission. Therefore, within thirty days after a request has been served the party who does not wish to admit it must deny it, explain why it is unable to admit or deny it, or file an objection to the propriety of the request.

Once the parties have completed the discovery process, the litigation will proceed to the pre-trial conference, the actual trial, the appeal and any post-trial proceedings. Although a comprehensive discussion of the mechanics of a trial is beyond the scope of this chapter, it is safe to say that this process consumes two of the most important resources of an emerging-growth business: time and money. As a result, if you are faced with litigation, either as a plaintiff or a defendant, consider less expensive and less time-consuming dispute resolution alternatives. (See the box on the next page for questions to consider if you're the defendant in a lawsuit.)

Alternatives to Litigation

When your growing business is faced with a legal conflict, there are a number of methods and procedures available to you that generally expedite the resolution of the dispute without the need for initiating or continuing litigation. In addition to serving as an expeditor for the res-

---

Questions to Consider if You've Been Sued

Questions to ask when assembling the dispute-management team:

- Who will be on the team?
- Who will act as our lawyer? (In-house counsel? Outside firm? Special attorney?)
- Who will act as our public-relations representative? (In-house person? Consultant?)
- Will the CEO be on the team? If not, who will represent the CEO?
- What technical expert(s) will be on the team?
- Will the director of public affairs be on the team?
- Will a consumer representative be on the team? If so, who will it be?
- Will a sales or marketing representative be on the team? If so, who will it be?
- What tasks will the team perform?
- What public-relations issues will the team need to handle? Which of these are short-term issues? Which are long-term?
- What internal investigation will the team need to conduct? How should it be conducted?
- What specific information should we give employees? What instructions should we give them for

---

olution of the problem or dispute, these alternatives tend to be more cost-effective than formal litigation. The alternatives are broadly referred to as alternative dispute resolution (ADR). They include arbitration, mediation, private judging, moderated settlement conferences, and small-claims court. Business owners often prefer ADR to litigation because with ADR, proprietary information, trade secrets and the like are not subject to the potentially intense scrutiny of the judicial process, where the right of access by the general public and news media can afford competitors the opportunity to misappropriate and use otherwise confidential information. Each type of ADR offers certain advantages and disadvantages. Therefore, before choosing the process appropriate for resolving a particular dispute, carefully review the procedures, costs and benefits of each ADR method with experienced legal counsel.

Arbitration

The most commonly known method of ADR is arbitration, in which a neutral third party is selected by the disputants to hear answering questions from family, friends and the media?

■ **What legal strategy should be followed?**

■ **What corrective action do we need to take?**

Questions to ask when attempting an amicable settlement:

■ **Have we conducted an internal investigation to find out all relevant facts?** (Remember, fingerpointing and written memos can later be discoverable as the litigation progresses.)

■ **Is the CEO involved in the nego-**tiations? If so, has he or she been properly briefed?

■ **If a settlement is not reached quickly,** have we left the door open for possible future negotiations?

■ **Are personality conflicts hindering negotiation?** If so, has the possibility of hiring a mediator been explored?

■ **Will a settlement encourage others to bring similar claims** against the company?

■ **Do our negotiators have a clear understanding of the costs,** benefits and goals of this litigation?

the case and render an opinion, which may or may not be binding on the parties, depending upon the terms of the arbitration clause or agreement.

There are many types of formal arbitration. Each involves a process whereby the parties to the dispute agree to submit arguments and evidence to a neutral person or persons for the purpose of adjudicating their claims. The evidentiary and procedural rules are usually not nearly as formal as in litigation, and there tends to be far greater flexibility in the timing of the proceeding and the selection of the actual decision makers.

Arbitration may be a voluntary proceeding, as when the parties to a contract have selected it as a means of dispute resolution, or it may be a compulsory, court-ordered procedure that is a prerequisite to full-blown litigation. If you wish to avoid the cost and delay of litigation, consider adding arbitration clauses to contracts prior to entering into them. The clause should specify:

■ **that the parties agree** to submit any controversy or claim arising from the agreement or contract to a binding (or nonbinding) arbitration;

- **the choice of location(s)** for the arbitration;
- **the method for selecting** the neutral third-party or parties who will hear the dispute;
- **any limitations on the award** that may be rendered by the arbitrator;
- **which party will be responsible** for the costs of the proceeding;
- **whether the loser will pay** the winner's attorneys' fees; and
- **any special procedural rules** that will govern the arbitration, such as those employed by the American Arbitration Association (AAA).

Due to the increasing battle over mandatory arbitration, it is advisable not to include a boilerplate arbitration provision in your key contracts. For example, in the August 1996 issue of the *ABA Journal*, it was reported that "Employment law has been one of the most significant sectors of ADR growth, as management lawyers have seized upon several Supreme Court decisions upholding mandatory arbitration clauses on statutory grounds." However, in its September 1996 issue the journal reported that "Consumer advocates are criticizing a U.S. Supreme Court decision invalidating a state law that required the prominent display of arbitration provisions in contracts." By 1999, in response to a series of court challenges, the National Association of Securities Dealers and the New York Stock Exchange had changed their rules to abolish mandatory arbitration of statutory employment-discrimination claims. The American Arbitration Association recommends the following arbitration clause:

Any controversy or claim arising out of or relating to this contract, or the breach thereof, shall be settled by arbitration in accordance with the Commercial Arbitration Rules of the American Arbitration Association, and judgment rendered upon the award rendered by the arbitrator(s) may be entered in any court having jurisdiction thereof.

Because arbitrators are usually lawyers whose expertise may be negotiating rather than adjudicating, arbitration often results in "splitting the baby down the middle," rather than in a clear award for one party. Additionally, because no jury is involved, the likelihood of recovering punitive or exemplary damages from a lawyer or experienced arbitrator—who is unlikely to be swayed by emotional appeals—is reduced.

A key consideration in drafting an arbitration contract is whether the decision of the arbitrator will be binding or non-binding. If you and the other party agree that the award will be binding, then you must live with the results. Binding arbitration awards are usually enforceable as written by the local court, unless there has been a defect in the arbitration procedures. On the other hand, the opinion rendered in a non-binding arbitration is advisory only. You and the other party may either accept the result or reject the award and proceed to litigation. The court may also order the arbitration as a non-binding proceeding in an effort to resolve the differences between the parties before moving further toward trial. The major drawback of non-binding arbitration is that after the award is made, the losing party often threatens litigation (a trial de novo, or new trial) unless the monetary award is adjusted. Thus, the party that wins the arbitration is often coerced into paying or accepting less than the award simply to avoid a trial after arbitration.

A key consideration in drafting an arbitration contract is whether the decision of the arbitrator will be binding or non-binding.

There are many sources of arbitration rules. Unless you and the other party have specific rules and procedures in mind that will govern the arbitration, the two best-known sources in the U.S. are the American Arbitration Association, or AAA (212-484-4000; www.adr.org), and the International Chamber of Commerce (212-206-1150; www.iccwbo.org). Both offer their rules at no cost; the fees for handling arbitration proceedings vary for these and other such organizations, depending upon the number of arbitrators and their level of expertise. Other sources for rules include the U.N. Commission on International Trade Law (www.uncitral.org), the Inter-American Commercial Arbitration Commission (part of the Organization of American States; see AAA's Web site for more information), and the CPR Institute for Dispute Resolution (formerly the Center for Public Resources; www.cpradr.org).

Whether arbitration is faster and cheaper than litigation really hinges on the parties. Determined or vindictive parties can escalate the costs and length of arbitration until they rival those of litigation. For example, in *Advanced Micro Devices Inc. v. Intel Corp.*, the proceeding lasted seven years, cost about $100 million, and included several rounds of collateral litigation, despite Intel's description of the case as a "basic contract dispute." Ultimately the arbitrator's ruling led the parties to settlement via a mediation proceeding.

Even in small, closely held companies, arbitration can turn into a high-stakes battle. For example, one of the country's first brewpubs was wildly successful from its opening day, in part due to its superb location next to a major-league ballpark. The company's growth stalled, however, when the three shareholders began to disagree on expansion plans. Two of them allied against the third and tried to remove him from the company through a forced buyout. When the minority shareholder sued, the others compelled him—via a clause in the shareholder's agreement—to abandon litigation and proceed to binding arbitration. When the arbitrator awarded the minority shareholder more than $1 million, plus attorneys' fees, and ordered an appraisal of the company for the purpose of recalculating the value of the shares, the majority shareholders reversed course and filed litigation in an effort to overturn the award. While the dispute dragged on, the company lost the opportunity to obtain a number of expansion sites near other major sports arenas—failing to capitalize on the strategy that led to its initial success.

> **Even in small, closely held companies, arbitration can turn into a high-stakes battle.**

Mediation

Mediation differs substantially from arbitration. An arbitrator renders a decision that is often binding. In the non-binding mediation process, the parties attempt to resolve their dispute by discussing their differences with a mediator, who makes suggestions or recommendations for an appropriate outcome. The mediator often tries to reach a settlement by reminding each side of its own weaknesses while pointing out the other party's strengths.

A sample mediation clause in an agreement would read as follows:

Any dispute arising out of or relating to this Agreement shall be resolved in accordance with the procedures specified in this Agreement, which shall be the sole and exclusive procedures for the resolution of such disputes. Each party shall continue to perform its obligations under this Agreement pending final resolution of any dispute arising out of or relating to this Agreement, unless to do so would be impossible or impracticable under the circumstances.

Upon becoming aware of the existence of a dispute, a party to this Agreement shall inform the other party in writing of the nature of such dispute. The parties shall attempt in good faith to resolve any dispute arising out of or relating to this Agreement promptly by negotiation between executives who have authority to settle the controversy. All negotiations pursuant to this Agreement shall be confidential and shall be treated as compromise and settlement negotiations for purposes of the applicable rules of evidence. If the dispute cannot be settled through direct discussions within _____ days of the receipt of such notice, the dispute shall be submitted to {Name of Mediator} (or such substitute mediation service specified by the parties in writing prior to receiving notice of the existence of such dispute) for mediation by notifying {Mediator} (or the specified substitute service) and the other party in writing. The notification shall specify: (1) the nature of the dispute, and (2) the name and title of the executive who will represent the party in mediation and of any other person who will accompany the executive. Following receipt of the notice, {Mediator} (or the specified substitute service) will convene the parties, in person or by telephone, to establish the mediation procedures and a schedule. If the parties are unable to agree on mediation procedures, {Mediator} (or the specified substitute service) will set the procedures. The mediation shall be completed within seven (7) days of submitting the dispute to mediation or such longer time as the parties may agree. Each party will participate in the mediation process in good faith, will use their best efforts to resolve the dispute within the seven (7) day time period and will make available executives or representatives with authority to resolve the controversy to participate personally and actively in the mediation. The parties shall share equally the fees, charges and expenses of {Mediator} (or the specified substitute service).

The mediation process typically consists of four stages:

- **presentation of positions;**
- **identification of interests;**
- **generation and evaluation of options;**
- **narrowing of options to resolve the dispute; and**
- **execution of a written settlement agreement.**

Mediation costs are minimal and generally include only payment on an hourly basis to the mediator for his or her services. However, because the mediator has no authority to render a binding decision, the mediation process will be effective only if both parties are committed to achieving a resolution. The participants always have the ultimate authority in the mediation process, and they are free to reject any suggestion by the mediator and proceed to litigation.

The controversies surrounding mediation typically involve the mediator's method of resolving disputes and the ethical standards governing the mediator's conduct.

The controversies surrounding mediation typically involve the mediator's method of resolving disputes and the ethical standards governing the mediator's conduct. Some experts believe that mediation should facilitate the parties' own resolution of the problem by digging deep into the interests and feelings underlying the surface dispute. Others say that the proper purpose of mediation is to bring the parties to an amicable accord. Still others contend that mediators should provide subject-matter expertise, acting essentially as sounding boards to help the parties evaluate the merits of the dispute or the proposed settlement. The American Bar Association's Section on Dispute Resolution, the Society of Professionals in Dispute Resolution and the AAA—in an attempt to draft ethical standards of conduct—concluded that mediators should simply try to facilitate the parties' own resolution of the matter. They admonished professionals who serve as mediators (including lawyers) to "refrain from providing professional advice." Florida, Hawaii and New Jersey are the only states that have adopted qualification requirements for mediators. Many states merely require completion of 40 hours of training, while in others a law license is enough. Florida is the only state to take the further step of implementing a disciplinary process for mediators.

Private Judging

In many communities, retired judges are available for an hourly fee (often as high as $350 per hour) to hear and resolve disputes. With this approach, parties may agree in advance whether the decision will be legally binding. The disadvantages of non-binding arbitration also apply to non-binding private judging. While private-judging costs are substantially higher than court-annexed arbitration costs, private judging is considerably more flexible. A private judge may be retained without court intervention and without litigation first being instituted. The parties are free to select a judge and a mutually convenient date for the hearing. The hearing itself tends to be informal, and the rules of evidence are not strictly applied. The private judge often uses a settlement-conference approach, as opposed to a trial approach, to achieve a resolution of the dispute.

Moderated-Settlement Conferences

If you're involved in litigation, after litigation begins, a court may insist that you and the other litigant participate in settlement discussions before a judge or a mediator located at the courthouse. If the court does not schedule a settlement conference, you or the other party to the case can usually request one, often with a particular judge.

The attorneys are usually required to prepare a memorandum jointly that informs the judge of each party's contentions, theories and claimed damages. Parties, as well as attorneys, attend the conference so that the judge may explain his or her view of the case and obtain the parties' consent to any proposed settlement. If a resolution is reached in the judge's chambers, the litigants often proceed to the courtroom so that the settlement—and the parties' consent to it—can be entered into the record. The creation of this written record helps eliminate any further disputes regarding what was promised. Aside from attorneys' fees, moderated-settlement conferences have no out-of-pocket costs. In addition, information obtained or revealed in the conference is deemed to be for settlement purposes only, making it inadmissible, if the litigation continues, for the purpose of determining liability. For these reasons, moderated-settlement conferences provide an excellent "last ditch effort" for resolving a dispute prior to trial.

Small-Claims Court

Very minor disputes, such as matters that involve a small monetary amount (typically no greater than $2,500), are often best resolved in small-claims court. Generally, litigants represent themselves and describe the dispute in an informal manner to a judge, who renders a decision at the time of the hearing. Court filing fees are moderate, and a trial date is usually set for two or three months after filing. Often a bookkeeper or credit manager may represent a company as long as he or she is knowledgeable about the particular dispute and has supporting documentation. Unfortunately, it is often difficult for a successful plaintiff to actually collect the judgment. As a result, many courts have small-claims advisers who can assist litigants in collecting the money awarded.

The Benefits of ADR

Regardless of which method you choose, ADR offers many advantages.

FASTER RESOLUTION OF DISPUTES. The need to reduce delays in resolving legal claims was one of the driving forces behind the ADR movement. As the number of civil filings continues to increase, it is clear that the courts cannot expeditiously accommodate the influx unless many parties obtain a final resolution of their disputes outside the courthouse.

COST SAVINGS. In a study by the accounting firm of Deloitte & Touche, 60% of all ADR users and 78% of those characterized as extensive users reported that they had saved money by using ADR. The amount of savings ranged from 11% to 50% of the cost of litigation.

PRESERVING RELATIONSHIPS. ADR offers the opportunity for parties to resolve a dispute without engendering the bitterness that may destroy a business or personal relationship.

PROTECTING CONFIDENTIAL INFORMATION. Traditional litigation often results in public disclosure of proprietary information, particularly in commercial disputes. Although one party may seek a protective order restricting the other party's access to its trade secrets, the mere process of obtaining such an order subjects the confidential information to outside scrutiny. ADR procedures allow the parties to resolve their disputes while better protecting confidential information.

FLEXIBILITY. ADR allows the parties to tailor the dispute-resolution process so that it is uniquely suited to the matter at hand. Parties can select the mechanism, determine the amount of information that needs to be exchanged, choose their own neutral third party, and agree on a format for the procedure, all in a way that makes sense for the issue in dispute.

DURABILITY OF THE RESULT. Resolutions achieved by consensus of the disputants are less likely to be challenged than resolutions imposed by a court.

BETTER, MORE CREATIVE SOLUTIONS. By giving litigants early and direct participation, ADR provides a better opportunity for achieving a resolution based on the parties' real interests. Such agreements often involve terms other than the distribution of dollars from one party to another, and may well produce a solution that makes more sense for the parties than one imposed by a court.

Is ADR a Viable Option?

The following situations are ones in which ADR is likely to be a successful alternative to litigation.

WHEN AN ADR CONTRACT CLAUSE IS IN PLACE. The most important indicator of possible ADR success is the existence of an effective contract clause that provides for the use of ADR in the event of a dispute.

IN CONTINUING RELATIONSHIPS. If a continuing relationship between the parties is possible (as with franchisors and franchisees or suppliers and customers), the chances of ADR success are greatly enhanced. It makes more sense for the parties to continue a profitable business relationship than to sever it because of litigation.

IN COMPLEX DISPUTES. If a case involves highly complex subject matter, such as advanced technology, there is a substantial chance that a jury and even a judge may become confused. Under these circumstances, ADR may be the best option, particularly if the proceedings are conducted before a neutral person who is an expert on the subject of the dispute. And because the parties themselves select the arbitrator or mediator, they will have the opportunity to choose a well-qualified candidate rather than accept the random assignment of a judge or be subjected to the caprices of the jury-selection process. In addition, the American Arbitration Association has enacted rules specifically designed for use in complex cases.

WHEN RELATIVELY LITTLE MONEY IS AT STAKE. If the amount of money in dispute is relatively small, the cost of litigation may approach or even exceed that amount, making ADR a much more sensible approach.

WHEN CONFIDENTIALITY IS AN IMPORTANT ISSUE. In an ADR proceeding, the parties can more easily maintain confidentiality, not just of business information but of the nature of the case. The need for confidentiality can prove to be more important than any other consideration in selecting a dispute-resolution process.

The following situations are ones in which ADR is not likely to be successful.

WHEN FACING A SKEPTICAL AND MISTRUSTING ADVERSARY. If the parties are sufficiently hostile, one side may refuse to agree to otherwise well-qualified arbitrators simply because they were suggested by the opponent, or may see the other side's efforts to employ ADR after a complaint has been filed as a ploy designed to get an edge in litigation.

WHEN PARTIES OR THEIR LAWYERS HAVE HARSH ATTITUDES. When the parties or their lawyers are particularly emotional, belligerent or abusive, instead of focusing on the expeditious resolution of the case, they are likely to be more interested inn airing their grievances, thereby significantly diminishing the chances for successful non-binding ADR.

WHEN THE CASE IS ONE OF MANY. If the case at issue is just one of many that is expected to be filed, then it is highly unlikely that the defendant will be motivated to agree at an early stage to the use of ADR, particularly if it is non-binding. This also may be one of those rare situations where full-blown litigation is actually more cost-effective due to the efficiency gained by the consolidation of multiple cases.

WHEN DELAYS ARE ADVANTAGEOUS. If a delay will benefit one of the parties, then the chances for the successful use of ADR are diminished.

WHEN THERE ARE MONETARY IMBALANCES. If there is a monetary imbalance between the parties and the wealthier party thinks it can wear down the other party through litigation, it will be difficult to obtain the wealthier party's agreement to ADR.

As the owner of a growing company, you must be committed to developing programs and procedures within your organization that are specifically designed to avoid the time and expense of litigation. Business conflicts are inevitable, but lengthy trials are not if you take prompt steps to resolve legal disputes. If you encounter conflicts that cannot be amicably resolved, then take the time to understand the costs and benefits of litigation and its alternatives well before the pleadings are filed. If litigation is, in fact, the only alternative available to your company, then you must work closely with your lawyers to establish specific strategies, objectives and budgets for each conflict that matures into a formal legal dispute.

Managing the Dark Side of Business Growth: Bankruptcy and Its Alternatives

T HE BUSINESS SUCCESS STORY THAT TURNS INTO A nightmare often goes like this: A growing company begins to achieve and exceed its projected growth plans. The company moves into new offices, recruits new employees, increases management salaries and benefits, hires a team of outside advisers and begins plans for acquisitions and eventually a public offering of its stock.

The founding entrepreneur has built a successful company, but has also created a challenge beyond his experience and capabilities. His ego and bullheadedness prevent him from accepting the fact that he needs to appoint a professional-management team.

A culture of growth at any price begins to build within the company. Most of the staff rides an emotional roller coaster, with feelings that range from excitement to fear to blind trust.

The cash-flow shortages are subtle at first, but with each new month of growth, expenses begin to exceed revenues at a quickening pace.

The company, in addition to not paying attention to the bottom line, is so caught up in its own growth that it is not paying sufficient attention to the aggressive steps competitors are taking or to the changes in the marketplace that are affecting its industry.

Failing to Manage
All Aspects of Business Growth

As you can see from this story, growth for growth's sake is not acceptable in today's competitive marketplace. In addition to managing and adapting to the more exciting aspects of business growth, you must also:

- **anticipate the financial problems,** particularly with a focus on cash flow—it is the slow-pay and no-pay customers in a weakened economic environment who will potentially kill your company;
- **monitor your company's business plan** and model to ensure that growth and profitability targets are met;
- **manage the costs and risks** associated with economic problems;
- **keep a close watch on business trends** that may require your business to change strategies; and
- **understand the methods and alternatives** available for resolving financial problems.

The rapid growth of the Internet-driven economy in the late 1990s and the harsh dose of reality in early 2000 lead to many high-profile bankruptcies. In many of these failures, management teams who had at one time been regarded as industry pioneers and leaders failed to manage these five key tasks.

Companies such as Cybercash.com (e-commerce systems), Lernout & Hauspie (voice-recognition technologies), eToys. com (business-to-consumer sales), Iridium (satellite-based mobile-phone services), and NorthPoint Communications (high-speed Internet services/DSL provider) filed for bankruptcy in 2000 and 2001. In fact, according to studies published by Webmergers.com, more than 300 dot.com and technology companies failed between 1999 and mid 2001, leaving thousands without jobs and without any value in their stocks. Some of these companies filed for bankruptcy, while others more informally shut down or sold to third parties at deep discounts

The problems facing leaders of growing companies who do not keep a close watch on the financial condition of their companies, or who ignore key trends that may quickly have an adverse effect on their plans or strategies, are not limited to technology. Other leading companies that have filed for bankruptcy in 2000 and 2001 include those in traditional industries, such as TWA, Fruit of the Loom, Sunbeam, Planet Hollywood, and Loews Cineplex Entertainment. As this book was going to press, many other companies were on the brink of bankruptcy, having lost hundreds of millions of dollars in market value as their stocks plunged into the single digits. Such companies include Xerox, CMGI (Internet incubator), VerticalNet (B2B vertical-exchange operator), Amazon.com, Friendly's Ice Cream and Revlon.

Many of these companies' losses resulted from misguided business strategies; misjudged markets; over-reliance on a given customer; fixed expenses ballooning out of control; accounts receivables overlooked that were 90+ days overdue; credit extended too easily or business continued with customers who were deep in arrears; obsolescent technologies; embarrassing accounting irregularities; or simply growth too fast to manage. Loewen Group is an example of the latter problem. It aggressively bought out its funeral-home competitors nationwide, paying too much and acquiring targets too quickly. The company did not allow time for integration of the companies it purchased, thus could not achieve post-acquisition operating efficiencies.

Other companies such as Owens-Corning and Armstrong World Industries, at one time healthy companies in the home-building and construction-supply business, faced financial problems and were forced to file bankruptcy to contend with the costs of product-liability and asbestos class-action lawsuits. The significant cost of defending these legal attacks drastically diluted what would otherwise have been healthy earnings.

Solutions for a Financially Troubled Company

When the economy is slowing and the capital markets tighten, the chances increase significantly that a rapidly growing company or even a market leader will face a cash-flow crunch or have trouble meeting its operating expenses. The solutions to these financial and operating problems are often found in the non-traditional or troubled-company/turnaround segment of the venture-capital markets. But because risk is high, the cost of borrowing capital or getting an equity infusion is often prohibitively high, offering the providers of this capital a tremendous upside, if either the company or the economy begins to improve dramatically.

Financiers who specialize in investing in companies on the brink of failure are known as "grave dancers" or "vulture investors."

Financiers who specialize in investing in companies on the brink of failure are specialty lenders or investors known as "grave dancers" or "vulture investors," because they pick through the bones of near-dead or dead companies to find the remaining morsels that may be of value. Where most investors would see virtually incurable problems, these troubled-company investors and lenders see opportunity and the chance to earn significant profits as a result of the growing company's distress. Often, they combine capital with turnaround management expertise to rebuild and restructure troubled companies and ensure a return on their investment.

But for this risky strategy to work there must be a core of residual value that can be tapped and harnessed. There must be a few sparks left in the ashes from which the company can be rebuilt and the sources of this high-risk financing rewarded. Naturally, reaching out to this pool of resources is quite expensive in terms of the cost of capital and potential loss of control.

The Importance of Risk Management

Commonly used in the insurance industry, risk management is the process of identifying and analyzing a company's exposure to risk, and then selecting alternatives for protecting against these risks. Once identified, certain types of economic and financial risks are predictable and can be managed, while other types of risks are usually beyond the control of even the best management team. Similarly, certain types of risks can be mitigated with insurance, while others, such as hostile acts by suppliers or competitors, are not insurable. To implement a risk-management program for your company, consider the following questions:

- **What aspects of your company's operations** could directly or indirectly cause an economic loss?
- **What is the likelihood** that such a loss will actually occur?
- **If the potential loss** you identify actually occurs, what tangible and intangible costs will be the result of such a loss?
- **To what extent are the potential losses insurable?** Does the cost of the insurance policies outweigh the cost of potential conflict or loss?
- **To what extent can you** and your management team implement internal financial controls to prevent or reduce the exposure to financial distress?

Effective risk management goes far beyond the installation of smoke detectors and a periodic safety check for all company-owned vehicles. From a management perspective, it means you must establish internal financial and managerial controls designed to ensure ongoing compliance with your company's strategies, policies and procedures. From an accounting perspective, it means you must ensure that accurate and comprehensive financial records are maintained so that periodic financial statements are produced on a timely basis in accordance with generally accepted accounting principles (GAAP). From a legal perspective, it means you must ensure that your company is in compliance with corporate-law formalities; labor and employment laws; antitrust and trade regulations; maintenance of all necessary business licenses and permits; material contractual obligations (such as vendor agreements, leases and loan documents); obligations to protect intellectual property; and any other laws and regulations which may be applicable to the company's operation and management.

As discussed in Chapter 10, periodic legal audits are one effective method of ensuring that a company remains in compliance with its legal obligations, the nature and extent of which are likely to change as the company grows and develops.

Anticipating Distress

The primary role of a risk-management and control system is to provide early-warning signs of financial distress. Early detection of business problems is vital to a company's continued growth and to the management of situations that are likely to cause economic distress. Business problems rarely occur suddenly. Most problems develop over a long period of time due to a series of financial, legal, operational and strategic mistakes or miscalculations that went largely undetected by management. Some obvious symptoms that a company is heading down the wrong course include:

- **persistent operating losses;**
- **the departure of several key employees;**
- **the loss of more than 5% market share** per quarter in two consecutive quarters;
- **recurring cash flow shortages;** and
- **a general loss of morale** and enthusiasm among workers at all levels.

Distressed companies often show an inability to service debt, a decline in profits and margins, or inefficiency in management structure, or in the delivery of services. It is often difficult to convince management to take the steps necessary to cure the problems. Many entrepreneurs mistakenly believe that they can remedy their company's problems by selling more products or services, when in fact this approach does not address the specific cause of the company's distress—and may even be part of it.

Recognizing the Warning Signs

To determine whether your growing company is on a course leading to disaster, see if you can spot any of these red flags.

LACK OF DEPTH IN THE MANAGEMENT TEAM. If your company depends on an overly centralized management team made up of the original founders, its risk of failure is greatly increased. Your company's long-term health lies in your (and your cofounders') ability to recruit and retain qualified personnel who are capable of taking and guiding the company to its next phase of growth.

OPERATING IN AN INDUSTRY WITH RAPIDLY CHANGING TECHNOLOGY. If your growing company operates in a marketplace where rapidly changing technology could render its products and services suddenly obsolete, the chances of business failure are very high. As a result, you and your management team must stay abreast of technological developments, attempt to establish product diversification, and ensure adequate capitalization for ongoing research and modernization of equipment.

DEPENDENCE ON A KEY CUSTOMER, SUPPLIER, LENDER OR CONTRACT. Many rapid-growth companies have been built and continue to flourish as a result of a single critical customer or supplier, or because of a special relationship with a lender or investor. But if you want to grow your business even more, you can't be a hostage to any third party that you cannot completely control. For example, if your company relies on a major customer for 35% to 60%t of its revenues, what will be the effect on your company if you lose that customer to a competitor? Worse yet, if that key customer is aware of your company's dependence on its business, how many demands will that customer make, and you be forced to grant, as a result of your need to preserve the account? Similarly, if your company is excessively dependent on patents, licenses, concessions, and related contractual advantages that may be terminated or expire, the chance of business failure significantly increases. The only way to help mitigate the risk of dependence on a third party is to diversify product lines, geographic trading areas, targeted markets, and distribution channels.

UNDERCAPITALIZATION FOR SPECIFIC PROJECTS. It's easy for rapidly growing companies to charge ahead and seek to take advantage of market opportunities even if they lack the capital necessary to complete the components of the project. For example, say your company manufactures a product that management deems necessary for staying competitive, but your company doesn't have the necessary capital for bringing the product to the market. Producing the product would only be a waste of time and resources. Under such circumstances, it often makes more sense to sell or license the technology to another company, then use the proceeds or licensing royalties to exploit an existing product or service your company offers.

DEFECTIVE INFORMATION AND MONITORING SYSTEMS. A growing company with an inadequate or defective management-information system is likely to have difficulty monitoring its competition, internal costs and budgets, changes in the economic and political environment, inventory controls, management problems and internal conflicts, cash flow, and sales growth. If your company lacks access to this information in an organized and timely fashion, then it is likely to experience difficulty in making informed day-to-day decisions or engaging in meaningful long-term strategic planning.

RETAINING NON-PRODUCTIVE DIVISIONS, ASSETS AND PEOPLE FOR NO GOOD REASON. Many fast-track growth companies will inevitably have an unproductive operating division, asset or person putting a strain on their overall profitability. If you see this happening, the only solution is to get rid of the deadwood. Especially dangerous to keep around are projects or people that remain for paternalistic or egotistical reasons. Chances are that such a lack of productivity is bleeding precious cash from your company. Any obsolete or idle equipment, unused real estate and unnecessary employee benefits (such as the company car, boat, condominium, or plane) should also be candidates for disposal when cash is at a premium.

ACCOUNTS-RECEIVABLE MANAGEMENT PROBLEMS. If with your company's tremendous increase in sales comes an equally growing accounts-receivable management problem, it's clear that your accounts-receivable procedures need to be revamped. Be sure that customers are carefully monitored, with no further goods or services provided when overdue accounts reach certain levels. As soon as a customer shows signs of difficulty paying, obtain collateral to secure the obligation. Use collection agencies and lawyers for larger problem accounts. If cash flow becomes a real problem, consider discounting the accounts receivable at a commercial bank, obtaining the services of a factoring company, or obtaining credit insurance to protect against excessive bad-debt losses.

The Costs of Financial Distress

When a company suffers from financial distress, the effects are felt by employees, customers, stockholders, creditors and suppliers, and often are compounded by their responses to the distress. For example, customers and vendors often attempt to avoid dealing with a troubled company, which is likely to further damage its financial performance and ability to raise capital. Vendors, to the extent that they are still willing to sell to a distressed firm at all, are likely to demand unreasonable sales terms to protect their risk. Key employees, fearful for their jobs, often flee to a more stable competitor, usually taking their enthusiasm, ideas and expertise with them. As a result, the distressed company will face even more difficulty attracting and retaining skilled personnel, who may be desperately needed to keep the company alive. Stockholders are likely to dispose of their securities, driving down the market price per share. Creditors of a troubled company often seek to accelerate obligations to protect against the risk of default. During this difficult period, it is likely that a company's inventory will become obsolete, building and machinery will deteriorate as result of lack of capital for upkeep, and equipment will not be maintained because the company lacks the resources to commit to servicing or replacing worn parts. Finally, competitors are likely to become more aggressive in taking advantage of the opportunities created by the company's financial distress.

Bankruptcy

If your company does get in a difficult financial situation, all hope is not lost. Bankruptcy (and its alternatives, discussed beginning on page 543) may offer you a way of salvaging your company. Bankruptcy does not carry quite the same stigma that it did 20 years ago. In fact, reorganization under the federal bankruptcy laws has emerged as an integral part of the long-term strategic planning process and as a viable alternative for a troubled project, subsidiary or entire company.

Bankruptcy can be extremely time-consuming and disruptive to management's responsibilities and morale, and often results in extensive negative publicity and loss of goodwill, involves substantial legal fees and causes a significantly weakened bargaining position with creditors and competitors. A formal bankruptcy proceeding usually results in:

- **a transfer** of the company's control to creditors;
- **a significantly reduced ability** to raise capital;
- **the need to terminate** a large percentage of the company's workforce; and
- **difficulty in attracting qualified employees** and service providers.

Carefully consider these costs and risks when considering bankruptcy as a solution to your company's financial distress.

Creditors tend to favor formal or informal reorganization when the principal cause is temporary (known as a Chapter 11 filing) and liquidation of the assets when the principal cause is permanent (known as a Chapter 7 filing), because the company is ultimately worth more to the stockholders dead than alive.

Petition for Relief Under Chapter 11

A troubled company may voluntarily petition for formal reorganization under Chapter 11 or be involuntarily forced into reorganization by at least three of its creditors (unless the company has fewer than 12 creditors, in which case even a single creditor can force a reorganization).

In a typical Chapter 11 proceeding, the debtor is essentially reclassified into a "debtor in possession." It is either permitted to continue to operate and manage its business, subject to certain restrictions imposed by the court and the federal bankruptcy statutes, or the court may determine that the company's management is so incompetent that a trustee or management committee must be appointed to full or partial control of the company during the period that the plan of reorganization is being developed and approved. Once the company has been reclassified as a debtor-in-possession, it has a fiduciary duty to protect the assets of the business on behalf of its secured and unsecured creditors. There is also the possibility that the court will deem the current management incapable of running the company and will appoint a "receiver" to manage the day-to-day affairs for the benefit of the creditors. Either way, restrictions will be placed on the company's ability to borrow and raise capital, enter into new contracts, hire new employees, implement management strategies and conduct certain business operations. The direct and indirect costs of these restrictions are high, in terms of both professional fees and management resources. It is likely that the founding entrepreneurs will be spending more time at court appearances, meetings with creditors and on the preparation of financial statements and schedules than they will actually operating and managing the business.

Although these costs associated with a Chapter 11 filing are high, if your company is facing financial distress, a Chapter 11 filing also offers benefits to your company against which these costs must be weighed. For example, upon the filing of the petition for reorganization, all actions against the company and its assets are subject to an automatic stay, which has the effect of delaying almost all immediate obligations and proceedings until the formal plan has been approved. In fact, creditors who attempt to violate the automatic-stay provisions may be held in contempt of court. Once the statutory requirements of the formal plan have been met and all necessary consents obtained, the plan is ready to be confirmed by the presiding bankruptcy judge. The confirmation of the plan has the following legal ramifications:

- **The plan has a binding effect** on the troubled company and its creditors.
- **All property of the bankruptcy estate** is vested in the reorganized debtor, free and clear of all liens and encumbrances unless otherwise stated in the plan.
- **All prior debts of the troubled company** are discharged except as may be provided in the plan.

■ **The debtor company commences** its operations pursuant to the terms of the plan.

If your company faces financial troubles, the development and approval of a formal plan of reorganization offers significant benefits; however, approval marks the beginning, not the end, of a successful turnaround. If the company is reorganized properly, then it may emerge and prosper even more effectively than prior to the bankruptcy proceedings. There are many emerging-growth companies, however, that survive the bankruptcy process, but that are subsequently unable to truly flourish under the terms and conditions of the approved reorganization plan. The change in control, management policies and operational freedom caused by the reorganization plan could result in an eventual collapse of the company, leading to another reorganization or even liquidation proceedings under Chapter 7.

Formal Liquidation Under Chapter 7

If the troubled company cannot be formally reorganized, or if the plan of reorganization proves to be unsuccessful, then a formal liquidation under Chapter 7 of the Bankruptcy Act must be considered. The proceedings under Chapter 7 begin with the filing of either a voluntary or involuntary petition for liquidation. Upon filing of the petition, the court will issue to the petitioner an "order for relief," which triggers the automatic stay provisions. At the same time, a trustee will be appointed to manage the company's assets, referred to as the "bankruptcy estate." Creditors must file a proof of claim within 90 days of the first meeting between the debtor, trustee and creditors. The appointed trustee then gathers together all available assets into the bankruptcy estate for liquidation, sets aside any fraudulent transfers, reviews the validity of all proof of claims submitted by creditors, separates the interests of secured and unsecured creditors, determines if any assets collected are exempt from liquidation, and arranges for the sale of the assets in the bankruptcy estate in a manner and on terms most advantageous to the creditors. Once the assets have been gathered, inventoried, appraised and sold, the trustee distributes the proceeds to the creditors according to the terms of the plan of liquidation, and virtually all obligations of the debtor are discharged.

Alternatives to Bankruptcy

If your company becomes financially troubled, you have several alternatives to bankruptcy, both under the federal bankruptcy laws and informally in a workout with major creditors. The alternative that is right for your company will be determined by whether the principal cause of failure is temporary or permanent.

Implementing a Turnaround Plan

To rescue your company from financial distress, weigh the viability of the development and implementation of a formal turnaround plan, which usually involves a critical evaluation and assessment from an outside adviser who can make recommendations for eliminating waste by downsizing and trimming the fat. This assessment may include:

- **intensive data-gathering;**
- **careful listening to key employees;**
- **tightening controls** (including reducing expenses and maintaining an "extra slim" inventory);
- **developing strong internal reporting systems;**
- **negotiating for extended terms with suppliers;**
- **reviewing materials, labor and engineering;** and
- **studying the administrative overhead.**

Many growing companies find that once the bleeding has stopped and the internal attitudes have been adjusted, the company can have a second chance as a profitable operation.

Informal Negotiations with Creditors

In almost all cases, an informal workout with creditors is more efficient and less disruptive than a formal Chapter 11 proceeding. An informal workout may include:

- **negotiating an extension;**
- **restructuring the overall costs or terms;**
- **composing an agreement** (under which all known creditors accept partial payment on a pro rata basis in full satisfaction of the obligation);
- **transferring partial control** of the company or even exchanging all or part of the debt for equity.

The cooperation of all known creditors is necessary for this alternative to be viable, because there is usually no way to force dissenting creditors to become parties to a composition or settlement agreement. This would not be the case, however, in a formal Chapter 11 proceeding, where the judge has the power of the "cram down" rules used to force a creditor to accept the terms of whatever the court deems to be a generally fair and equitable plan of reorganization.

Informal Reorganization

With this alternative to bankruptcy, you may seek to voluntarily reorganize or restructure your company in order to achieve more efficient and more profitable operations. For instance, your board of directors may choose to merge or be acquired by another company that could make more effective use of your company's remaining assets. Alternatively, your company could separate one of its profitable divisions from the unprofitable division and create two different subsidiaries. Capital formation efforts could then be placed on the profitable subsidiary with plans to rebuild the unprofitable subsidiary at a later date. Finally, you could simply "spin off" certain assets to third parties and then use the proceeds of the sale to repay debts and concentrate on the growth and development of the remaining operations. Each of these basic methods of informal reorganization usually can be implemented more quickly and inexpensively than a formal proceeding under Chapter 11, provided, however, the principals of the company can obtain the cooperation and support of stockholders and creditors.

The benefits of implementing an informal workout or

reorganization plan as an alternative must not be underestimated. This is especially true for owners and managers of closely held companies, where the list of trade creditors and lenders is likely to be far shorter than for a large, publicly traded corporation. Small companies are much more likely to be able to gather their creditors for the purpose of negotiating a composition agreement than would a multinational corporation which has thousands of creditors.

To safeguard your growing company against situations that are likely to lead to financial distress, work closely with your accountants and attorneys to identify and manage risks. The costs of financial distress are very high, and can even be fatal. If your company does face financial distress, carefully analyze and assess the formal and informal legal strategies available to you, so that the recovery path you select and the lessons you and your management team learn will ultimately lead to a successful turnaround and continued growth for your company.

Growing Up Too Fast: Antitrust and Related Regulatory Aspects of Business Growth

A S MICROSOFT, INTEL AND OTHER RAPID-GROWTH companies learned the hard way in the late 1990s, one of the few downside risks of business growth is having federal or state regulators decide that you have grown too much too fast or through strategies or practices that are anticompetitive in nature. It can also be frustrating if and when your plans to grow via mergers and acquisitions are ultimately blocked by federal regulators due to antitrust concerns, as Worldcom learned when its plans to acquire Sprint broke down. As an entrepreneur, you may dream of achieving a fast-track growth level and market-share dominance that would put you on the radar screen of a potential antitrust action. But those dreams quickly fade when you must actually deal with the time and expense of reporting to regulatory inquiries or when your proposed transaction is held up for months by government lawyers. Even if you are never on the defending end of an antitrust dispute, it is critical that you understand the basics of the antitrust laws as a potential plaintiff in the event that your efforts to expand are being restricted by the anticompetitive practices of the dominant player in your marketplace. This chapter provides a brief overview of the federal antitrust laws as well as some related laws that may affect certain types of business-growth strategies.

Federal Antitrust Laws

The federal antitrust laws, beginning with the Sherman Act of 1890, the Clayton Act of 1914, the Federal Trade Commission Act of 1914 and the Robinson-Patman Act of 1936, have been designed to promote a free-market system and protect against restraints of trade. Conflicts have arisen, however, between the two themes at the heart of antitrust policy. On the one hand, political theory supported a body of law that promoted equality and fair play among businesses. (Under this view, the interests of the entrepreneur are paramount, even if the end result was economic inefficiency. This view essentially states that the interests of the small-business owner are paramount to the interests of the consumer.) On the other hand, antitrust laws have also been developed based on economic theory. (Economists view antitrust as a body of law designed to protect competition and production efficiency, with the emphasis on the consumer and not the interests of individual competitors.) No matter which theory is currently at the forefront, if you are adopting aggressive strategies to expand your company's market share, you must be aware of the pricing, customer relations, marketing practices and distribution methods that will not be tolerated by federal antitrust regulators.

Restraints Prohibited by Antitrust Laws

There are essentially two general categories of restraints of trade that are prohibited by antitrust laws: vertical restraints and horizontal restraints.

VERTICAL RESTRAINTS. These are restraints on trade that develop between firms at different levels in the production and distribution network. Examples include resale-price maintenance, such as an attempt to fix the prices at which the retailer could offer the manufacturer's products; geographic and customer limitations, such as limiting a distributor to an exclusive territory; exclusive dealing arrangements, such as forcing a distributor to sell only a particular line of products; tying, which forces a distributor to buy products A and B, when all he really wants is B; and price discrimination, such as selling to one wholesaler in a given area under terms and conditions primarily designed to drive out regional competition. In certain cases, these arrangements are contractual and voluntary, such as in a franchise agreement, or are necessary to protect against free-riders (so-called because they want the benefits of access to a given product or service without the burdens of the protections imposed by the manufacturer), who threaten product quality and pricing formulas. However, if the government determines that a growing company is implementing these restraints in bad faith merely to protect and expand its market share, antitrust violations are likely to be triggered.

HORIZONTAL RESTRAINTS. The laws against horizontal restraints are designed to protect against large portions of market strength and market share being concentrated in one or only a few firms. Monopolistic practices, such as predatory pricing (underselling rivals in order to acquire or preserve market share) or price fixing among market leaders (in order to squeeze out smaller firms and create greater barriers to market entry), production and output agreements, and other forms of collusion among market leaders and restrictions on mergers and acquisitions, all generally fall within the category of horizontal restraints.

Specific Growth Strategies and Marketing Practices Under Federal and State Antitrust Laws

The penalties for failure to obey the federal antitrust laws can be severe, and in the past have included criminal sanctions, injunctive relief, damages for lost profits and in certain cases triple damages. The following discussion of specific marketing practices that run afoul of the antitrust laws should be of interest to you not only as the owner of a growing company seeking to avoid these sanctions, but also to ensure that you are not injured by such practices on the part of one of your competitors.

There are a wide variety of growth strategies and specific marketing, distribution and pricing practices that are closely scrutinized by federal and state antitrust laws. For example, suppose that a rapidly growing electronics manufacturer adopted a marketing strategy that called for entry into new geographic markets, either by means of acquisition of other consumer-electronic product manufacturers or by developing a below-cost pricing structure in new territories. Although such a strategy appears on its face to be perfectly legitimate, it may trigger horizontal-restraint problems under the Sherman Act or predatory-pricing problems (if an anticompetitive intent is proven) under the Robinson-Patman Act, both of which carry civil and even criminal penalties. Therefore, it is the responsibility of the company's marketing department to develop strategies and objectives that comply with applicable antitrust laws and to recognize when legal advice is needed. When you are developing marketing strategies for your company, you and your marketing team should consider the following specific practices, which have been deemed to be anticompetitive or in restraint of trade under federal and state antitrust laws.

The company's marketing department is responsible for developing strategies and objectives that comply with applicable antitrust laws.

Monopolistic Practices

It may seem ironic that a capitalistic society that fosters entrepreneurship and business growth also has laws to penalize companies who manage to acquire substantial market power. Nonetheless, the antitrust laws have struggled over the last century to draw a line between practices that are permissible because market power was achieved due to a superior product or business skill, and practices that must be condemned as being anticompetitive and harmful to our economy and society because market power was achieved due to a conscious effort by a growing company to reduce output and raise prices. The current approach for striking this balance involves the application of a "rule of reason" test to the conduct in question. The rule-of-reason" test examines all relevant facts and circumstances in an attempt to determine whether the particular act by the company was exclusionary and harmful to competition or whether the act should be permitted as actually fostering and promoting competition. A wide variety of acts could be deemed to be monopolistic. These would include price discrimination, a refusal to do business with a given customer or supplier (often referred to as a refusal to deal), certain customer and territorial restrictions, mergers of rivals, tying arrangements and conspiracies among competitors (some of which are discussed in greater detail below). Courts have consistently stated that size and growth alone, even at the expense of competitors, is not enough to determine guilt under the antitrust laws; rather, there must be some wrongful intent or illegal conduct by which the company seeks to either obtain or sustain market power.

Courts have consistently stated that size and growth alone, even at the expense of competitors, is not enough to determine guilt under the antitrust laws.

Price-Fixing

The Sherman Act specifically prohibits "contracts, combinations or conspiracies" in restraint of trade. Under Section 1 of the Sherman Act, if two or more competitors conspire to fix prices or methods of price computation (e.g., base-point pricing) at a certain level, then such conduct is illegal per se. This means the courts will not tolerate such practices regardless of the facts and circumstances, even if prices are fair, reasonable and in the best interests of all competitors within the industry or geographic area. This "per se" approach not only affects any agreements among competitors as to price, but also covers any terms and conditions of sale, such as credit terms, shipping policies or trade-in allowances. Another practice closely related to horizontal price-fixing is known as *conscious parallelism,* where companies follow the acts of a dominant market leader, such as a change in price or sales terms, even in the absence of a formal agreement to fix prices among competitors. For example, in the airlines industry, a price cut by one carrier usually triggers a price cut by the others, and vice-versa for price increases. If these price adjustments are in response to competition and market forces, they are typically legally acceptable, but if they follow a pattern that over time is harmful to the consumer, then they are likely to be challenged.

Similar legal principles apply to price-fixing attempts in the vertical chain of distribution, generally known as resale price maintenance (RPM). Attempts by a company to impose RPM policies on its distributors and retailers are also illegal per se, with a few limited exceptions for non-price vertical restraints, such as unilateral refusals to deal, customer restraints, and the designation of exclusive territories. Perhaps the most noted exception to the per se illegality of vertical price-fixing is the unilateral refusal-to-deal-rule. This rule allows an objective decision by a manufacturer that it will not deal with distributors who cut prices below suggested levels, provided that the decision to refuse to deal is both truly unilateral (that is, not at the urging of another distributor) and is not the result of threats or intimidation. The only other well-recognized exception to the per se rule against RPM is when a manufacturer essentially retains ownership of the product by distributing on a consignment basis. These consignment arrangements make the reseller a mere "agent" of the manufacturer and thus create a legal and business justification for controlling prices.

> **Attempts by a company to impose resale price maintainence policies on its distributors and retailers are also illegal per se, with a few limited exceptions.**

Price Discrimination

Most price-discrimination issues arise under the Robinson-Patman Act, when a seller offers its otherwise uniform products at different prices due to size or geographic location of the buyer. The Robinson-Patman law is designed to ensure fair pricing among the various buyers of the seller's products and to protect against pricing strategies that are intended to drive out local competition.

Here again, the antitrust laws attempt to draw a line between competitive practices that will be encouraged and anticompetitive practices that will be prohibited. For example, the Robinson-Patman Act does not expressly prohibit a seller from charging a lower price to a customer if the actual costs of the sale are lower due to the quantities purchased by the buyer or the geographic proximity of the buyer. Similarly, a seller is permitted to drop its prices under certain circumstances if necessary to meet changing market conditions—to compete with a rival's equally low price, for example—as long as products are not sold below cost. As with certain related monopolistic practices, Robinson-Patman must be considered not only for direct pricing issues, but also for non-price considerations such as promotional allowances and credit terms.

Vertical Non-Price Restraints

Manufacturers may attempt to implement a variety of restraints on distribution channels that trigger antitrust considerations. The three most common forms are "tying," "exclusive dealing," and "territorial and customer restrictions."

TYING. In this arrangement, the sale or lease of Product X (which the buyer wants) is conditioned on the buyer also purchasing Product Y (which the buyer may not necessarily want). Recent cases have established a clear test for distinguishing when a tie-in arrangement will be permitted and when it will be prohibited, although the exact elements of the test vary among jurisdictions. A threshold condition to finding an illegal tying arrangement has always been that the seller has sufficient market power and exercises enough coercion to truly force the buyer to purchase Product Y as a condition to getting Product X.

EXCLUSIVE DEALING. This involves a situation where a buyer contracts to purchase all of its requirements of a given product exclusively from a particular seller.

If the buyer is entering into such an arrangement merely to meet its requirements for a given product in a period of market-supply uncertainty, the agreement would not be classified as anticompetitive. However, if the exclusive-dealing contract is designed to suppress competition, then it will be examined by the court in light of all relevant facts and circumstances under the "rule of reason" test, and is likely to be found anti-competitive.

TERRITORIAL AND CUSTOMER RESTRICTIONS. These usually involve attempts by sellers to divide the targeted market into distinct territorial segments and grant geographic or customer exclusivity to a given buyer.

Courts have struggled with the antitrust implications of such arrangements primarily because of the dual effect on competition that territorial and customer restraints tend to have—namely, that interbrand competition (competition among different manufacturers) is generally increased at the same time that intrabrand competition (competition among different retailers of the same manufacturer) is generally adversely affected. The courts have attempted to balance this conflicting effect on competition by analyzing all of the surrounding facts and circumstances of a territorial or customer restraint under the "rule of reason" test.

State Antitrust Statutes

As a general rule, state antitrust statutes closely parallel federal antitrust laws; however, specific rules and regulations often vary widely from state to state. When developing marketing and distribution strategies for your growing company, there are three key trends in state antitrust statutes that you must consider.

First, as federal enforcement of the antitrust laws becomes more relaxed, many state attorneys general have become more vigilant in their enforcement of civil and criminal state antitrust statutes. These statutes are being used as vehicles to enforce economic and political positions regarding antitrust-enforcement policies within the given state's jurisdiction as well as to pursue white collar and organized criminals whose business practices may be, among other things, in restraint of trade. A second important trend has been the willingness of state courts and juries to interpret the state antitrust statutes more broadly and the exceptions to antitrust violations more narrowly. For example, in a case where a large local employer is being adversely affected by the trade practices of an unknown out-of-town conglomerate, arguments concerning the economic efficiency provided by the conglomerate are unlikely to be effective in persuading a jury to rule in favor of the conglomerate. Finally, many recent state anti-takeover statutes designed to protect local business have also fostered an environment where state antitrust-enforcement officials more often than in the past are challenging proposed mergers on anticompetitive grounds.

Establishing an Antitrust-Compliance Program

As your company's growth leads it into new product lines, expanded geographic territories and increased market share, establishing and maintaining a formal antitrust-compliance program becomes of increased importance, and even a virtual necessity for avoiding antitrust problems and penalties.

The first step in implementing an antitrust-compliance program is to conduct an antitrust audit, which consists primarily of a questionnaire circulated to all key employees responsible for marketing, distribution and pricing decisions within your organization. The purpose of the questionnaire is to identify existing company policies, objectives, activities, contracts, practices or even attitudes that could create problems under the antitrust laws if not promptly corrected. The audit should address the following issues:

- **Does the company have an oral or written understanding** with any direct or indirect competitor with respect to pricing, warranties, discounts, shipping and credit terms, promotional contributions or service policies in connection with any of the company's products?
- **What are the exact product and geographical markets** in which the company competes? What is the respective market share of the company in each of these markets?

- **Has the company experienced any actual or threatened antitrust litigation or investigation** in the past? What were the specific company practices on which these claims were based? What steps, if any, have been taken to resolve any of the problems previously identified?
- **How are the company's pricing policies developed?** Is the same product ever sold to different customers at different prices? What is the rationale or justification for such a price disparity?
- **What distribution channels have been selected** for the marketing of the company's products and services? What oral or written agreements have been developed with wholesalers and retailers? Do any of these agreements include specific provisions or understandings as to price, territory or customer restrictions? Does the company engage in dual distribution? Are any buyers of the company's products or services forced to purchase unwanted products and services as a condition to dealing with the company?
- **To what trade associations does the company belong?** What types of information are exchanged among members? Why?

Have your lawyer review the answers to the completed questionnaires to determine whether any changes are needed in your company's policies or practices.

A Brief Introduction to Consumer-Protection Laws

There are an infinite number of federal, state and local consumer-protection laws that directly and indirectly affect a business's marketing and distribution planning and decision-making. This section is not intended to address all of these laws but to underscore the importance of carefully reviewing legal restrictions on product manufacturing, packaging and labeling and false advertising when you develop your company's marketing strategies. In addition to laws of general applicability, the Federal Trade Commission (FTC), the Food and Drug Administration (FDA) and other federal and state regulatory agencies have developed a wide variety of industry-specific regulations in businesses such as textiles, pharmaceuticals and food products.

The consumer-protection laws that generally apply to growing companies tend to fall into one of two categories: laws affecting design and production, or laws affecting sales and advertising.

Laws Affecting Design and Production

Companies of all sizes and in all industries that manufacture consumer or industrial products have a legal as well as a social responsibility to offer products that are safe for their intended use. This commitment to product safety must begin with the design of the product by the research and development department, then becomes the responsibility of the manufacturing department, which ensures that products are produced without defects or hazardous parts. Finally, the marketing department must ensure that the product is packaged in a manner that is not misleading, either in terms of the product's range of capabilities or in the instructions for its use.

Consumer product-safety laws have attracted significant attention in the last decade as a result of increased litigation (resulting in excessive damages awarded to plaintiffs) and insurance costs (resulting in excessive and even unaffordable insurance rates for small companies). At state and local levels, the laws governing product liability, negligence and personal injury determine the manufacturer's responsibility to produce safe products and the penalties for failure to do so. Liability may be imposed due to an act of negligence by the company, a breach of a warranty or even as a result of strict liability. This is a theory that forces a manufacturer to pay damages even if there were neither the intent to produce a faulty product nor a breach of the duty of reasonable care, which is at the heart of all negligence law. The scope and limitation of these state laws are constantly changing; therefore, manufacturers of products, especially at the small-business level, should pay careful attention to the state product-liability laws in the various jurisdictions where their products are manufactured and distributed.

At the federal level, the Consumer Product Safety Commission (CPSC), the FDA and the FTC develop most of the consumer-product safety laws. The CPSC was created in the early 1970s as part of the Consumer Products Safety Act to develop federal regulations to reduce the hazards posed to consumers by unsafe products. CPSC regulations now affect the design, manufacture and marketing of a wide variety of consumer products offered by companies of all sizes. CPSC has the power and authority to:

- **inspect a company's manufacturing facilities;**
- **publicize information about companies** and products that it has determined are in violation of its regulations;
- **force a manufacturer to order a recall,** pay a refund or offer the replacement of a hazardous product;
- **establish regulations for minimum standards of safety** and quality control for specific products; and
- **impose a complete ban** from the marketplace on a given hazardous product.

The FDA represents a second major federal regulator in this area. The principal statute enforced by the FDA is the Federal Food, Drug and Cosmetic Act (FFDCA). The FFDCA is intended to ensure that:

- **food products are pure and wholesome,** safe to eat and produced under sanitary conditions;
- **drugs and medical devices are safe** and effective for their intended uses;
- **cosmetic and beauty-aid products are safe** and made from appropriate ingredients; and
- **packaging and labeling of all types of food, drug and cosmetic products is truthful and informative.** In addition, the Fair Packaging and Labeling Act (FPLA) regulates the contents and placement of information required on the packaging of all consumer and industrial products. The FDA is also charged with the regulation of manufacturing and distribution of certain biological products and electronic devices.

The FFDCA prohibits interstate distribution or international importation of products that are either adulterated or misbranded. An adulterated product is defined by the statute as one that is defective, unsafe, filthy or produced under unsanitary conditions. A misbranded product is defined by the statute as one that includes packaging or labeling that is false, misleading or incomplete. There are a wide variety of federal regulations and court cases that have attempted to interpret the scope of these two broad prohibitions as applied to the facts and circumstances surrounding each alleged violation of the statute. The FFDCA also prohibits the distribution of any product that requires FDA approval prior to such approval, the refusal or failure of a company to provide the FDA with reports, and refusals by a manufacturer to allow FDA officials to inspect facilities regulated by the statute.

Laws Affecting Sales and Advertising

Emerging-growth companies usually develop sales and advertising campaigns to:

- **introduce the company's products** and services to the marketplace;
- **build goodwill** and consumer loyalty; and
- **increase the company's revenues** and profits once a market is developed.

Advertising must communicate the benefits, features and competitive advantages of a company's products and services in a clear, concise and accurate manner. Companies that include false or misleading information in their advertising materials are likely to rapidly lose market share, consumer goodwill and the dedication of their distribution network. In addition, it is likely that suppliers, creditors, consultants, shareholders and lenders will become disenchanted with the company's credibility and reputation if deceptive practices play a role in its advertising. But the costs of false and deceptive practices go beyond problems affecting the operation and management of the company from a business perspective. Using false or misleading advertising will also trigger legal problems at federal and state levels due to the consumer-protection laws that regulate advertising and sales strategies.

At the heart of the legal regulation of sales and marketing practices is the FTC, which, through Section 5 of the Federal Trade Commission Act, has the authority to prohibit all unfair or deceptive acts or practices in interstate commerce. The following three elements must be present for the FTC to bring a formal enforcement action against a company for a deceptive act:

- **there must be a representation,** commission or practice that is likely to mislead the consumer;
- **the specific act will be analyzed** from the perspective of the consumer acting reasonably under the circumstances; and
- **the act in question must be material.**

The broad nature of these elements vests the FTC with considerable discretion in determining whether a particular act is unfair or deceptive.

The primary safe harbor available to a growing company in developing aggressive sales and marketing strategies is known as "puffing." Puffing may be understood as "a seller's privilege to lie his head off, as long as he says nothing specific, on the theory that no reasonable person would be influenced by such talk." To fall within the parameters of this safe harbor, the contents of the specific advertisement should discuss the company's products and services using only subjective opinions, superlatives or exaggerations and not claim to be based on any specific facts, unless such facts have been reasonably substantiated.

To avoid a claim for false or deceptive advertising under federal or the various state laws, follow these general guidelines:

- **Use only true statements in advertising.**
- **Accurately identify any competitive products** appearing in the advertisement.
- **Do not make express** or implied disparagements of the competitor.
- **Use objective statements of a type that can be substantiated** by the consumer or a regulatory body.
- **Avoid making subjective statements in the advertisement.** Be sure to use an independent testing company to substantiate com-

parisons based upon actual tests among competing products. It is important to have the testing company maintain accurate records of any tests.

■ **Be sure to comply with the advertising codes** of a particular association, industry, or media. Television and radio stations usually have policies for accepting comparative advertisements.

■ **Avoid using claims and statements** that are mere puffery, and thus can't be protected.

■ **Respect the intellectual-property rights** (e.g., trademarks and trade secrets) of your competitors who are mentioned in comparative advertising.

Business-Growth Resources Directory

T HERE ARE LITERALLY THOUSANDS OF TRADE ASSOCI-
ations, networking groups, venture clubs, and
other organizations that directly or indirectly
focus on the needs of small-business owners,
entrepreneurs, growing companies, women-
owned businesses, minority-owned businesses, importers and
exporters, and virtually every other group that shares common interests. Some of the more established groups with a
genuine nationwide presence and solid track record include:

ORGANIZATIONS DEDICATED TO BUSINESS GROWTH
U.S. Chamber of Commerce
1615 H St., N.W.
Washington, DC 20062
(202) 659-6000, www.uschamber.com

The U.S. Chamber of Commerce represents 3 million businesses, 3000 state and local chambers of commerce, 830 business associations, and 87 American Chambers of Commerce
abroad. It works with these groups to support national business
interests and includes a Small Business Center (202-463-5503).

Association for Corporate Growth
International Headquarters
1926 Waukegan Rd., Suite 1
Glenview, IL 60025
(800) 699-1331, www.acg.org

The Association for Corporate Growth provides programs, education, and networking in the areas of middle-

market corporate growth, corporate development, and mergers and acquisitions. The Association has about 5,500 members representing 2,500 companies in 36 chapters throughout North America and the United Kingdom.

Young Entrepreneurs' Organization

1199 N. Fairfax St., Suite 200
Alexandria, VA 22314
(703) 519-6700, www.yeo.org

The Young Entrepreneurs' Organization is made up of young business professionals under the age of 40 who have founded, co-founded, own, or control businesses with annual sales of $1 million or more. The organization provides support, education, and networking opportunities to its members.

Alliance of Independent Store Owners and Professionals (AISOP)

P.O. Box 2014, Loop Station
Minneapolis, MN 55402
(612) 340-1568

AISOP was organized to protect and promote fair postal and legislative policies for small business advertisers. Most of its 4,000-plus members are independent small businesses that rely on reasonable third-class mail rates to promote their businesses and contact customers in their trade areas.

American Entrepreneurs Association

2392 Morse Ave.,
Irvine, CA 92714
(800) 482-0973

The American Entrepreneurs Association was established to provide small-business owners with benefits and discounts that are generally reserved for big businesses, such as express shipping, health insurance, and long-distance telephone rates.

American Small Businesses Association (ASBA)

8773 IL Rte. 75E
Rock City, IL 61070
(800) 942-2722, www.asbaonline.org

ASBA's membership base consists of small business owners

with 20 or fewer employees. ASBA members have access to the same advantages that larger corporations enjoy through member benefits and services.

Council of Growing Companies
8260 Greensboro Dr., Suite 260
McLean, VA 22102
(800) 929-3165, www.ceolink.org
The Council of Growing Companies extends invitations to CEOs of firms in order to promote the entrepreneurial growth sector of the economy, to give CEOs the resources they need to lead their companies in the growing economy, and to provide a forum for CEOs to express their positions on local and national policies that could affect the growth of their companies.

Ewing Marion Kauffman Foundation
4801 Rockhill Rd.
Kansas City, MO 64110
(816) 932-1000, www.emkf.org
The Kauffman Center for Entrepreneurial Leadership sponsors the entreworld.org Web site, which serves as a critical resource for those entrepreneurs starting and growing businesses, and provides links to other resources on the Web.

International Franchise Association (IFA)
1350 New York Ave., N.W., Suite 900
Washington, DC 20005
(202) 628-8000, www.franchise.org
The IFA serves as a resource center for current and prospective franchisees and franchisors, the media and the government. The IFA has promoted programs that expand opportunities for women and minorities in franchising.

National Association of Development Companies (NADCO)
6764 Old McLean Village Dr.
McLean, VA 22101
(703) 748-2575, www.nadco.org
NADCO is the trade group of community-based, nonprofit organizations that promote small-business expansion

and job creation through the SBA's 504 loan program, known as Certified Development Companies (CDC).

National Association of Manufacturers (NAM)
1331 Pennsylvania Ave., N.W.
Washington, DC 20004
(202) 637-3000, www.nam.org

NAM serves as the voice of the manufacturing community and is active on all issues concerning manufacturing, including legal system reform, regulatory restraint, and tax reform.

National Association for the Self-Employed (NASE)
P.O. Box 612067, DFW Airport
Dallas, TX 75261
(800) 232-6273, www.nase.org

NASE helps its members become more competitive by providing more than 100 benefits that save money on services and equipment. NASE's members consist primarily of small business owners with few or no employees.

National Association of Small Business Investment Companies (NASBIC)
666 11th St., N.W., Suite 750
Washington, DC 20001
(202) 628-5055, www.nasbic.org

The National Association of Small Business Investment Companies is dedicated to promoting a strong small-business investment company industry. NASBIC provides professional programs and representation in Washington to promote the growth and vitality of this sector of the business community.

National Commission on Entrepreneurship
444 North Capital St., Suite 399
Washington, DC 20001
(202) 434-8060, www.ncoe.org

The National Commission on Entrepreneurship provides governmental and private-sector leaders with information and resources regarding the entrepreneurial sector, and seeks to recommend new public policies to protect and stimulate the creation and growth of an entrepreneurial economy and culture.

National Federation of Independent Business (NFIB)

53 Century Blvd., Suite 250
Nashville, TN 37214
(800) 274-6342, www.nfib.org

NFIB disseminates educational information about free enterprise, entrepreneurship, and small business. NFIB represents more than 60,000 small and independent businesses before legislatures and government agencies at the federal and state level.

National Small Business United (NSBU)

1156 15th St., N.W., Suite 1100
Washington, DC 20005
(202) 293-8830, www.nsbu.org

The NSBU is a membership-based association of business owners that presents the small business point of view to all levels of government and the Congress.

Let's Talk Business Network

54 W. 39th St.
12th Floor
New York, NY 10018
(212) 742-1553. www.ltbn.com

Let's Talk Business Network acts as an entrepreneurial support community, providing products, a radio network and a support network of more than 5,000 contacts for entrepreneurs who wish to discuss common business experiences and challenges.

National Venture Capital Association

1655 N. Fort Myer Dr., Suite 850
Arlington, VA 22209
(703) 524-2549, www.nvca.org

The National Venture Capital Association's mission is to define, serve, and promote the interests of the venture-capital industry, to increase the understanding of the importance of venture capital to the U.S. economy and to stimulate the flow of equity capital to emerging-growth and developing companies.

National Association of Investment Companies (NAIC)
733 15th St., N.W., Suite 700
Washington, DC 20005
(202) 289-4336, www.naichq.org

NAIC is the industry association for venture-capital firms that dedicate their financial resources to investment in minority businesses.

National Association of Women Business Owners (NAWBO)
1595 Spring Hill Rd., Suite 300
Vienna, VA 22182
(703) 506-3268, www.nawbo.org

NAWBO uses its collective influence to broaden opportunities for women in business, and is the only dues-based national organization representing the interests of all women entrepreneurs in all types of business.

National Association for Female Executives (NAFE)
P.O. Box 469031
Escondido, CA 92046
(800) 634-6233, www.nafe.com

Through education and networking programs, NAFE helps women share the resources and techniques needed to succeed in the competitive business world.

National Business League (NBL)
1511 K St., N.W., Suite 432
Washington, DC 20005
(202) 737-4430, http://thenbl.com

NBL is primarily involved in business development among African Americans and serves as a voice for black business on Capitol Hill and in the federal government.

U.S. Hispanic Chamber of Commerce
2175 K St., N.W., Suite 100
Washington, DC 20037
(202) 842-1212, www.ushcc.com

The U.S. Hispanic Chamber of Commerce advocates the

business interests of Hispanics and develops minority business opportunities with major corporations and at all levels of government.

National Foundation for Teaching Entrepreneurship Inc. (NFTE)
120 Wall St.
29th Floor
New York, NY 10005
(212) 232-3333, www.nfte.com

NFTE is an international nonprofit organization that introduces poor and at-risk young people to the world of entrepreneurship by showing them how to operate their own small-business enterprises.

Opportunity International
2122 York Rd., Suite 340
Oak Brook, IL 60523
(800) 793-9455, www.opportunity.org

With partner organizations, Opportunity International provides loans and basic training in business practices to the poor, thereby breaking the cycle of poverty.

American Farm Bureau Federation
225 Touhy Ave.
Park Ridge, IL 60068
(847) 685-8600, www.fb.com

As the nation's largest farm organization, the American Farm Bureau Federation promotes policies and provides programs that improve the financial well-being and quality of life for farmers and ranchers.

American Electronics Association
601 Pennsylvania Ave., N.W., Suite 600 N.
Washington, DC 20004
(202) 682-9110, www.aeanet.org

The American Electronics Association offers human-resources services, management-development programs, executive networking, public-policy leadership, and other services.

American Financial Services Association
919 18th Street, N.W., Suite 300
Washington, DC 20006
(202) 296-5544, www.afsaonline.org

The American Financial Services Association acts as the national trade association for market funded providers of financial services to consumers and small businesses.

American Society of Association Executives (ASAE)
1575 I St., N.W.
Washington, DC 20005
(202) 626-2723, www.asaenet.org

The American Society of Association Executives serves as an advocate for the nonprofit sector of the economy.

Association of American Publishers
50 F St., N.W.
Washington, DC 20001
(202) 347-3375, www.publishers.org

Assists publishers by expanding the market for American books both nationally and abroad, promotes intellectual freedom and opposes censorship, and offers practical advice and information to assist members in the management and administration of their companies.

National Association of Convenience Stores
1605 King St.
Alexandria, VA 22314
(703) 684-3600, www.cstorecentral.com

The National Association of Convenience Stores is an international trade association representing 2,300 retail and 1,700-supplier company members, assisting these entities to increase their current effectiveness and profitability.

National Association of Wholesaler–Distributors
1725 K St., N.W., Suite 300
Washington, DC 20006
(202) 872-0885, www.naw.org

The National Association of Wholesaler-Distributors is a

trade association that represents the wholesale-distribution industry, and is active in the areas of government relations and political action, research and education, and group purchasing.

National Restaurant Association
1200 17th St., N.W.
Washington, DC 20036
(202) 331-5900, www.restaurant.org

Represents, promotes, and educates the restaurant industry. The National Restaurant Association is comprised of 43,000 member companies and 220,000 restaurant establishments.

National Retail Federation
325 7th St., N.W., Suite 1100
Washington, DC 20004
(202) 783-7971, www.nrf.com

The National Retail Federation is the world's largest retail trade association, providing programs and services in education, training, information technology, and government affairs to advance its members' interests.

Business Software Alliance
1150 18th St., N.W., Suite 700
Washington, DC 20036
(202) 872-5500, www.bsa.org

The Business Software Alliance is an international organization representing software and e-commerce ventures in 65 countries around the world. The Alliance educates consumers and governments about the positive impact software has on our lives, fights software piracy and Internet theft, and promotes greater trade opportunities.

American Intellectual Property Law Association
2001 Jefferson Davis Highway, Suite 203
Arlington, VA 22202
(703) 415-0780, www.aipla.org

The American Intellectual Property Law Association is a national bar association composed mainly of lawyers that strives to improve the nation's intellectual property laws and their interpretation by the courts, and provides legal education to the public and to organization members on matters involving intellectual property.

International Trademark Association
1133 Avenue of the Americas, 33rd Floor
New York, NY 10036
(212) 768-9887, www.inta.org
The International Trademark Association is a worldwide membership organization of trademark owners and advisors, and seeks to shape public policy, advance practitioners' knowledge, and educate the public and the media about the significance of trademarks in today's commercial environment.

Morino Institute
11600 Sunrise Valley Dr., Suite 300
Reston, VA 20191
(703) 620-8971, www.morino.org
The Morino Institute attempts to explore and understand the opportunities and risks of the Internet and the New Economy to expand social progress, and seeks to create a dialogue on such issues among entrepreneurs and others.

National Association of Professional Employer Organizations (NAPEO)
901 N. Pitt St., Suite 150
Alexandria, VA 22314
(703) 836-0466, www.napeo.org
NAPEO is the recognized voice of the professional employer organization industry and is dedicated to working towards the goals of PEOs, their clients, and the regulatory and legislative bodies that monitor the industry.

Turnaround Management Association
541 N. Fairbanks Ct., Suite 1880
Chicago, IL 60611
(312) 822-9700, www.turnaround.org
The TMA publishes the *Journal of Corporate Renewal* six times per year.

FEDERAL AGENCIES

U.S. Small Business Administration (SBA)

409 Third St., S.W.
Washington, DC 20416
(800) 827-5722, www.sbaonline.sba.gov

The SBA offers a wide variety of financing programs, workshops and seminars, management and technical assistance, typically through its many district offices.

Export-Import Bank (Eximbank)

811 Vermont Ave., N.W.
Washington, DC 20571
(800) 565-3946, www.exim.gov

The Export-Import Bank offers financing assistance for potential exporters and companies of all sizes interested in doing business abroad.

U.S. Department of Commerce (DOC)

1401 Constitution Ave., N.W.
Washington, DC 20230
(202) 482-2000, www.doc.gov

This agency offers a wide variety of programs and services relating to economic development, international trade and minority business. The U.S. Patent and Trademark Office (800-786-9199) is a division of the DOC that processes federal patent and trademark applications and publishes various resources on the protection of intellectual property.

Federal Trade Commission

600 Pennsylvania Ave., N.W.
Washington, DC 20580
(202) 326-2222, www.ftc.gov

The FTC provides guidance to businesses that may need to comply with a variety of federal rules and regulations.

National Trade Data Bank on the Internet

(800) 782-8872, (202) 482-1986 (to subscribe),
www.stat-usa.gov, email: statmail@mail.doc.gov

Trade Information Center
International Trade Administration
U.S. Department of Commerce
Washington, DC 20230
(800) 872-8723, (202) 482-0543, TDD: (800) 833-8723,
www.ita.doc.gov/TICFramesel.html

Export Assistance Center
(800) 872-8723 (call for local center), www.usatrade.gov

The Trade Information Center provides comprehensive resources for information on all U.S. federal government export-assistance programs.

Bankers Association for Finance and Trade
2121 K St., N.W, Suite 701
Washington, DC 20037
(202) 452-0952, www.baft.org

Bureau of Export Administration
Department of Commerce
1401 Constitution Ave., N.W.
Washington, DC 20230
(202) 482-0436, www.bxa.doc.gov

International Business Exchange Network
(Contact your local Chamber of Commerce)

In addition to the agencies listed above, all major federal departments and agencies have an Office of Small and Disadvantaged Business Utilization (OSDBU), which is responsible for ensuring that an equitable share of government contracts are awarded to small and minority businesses. Below are listed OSDBU office phone numbers within selected agencies:

Department of Agriculture
(202) 720-7117, www.usda.gov

Department of Defense
(703) 545-6700

Department of Justice
(202) 616-0521, www.usdoj.gov/jmd/osdbu

Agency for International Development
(202) 712-4810, www.usaid.gov/procurement_bus_opp/osdbu

Office of Personnel Management
(202) 606-2180

DIRECTORY OF INTERNATIONAL FRANCHISE ORGANIZATIONS
Argentine Franchise Association
Santa Fe 995, Piso 4
Buenos Aires 1059, Argentina
Attn: Richard Rivera, President
Tel: (54) 1-393-5263, Fax: (54) 1-393-9260

Association de Franchising de Chile (AFICH)
Hernando de Aguirre 128, of. 704
Providencia, Santiago, Chile
Attn: Carlos Fabia, President-Elect
Tel: (56) 2-234-4189, Fax: (56) 2-232-7759

Franchisors Assn. of Australia & New Zealand
Unit 9, 2-6 Hunter Street
Parramatta, NSW 2150, Australia
Attn: Berridge Hume-Phillips, Executive Director
Tel: (61) 2-891-4933, Fax: (61) 2-891-4474

Austrian Franchise Association
Nonntaler Hauptstrasse 48
Salzburg 5020, Austria
Attn: Mrs. Waltraud Frauenhuber
Tel: (43) 662-83-21-64, Fax: (43) 662-83-21-64

Belgium Franchise Federation
Boulevard de L'Humanite, 116/2
B-1070 Brussels, Belgium
Attn: Pierre Jeanmart, Chairman
Tel: (32-2) 523-9707, Fax: (32-2) 523-3510

Brazil Franchise Association
Rua Professor Ascendino Reis, 1548
Sao Paulo 04027-000, Brazil
Attn: Bernard Jeger, President
Tel: (55) 11-5711303, Fax: (55) 11-5755590

British Franchise Association
Thames View, Newton Rd., Henley-on-Thames
Oxfordshire RG9 1HG, United Kingdom
Attn: Brian Smart, Director
Tel: (44) 1491-578-049, Fax: (44) 1491-573-517

Bulgaria Franchise Association
P.O. Box 20
9010-Varna, Bulgaria
Attn: Ms. Lubka Kolarova, President
Tel: (359) 52-256-891, Fax: (359) 52-256-891

Canadian Franchise Association
5045 Orbitor Drive, Suite 401, Bldg. 9
Mississauga, Ont. L4W 4Y4, Canada
Attn: Richard B. Cunningham, President
Tel: (905) 625-2896, Fax: (905) 625-9076

Ceska Asociace Franchisingu
Rytirska 18-20, P.O. Box 706
11000 Prague, Cezech Republic
Attn: Gosef Fidler, President
Tel: (42) 2-242-30-566, Fax: (42) 2-242-30-566

Chile Franchise Association
Rafael Canas 16, of. 1
Providencia, Santiago, Chili
Attn: Mr. Fernando Kaminetsky, President
Tel: (56-2) 236-3622, Fax: (56-2) 264-9134

China Chain Store and Franchising Association
No. 25 Yuetan North St.
Beijing 100834, P.R. China

Attn: Mrs. Guo Geping, President
Tel: (86-10) 6839-2260, Fax: (86-10) 6839-2210

Association Colombiana De Franquicias
Apartado Aereo 25200
Cali, Colombia
Attn: Jorge Barragan, President
Tel: (57) 2-339-2163, Fax: (57) 2-339-2166

Denmark Franchise Association
Amaliegade 37
Copenhagen K 1256, Denmark
Attn: Peter Arendorff, President
Tel: (45) 33-156011, Fax: (45) 33-910346

Dominican Republic Franchise Association
Plibio Diaz #74, Apt. C-1
Edificio Alfonso X, Cuaristo Morales
Santo Domingo, Dominican Republic
Attn: Mr. Oscar Luis Monzon, Executive Director
Tel: (809) 549-6383, Fax: (809) 563-1916

Ecuador Franchise Association
Ave. 9 de Octubre y Los Rios Ed. Finansur, p. 16
Guayaquil, Ecuador
Attn: Dr. Leonidas Villagran-Cepeda, Director
Tel: (593-4) 450-150, Fax: (593-4) 280-078

European Franchise Federation
Boulevard de l'Humanite 116/2
Brussels, Belgium
Attn: Ms. Carol Chopra, Executive Director
Tel: (32-2) 520-1607, Fax: (32-2) 520-1735

Finland Franchise Association
Laurinkatu 47
08100 Lohja, Finland
Attn: Mr. Rolf Granstrom, Executive Officer
Tel: (358) 19-331-195, Fax: (358) 19-331-075

France Franchise Federation
60, rue La Boetie
Paris 75008, France
Attn: Ms. Chantal Zimmer, Executive Director
Tel: (33) 1-5375-2225, Fax: (33) 1-5375-2220

Germany Franchise Association
Paul Heyse Str. 33-35
Munchen 80336, Germany
Attn: Prof. Utho Creusen, President
Tel: (49) 89-53-50-27, Fax: (49) 89-53-13-23

Greece Franchise Association
Skoufou 10
105 57 Athens, Greece
Attn: Ms. Anna Trigetta, Secretary
Tel: (30-1) 323-4620, Fax: (30-1) 323-8865

Hong Kong Franchise Association
22/F Unit A United Centre, 95 Queensway
Hong Kong
Attn: Charlotte Chow, Senior Manager
Tel: (852) 2529-9229, Fax: (852) 2527-9843

Hungary Franchise Association
Secretariat: c/o DASY
P.O. Box 446
Budapest H-1537, Hungary
Attn: Dr. Istvan Kiss, CEO
Tel: (361) 212-4124, Fax: (361) 212-5712

Indonesia Franchise Association (AFI)
A19 Darmawangsa
Kebayoran Baru, 12150 Indonesia
Attn: Mr. Anang Sukandar
Tel: (62) 21-739-5577, Fax: (62) 21-723-4761

Ireland Franchise Association
Hambleden House 19/26 Lower Pembroke Str.

Dublin 2, Ireland
Attn: Mr. Bill Holohan, Director
Tel: (353-1) 678-5199, Fax: (353-1) 678-5146

Israel Franchise & Distribution Association
P.O. Box 3093
Herzeliya 46590, Israel
Attn: Michael Emery, Chairman of the Board
Tel: (972) 9-576-631, Fax: (972) 9-576-631

Iberto American Franchise Federation (FIAF)
La Otra Banda #74/col. Tizapan San Angel
Mexico 01090 D.F.
Attn: Juan Manual Gallastegui, Secretary General
Tel: (52-5) 616-0112, Fax: (52-5) 550-4965

India Franchise Association
1-C, Vulcan Insurance Bldg.
Veer Nariman Road
Churchgate, Mumbai 400-020, India
Attn: Mr. C. Yoginder Pal, Chairman SIG
Tel: (91-22) 282-1423, Fax: (91-22) 204-6141

Italy Franchise Association
Corso di Porta Nuova, 3
Milano 20121, Italy
Attn: Michele Scardi, General Secretary
Tel: (39) 2-29003779, Fax: (39) 2-6555919

Japan Franchise Association
Elsa Bldg. 602, Roppongi, 3-13-12, Minato-ku
Tokyo 106, Japan
Attn: Mr. Ojiri Keisuke, Exec. Director
Tel: (81) 3-34010421, Fax: (81) 3-34232019

Korea (South) Franchise Association
Zipcode 143-202, Hyosan B/D 3F
57-80, Gui-2Dong, Kwangjin-Gu
Seoul, South Korea

Attn: Kyoung Woo, Lee, CEO
Tel: (82-2) 447-6094, Fax: (82-2) 3436-2162

Mexico Franchise Association
Insurgentes Sur 1783, #303, Col. Guadalupe Inn
Mexico, 01020 DF, Mexico
Attn: Mrs. Lorenzo Reynaud, General Manager
Tel: (52) 5-661-0655, Fax: (52) 5-663-2473

Malaysia Franchise Association
No. 79, Damai Complex, Dato Haji Eusoff Road
Kuala Lumpur 50400, Malaysia
Attn: Awalan Abdul Aziz, Secretary
General
Tel: (60-3) 445-4700, Fax: (60-3) 44-4711

Norway Franchise Association
P.O. Box 2900
Solli 0230, Oslo, Norway
Attn: Mr. Torild Brende, Managing Director
Tel: (47-2) 254-1700, Fax: (47-2) 256-1700

Middle East Franchise & Distribution Association
P.O. Box 3093
Herzeliya 46590, Israel
Attn: Michael Emery, Chairman of the Board
Tel: (972) 9-576-631, Fax: (972) 9-576-631

Netherlands Franchise Association
Boomberglaan 12
Hilversum 1217 PR, The Netherlands
Attn: Mr. A.W.M. Brouwer, Managing Director
Tel: (31) 35-624-2300, Fax:(31) 35-624-9194

New Zealand Franchise Association
1st Floor, 26 St. Heliers Bay Road
St. Heliers, Auckland, New Zealand
Attn: Mr. Winston Robinson, Chairman
Tel: (64-9) 575-3804, Fax: (64-9) 575-3807

Peru Franchise Association
Gregorio Escobedo 398
Lima 11, Peru
Attn: Mr. Samuel Gleiser Katz, President
Tel: (51-1) 562-1000, Fax: (51-1) 562-1020

Polish Franchise Association
Krolewska 27
00-670 Warsaw, Poland
Attn: Jolanta Kramarz, Chairman
Tel: (48) 22-27-78-22, Fax: (48) 22-27-78-22

Portugal Franchise Association
Rua Viriato, 25-3
1050-234 Lisboa, Portugal
Attn: Mr. Raoul Neves, President
Tel: (351-1) 319-2938, Fax: (351-1) 319-2939

Romanian Franchise Association
Calea Victorieri Nr. 95, Et. 4, Ap. 16, Sect. 1
Bucharest, Romania
Attn: Violeta Popovici, Chief Executive
Tel: (401) 3126889/6180186, Fax: (401) 3126890

Singapore Franchise Association
Informatics Building 5 International Business Park
Singapore 609914
Attn: Mr. Wong Tai, Chairman
Tel: (65) 568-0802, Fax: (65) 568-0722

Russia Franchise Association
2-nd Proezd Perova Polya, 9
Moscow 111141, Russia
Attn: Mr. Alexander Mailer, President
Tel: (7-095) 305-5877, Fax: (7-095) 305-5850

Spain Franchise Association
Avda. de las Ferias S/N
P.O. Box 476, 46035 Valencia, Spain

Attn: Mr. Xavier Vallhonrat, President
Tel: (34-96) 386-1123, Fax: (34-96) 363-6111

South Africa Franchise Association
24 Willington Road
2193 Houghton, South Africa
Attn: Mr. Nic Louw, Executive Director
Tel: (27-11) 484-1285, Fax: (27-11) 484-1291

Swedish Franchise Association
Box 5512-S., Grevgatan 34
Stockholm 11485, Sweden
Attn: Mr. Stig Sohlberg, Chief Executive Officer
Tel: (46) 8-6608610, Fax: (46) 8-6627457

Switzerland Franchise Association
Lowenstrasse II, Postfach CH-8023
Zurich, Switzerland
Attn: Dr. Christopher Wildhaber
Tel: (41) 41-225-4757, Fax:(41) 41-225-4777

Turkey Franchise Association
Ergenekon cad. Pangalti Ishani 89/15
Istanbul 80240, Turkey
Attn: Mr. Serdar Yanasan, Chairman
Tel: (90-212) 296-6628, Fax: (90-212) 224-5130

Yugoslavia Franchise Association - YUFA
21000 Novi Sad
Mokranjceva 28, Yugoslavia
Attn: Dr. Zdravko Glusica, General Secretary
Tel: (381) 21-614-232, Fax: (381) 21-614-232

Uruguay Franchise Association
Daniel Munoz 2240, CP 11.200
Montevideo, Uruguay
Attn: Mr. Rodolfo Montesdeoca, President
Tel/Fax: (598-2) 408-5189

Venezuela Chamber of Franchising
Oficentro Neur, 3-Altamira, Oficina N 5
Caracas, Venezuela 1060
Attn: Mr. Rolando Seijas S., President
Tel: (58-2) 261-8596/6855, Fax: (58-2) 261-9620

Venezuela Franchise Association
Av. La Estancia, Torre Diamen, Pisa 8, of. 88-B
Chuao, Caracas, Venezuela
Attn: Mr. Arquimides Beliz, President
Tel: (58-2) 991-4078, Fax: (58-2) 991-1401

Zimbabwe Franchise Association
c/o The ZNCC
P.O. Box 1934
Harare, Zimbabwe
Tel: (263-4) 753-444, Fax: (263-4) 753-450

BUSINESS-GROWTH RESOURCES ON THE WEB

Hundreds of Web sites have been developed to provide support to entrepreneurs and growing companies. Web sites come and go quickly and change often, so it's probably best to use one of the popular search engines and enter key words that will narrow the scope of your search or particular resource need. Some current Web sites worth visiting include the following:

National Survey of Small Business Finances
www.federalreserve3.gov/Pubs/Oss/Oss3/nssbftoc.htm
Provides a wealth of information on American small businesses, including financial characteristics, firm size, and income and balance sheets.

The Small Business Journal
www.tsbj.com
A free online magazine for small businesses, containing an indexed archive of articles and a discussion group.

NetBusiness

www.netbusiness.com

Run by Netscape and designed specifically for the small-business owner, this site includes articles, business-management tools, industry information, and many useful links to other Web sites.

IdeaCafe

www.ideacafe.com/welcome.html

A small-business meeting place

International Franchise Association

www.franchise.org

Provides information on franchising opportunities, trends, and developments.

Centercourt Franchise and Business Opportunities

www.centercourt.com

Articles and information on franchising

IFA Online

www.franchise.org

Offers IFA's *Franchise Opportunities Guide, Franchising World,* bulletin boards, a calendar of events and more for franchisors and franchisees.

Legaldocs

http://legaldocs.com

Low-cost legal forms

Venture Capital Institute

http://vcinstitute.org

A wide range of venture-capital resources

Small Business Resource Center

www.seaquest1.com/sbrc/

Offers tips to help make a small business successful.

Dun & Bradstreet Information

www.dnb.com

A comprehensive source of financial and demographic data.

National Financial Services Network

www.nfsn.com

Offers a directory of investment-related information on such topics as the stock market, brokerage firms, mutual funds, and dividend and reinvestment plans.

The American Association of Individual Investors

www.aaii.org

Offers a basic guide to computerized investing and articles from the *AAII Journal* and *Computerized Investing*

Quicken.com

www.quicken.com/investments

Offers information and links to mutual fund companies and online access to fund prospectuses.

EDGAR

www.sec.gov/edgarhp.htm

A database that contains all corporate annual and quarterly reports (and exhibits) filed with the Securities and Exchange Commission.

The *Wall Street Journal's* Interactive Edition

www.update.wsj.com

Allows subscribers to access news and financial information about specified companies

Inc. Online

www.inc.com

Allows users to (1) build their own Web sites; (2) read the current issue or browse through *Inc.* magazine's extensive archives; and (3) interact with other entrepreneurs, experts and *Inc.* editors.

Ask the Lawyers

www.fairmeasures.com/asklawyer/index/htm

A Web site that offers practical advice for complying with employee law and preventing lawsuits.

Bizjournals.com

http://bizjournals.bcentral.com

Features expert advice for small businesses on topics such as sales and marketing, technology, business financing, and tips on shopping for business products and services.

Headhunter.net

www.headhunter.net/JobSeeker.

Offers a database of national job openings.

JobOptions.com

ww1.joboptions.comjo_main/index.asp

Used by human-resource professionals to post jobs world-wide. Offers reference materials for HR practitioners.

Monster.com

www.monster.com

Offers a variety of issues, from hiring to staffing and other related topics for human-resource executives.

Interbiznet

www.interbiznet.com/top100.html

Lists the top 100 recruiting sites

CareerBuilder

www.careerbuilder.com

Features jobs from more than 70 career sites, personalized job-hunting tools, skills certification and articles from several publications.

OfficeNET

www.officenet.com

Offers administrative, secretarial and professional support services.

Society for Human Resource Management (SHRM)

www.shrm.org

Lists a variety of services and products for human-resource professionals

SBA Office of Women's Business Ownership

www.sba.gov/womeninbusiness

Provides training, advice, and guidance to women who may be starting businesses.

American Society of Association Executives

www.asaenet.org

Provides a newsroom, a bookstore, and links to various upcoming events and meetings.

eIncomeOpportunities.com

www.eincomeopportunities.com

Provides advice and tips on starting and succeeding in your own e-commerce venture.

Spanlink Communications

www.spanlink.com

Provides a broad range of communications products and services to businesses and enterprises.

Switchboard

www.switchboard.com

Contains a searchable database to locate businesses nationwide.

American Demographics

www.inside.com/default.asp?entity-AmericanDemo

Subscription service that provides timely and useful marketing and demographic information for all types of businesses.

Red Herring magazine

www.redherring.com

Contains news, research, event listings and other information for investors and entrepreneurs.

GreatIdeasRadio.com
www.greatideasradio.com

Contains a searchable archive of radio interviews conducted with prominent people in business and technology.

Info Franchise News Inc.
www.infonews.com/franchise

Provides useful information on franchising opportunities.

The Small Business Advocate
www.smallbusinessadvocate.com

Provides access to a live radio talk show, audio archives of past shows, links to small business-related articles, and links to related small-business Web sites.

CFO.com Mergers & Acquisitions Center
www.cfo.com

A collection of articles, resources and an M&A Discussion Group from *CFO Magazine*.

International Mergers & Acquisitions Benchmarking Consortium
www.imabc.com

MergerNetwork.com
www.mergernetwork.com/index.cfn

Database of M&A leads

MergerStat
www.mergerstat.com

Global mergers and acquisitions information

The Online Investor Mergers
www.theonlineinvestor.com/mergers.phtml

Weekly information on new M&A announcements

NVST.com's World M&A Network
www.nvst.com/pubsworldma-pub.asp

Pay service listing sellers and buyers

TradePort
www.tradeport.org

Comprehensive trade information, trade leads and company databases.

STAT-USA/Internet
www.stat-usa.gov

U.S. Dept. of Commerce site for economic, business and international trade information.

International Business Resources on the WWW
http://ciber.bus.msu.edu/busres.html

Michigan State University Center for International Business Education and Research.

MSU Export Academy
http://ciber.bus.msu.edu/outreach/export

Michigan State University program in international trade.

Export Process Assistant (ExPa)
www.cob.ohio-state.edu/citm/expadocs

Electronic guide to the export process.

Trade Compass
www.tradecompass.com/

Trade Resources
www.usitc.gov/tr/tr.htm

American Computer Resources, Inc.
www.the-acr.com/

is-Trade
www3.is-trade.com

Provides non-Japanese vendors with real time access to the Japanese retail market.

INTERNATIONAL FINANCE INSTITUTIONS ON THE WEB

All of the international finance institutions maintain Web sites with extensive information and data on the countries in which they work. These sites also provide detailed listings of projects under consideration and contact information for businesses interested in working with the institutions.

Africa Business Network

www.ifc.org/abn

International Finance Corp.'s site of basic economic and investment data for individual countries in sub-Saharan Africa; also provides country information with economic data and contact information, and guidance on investment procedures.

The African Development Bank Group

www.afdb.org

Economic statistics, including major indicators, updated annually for individual countries.

Asian Development Bank (ADB)

www.adb.org

Quarterly economic analyses with major economic indicators reported for most Asian nations; ADB's Asian Recovery Information Center (www.aric.adb.org) provides detailed economic data for East Asian countries and in-depth reports on the Asian recovery.

Asiaweek

www.asiaweek.com

CNN's economic and business data and news site; provides weekly comparative data on major economic indicators by country, and top business stories from the region.

Asia in the World Economy

www.ap.harvard.edu/awe

A Harvard University site with a collection of statistics for each country, including economic indicators, trade data and information on economic zones and links to public and private online resources for the region.

Banco de Mexico

www.banxico.org.mx-siteBanxicoINGLES/index.html
Economic and financial indicators and statements on monetary policy.

ChinaOnline

www.chinaonline.com
Daily updates on economic and business developments with breakdowns by industry, reports on economic data as they are released from major sources, and detailed coverage of financial services.

China Economic Information Network

www.ce.cei.gov.cn
Business and economic news; information on investments, laws and regulations; extensive data on trade, finance, employment, prices, wages, major industries and population, with most data lagging by one quarter; and forecasts for six months ahead.

Company Annual Reports Online (Carol)

www.carol.co.uk
Annual reports for companies in Europe, Asia and the United States. Users can search by company name or industry.

DRI-WEFA

www.dri-wefa.com
WEFA, formerly Wharton Econometric Forecasting Associates, focuses on privatization, globalization, trade, finance and technology developments in established and emerging markets.

Europa—The European Union Online

www.europa.eu.int
The European Commission's server for the European Union's 15 member countries. Includes Eurostat, the official statistical agency for the EU, which provides data for the EU-15 and for each member nation on imports, exports, consumer prices, GDP, industrial production, employment and current living conditions, with most data lagging by two

months; legal instruments in force and official euro rates.

European Central Bank

www.ecb.int

Euro conversion rates; daily euro foreign exchange; balance of payments and international investment position of the euro area; retail bank interest rates, financial markets; government bond rates and stock market indexes; and monetary policy decisions. Most data lags by one month.

European Investment Bank

www.eib.org

Detailed research reports by industry sector; information on capital markets; and developments in European banking.

Europe Profile

www.europeprofile.com

Monthly reports on the European Internet market, including the overall European market, specific country markets, and e-business trends and sectors.

Export-Import Bank of the United States

www.exim.gov

The Export-Import Bank Web site posts information about the Bank's program, including detailed information for companies interested in the Working Capital Guarantee Program. The Bank also offers a 24-hour Asia hotline (800) 565-3946, ext. 3905) which gives current information on Bank programs by country and can provide faxes with additional information.

Global Financial Network

www.wallstreeter.com

World market indexes; American depositary receipts for many countries; links to 107 central banks and 135 exchanges; links to ministries of finance and economy for most nations.

Hong Kong Government Information Center

www.info.gov.hk/index_e.htm

From Hong Kong's central statistical agency; data on national accounts and balance of payments, prices, trade, industrial production, construction and the labor force.

Hoover's
www.hoovers.com
This megasite for company information, well known in the United States, has added sites for the U.K., France, Germany, Italy, and Spain. The sites allow users to search by industry and provide a list of companies in each industry. Information for companies covered on each site includes capsule summary of the company's main line of business, a link to the company's Web site and a list of major competitors, plus financial data, officers and contact information. In addition to company information, the site posts market news on emerging markets, IPO updates, and news about earnings and forecasts. Additional information is available for subscribers.

Instituto Nacional de Estadistica, Geografia e Informatica
www.inegi.gob.mx/difusion/ingles/portadai.html
The Mexican central statistical agency's data on GDP, inflation, capital formation and trade, with real GDP data broken down by major industries. Data generally lags by one quarter.

Inter-American Development Bank
www.iadb.org
Detailed economic, trade and demographic data for Latin American and Caribbean countries.

International Finance Corp.
www.ifc.org
Statistics on private investment in developing countries and technical papers on finance topics.

International Institute for Management Development (MD)
www.imd.ch/wcy
From the IMD, an executive management school based in Lausanne, Switzerland, this site posts the results of the IMD's annual *World Competitiveness Yearbook,* which analyzes and ranks

47 nations using 290 criteria for competitiveness in the global economy.

International Labour Organization

www.ilo.org

Comparative labor statistics for employment and unemployment, average earnings, labor costs, consumer prices, occupational injuries, union membership, and industrial disputes; wages and hours of work by detailed occupation and industry group; projections for employment levels; legal minimum-wage laws for 55 countries; international guidelines for working conditions and child labor. Some of the data lags by a year but is still valuable because it is converted for better comparability.

International Monetary Fund (IMF)

www.imf.org

The IMF's Web site is loaded with statistical information on the economies of most countries, including detailed forecasts for growth and reports on business conditions. It also includes links to many important regional institutions and other sources of data.

LatinFocus

www.latin-focus.com

Economic indicators on a comparative basis for Latin American countries (including data on inflation, GDP, industrial production and trade) with most data lagging by one to two months; business and economic news; consensus forecasts for the region and individual countries.

Latin America Research Group

www.frbatlanta.org/econ_rd/larg

The site for the Federal Reserve Bank of Atlanta's center for economic analysis of Latin countries; reports on economic, financial and political developments and an extensive list of links to other Latin America sources. (see also the Dallas Fed's Center for Latin American Economics: www.dallasfed.org/htm/latin/center.html).

Organization for Economic Co-operation and Development (OECD)

www.oecd.org

Main economic indicators, including GDP, industrial production, retail sales, trade, price and interest-rate data for the 29 member OECD countries (primarily from Europe and the Americas); labor-force statistics; national accounts; purchasing-power parties; economic forecasts for member countries and other major economies; information on insurance, pensions and taxes; industry analysis, including agriculture and food, biotechnology, e-commerce, energy, finance and investment; special reports on capital movements and international investment; and OECD guidelines for multinational enterprises.

Overseas Private Investment Corp. (OPIC)

www.opic.gov

OPIC is an independent U.S. government agency that sells investment services to U.S. companies investing in 140 emerging economies. Its Web site includes detailed investment information, including special information on opportunities for small businesses, plus descriptions of OPIC's political-risk insurance and project-finance and investment funds.

State Committee of the Russian Federation on Statistics

www.gks.ru/eng

Goskomstat, the central Russian agency for economic data reported at the federal, regional and district levels, posts quarterly data on GDP, employment, population, enterprises and organizations, industry, agriculture, construction, transportation and communications, trade, finance, investment, prices, and tariffs. Six-month lag in most data.

S&P Global

www.spglobal.com

The Standard & Poor's global site, with real-time and closing values for a number of global indexes, including the S&P Global 1200, the S&P Europe 350, the S&P United Kingdom 150, the S&P Asia Pacific 100 and the S&P Latin America 40. These indexes were acquired by S&P from the International Finance Corp. and are now maintained by S&P.

Statistics Canada

www.statcan.ca

Canada's national statistical agency's data on economic indicators, primary industries, employment, trade and finance, plus a statistical profile of Canadian cities. Three-month lag in data.

United Nations Statistics Division

www.un.org/depts/unsd

Detailed population and vital statistics for 229 countries and areas, including a monthly bulletin of economic statistics; quarterly data on long-term economic trends.

U.S. Agency for International Development (USAID)

www.info.usaid.gov

USAID is the federal agency for foreign-assistance programs, which include agency-financed procurement opportunities. Its Web site posts notices for procurement projects and recent awards, plus contact information.

U.S. Department of Commerce

www.commerce.gov

The Commerce Department and its International Trade Administration (www.ita.doc.gov) post extensive information on the levels of direct investment and trade with other countries and provide contacts for assistance.

U.S. Department of State

www.state.gov

Country commercial guides prepared by U.S. embassy and agency staff with economic and political analyses; key information for U.S. companies exporting to or investing in most countries, including laws, trade regulations, investment climate, trade and project financing, business travel conditions, trade contacts, and major imports and exports; country reports on economic policy and trade; and key economic indicators for each country for the past three years.

U.S. Trade and Development Agency (TDA)
www.tda.gov
The TDA site offers trade and export news, reports on agency programs by region and sector, dates for business briefings and announcements of export opportunities.

The William Davidson Institute
www.wdi.bus.umich.edu
The William Davidson Institute is a nonprofit, independent institute that works with international finance institutions and private companies interested in investing in emerging economies. The Institute offers management training, executive education, consulting expertise and project-based assistance to corporations operating abroad.

World Bank
www.worldbank.org
The World Bank site is a huge source of information on economic and business conditions in developing nations, plus the Bank's programs for procurement, investment and risk management. The Bank's Business Partnership Center posts detailed information about working with the Bank to finance projects, obtain insurance and identify private partners. The site also offers contact information and links to the Bank's regional institutions.

GUIDEBOOKS, PUBLICATIONS AND NETWORKS
(INCLUDING COMPUTER SOFTWARE)
The Export Assistance Center distributes, for a charge, guide books that include, among others:
- A Basic Guide to Exporting
- How to Build a Successful Export Business
- Breaking Into the Trade Game: A Small Business Guide to Exporting
- North American Free Trade Agreement: A Guide to Customs Procedures

The U.S. Department of Commerce distributes the *Journal of Commerce*. To subscribe, contact them at (202) 482-1986.

High-Tech Exporting Assistance Software

- The Export Expert ($169.95), Columbia Cascade Inc. (703- 620-9403)
- Quick Assistance for Export Documentation ($895), Export-Import Trade Software Inc. (203-396-0022)
- Export Software: Version II.2 ($529), Unz & Company, (800-631-3098)
- Export America, The Complete Guide to Export for American Business ($195), M. Thorne & Company (360-853-7099)
- Worldwide Express Guide, free from DHL Worldwide Express, or call 800-225-5345.

CD-ROM's

- National Trade Data Base: The Export Connection ($59 for one monthly issue; $575 for an annual subscription), U.S. Department of Commerce (800-782-8872)
- Eastern Europe Business Database ($395), American Directory Corp., Order number PB93-506210INC; call National Technical Information (703-487-4650)
- Latin America 25,000; Asia Pacific 25,000; Western Europe 25,000; Manufacturing 25,000; Service 25,000; Worldwide 25,000 ($295 each), D-B Worldbase Services, Dun & Bradstreet Information Services, (800-624-5669)
- PIERS (Port Import Export Reporting Service) Export Bulletin ($175 per month), *The Journal of Commerce*, (212-837-7051)

A

provisions, 84–85

wrongful-termination lawsuits, 99

"Angels" or "bands of angels," as
equity capital sources, 184

Anti-Cybersquatting Consumer
Protection Act, 317–318

Anti-dilution provisions, 216, 317

Antitrust audits, 555–556

Antitrust laws

antitrust audits, 555–556

conscious parallelism, 551–552

economic theory, 548

exclusive dealing, 553–554

federal laws, 548–554

free-riders and, 549

horizontal restraints, 549

litigation and, 506

monopolistic practices, 549,
550–551

penalties for failure to obey, 549

"per se" approach, 551–552

political theory, 548

price discrimination, 552–553

price-fixing, 549, 551–552

refusal to deal, 551, 552

resale price maintenance, 552

"rule of reason" test, 550–551,
554

state laws, 554–555

territorial and customer
restrictions, 554

tying, 553

vertical restraints, 548–549,
553–554

Application hosting, 333–334

Application service providers, 74, 78,
305

business models, 333–334

downside risks of, 333

overspending and, 332–333

responsibilities, 332

Applications management outsourcing,
334

Arbitration, 70

binding, 521

compulsory, 519

contract clauses, 519–520

costs, 521–522

description, 518–519

non-binding, 521

recovering punitive or
exemplary damages, 520–521

sources of rules, 521

voluntary, 519

Area-development agreements,
435–436

Ariba, 47–48

Armstrong World Industries, 533

ARPANET, 304

ASPs. *See* Application service
providers

AT&T, 278

B

"Bad faith intent to profit," 317–318

BankersTrust Corp., 278

Bankruptcy

accounts-receivable management
problems and, 538–539

alternatives to, 543–545

Chapter 7 type, 542–543

Chapter 11 type, 540–542, 544

costs of financial distress, 539

defective information and
monitoring systems and, 538

dependence on a key customer,
supplier, lender or contract and,
537

dot.com and technology
companies, 532

S